50 Cases in International Finance

Gunter Dufey ▪ **Ian H. Giddy**

The University of Michigan   New York University

 Addison-Wesley Publishing Company
Reading, Massachusetts ▪ Menlo Park, California ▪ Don Mills, Ontario
Wokingham, England ▪ Amsterdam ▪ Sydney ▪ Singapore
Tokyo ▪ Madrid ▪ Bogotá ▪ Santiago ▪ San Juan

With contributions by: M. Edgar Barrett, Christine R. Hekman, Robert C. Higgins, Thomas R. Hofstedt, Jarl G. Kallberg, Richard W. Moxon, H. Lee Remmers, Arthur I. Stonehill, Raymond Vernon, and Ingo Walter.

Library of Congress Cataloging-in-Publication Data

50 cases in international finance.

    1. International finance—Case studies.   I. Dufey, Gunter. II. Giddy, Ian H.   III. Title: Fifty cases in international finance.
HG3881.A125   1987   332'.042   86-3424
ISBN 0-201-05127-3

CDEFGHIJ–MA–89

Preface

International finance is a dynamic area of study. Wittingly or unwittingly business firms, large and small, find themselves involved in international competition and affected by currency values and other international variables. Thus, business executives and those who work in the financial service industry are compelled to absorb the international dimensions of corporate financial management.

Almost one half of the cases in this book focus on the management of international corporate finance—issues ranging from foreign direct investment strategy to international accounting to cash management in an international context. Core areas, such as the analysis and management of corporate foreign exchange risk, are covered by several cases. Hence, this case collection comprehensively covers all relevant areas of financial management for international companies.

In addition, however, our work covers another dimension of international finance: during the past decade, there has been a revolution in international financial markets, characterized by the introduction of a number of new instruments and techniques. More than half of all cases focus on the mechanics and applications of "innovations" ranging from swaps to synthetic securities (options, futures). Further, a number of cases are designed to foster an understanding of international capital markets, including the recognition and exploitation of arbitrage opportunities.

In this collection we also introduced a new pedagogical element: the mini-case. While our full length, "Harvard" style cases provide the traditional challenge of identifying the information relevant to reaching a decision, we found this objective to be inappropriate in many applications, especially executive seminars. The mini-cases are not simply "examples" or "problems", but—if taught by a skilled instructor—present material as rich as the fuller cases without allocating precious time to digging through information of marginal relevance.

Last, but not least, all of the cases have been successfully tested. In over 25 years of teaching international finance to thousands of MBA students, corporate executives, and bankers in perhaps thirty countries, the authors have received a wide range of responses to the cases and caselets they have employed. It is these students and seminar participants who are to be thanked for providing the raw material for this book, and for prompting the many revisions that have been made to the written cases. These individuals' feedback, too, guided the authors' selection of cases written by other colleagues, many of which appeared in Addison-Wesley's *International Finance: Cases and Simulation*. To these collaborators, to our students, and to the corporate executives who provided information for the case studies, the authors say "thank you". To readers who have further suggestions, the authors say "write to us", directly or through our publisher.

Ann Arbor, Michigan   G. D.
New York, New York   I. G.

Contents

II *International Funding and Hedging Decisions* 95

III *Hedging and Positioning in International Markets for Financial Assets* 289

IV *International Banking and Financial Intermediation* 341

V *Multimarket Financial Packaging* 403

VI *Organization, Control, and Financial Reporting* 417

I

International Investment Decisions

1.1

Direct Investment and Capital Budgeting

Gunter Dufey

Case 1

Compãnia Nacional de Tubos Ltda. (CNT)

THE FOUNDING OF THE COMPÃNIA NACIONAL DE TUBOS LTDA. (CNT)/ACQUISITION OF AN EQUITY PARTICIPATION IN COMPÃNIA MEXICANA DE ACERO S.A. (CMA).

In the early 1950s, German industry, for the first time since the war, was again faced with the question of investment abroad. Metall AG (Metal Corporation), whose operations primarily involved the manufacture of

The original case from which this translation was made was prepared by Messrs. Storck and Wussow under the direction of Professor Busse von Colbe of Universitätsseminar der Wirtschaft as the basis for discussion in seminars rather than to illustrate either effective or ineffective handling of an administrative situation.

steel pipe, had traditionally been oriented toward investment abroad and hence was one of the first German enterprises to resume foreign operations after World War II.

At this time Mexico was at the beginning of a period of intense industrial development. Characterized by a stable political climate and an ample labor supply, Mexico was especially receptive to German industrial investments.

Because of a shortage of domestic production facilities, the Mexican market for pipe was supplied primarily by imports from the United States. A rapidly growing market for pipe material was taken for granted, an expectation reinforced because of the country's size. Consequently Metall AG decided to establish a plant in Mexico for the production of seamless pipe. Tampico, which is located on the Gulf of Mexico about three hundred miles northeast of Mexico City and approximately the same distance from the U.S. border, was chosen as the location for the new plant. Here it was possible to work in cooperation with a Mexican foundry, Compãnia Mexicana de Acero S.A. (CMA), which would supply the necessary preworked metal stock from which piping is formed. Availability of such metal stock is typically a decisive factor in the selection of a site for a seamless metal pipe plant. A preliminary long-term contract for the supply of pipe material was agreed upon by CMA and Compãnia Nacional de Tubos Ltda. (CNT), the new wholly owned subsidiary of Metall AG. At the same time, CMA agreed to lease, for 99 years, 75 acres of real estate conveniently located to CNT for the construction of the new pipe plant. The ties between Metall AG and CMA strengthened over several years as Metall AG gradually acquired a 25 percent interest in CMA. In the long run, the acquisition of a majority holding was contemplated.

The new plant was equipped with automated pipe-forming machinery on which seamless pipes of diameters ranging between 4″ and 12¾″ could be produced. The plant was designed for an eventual maximum production of 300,000 tons per year. Initial production was to start at 90,000 tons per year and to eventually be increased to 180,000 tons per year within five years. The results of a market study showed these tonnages to be saleable. The capacity for finished output and other aggregates was estimated to be about 225,000 tons per year. Approximately six hundred laborers and office workers were to be initially employed.

From an analysis of the production costs and net revenues, it was expected that sales of 120,000 tons per year would be necessary to break even, and that anticipated future sales indicated that the operation would have earnings after about two years.

The market analysis was based on the feasibility of virtually displacing the U.S. imports by approximately 120,000 tons per year and the possibility of retaining 60 to 70 percent of the annual market size growth within

Mexico. The market analysis predicted an annual growth of the market by 10 to 15 percent. The pipes were to be distributed via two CNT sales corporations, in Mexico and in the United States respectively. Investment in plant and equipment for the new plant amounted to DM150 million ($32 mil) during 1956 and 1957. The equity portion of this investment amounted to DM100 million, which at the current exchange rate corresponded to $24 million.

CNT'S PROGRESS

1. The strategy which led to the founding of CNT failed for two reasons:
   a) The Mexican market in general, and the pipe market along with it, did not attain the growth rates anticipated in the preliminary market study.
   b) A much more serious problem was that the rolling process for pipe production advanced more rapidly than had originally been anticipated. Seamless pipe could now be manufactured at a lower cost and sold at a lower price, which led to cut-throat competition in the pipe market.
2. The corporation attempted to adapt to this new development by slowly retreating from the market for standard, average quality piping and by switching to the manufacture of high-grade, specialized pipes, in particular highly refined casings for oil drilling. This specialization made it necessary to extend the market area beyond the Mexican border. Consequently the U.S. market, with its heavy demand for such casings, presented itself.

The corporation was successful in adapting to this specialized pipe market, and by 1965 production and sales had increased to 210,000 tons per year. Of this amount, 50 percent was sold in Mexico, 40 to 45 percent in the United States, and 5 to 10 percent at lower prices in other countries. CNT's share of the Mexican seamless pipe market was about 80 percent.

Despite the sales level attained by 1965 through the adoption of the altered market strategy the earnings level of the corporation still remained unsatisfactory.

Results for the years 1965 to 1970 were as follows:

	1965	1966	1967	1968	1969	1970
Sales	50.3	47.6	34.2	48.0	50.1	52.3
			($000,000)			
Earnings Before Taxes	3.0	1.7	(1.7)	.6	.8	.4

The corporation cited the following reasons for its unsatisfactory earnings:

a) The constant development of higher grade specialized pipes necessitated considerable research and development expenditures and various additional investments.

b) The extensive specialization in highly refined pipes led to a strong dependence on the drilling activities of large oil companies, and a dependence on exports to the United States, which were less profitable due to tariffs and freight costs.

c) The production of highly refined pipes placed specific quality requirements on the preworked metal stock. CMA was not equipped to meet these quality standards, so high quality production could be achieved only with added expense and difficulty.

d) In deciding to service this specialized market, CNT had to conform to the industry practice of maintaining warehouses in all localities with major drilling operations in order to be prepared to deliver at any time. As a result, liquid assets were tied up and interest costs were incurred for funds invested in nonearning assets.

e) The poor earnings as a percent of sales in 1967 were attributed to lengthy periods of plant shutdown at CNT.

f) In selling 40 percent of its production of highly refined pipes in the United States, the firm competed with large U.S. manufacturers. In comparison to these competitors, who generally worked in affiliation with steel manufacturing and rolling mills, CNT controlled a very small plant and had an equally low sales volume. The company's costs for development, technical management and administration, purchasing, supply maintenance, and distribution as a percentage of sales were all very high. The supply of metal stock from CMA was also very expensive when compared to the in-house production of the competitors.

3. In addition to the unsatisfactory earnings yield of the firm, Metall AG was adversely affected by changes in the par values of various currencies that paralleled the revaluation of the Deutsche mark, because the DM equivalents of the transferred profits sank accordingly.

CMA'S POSITION WITH RESPECT TO CNT/METALL AG

1. Deliveries of metal stock to CNT for the planned production of 300,000 tons of piping in 1971 meant a possible contribution to overhead of about $6 million for CMA. If deliveries were discontinued,

CMA would have no way for the next five years of recovering this amount through increased sales of existing and new products.

2. Upon completing commitments to expand the capacity for steel output, CMA was interested in expanding the breadth of its operations and particularly in taking on the production of piping. Cooperation with Metall AG would simplify this process through the transfer of know-how, patents, licenses, and the like. However, the heavy financial burden of the commitments to expand output capacity left no margin for further investments during the next five years.

METALL AG'S POSITION WITH RESPECT TO CMA

The originally planned purchase of a majority interest in CMA required reconsideration as it became apparent that the Mexican government might take measures to protect domestic industry from foreign takeovers.

Exhibit 1 Compãnia Nacional de Tubos Ltda.

June 1970

Board of Directors
Metall AG

Dear Sirs:

In compliance with your request, we have drawn up a plan for sales, production, and earnings of Compãnia Nacional de Tubos Ltda. (CNT), which is enclosed.

As you can see from our planning, we are forecasting an improvement in our earnings on a long-term basis, which would result from increasing sales and simultaneously decreasing costs due to economies of scale.

We point to the fact that the realization of these plans depends on whether the additional sales intended particularly for the Mexican market can be achieved without price concessions and without such extraordinary factors as political unrest or worsening of export proceeds.

On this basis we will attain an average return on investment of only 8.4 percent or 9.6 percent, depending on alternative shipping projections for the period 1971–1975, and therefore will not attain the target return that you require. Even in consideration of an optimistic forecast regarding the volume of shipments, we would realize a ROI of only 14 percent by 1975 and thus be below your expected goal of 15 percent.

TABLE 1 Sales and profit plan, CNT 1971–75

	1971	1972		1973		1974		1975	
		pessimistic	optimistic	pessimistic	optimistic	pessimistic	optimistic	pessimistic	optimistic
— in 1000 t —									
Shipments									
Mexico	120	128	128	135	135	141	143	147	150
United States	90	90	95	92	99	95	102	98	105
Offshore	23	27	29	30	35	30	39	30	45
Total	233	245	252	257	269	266	284	275	300
— in Million $ —									
Net sales	*54.83*	*57.6*	*59.0*	*60.5*	*63.2*	*62.6*	*66.5*	*64.8*	*70.4*
Material cost	31.40	33.0	33.8	34.7	36.3	35.9	38.3	37.1	40.5
Processing cost	21.86	22.5	23.0	23.3	24.0	23.9	24.9	24.5	26.0
Cost of goods sold	53.26	55.5	56.8	58.0	60.3	59.8	63.2	61.6	66.5
Gross margin*	1.57	2.1	2.2	2.5	2.9	2.8	3.3	3.2	3.9
Adjustments	./.0.37	./.0.5	./.0.5	./.0.5	./.0.5	./.0.5	./.0.5	./.0.6	./.0.6
Earnings before taxes	1.20	1.6	1.7	2.0	2.4	2.3	2.8	2.6	3.3
Earnings after taxes in CNT (tax rate 42%)	0.70	0.9	1.0	1.2	1.4	1.3	1.6	1.5	1.9
Earnings after taxes in Germany**	0.56	0.7	0.8	1.0	1.1	1.0	1.3	1.2	1.5

* Differences between estimated and book values.

** The dividend paid to the German parent is subject to a 20 percent withholding tax in Mexico and is not taxable in Germany.

Basis: Price level of 1970, no significant shifts between market sectors.

Assumption: Increased cost can be offset through increases in productivity or, alternatively, they can be passed on to customers.

Pessimistic and optimistic planning data are solely due to different estimates of shipments. Other risks (price discounts, cyclical fluctuations) should be compensated for by a special factor.

The continued realization of 1975 results cannot realistically be expected.

9

The well-known difficulties with the Compãnia Mexicana de Acero S. A. (CMA) concerning the quality, quantity, and timely delivery of metal stock supply still exist. Owing to the long-term supply contract, we can see no way to improve this situation decisively.

In view of the difficult situation with CMA, we have also contemplated establishing our own production facilities for metal stock. The management of CNT, however, has reached a unanimous decision on the basis of its analyses that this alternative must be discarded. Considering the limited demand for metal stock, it is felt that the proposed facilities could not be operated economically.

We have also recently concluded a study which investigated the possible expansion of production of welded pipes and cold-rolled steel pipes. In addition to the difficulties which could arise from the construction of the facilities on land leased from CMA and the already mentioned metal stock supply acquisition problems with CMA, our investigation has also revealed that considerable funds would be required to bring the proposed facilities into operation. The investment necessary would amount to approximately $10 million for the welded pipe facility and $12 million for the cold-rolled steel pipe facility. The ROI for these investments would only be 9 percent or 10 percent.

In addition, the construction of a welded pipe facility would be of limited value since even our present production facilities are not operating at full capacity.

We suggest that the problems mentioned should be discussed at the next Board meeting.

Sincerely yours,

CNT Management

Enclosures

Exhibit 2   Metall AG

July 1970

Management
Compãnia Nacional de Tubos Ltda.

Dear Sirs:

We thank you for your exposition of your economic situation along with the possible alternative courses of action for your company. As you know, we emphasized the difficulties in metal stock shipments during the last CMA Board meeting. It seems, however, that the solution to this problem cannot be reached in the present way of operating.

Based on experiences in our other plants, we view the present form of cooperation agreement as the primary cause for the difficulties. Directly coordinating metal stock material requirements with the appropriate departments in the rolling mills could result in an improvement.

We are convinced that the structural disadvantage of your operation, as well as the lack of your own metal stock supplies and the unfavorable ratio of overhead expenses to sales, can be eliminated only through close cooperation with CMA.

We therefore agree to discuss these points during the next Board meeting. Preliminary to this meeting we request that you consider possible benefits which would result from closer cooperation with CMA and then prepare the following material.

1. Quantify changes in earnings of CNT and CMA which would result from consolidating both stages of production.
2. Comment on the new Mexican legislation on foreign takeovers, which is presently being drafted.

In view of the legal question we ask that you invite your lawyer to the next Board meeting.

Sincerely yours,

Metall AG

Exhibit 3 *Excerpt from the minutes of CNT board meeting on September 30, 1970 Third point on the agenda*

GENERAL CONDITION OF CNT AND POSSIBLE COURSES OF ACTION

In connection with CNT's unsatisfactory situation, its report explains in detail sales and profit plans from 1971 to 1975 and medium-term alternatives.

The material requested by Metall AG is presented and explained. After a detailed inquiry, a $2.2 million reduction in annual overhead expenses at CNT was considered feasible on a long-term basis (Exhibit 1). Moreover, this reduction in expenses in the steel production and rolling stage and metal stock preworking stage has been determined to amount to approximately $1.8 million per year (Exhibit 2). CMA's expected economic benefits from the combined responsibility for production from raw material to the finished pipe are based on the data that have been attained in Metall AG's integrated foundry, rolling mill, and pipe works. As a consequence of integration, savings will also be made in the inventory of metal stock (Exhibit 3).

The detailed discussion on the potential to economize on overhead expenses shows that CNT's estimates are optimistic, but that at least 60 percent should be attainable.

The participants of the discussion all agree that cooperating with CMA is the best course of action. Therefore, CNT and CMA should be consolidated.

The expected profits for 1971–1975, according to the plan, make a takeover of CNT by CMA very interesting, especially in combination with the synergistic effects considered possible.

Mr. Fulano, the corporate legal counsel, presented the following views: The draft of the bill limiting foreign influence on domestic industries that is presently under consideration in Parliament provides for considerable limitations on foreign capital. In particular, foreign companies shall no longer be permitted to acquire a majority ownership share of Mexican companies. The date on which the bill is to be passed has not yet been set; however, an increase of Metall AG's share in CMA could accelerate this legislation and create considerable opposition. Already, any intended acquisition of additional shares by foreign companies must be registered.

Mr. Shultz, Senior Vice-President of Finance at Metall AG, states that this information, together with other intelligence reports available in Germany, confirms the change in attitude of Mexican officials toward foreign investment. For this reason, an increase in CNT's ownership share in CMA must be eliminated as an alternative as far as the Board of Metall AG is concerned, even though it would be the most rational solution economically.

In addition, Mr. Fulano refers to the following matters:

1. Consideration of the benefits of the consolidation under discussion in connection with this type of valuation study is new in Mexico.
2. During negotiations on cooperation with CMA, the impression should not be left that Metall AG, as major shareholder of CMA, could gain unfair advantage (reference to arm's-length clause).
3. Also, with regard to its own Board of Directors, CMA will request that a valuation study be made.
4. Because of its own plans for expansion and the restriction conven-

TABLE 2 Compãnia Nacional de Tubos Ltda., Tampico, August 1970
(Summary of possible cost savings, especially in overhead expenses when steel and rolling operations are integrated)

| Cost center ledgers | Actual 1.1–6.30.70 × 2 = expenses budget 1970 | Compound effect (CNT)* | | | Remarks |
| | | Compound effect (at CNT) | | | |
		Profit per year**	Loss per year**	Investment savings***	
4 Plant service I.	$ 10,532	—	—	—	
40 Roads and parking	607,170	—	—	—	
41 Tube mill buildings					
42 Utility systems					
4201 Water distribution system	$ 38,576			$100,000	Water settling basin and oil skimming facility
4202 Compressed air	14,914	—	—	—	
4203 Gas system	8,156				
4204 Heating	63,302	$ 6,000	—	—	Natural gas (difference in contract price) (difference in contract price)
4205 Electric power	469,402	150,000	—	—	
4206 Butane plant	13,914	—	—	—	
4207 Trolley wire system	750	—	—	—	
4208 Waste heat boiler	609,014	—		—	
43 Plant protection and safety	104,398	20,000		—	1 messenger, 2 guards
44 Plant cleaning	36,008	18,000		—	Reduction of office space
45 Stores	212,698	180,000		—	15 men
46 Hot mill offices	198,398	12,000		—	1 assistant superintendent
47 Hot mill tool processing	148,570	10,000		—	1 foreman
49 Grounds maintenance	59,996	20,000		—	Lower billet inventory
Subtotal	*$1,986,784*	*$416,000*	*—*	*$100,000*	

13

TABLE 2 (Cont.)

		Compound effect (CNT)*			
Cost center ledgers	Actual 1.1–6.30.70 × 2 = expenses budget 1970	Compound effect (at CNT)			Remarks
		Profit per year**	Loss per year**	Investment savings***	
5 Plant Service II.					
50 Inspection department	1,002,732	100,000	—	—	1 superintendent, 1 foreman, 8 men
51 Mechanical maintenance	1,431,036	36,000	—	—	4 operators
52 Machine shop	147,994	10,000	—	—	1 foreman
53 Labor pool	163,052	10,000	—	—	
54 Electrical maintenance	442,778	—	—	—	
55 Finishing mill tool grinding	74,526	—	—	—	
56 Cold straighteners	125,170	—	—	—	(Operating cost center)
57 Test preparation	85,684	20,000	—	—	Test department (2) for special investigations
58 Shipping department	465,788	30,000	—	50,000	1 foreman and 3 men, 1 diesel locomotive
59 Finishing mill offices (foreman)	211,268	—	—	—	
Subtotal	*4,150,028*	*206,000*	*—*	*50,000*	
6 Operating cost centers (Hauptkostenstellen)					
60 Billet department	385,1⁴	?,000	—	45,000 / 20,000 / 10,000	Based on lower inventory: 1 straddle-carrier, 1 Michigan front loader, 1 Caterpillar, and 2 men
61 Hot mill	2,681,184	36,000	—	—	Natural gas (difference in contract price)
62 Finishing department cut-off A	543,964	—	—	—	
63 Reclaim department A (Grinding)	461,608	—	—	—	

No.	Item	Amount			Notes
64	Finishing Department Threading B	310,394	—	—	
65	Testing Department	574,166	—	—	
68	Heat Treat Department	766,274	22,000	—	Natural gas (difference in contract price)
69	Nondestructive Testing	803	—	—	
70	Ultrasonic Testing	1,925	—	—	
71	Reclaim Department C (Adjustage)	63,660	—	—	
72	Finishing Dept. Cut-off C	69,016	—	—	
76	Coupling Department—Cut-off	40,882	—	—	
77	Coupling	162,890	—	—	
78	Department—Boring Coupling Department Tapping	166,270	—	—	
79	Coupling Department Electric Plant and Paint	62,954	—	—	
	Subtotal	*6,291,904*	*98,000*	*75,000*	
8	*Plant Administration Cost Centers*				
80	General operating	103,570	103,570	—	
81	Production planning department	87,030	25,000	—	1 superintendant and 1 man
82	Metallurgical department	216,932	60,000	—	1 superintendent and 2 phys. testers, and 1 metallurgist
83	Engineering department	102,472	30,000	—	1 superintendent and 1 man
84	Industrial engineering	168,146	75,000	—	1 superintendent and 5 men
89	Customer complaints	44,026	—	—	1 superintendent and 1 man
	Subtotal	*722,176*	*293,570*	—	

TABLE 2 (Cont.)

		Compound effect (CNT)*			
	Actual 1.1–6.30.70 × 2 = expenses budget 1970	Compound effect (at CNT)			
Cost center ledgers		Profit per year**	Loss per year**	Investment savings***	Remarks
9 General Admin. and Sales Cost Center					
90 Corporate Management	262,912	262,912	—	300,000	Office building
91 Industrial relation department	66,212	50,000	—	—	except 1 man
92 Office service department	150,720	100,000	—	—	Communications, Depreciation on office equipment
93 Administration and finance expenses	447,712	165,000	—	—	Reduction of Interest due to lower Billet Inv. (7,000 t) and Compt. office.
94 Accounting department	214,680	170,000	—	—	except 4 people
95 Data processing department	214,976	170,000	—	—	
96 Purchasing department	40,616	40,616	—	—	except 4 people
97/98 Sales department	286,242	219,744	—	—	except "Traffic-Billing"
99 Outside pipe storage	285,720	—	—	—	
Subtotal	1,969,790	1,178,272	—	300,000	
Total	**15,120,682**	**2,191,842**	**—**	**525,000**	

The savings shown represent optimistic assumptions and can be realized to a certain extent only over an extended period of time.
*Synergistic effects
**Current cost savings with respect to increases p.a.
***Savings of investment funds when it is possible to rely on appropriate, sufficiently large-scale operations in another plant (which is the rule in an integrated steel and rolling mill).

ants[1] associated with long-term borrowing, CMA has no funds for such investments. CMA must not incur any additional debt that would show on its balance sheet.

5. A general increase of the equity capital for CMA is not considered feasible because of the presently low price of CMA common stock on the exchange.
6. CMA has no experience in the production and marketing of pipe.
7. Basically, CMA expects a before-tax return on equity of 18 percent, in which case the current balance proportions would be considered as adequate.

Talks with CMA concerning a consolidation of CMA and CNT have been decided upon. Upon convening a meeting, Mr. Shultz will speak to CMA's Board of Directors and will suggest that CMA appoint a committee for the negotiations. It shall be proposed that the committee consist of three members from each of the two parties.

For the time being, the committee members of CNT/Metall AG are to develop suggestions that might serve as a basis for the negotiations on CMA's takeover of CNT. Among other things, CMA's financial situation and its lack of know-how in the area of pipe production and sales must be specifically taken into account.

Enclosures

Exhibit 4 *Tampico, Mexico*

September 1970

Memorandum

TECHNOLOGICAL ADVANTAGES OF AN INTEGRATED FOUNDRY AND PIPE FACILITY (IMPROVEMENT OF OUTPUT, MANUFACTURING METHODS, AND PRODUCTION FACILITIES)

1. Improvement of output in the steel plant through increased use of exothermic hot tops. These are special covers for the molds into which the liquid steel is poured. They permit the slowest possible

---

[1] Regarding the structure of the balance sheet: the fixed assets, when increased by the amount of an additionally planned debt, must add up to at least two and one-half times the long-term debt (including the new loan). Regarding earning capacity: the earnings after tax must amount to at least three and one-half times the interest for long-term debt (including new loan) in the year prior to receipt of the additional debt. CMA was not in compliance with this restrictive condition.

hardening of the liquid steel on the surface so that impurities can rise, thus avoiding the formation of air pockets inside the steel block.

Normally, the application of exothermic hot tops improves the output. However, the reduction in the quality of the surface must be taken into account when the steel is rolled. Metall AG has considerable know-how in this area and can use these exothermic hot tops specifically for molding up to 90 percent of the different qualities of metal stock for pipe material. This exchange of know-how is consistently possible only if the production of both metal stock supply and pipe is under centralized control, since decisions on the most practical methods of the process demand thorough knowledge of pipe production and since specific decisions are necessary for each production run.

2.   Matching of quality requirements of specific orders better throughout the individual stages in production particularly affects the finishing of the pipe output. In order to satisfy the *general* quality requirements of the customer CNT, the metal stock must be "soaked" or kept in a high temperature oven for a period of time. By taking the specific quality requirements into consideration, the extent of the soaking process can be calibrated much more precisely and the output can thus be improved. To that extent it would also be more practical to integrate the pipe material soaking process with the pipe manufacturing plant when combining foundry and pipe production. For reasons of pipe quality control, this is not possible without integrating all processes.

3.   Leftover piping, which without consolidation has to be scrapped or at least depreciated in value, could be used partially for pipe manufacture when operations are integrated. Moreover, with integrated plants it is possible to deliver piping in roll-lengths and divide them up according to exact information on how they are to be employed, which would considerably reduce the amount of scrap lengths left over.

Furthermore, in integrated plants it is possible, within certain limits, to produce pipes from piping which does not fully meet the quality demanded.

To a considerable extent, good pipe can still be produced from this lower grade material.

With respect to the production of about 300,000 tons of piping the following quantifiable advantages would result from the above change.

Item 1   Approximately $0.6 million per year
Items 2 and 3   Average between pessimistic and optimistic estimate: approximately $1.2 million per year.

Exhibit 5 *Compānia Nacional de Tubos Ltda., Tampico*
August 1970

INVENTORIES

The special situation of CNT, which was characterized by its dependence on a third party for the supply of metal stock and by correspondingly long lead times for scheduling the semifinished metal stock, demanded a considerably higher inventory compared to our other integrated pipe plants.

The volume of additional inventory required was estimated at about 15,000 tons and, according to a cautious assessment, was worth around $100 per ton. The expenses resulting from this (interest and warehouse costs) amounted to at least $0.15 million (10 percent).

Study Questions
1. What are the problems facing MAG's management?
2. Does MAG still have a foreign direct investment strategy?
3. What are MAG's alternatives?
4. How would you go about quantifying these alternatives?
5. What are the key issues of each alternative?
6. Which is your suggestion? Summarize the arguments you will use to sell it to your top management.
7. Would you lend to CMA for the purpose of acquiring CNT?

Exhibit 6 Compãnia Nacional De Tubos Ltda., balance sheet, December 31, 1970

Assets	$	$	Liabilities	$	$
CURRENT			**CURRENT**		
Cash		171,000	Bank loan		11,289,000
Accounts receivable		5,805,000	Accounts payable and accrued liabilities		7,479,000
Due from subsidiary companies		1,665,000	Employees' withholding and other taxes payable		336,000
Inventories, at lower of cost or market			Due to subsidiary companies		357,000
Finished goods*	7,563,000				
Work in process	2,121,000		Total current liabilities		19,461,000
Raw materials	2,880,000				
Spare parts and supplies	1,353,000		Deferred income taxes		306,000
Total inventory		13,917,000			
			Shareholders' equity:		
Production tools		426,000	Capital		24,000,000
Prepaid expenses		228,000	Retained earnings		444,000
Total current assets		22,212,000			
Investment in subsidiary companies, at cost		312,000			
Fixed assets, at cost	43,509,000				
Accumulated depreciation	21,822,000				
Net book value		21,687,000			
		44,211,000			44,211,000

* As to final product inventories in the U.S. they are on the books of the U.S. sales company ($7.2 mil on Dec. 31, 1970).

Exhibit 7 *Compãnia Nacional De Tubos Ltda., statement of profit and loss and retained earnings, year ended December 31, 1970*

	1970 $
Sales, less discounts and allowance	52,254,000
Interest charged to subsidiary company	615,000
	52,869,000
Cost and expenses:	
Cost and expenses excluding the following	49,386,000
Depreciation	2,520,000
Interest	543,000
	52,449,000
Net profit before taxes and extraordinary items	420,000
Income taxes	240,000
Net profit before extraordinary items	180,000
Add extraordinary items:	
Income tax credit	87,000
Net profit for the year	267,000
Retained earnings, beginning of the year	177,000
Retained earnings, end of the year	444,000

Exhibit 8 Compañía Mexicana De Acero S.A., consolidated balance sheet, December 31, 1970

Assets	$	Liabilities	$
Current:		Current:	
Cash	3,957,000	Accounts payable and accrued	43,026,000
Short-term investments, at cost	28,595,000	Provision for income and other taxes	14,381,000
Accounts receivable	53,911,000	Dividend payable	3,650,000
Inventories	79,389,000	Current portion of long-term debt	1,172,000
Prepaid expenses	881,000		
Total current assets	166,733,000	Total current liabilities	62,229,000
Investments in associated companies, at cost	11,117,000	Long-term debt	55,113,000
Unamortized debenture issue expense	482,000	Provision for deferred income tax	76,000,000
Fixed assets		Shareholders' equity	
Raw material properties, at cost	77,010,000	Capital	65,700,000
Manufacturing plants and properties, at cost	461,722,000	Retained earnings	201,565,000
	538,732,000		
Accumulated depreciation	256,457,000		267,265,000
	282,275,000		
	460,607,000		460,607,000

Exhibit 9 *Appraisal, RCN value and RCLD value, summary classified by accounts, October 1970*

Accounts	Reproduction cost new (RCN)	Reproduction cost less depreciation (RCLD)
Buildings and structures	$16,945,484	$12,985,725
Residences	230,220	163,692
Misc. construction (paving, etc.)	550,607	442,950
Machinery and equipment	36,544,046	26,714,186
Misc. equipment	2,841,873	1,231,405
Power feed wiring*	240,225	215,549
Office furniture and equipment	442,463	309,725
Transportation equipment	960,218	641,863
Hot mill rolls	1,685,005	405,585
Subtotal	*$60,440,141*	*$43,110,680*
add:		
General overheads (Organization, administrative, and legal expenses, engineering and supervision, interest, taxes, and insurances during period of construction and installation)	10,758,150	7,674,750
Subtotal	*$71,198,291*	*$50,785,430*
Property in construction	1,947,972	1,947,972
Total	*$73,146,263*	*$52,733,402*

* These accounts include miscellaneous items of wiring and piping, as the major portion of this material is included with buildings and structures.

The revenue from the sale of individual pieces of equipment has been estimated at $10.2 mil.

Ian H. Giddy

Case 2

Imperial Power — Spain

Late in 1978 Imperial Power Company (IPC) management was considering expansion of the firm's involvement in international business. IPC was a Chicago manufacturer of a variety of electric motors for use in automobiles, household goods, and industrial equipment. All of the company's sales were to other manufacturers, primarily in the automobile industry. IPC's worldwide market was supplied from subsidiaries in France, Germany, Brazil and the Philippines as well as the United States. The company's success in Europe was based primarily on its technical expertise and prompt delivery of equipment meeting a variety of industrial needs. This success led top management to believe an expansion of IPC's European capacity was needed.

Imperial Power Company was written by Professor Ian Giddy of the New York University Graduate School of Business and revised by David Eiteman with the permission of the author.

The French and German subsidiaries of IPC distributed and assembled electric motors. They also performed a limited amount of manufacturing when special adaptations were required. With the maturing of European markets, particularly that for automobiles, an expansion of capacity to produce standard five-horsepower motors was required. The French subsidiary's management had urged IPC (U.S.) to expand facilities in France. However, Spain had much lower labor costs and certain government incentives that were not available in France, so IPC's president had asked the treasurer's staff to prepare a financial evaluation of a possible investment in Barcelona, Spain.

The proposed Spanish subsidiary of IPC would be a wholly owned venture producing electric motors for the Spanish domestic market as well as for export to other European countries. The initial parent-supplied equity investment would be $1.5 million, equivalent to Pts. 105 million at the current exchange rate of Pts. 70 to the U.S. dollar. An additional $600,000 would be raised by borrowing from Banque de la Société Financière Européenne, Paris-based consortium bank. Interest of 10 percent would be payable annually, and the entire principal would be due in ten years. However IPC-Spain did not anticipate any difficulty in renewing the loan indefinitely. The combined capital of $2.1 million would be sufficient to purchase equipment of $1 million and finance working capital requirements. No new working capital would be needed in the foreseeable future, and ten-year straight-line depreciation would be applied to the original cost of the equipment.

The project was regarded as an ongoing operation and therefore should, in principle, be evaluated for an indefinite time horizon. However, because of the difficulty of forecasting demand beyond a few years, the procedure used by IPC was to make cash flow forecasts only four years into the future and to treat the value of the subsidiary at the end of the fourth year as the present value of a constant annual cash inflow equal to that forecast for the fourth year.

(If, for example, the cash inflow forecast for year 4 were $150,000, then that amount was assumed to be the inflow for years 5, 6, and so forth. The net present value of this annual inflow can be found from the formula for the present value of a constant annuity:

$$\text{NPV} = \frac{\text{annual cash inflow}}{\text{discount rate}}$$

Assuming a 10 percent discount rate, the net present value at the end of the 4th year in this instance would be $150,000/0.10 = $1,500,000.)

The firm's overall marginal after-tax weighted-average cost of capital was about 12 percent. However, because of the higher risks associated with a Spanish venture IPC decided that a 16 percent discount rate would be applied to the project.

The initial sales price of an electric motor was to be Pts. 1,300 in Spain. Because of Spain's high tariffs on competing imports, this price would enable the Spanish operation to sell 50,000 units domestically and 150,000 in the export market. Spanish inflation would probably force the company to raise its sales price by 15 percent per annum, which would not affect domestic demand but might reduce forecast export sales unless the inflation were offset by a depreciation of the peseta. Discussions with the manager of the French subsidiary suggested that the price elasticity of demand in Europe was about 1.5; that is, for each 1 percent increase in the relative price of IPC's electric motors over the immediately prior year, demand would fall by 1.5 percent. Inflation in all Europe (except Spain) and in the United States was expected to run at a 5 percent annual rate.

For convenience, start-of-year prices and exchange rates would be used to calculate demand, sales prices, and operating costs for each year. However, interest (to the consortium bank) and royalty fees (to the parent) would be paid on December 31st at the year-end exchange rate.

In the absence of any price change or exchange rate change, sales for the first four years were forecasted as follows:

Year	Price (pesetas)	Price (French francs) (16.67 ptas/FF)	Domestic sales (units)	Export sales (units)
1979	1,300	77.98	50,000	150,000
1980	1,300	77.98	60,000	165,000
1981	1,300	77.98	65,000	181,500
1982	1,300	77.98	70,000	199,650

The capacity of the Spanish plant would be 350,000 units per year.

Variable cost per unit was estimated to be Pts. 840. Of this, 20 percent was for materials imported from the United States, 40 percent for domestic materials and the remainder for labor. Domestic costs could be expected to rise at the forecast inflation rate of 15 percent per annum. Annual fixed costs consisted of manufacturing overhead of Pts. 75 million, depreciation of the equipment over ten years with no salvage value, and royalty fees to the parent of $30,000 per year.

Spanish taxes consist of a 30 percent corporate income tax and a 10 percent witholding tax on dividends. No carry forward of losses is allowed. The U.S. income tax rate is 50 percent, with a credit allowed for foreign income and withholding taxes paid. Although the company expected that some of the subsidiary's earnings might be reinvested, for the purpose of evaluation, all profits were to be treated as if repatriated at the end of the year.

The project evaluation team at IPC was asked to evaluate the project on the basis of the above information, together with the following exchange rate forecasts received from the company's bank:

Currency Forecasts, 1978–1982 (Units of Foreign Currency Per U.S. Dollar)

December 31	Spanish pesetas/$	French francs/$
1978	70.0	4.20
1979	70.0	4.00
1980	85.0	3.50
1981	95.0	3.50
1982	110.0	3.50

Robert C. Higgins

Case 3

Wiley International

In early 1984, Richard Esposito, newly appointed Vice President Finance for Wiley International, instituted a new format for the evaluation of offshore capital projects. Henceforth, all proposals with a total cost exceeding $100,000 equivalent were to be submitted to Chicago headquarters for approval by the Capital Budget Review Committee. Among other items, proposals were to include a forecast of project cash flows and an estimated net present value or internal rate of return. In substance, the new format eliminated all distinctions between domestic and offshore projects in the approval process.

Domestic projects at Wiley had been evaluated in the manner de-

© by the Graduate School of Business Administration, University of Washington, 1984. This case was prepared by Professor Robert C. Higgins as a basis for class discussion. Cases are not designed to present illustrations of either effective or ineffective handling of administrative problems. Written by Robert C. Higgins, Professor of Finance, University of Washington.

scribed for a number of years, but for various reasons, foreign projects had historically been treated in a more decentralized, qualitative way. The roots of this differing treatment were several. During the late 1950s and throughout the 1960s, when Wiley began serious expansion outside the United States, many of the company's best managers were assigned to foreign divisions. (Wiley changed its name from Wiley, Inc. to Wiley International in 1971.) In addition, senior management in Chicago, most of whom had no foreign management experience, felt too far removed from foreign markets and products to evaluate specific capital projects. This encouraged a perception that foreign investments were fraught with so many non-quantifiable variables, such as exchange risk and political risk, that rigorous numerical analysis of foreign investments was not particularly valuable.

In recent years, the environment had changed considerably. Managers with significant foreign experience were reaching senior positions in Chicago. Foreign divisions were being staffed increasingly with foreign nationals who tended to have diverse educational backgrounds and approaches to business decision making. And the company was finding it increasingly necessary to allocate scarce investment capital among divisions. All of these trends suggested to Esposito that Chicago should take a more active role in offshore resource allocation decisions. Senior executives now had the expertise to contribute to project analysis, a formal approval process would encourage foreign divisions to analyze capital projects in a uniform, systematic manner, and as a result of the more formalized system, Chicago would be in a better position to allocate investment funds across divisions.

THE KOREAN PROPOSAL

Among the first offshore proposals submitted according to the new format was a request from Wiley's Korean division for the equivalent of $3.8 million to expand production of five-horsepower motors. Because the project's forecasted internal rate of return of 29.5 percent well exceeded the company's hurdle rate of 13 percent for product-line expansions, the Korea division manager strongly recommended the expenditure. (See Exhibit 1 for details.)

Esposito was troubled by several aspects of the Korean proposal. One concern was that the project's internal rate of return was calculated using won-denominated cash flows, while the hurdle rate employed had traditionally been applied to U.S. dollar cash flows. Inasmuch as the cash flow projections were based on an expected Korean inflation rate of 18 percent as opposed to a consensus forecast of 5 percent for the United States, Esposito believed this comparison was inappropriate. As a point of comparison, he noted that the Korea division was paying 22 percent interest on local currency financing. It did not seem appropriate that the hurdle rate for new investment should be below the firm's borrowing rate.

A second concern was the division's handling of favorable supplier financing. Almost 80 percent of the project's cost would be financed by Japanese equipment suppliers with a yen-denominated loan at a very attractive 6 percent interest rate. This rate was 7.5 percentage points below the yield on Wiley's recent dollar borrowings. The proposal incorporated this benefit by adding 7.5 percentage points to the project's stand-alone return of 22 percent, yielding the above-mentioned 29.5 percent return. Esposito doubted that 7.5 percent was an accurate measure of the value to Wiley of the supplier financing, and he questioned whether this number should be added to the stand-alone return when measuring the overall worth of the project. At a more fundamental level, Esposito was concerned that the project's return in the absence of favorable financing did not appear to exceed the local currency borrowing rate.

A final worry was the degree of leverage associated with the supplier financing. Wiley's stated policy was to maintain a target debt-to-equity ratio of no more than 1.5 to 1.0. The debt-to-equity ratio for this project was almost 4.0 to 1.0. It appeared that, if this project were accepted, future projects would have to be financed with proportionally more equity than implied by the 1.5 to 1.0 ratio in order to bring the average back down to the target. Esposito wondered how, if at all, this should be reflected in the analysis.

Esposito was convinced that the complexities evident in the Korean proposal would be recurring ones under the new capital approval format. Beyond approving or rejecting this particular proposal, therefore, he was anxious to develop a well-reasoned methodology for analyzing offshore capital projects.

Exhibit 1 *Korea division proposal for second five-horsepower production line (excerpts)*

PURPOSE

Wiley Korea has been manufacturing and marketing five-horsepower motors in Korea for the past four years. Profits from this activity have been moderate. Competition has been principally from foreign manufacturers, who face trade barriers in the form of informal quotas, and from small domestic manufacturers who have a history of quality problems. Our profits, while adequate, have been retarded by an aggressive pricing strategy designed to gain market share and also by some difficulty in acquiring local skilled labor.

We see a major increase in the demand for five-horsepower motors from Korean auto manufacturers. Our projections indicate that American and Japanese auto makers will significantly expand production in Korea as labor cost differentials continue to favor Korea. We further believe that the Korean government will encourage such expansion as a means of increasing skilled employment and of increasing exports. We anticipate that over three-quarters of cars manufactured in Korea in the next decade will be exported.

We are requesting 3 billion won ($3.8 million at the current exchange rate of 790.40 won/$) for the purpose of expanding production of five-horsepower motors. Major expenditures will be:

Building and site preparation	500 million won
Employee training/development	500
Production assembly equipment	2,000
	3,000 million won

FINANCIAL JUSTIFICATION

The new facility will enable us to expand production by 200,000 units in the first year, rising to 270,000 units in the fifth year. Exhibit 2, entitled Project Evaluation, presents the forecast cash flows over a five-year life, the project net present value, and the internal rate of return. Note that the NPV at Wiley's standard cutoff rate for expansion projects of 13 percent is a very healthy 8.65 million won, while the IRR is approximately 22 percent.

In the investment outlay of 3 billion won we have allocated 500 million won to the acquisition and training of a skilled workforce. This should obviate the kind of problems we have experienced in bringing our existing production line up to present efficiency. Unfortunately, this expenditure will not be depreciable. The remaining 2.5 billion won will be depreciated on a straight-line basis over five years to zero salvage value for taxes.

Pricing of the motors reflects a movement to a more attractive before-tax margin on sales of 12 percent. Price increases over time due to inflation are estimated to be 18 percent per annum over the forecast period.

Exhibit 2 *Project evaluation (in won millions)*

	Year					
	0	1	2	3	4	5
Initial investment	(3,000)					
Units sold (in thousands)		200	220	240	260	270
Price/unit (in thousands)		12	14.2	16.7	19.7	23.3
Revenue		2400	3124	4008	5122	6291
Operating cost		1400	1822	2338	2988	3670
Gross profit		1000	1302	1670	2134	2621
Administrative cost		212	276	354	452	556
Depreciation		500	500	500	500	500
Profit before tax		288	526	816	1182	1565
Tax at 40%		115	210	326	473	626
Profit after tax		173	316	490	709	939
Depreciation		500	500	500	500	500
After-tax cash flow		673	816	900	1209	1439
Salvage value after tax						776
Total cash flows	(3,000)	673	816	990	1209	2215

NPV at 15% = won 647
IRR   ≅ 22%

Although the building has an expected life of twenty to thirty years, the equipment will likely become physically and technologically obsolete in approximately five years. Consequently, we have chosen a five-year horizon for analysis. The salvage value of 776 million won in the fifth year is our forecast of the market value of the building at that time given an 18 percent inflation rate.

Based on discussions with Korean tax authorities, we believe that income taxes on this project will be at approximately the 20 percent rate. However, consistent with Chicago's requirements and in the interests of conservatism, we have used the higher U.S. rate, which we estimate to be 40 percent. This is the tax rate Wiley Chicago would pay if it repatriated all of the investment's profits. Given the rate of Wiley's expansion in Korea, we do not feel all profits would be repatriated.

PROJECT FINANCING

Our discussions with Japanese equipment suppliers indicate that, as part of the purchase of their production equipment, we will be able to finance almost 80 percent of the project with a five-year uniform paydown loan denominated in yen at an interest rate of 6 percent. (See Exhibit 3, entitled Project Financing, for details.) This is well below the yen borrowing rate of approximately 9 percent experienced by companies comparable to Wiley, and is certainly below the 13.5 percent it cost the company recently to borrow intermediate term in New York.

We were suspicious of such favorable terms at first, but the suppliers explained to our satisfaction that a sale would qualify for Japanese Ex-Im Bank loan guarantees. In addition, the suppliers appear to have cut the interest rate even further as a covert price reduction. Our technical people assure us the Japanese equipment is as good as any available, and it is available at an attractive "all-in" price.

Adding the financing "spread" of 7.5 percent over New York financing (13.5–6 percent) to the project's IRR of 22 percent, we calculate a return of 29.5 percent including the favorable financing. We are sure you will agree this makes the project very attractive indeed.

Exhibit 3 Project financing (in yen millions)

Year	Beginning of period loan balance	Interest expense at 6%	Principal payment*	End of period loan balance
1	680	36	125	555
2	555	33	128	427
3	427	26	135	292
4	292	18	143	149
5	149	9	152	0

*Annual interest + principal payment = 161 million yen
Exchange rates mid-March 1984:

$$1 \text{ US dollar} = 790.40 \text{ won}$$
$$1 \text{ US dollar} = 224.30 \text{ yen}$$
$$1 \text{ yen} = 3.5239 \text{ won}$$

Christine R. Hekman

Case 4

Vick International-Latin America/Far East

INTRODUCTION

In the summer of 1973, after three years of study and market testing, Tom McGuire had to decide whether to submit to the Indonesian government a final application to build a plant. McGuire, General Manager of Vick International-Latin America/Far East, a division of Richardson-Merrell, Inc. (RMI), knew that if the application was accepted the company would be expected to live up to the proposal as written. Because of the "binding" nature of the proposal he needed a firm commitment from RMI's Board of Directors before actually filing the application with the Indonesian government.

RICHARDSON-MERRELL, INC.

Richardson-Merrell is a diversified pharmaceutical manufacturer with plants, offices, and research laboratories in thirty-four countries. The company's three major product groups are 1) Consumer Products, 2) Merrell ethical pharmaceuticals (prescription drugs), and 3) a variety of smaller product lines including chemicals, veterinary products, and plastic products. The company had shown steady growth in sales and earnings of about 10 percent since 1969. In fiscal 1973 net sales were $505.4 million, earnings were $42.7 million, and total assets were $445.6 million. (See Exhibit 1.)

The Consumer Products group, the largest and most profitable of the groups (see Exhibit 2), is organized into four divisions: Vicks Health Care, Vicks Toiletry Products, Vick International-Europe/Africa (E/A), and Vick International-Latin America/Far East (LA/FE). The Vicks Health Care and Toiletry Products divisions manufacture and market all health and toiletry product lines in the United States and Canada. These include such familiar products as Vicks VapoRub, Lavoris mouthwash, Clearasil, and Oil of Olay. The international divisions, Vicks International E/A and Vicks International LA/FE, market Vick products in 160 other countries. These divisions also manufacture in 27 foreign countries more than 90 percent of the international sales volume; the remaining 10 percent is supplied

Exhibit 1 *Five year financial summary of Richardson-Merrell, Inc. ($000)*

Fiscal year ending June 30	1973	1972	1971	1970	1969
Sales	$505,384	$446,478	$408,520	$380,620	$340,262
Earnings for the Year	42,707	37,911	30,107	30,880	27,001
Research Expenditures	23,607	19,986	18,024	16,822	15,550
Advertising & Promotional Expenditures	74,816	65,576	60,101	56,334	49,724
Total Assets	445,607	401,159	374,305	331,188	311,538
Current Assets	236,215	203,734	188,128	174,211	168,104
Current Liabilities	100,987	83,685	79,970	60,678	58,278
Stockholders' Interest	296,063	264,477	237,408	220,154	207,666
Total Debt	149,544	136,682	136,897	111,034	103,872

Exhibit 2 *Richardson-Merell, Inc. Sales by major product group* (1972/1973)

Group	Group sales ($000)	Percent of total sales	Percent of group sales outside the U.S.
Consumer Products	$274,453	54	48
Ethical Pharmaceuticals	166,571	33	53
Other Products	64,360	13	12
Total	$505,384	100%	45%

Income by major product group (1972/73)

Group	Income* (millions)	Percent of total income
Consumer Products	$24.5	57
Ethical Pharmaceuticals	15.3	36
Other Products	2.9	7
Total	$42.7	100%

* Before taxes and allocation of central administrative expenses.

from domestic or international locations. Unlike the domestic divisions, the Europe/Africa and Latin America/Far East divisions also produce and sell various haircare, household, and nutritional products.

The divisions operate independently of each other but divisional plans and policies are subject to approval by Corporate Management or the Board of Directors dependent upon the size and nature of the investment. For example, routine expenditures for advertising and new product promotion are financed within the division. However, an investment in a new plant is of a magnitude requiring approval from the RMI Board of Directors.

International sales had been a major contributor to RMI's growth. For the period from 1967 to 1973 international sales grew twice as fast as domestic sales. This international success was primarily due to Vick's willingness and ability to tailor specific products and marketing programs for individual overseas markets. For example, the division had acquired such products as "ChocoMilk," a powdered milk supplement, for Mexico, and "Pea-Beu," a household insecticide, for Australia and New Zealand. Vick often tailored marketing techniques to each foreign culture, sometimes going so far as to create complex distribution systems. As a result, products usually captured primary market shares quickly and generated substantial income.

These abilities had proven especially important in developing countries. For example, Vick had entered the Indian market with a series of relatively high priced products. The quality of the products was communicated through a sophisticated marketing program and the company had been forced to build an entire distribution system. These efforts were rewarded, however, by tremendous consumer acceptance and Vick became one of the few companies that could boast a successful Indian subsidiary. McGuire hoped to put the same marketing skills to work in Indonesia.

INDONESIA

Indonesia seemed an attractive medium- to long-range investment opportunity for RMI because of its natural resources and its potential for rapid economic growth.

The five main islands of Indonesia are surrounded by the South China Sea, the Indian Ocean, and the Pacific Ocean. Jakarta, the capital city, is located on Java, the most densely populated of the five islands. It is 600 miles south of Singapore, and 1200 miles south of Thailand and Indo-China (Cambodia, Laos, and Vietnam).

The total population of Indonesia, two-thirds of which live on Java, was estimated at 120 million in 1973. Approximately 40 percent of the population over ten years old had received no schooling and nearly 60 percent of the labor force was employed in agriculture, fishing, and related industries. Only 9 percent of the labor force could be classified as administrative, technical, or clerical. Daily wages varied between laborers' wages of Rp 400 (US $0.95) and clerical wages of Rp 4167 (US $10.00).

The islands, which are covered with plush forests and mineral-rich soil, are also endowed with vast natural resources, including oil. In fact, Indonesia depended on these resources for most of its foreign trade which in turn supported most of the country's economic activity.

Indonesia's foreign trade patterns were very characteristic of a mineral-rich developing country. Machinery, fertilizer, and rice were the largest imports, coming primarily from the United States, Japan, and West Germany. Imports were partially financed by exports of oil. Indonesia was the world's twelfth largest producer of oil and exported 1.5 million barrels per day in 1973. At this rate oil comprised half of Indonesia's exports. Her largest export markets were Japan and the United States.

The strength of oil exports was reflected in a trade balance that was historically in surplus. (See Exhibit 3.) Huge shipping costs and other invisibles had contributed to current account deficits but in the 1970's these had been offset by foreign aid and private capital flows. Capital flows together with oil revenues had supported rapid growth of the Indonesian economy and real GNP had risen an annual average rate of 15.4 percent between 1969 and 1972. (See Exhibit 4.)

Exhibit 3 *Indonesian balance of payments (millions of U.S. dollars)*

Year	Balance of trade	Current account	Capital, allocation of SDR's and net errors and omissions	Balance of payments (official settlements balance)
1960	132	−58	126	−68
1961	−290	−466	235	231
1962	−26	−212	166	46
1963	54	−201	77	124
1964	42	−205	229	−24
1965	24	−222	252	−30
1966	118	−108	126	−18
1967	−34	−254	257	−3
1968	41	−225	213	12
1969	—	−336	316	20
1970	57	−310	345	−35
1971	81	−372	315	57
1972	347	−334	756	−422
1973	552	−475	803	−328

Note: Negative sign indicates a deficit.
Source: International Financial Statistics, lines: 77abd, 77a.d + 77tad + 77tgd, 78add + 78k.d + 78pbd + 78w.d + 79w.d, −1* 79a.d.

Exhibit 4 *Indonesian economic statistics*

	Gross national product (billions of Rupiahs)	Consumer price index (1970 = 100)	Annual rate of inflation (%)	Exchange rate (Rupiahs per dollar, end of year)
1966	838	12	N/A	78
1967	2,068	34	183%	235
1968	2,683	76	123	326
1969	3,290	89	17	326
1970	3,605	100	12	378
1971	4,405	104	4	415
1972	6,508	111	7	415

Source: International Financial Statistics.

In the present decade the economy had also exhibited relative stability. Inflation had been brought down from a 1967–1969 annual average of 108 percent to an annual average of 7.7 percent for 1970 through 1972. The rupiah, which had lost 76 percent of its dollar value between 1966 and 1969, had remained at 415 Rp/$ since 1971. (See Exhibit 5.)

The Indonesian economic system and government had been plagued with corruption and mismanagement, with at least 30 percent of national income lost to graft annually. But by 1973 the economy had strengthened remarkably, the government appeared to be in control, and much of the violent domestic strife had begun to fade into the past.

Of course, the government was anxious to continue these trends and encouraged foreign investment. A tax holiday of two years, beginning with the first year of plant operation, was granted for the initial investment. One additional year could be obtained for locating the plant outside Jakarta, and another year if the investment would generate foreign exchange savings of at least $250,000 per annum. The tax holiday exempted the investment from the normal 45 percent corporate tax rate. In addition, losses incurred prior to plant start-up, or during the tax holiday, could be carried beyond the tax holiday period without limitation until sufficient covering

Exhibit 5 *Indonesia, relative prices and exchange rates*

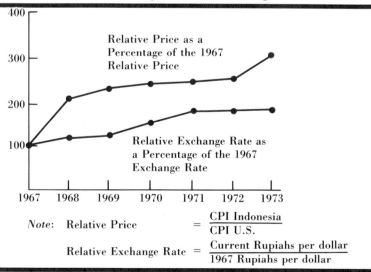

Source: International Financial Statistics.

profits were generated. Normally tax loss carry forwards were limited to five years.

RMI IN INDONESIA

Vick entered the Indonesian market late in the 1940s by importing and selling products through a Dutch distributor. In 1951, a Promotion Supervisor was hired to supervise the posting of tin signs on buildings, point-of-sale display, and consumer sampling, and to improve the effectiveness of the distributor's salesmen.

In the aftermath of having gained independence from the Dutch in December 1949, Sukarno badly mismanaged Indonesia's economy and the country became almost bankrupt. Import restrictions necessitated a change in Vick's strategy by the mid-1950s. Vick responded by licensing its Dutch distributor to both manufacture and sell, but restricted the license to one size of Vicks VapoRub — the overwhelmingly popular nine-gram tin package for which there was an Indonesian source of supply. Within two years, the Dutch distributor was nationalized as part of the Sukarno program to nationalize foreign-owned investments. Throughout the remaining nine years of the Sukarno regime, the government agency continued to manufacture and sell Vicks VapoRub, with the Promotion Supervisor continuing his activities, even though unable to communicate directly with Vick management.

After two years of mob violence, Sukarno was deposed in early 1967. Shortly thereafter, the new government under President Suharto promulgated Foreign Investment Law No. 1. This new law required that all new foreign investments be approved by the Investment Coordinating Board and that they include at least 10 percent Indonesian equity initially, and increase the Indonesian equity to 30 percent within five years from plant start-up.

Having reestablished direct communication with the Promotion Supervisor during 1968, McGuire sent in teams to assess the market for Vick products, the performance of the government agency that was the licensee, and the overall business and investment climate. The conclusion was that Indonesia offered a major opportunity for self-medication products, but that Vick would not be able to exploit this in any relationship with the government agency, which lacked any skilled distribution and promotional personnel and whose plant facilities were limited.

McGuire recognized that the investment climate was risky, but he was equally convinced that government regulations would start increasing the minority participation requirements. Response of foreign investors to Foreign Investment Law No. 1 was very favorable. From his standpoint, investment in Indonesia with majority foreign ownership was rapidly going to become a now-or-never situation. This reasoning prompted McGuire to move simultaneously on two fronts.

McGuire had found a potential partner, E. Trimistro, a well-respected Indonesian businessman who owned a consumer product distribution company, Perdoni. This was a vital asset since Indonesian law prohibits non-Indonesians from engaging in direct distribution. Vick retained the service of Perdoni as its distributor, and terminated its license with the government agency. Vick returned to an importing strategy — this time from RMI Philippines — but with a range of sizes of Vicks VapoRub and an expanded line of products to test the market.

The importing strategy was clearly temporary: as industrialization accelerated, so would the demand for imported raw materials, placing a strain on the availability of exchange. At the same time the Indonesian government, like most other countries, had stated its aim was to be self-sufficient in pharmaceutical products. Therefore, simultaneous with implementing the importing strategy, McGuire decided to approach the Board of Directors of RMI with a proposal to invest in a plant in Indonesia, with Mr. Trimistro as the holder of the 10 percent minority Indonesian equity. While the proposal was being developed, the Investment Coordinating Board announced that after December 31, 1969, investment proposals would only be accepted with minority foreign ownership.

This proposal requested $1.1 million to purchase land in Indonesia, to build and equip a pharmaceutical plant, and to provide enough working capital to begin operations by January of 1972. The plan was to manufacture and market the four cough and cold products which Vick had been importing: Cough Drops, VapoRub, Inhalers, and Formula 44.

The proposal was approved and financed as follows:

$ 900,000	RMI 90% equity
100,000	Minority interest
100,000	Local bank loans with RMI guarantee
$1,100,000	

The application was filed before the December 1969 deadline, an investment license was granted in August 1970, and a sixteen-acre site was purchased.

For the next two years, McGuire attempted to work with Perdoni, the local distributor, to increase sales. However, sales continued to lag due both to the inadequate sales force and to Perdoni's lack of enthusiasm. In addition import costs were much higher than predicted. Vick had planned for duties and shipping costs totaling 58–60 percent of the cost of products in Manila; in actuality they exceeded 100 percent on some products.

Because sales continued to fall far below projections, McGuire began

Exhibit 6 Richardson-Merrell, Inc.-Indonesia* Income statements ($000)

	1970/71	1971/72	1972/73
Net Sales			469
Total Cost of Goods Sold	5	10	288
Gross Margin	5)	(10)	181
Market Research			37
Advertising/Promotion			110
Total Marketing Expense	—	—	147
Sales/Advertising Admin.			31
Selling Expenses/Commission			82
Total Marketing Overhead	58	62	113
Administration and General			99
Total Overhead	58	62	212
Operating Profit	(63)	(72)	(178)
Total Non-Operating Expense	(1)	10	6
Profit Before Taxes	(62)	(82)	(184)

Balance sheets as of June 30 ($000)

Assets	1971	1972	1973
Cash	$102	$ 53	$138
Accounts Receivable	13		6
Prepaid Expenses	27	12	30
Total Current Assets	142	65	174
Net Fixed Assets	25	117	123
Total Assets	$167	$182	$297

Liabilities			
Accounts Payable	29	26	25
Net Worth:			
Capital Stock	200	300	600
Retained Earnings	(62)	(144)	(328)
Total Net Worth	138	156	272
Total Liabilities and Net Worth	$167	$182	$297

* Statements for 1970 through 1971/72 reflect financial activity for only the Indonesian investment project. Activity for the importing business was reflected in the books of RMI Philippines. The 1972/73 statements include the importing activity.

to question the wisdom of the investment. He decided to postpone further outlays and construction until he could be more confident of success in the Indonesian market. Vick requested and received approval of the Indonesian government for a deferral of the deadline for plant start-up.

McGuire decided to try yet another distributor. In 1972, Vick chose the Indonesian subsidiary of the Borneo Trading Company to distribute its products. Borneo was a large, established trading house with extensive experience in the distribution of consumer goods in Southeast Asia. However, even with Borneo's expertise sales and margins remained weak.

McGuire immediately authorized the development of a strong advertising campaign and heavy consumer testing. In September 1972 radio spots and magazine ads launched the program in five major urban areas. In addition, Vick took steps to solve the distribution problems. Inventories of key wholesalers were monitored and Vick personnel even began checking the visibility of Vick products on store shelves.

The results of the marketing effort were dramatic! In spite of severe stock-out problems, sales of Vick inhalers and Vick Cough Drops, a product new to Indonesians, were up by 72 percent and 227 percent, respectively. Sales of Formula 44 rose an amazing 270 percent. These results confirmed McGuire's feeling that the Indonesian taste for "self-medication" provided a large potential market for Vick products.

By June of 1973, the construction project remained stalled and Vick assets in Indonesia totaled only $123,000, mostly land. On the other hand, marketing and other expenses had generated $328,000 in losses. (See Exhibit 6.) However, the astonishing results of the marketing efforts prompted McGuire to dust off the original investment proposal and consider a final commitment to the investment.

THE REVISED PROPOSAL

Armed with the new and promising survey data, McGuire updated the original proposal. Vick would finish the Indonesia plant and plan to open it in 1975. Four products would be produced and sold in local markets: VapoRub, Cough Drops, Inhalers, and Formula 44.

Projected sales reflected a substantial increase above earlier forecasts. The final forecasts were still very conservative, but followed patterns similar to those experienced in similar markets. (Sales projections for Indonesia and experience in other markets are shown in Exhibit 7. Profit projections and pro-forma balance sheets are Exhibits 8 and 9.)

New promotional techniques had been modeled after those that were so successful in India. Radio and the press would be used heavily in urban areas and the effectiveness of television would be tested. Mass consumer

Exhibit 7
Vick sales projections in Indonesia

Sales growth			1972/73	1978/79	Six year % growth
VapoRub :	Total Grams	(000's)	20,910	59,280	183
	Total Dollars	(000's)	$ 213	$ 1,031	384
Cough Drops :	Total Drops	(000's)	15,200	56,660	273
	Total Dollars	(000's)	$ 116	$ 892	668
Inhalers :	Total Units	(000's)	120	272	227
	Total Dollars	(000's)	$ 35	$ 96	274
Formula 44 :	Total Mℓ	(000's)	19,200	67,800	353
	Total Dollars	(000's)	$ 112	$ 615	449

Note: Dollar sales growth outstrips real growth reflecting consumer price increases in 1973/74 and at a rate of 5% per year beginning 1975/76 to offset inflation.

Projected Vick reach of economically active population in Indonesia

	Total population (millions)	Millions Vick reach of economically active population	VapoRub gram/1000	Cough drops drops/1000	Inhalers /1000	Formula 44 Mℓs/1000
Indonesia 1972/73	120	14	1,493	1,085	9	1,371
Indonesia 1978/79	149	28	2,117	2,023	10	1,653
India 1972/73	550	90	2,769	1,665	13	1,143
Philippines 1972/73	37	28	5,849	1,522	15	2,851
Malaysia 1972/73	12	8	1,325	2,580	NA	NA

Exhibit 8 *Richardson-Merrell, Inc.-Indonesia, projected income statements ($000)*

	73/74	74/75	75/76	76/77	77/78	78/79
Net Sales	845	1,152	1,468	1,825	2,224	2,634
Total Cost of Goods Sold	553	532	618	714	863	1,022
Gross Margin	292	620	850	1,111	1,361	1,612
% of Sales	34.6	53.8	57.9	60.9	61.2	61.2
Market Research	31	17	15	17	10	12
Advertising/Promotion	187	197	249	310	371	440
Total CME	218	214	264	327	381	452
Sales/Advertising Admin.	92	96	108	119	131	146
Selling Expense/Commission	148	201	220	274	333	395
Total Marketing Overhead	240	297	328	393	464	541
Administration and General	105	122	134	150	165	181
Total Overhead	345	419	462	543	629	722
Operating Profit	(271)	(13)	124	241	351	438
Total Non-Operating Expense	7	151	186	228	256	280
Profit Before Taxes	(278)	(164)	(62)	13	95	158
Income After Taxes	(278)	(164)	(62)	13	95	158

contact programs were also planned. These included providing information from traveling vans and a massive sampling effort. For example, one million samples of VapoRub were to be distributed yearly for five years and 1.5 million samples of cough drops a year for six years.[1]

In addition, Vick personnel would build a distribution system from the ground up. Current distribution was incredibly weak even in areas surrounding the largest cities.

Because of these ambitious plans, projected marketing and distribution expenses far exceeded those in the earlier proposal. However, these expenditures were a crucial part of McGuire's "preemptive" strategy. Vick's only major competitor was in the process of negotiating for the return of its plant, which had been nationalized. McGuire hoped to blitz Indonesian consumers and capture a large market share early on. Competitors anxious to capture part of that market would be forced to invest heavily in both marketing and manufacturing capacity.

[1] Sampling of Formula 44 at homes was prohibited by law, but the Vick management planned to explore other sampling strategies.

Exhibit 9 *Richardson-Merrell, Inc.-Indonesia, projected balance sheets at June 30 ($000)*

	1974	1975	1976	1977	1978	1979
Assets						
Cash	$ 113	$ 96	$ 93	$ 80	$ 80	$ 96
Accounts Receivable		236	300	374	456	540
Inventories	86	216	268	314	382	450
Prepaid Expenses	46	40	32	28	20	20
Total Current Assets	245	583	693	796	938	1106
Net Fixed Assets	993	907	822	739	657	577
Total Assets	$1238	$1495	$1515	$1535	$1595	$1683
Liabilities						
Notes and Loans Payable		150	225	275	225	150
Accounts Payable	244	115	122	79	94	99
Total Current Liabilities	244	265	347	354	319	249
Notes Payable— Intercompany	600	1000	1000	1000	1000	1000
Net Worth:						
Capital Stock	1000	1000	1000	1000	1000	1000
Retained Earnings	(606)	(770)	(832)	(819)	(724)	(566)
Total Net Worth	394	230	168	181	276	434
Total Liabilities and Net Worth	$1238	$1495	$1515	$1535	$1595	$1683

The problems of the early 1970s underscored the value of a qualified staff. Vick planned to solve its personnel problem in Indonesia by transferring to key positions people with experience in similar markets, primarily India, the Philippines and Malaysia. These personnel had already been identified and their transfers had been planned.

The project was not expected to generate profits until fiscal 1977 and accumulated losses were expected to reach a total of $832,000 for this first six years of investment. Of these losses $606,000 would be generated before 1974, when the tax holiday began, but could be carried forward without limitation until absorbed by profits.

The proposal requested an additional $1.2 million and would bring Vick's investment in Indonesia to $2.3 million. Funds would be invested in advertising, higher than expected construction costs, interim losses on the

Philippines imports, and added staff. The total resources would be applied as follows:

Operating Losses		
Pre-Plant Start-Up		$ 606,000
Plant Operation: First Year		164,000
Total		$ 770,000
Fixed Assets		
Land		$ 142,000
Plant and Equipment		775,000
Other		159,000
Total		$1,076,000
Net Working Capital		$ 454,000
TOTAL		$2,300,000

The investment was to be financed initially by equity ($1,000,000), a $1 million loan from RMI, and $300,000 in local bank loans with RMI guarantees.

GAINING THE BOARD'S APPROVAL

McGuire anticipated serious problems moving this proposal through the RMI Board. Several members of the Board had already voiced strong opposition. "We don't need the additional risk of another developing country. If it's diversity you're looking for — we've already got Venezuela, Australia, India, the Philippines . . ."

The ownership issue was another sore point. The new investment act would require RMI to reduce its equity holdings in the proposed Indonesian company from 90 percent to 70 percent by February, 1980. This short-term loss of equity certainly reduced the value of the investment.

It was hard to argue that the cash flow projections outweighed these disadvantages. In fact, the project would generate almost no cash for ten years. One reflection of these projections was an estimated payback period of 14.4 years. (Exhibit 10 shows the details of the payback calculation.) In contrast, other consumer product investments had paid back within five years and the Board had become accustomed to proposals that projected payback within this range.

McGuire planned to stress, however, that the project was a strategic

Exhibit 10 Richardson-Merrell, Inc.-Indonesia, projected payback at July 1, 1974

	Investment Base: $1,394						$000's	
	74/75	75/76	76/77	77/78	78/79	83/84	87/88	88/89
Cash flows								
Interest—RMI	50	50	50	50	50	50	43	35
Royalties—5%	58	73	92	111	132	194	263	284
Technical Service Fee	22	29	37	45	57	77	105	114
TOTAL	130	152	179	206	239	321	411	433
U.S. Tax at 48%	62	73	86	99	115	154	197	208
Net	68	79	93	107	124	167	214	225
Loan Repayment	—	—	—	—	—	—	150	150
Dividends Gross	—	—	—	—	—	—		
Dividends Net	—	—	—	—	50	—		
Minority Interest								
Participation—10%	—	—	—	50	—	—		
Additional—20%	—	—	—	—	—	—		
TOTAL CASH PROCEEDS	68	79	93	159	174	167	364	375
Payback								
Capital, June	394	1,465	1,533	1,593	1,595	882	440	120
Net RMI Loan	1,000	—	—	—	—	—	—	—
TOTAL—Investment Base	1,394	1,465	1,533	1,593	1,595	882	440	120
10% Interest Cost	139	147	153	159	160	88	44	12
TOTAL	1,533	1,612	1,686	1,752	1,755	970	484	132
Net Cash Flow	68	79	93	157	174	167	364	375
Investment Balance	1,465	1,533	1,593	1,595	1,581	803	120	(243)

Payback 14.4 YEARS

Calculation of Payback: Projected net worth in July 1974, $394,000 plus RMI loans of $1,000,000 constitute the initial investment. An opportunity cost of 10% increases the investment base annually. The investment base is reduced by the projected cash proceeds to RMI.

investment for growth, not a short-term moneymaker. One should not expect an immediate return in a developing country. Instead, by capturing primary market share now, Vick would position itself to participate in the coming prosperity. He also intended to point out that failure to move now not only would cost the majority ownership approval, but probably the ability to enter the market. McGuire was convinced that Indonesia would close categories to new foreign investment, and that the pharmaceutical industry was a prime candidate for such action.

McGuire was sure that Indonesia was a future "hot spot." All indicators pointed to future success:

- Indonesia had rejected state socialism, opting for free enterprise.
- The population was large and growing.
- Personal consumption expenditure had doubled in the last five years. This rate of growth was the third highest rate in the world.
- Progress was obvious, even to the casual observer. One saw building construction, highways, electrification, restaurants, automobiles, port activity, better dressed population, etc.
- Inflation had been brought under control.
- Oil revenues would continue to finance growth.

In short Indonesia was one of the last major undeveloped markets in the free world. "For a $2 million investment like that, a billion dollar company can't afford to pass it by," McGuire reasoned.

Apparently, McGuire was not alone in his assessment. Thirty-three other pharmaceutical companies had already approved investments in Indonesia; twenty-one had plants under construction or had purchased land, and ten had plants in operation. After meeting with representatives from Chase Manhattan, First National City Bank, and Morgan Guaranty, an RMI Assistant Treasurer reported that

> *"The banks are extremely bullish on investing in Indonesia. They feel under current conditions, that Indonesia provides one of the few bright spots for investment in the Far East."*

In McGuire's opinion, the marketing results were promising and, since the sale projections were conservative, the income figures represented the company's downside risk. In other words, the project would have a payback of fourteen years at worst. McGuire felt that he was now prepared to move on the project, but there was no doubt in his mind that the Board would be less eager than he.

Ian H. Giddy

Case 5

Dallas Semiconductor Company
An exercise in international tax planning

Don Mardick, Assistant Treasurer of the Dallas Semiconductor Company, was considering a discussion he had just had with his new assistant. This young fellow, newly graduated from business school, was brimming over with suggestions for the improvement of the international cash management function. He had no idea, Don thought, how difficult it was to manipulate the accounting and transfer pricing practices of some well-entrenched overseas subsidiaries. Nevertheless Don was intrigued by the suggestion that the company's international tax burden could be reduced by altering the legal structure or the intracompany pricing policies of the worldwide company.

Don decided that he would have to undertake a systematic review of the earnings, foreign taxes paid, and U.S. taxes associated with each of the firm's foreign affiliates. This done, he could assess his assistant's suggestion that after-tax profits could be increased by persuading the firm's Belgian subsidiary to lower prices on components shipped to the Taiwanese assembly plant. Tapping out some numbers on his calculator, Don figured that so doing might increase the Taipei unit's pre-tax profits by $10 million (and reduce profits in Belgium by the same amount). He decided to try to compute the effect of this change in transfer pricing on 1980 taxes and net income, assuming nothing else had changed.

Don glanced at the Dallas Company's 1980 results for overseas operations. Forty-eight percent of the company's total pre-tax profits, amounting to $398.14 million, had been earned abroad. At the end of 1979, Dallas had accumulated $25.5 million in excess tax credits which, according to current rulings, could be "carried forward" into 1980. As in the past, and in accordance with the Tax Reform Act of 1976, the firm employed the "overall" method of computing the limitation on foreign tax credits.[1]

In 1980 the German subsidiary had an income before taxes of $80 million. The German subsidiary declared a 100 percent dividend, in order to take advantage of the lower corporate tax rate on paid-out earnings (see Exhibit 1). This meant, however, that the 15 percent German withholding tax had to be paid on the full amount of after-tax earnings. Eighty percent of the earnings were reinvested in Germany. The subsidiary also reported that it had paid $40 million in value-added taxes to the German government in 1980; however, Don believed that VAT could not be counted toward the tax credits to offset U.S. taxes on foreign income.

Dallas Semiconductor's biggest operation was the European headquarters and manufacturing plant, located outside Brussels. In 1980 the before-tax profit of this subsidiary had been $260 million, but because it was located in a high-tax country, it declared a dividend of only 50 percent. The

---

[1] The Tax Reform Act of 1976 repealed the use of the "per-country" limitation for taxable years beginning after 1975; so taxpayers (with the exception of certain existing ventures in U.S. possessions and certain existing mining operations) must now use the "overall" method. The foreign tax credit on interest income, already required to be computed separately under the law, must also now be computed under the overall method.

The Act permits taxpayers who had been using the per-country limitation in the past to carry over some excess credits from pre-1976 years to post-1975 years as if the per-country limitation rules were still in effect. However, the taxpayer must compute his foreign credits for the pre-1976 year under the overall limitation method, and if such computation results in a lower amount of total credits, only the lower amount can be utilized in the current year. This reduction in the amount of credits available for carryover must be allocated to each of the foreign countries in the ratio of credits allowable under the per-country limitation for each country to the total credits allowable under the overall limitation. These unused credits can be carried forward over the remainder of the five-year period to the extent the limitation in the carryover year is not exceeded.

company also had a minor (seven percent) interest in a French electronics company, which had declared dividends totalling $105 million (out of $150 million after-tax profit) in 1980. Don Mardick had heard that Dallas was considering increasing its share in this firm to 10 percent, at a cost of $16 million, and he wondered what the tax effects would be.

The company had two subsidiaries in the Far East. One, located in Singapore, was a 50 percent joint venture with a local company and manufactured standard electronic components for export to the United States. In 1980 this company had declared a dividend of $10 million. The other, a wholly owned embryonic assembly operation in Taiwan, had reported $30 million in before-tax profits in 1980. It was the company's policy that this firm should pay 100 percent dividends.

Don knew, of course, that shifting income from one subsidiary to another could reduce foreign taxes, but he wondered whether any savings in Belgium would not be offset by increased taxes payable to the U.S. authorities. He recalled that the U.S. credit for foreign taxes paid was limited to the amount of taxes that would have been paid had the income been generated within the United States.

As he began his computations, Don Mardick pondered some of his assistant's other suggestions. Of what benefit, he wondered, would be certain changes in the legal form of certain overseas operations, all of which were locally incorporated subsidiaries? Under what circumstances would a branch form be more advantageous from the tax viewpoint? And could worldwide taxes be reduced by setting up a holding company for the German subsidiary, one incorporated in a low-tax location such as the Bahamas, and channelling Germany's income into that subsidiary? Don knew that in many instances changes such as these required the approval of the U.S. tax authorities, and he wanted to ascertain the possible benefits and obstacles of the proposed changes.

Exhibit 1   Dallas Semiconductor Co.

Country	Corporate tax rate	Withholding tax rate
U.S.A.	48% (earnings)	—
Germany	56% (retained earnings) 36% (paid out earnings)	15%
Belgium	48%	15%
France	50%	5%
Singapore	30%	10%
Taiwan	35%	8%

1.2

International Portfolio Investment

Gunter Dufey

Case 6

All-World Investment Management, Ltd.
International portfolio diversification

Janet Smith is the executive assistant to the treasurer of a large domestic manufacturing corporation. The treasurer has been recently appointed to this position, and consequently all areas of treasury operations are being reviewed, including the appointments of (external) managers of the company's pension funds.

The company has solicited proposals on investment strategy from current investment advisers as well as organizations whose services have not been used in the past.

One of the proposals has attracted the attention of the treasurer. It came from the firm of All-World Investment Management, Ltd., a joint

This case was prepared by Gunter Dufey while at Stanford University, Graduate School of Business, 1981. The case has been prepared as a basis for class discussion only; it is not designed to present illustrations of either effective or ineffective management. Revised May 1985.

venture whose prestigious parents comprise an old line Banque d'Affairs in Paris and a British merchant bank with a long history in international finance. The proposal purports to show a superior performance record in terms of returns (higher) and risk (lower) than any of the usual comprehensive yardsticks such as Standard and Poor's Composite Index of 500 Stocks (S & P 500).

The treasurer told Janet to look into this firm, having been particularly impressed by the performance record of the investment adviser. He reasoned that the superior portfolio performance would easily compensate for the investment adviser's fees, which were almost three times that charged by managers of domestic portfolios.

INVESTMENT PERFORMANCE: U.S. CLIENTS' TAX-EXEMPT PORTFOLIOS

Exhibits 1 and 2 set out the total returns for the portfolios managed by All-World Investment Management Ltd. (AWIM) for its tax-free U.S. clients. These portfolios are permitted to invest both in equities and in bonds and are valued in U.S. dollars. Returns are given for portfolios invested outside the U.S. securities markets and are computed from the data for a "global fund" consisting of all the U.S. client's funds invested outside the United States.[1-5]

[1] The data given are historical information, and it cannot be inferred that similar results will be obtained in the future. These results have been affected by variations in the rate of exchange of the U.S. dollar against the currencies of various foreign countries, and such variations may not occur in a similar way in the future.

[2] During 1975 and 1976 these funds have not always been valued at the exact quarter-end date.

[3] These returns have been computed after the impact of withholding taxes and commissions have been assessed where applicable. No allowance for withholding taxes or commissions has been deducted from the returns of the Capital International Index or the S & P 500.

[4] These returns have been computed after certain but not all custody fees have been charged, most of which have been paid directly by clients.

[5] These returns have been computed after certain but not all of AWIM's investment management fees have been charged. Most of such fees have been paid directly by clients.

Exhibit 1 *Rates of return for the current year*

Funds under management by AWIM		Quarterly returns			
	3 months ended Dec 1984 (%)	3 months ended Mar 1985 (%)	3 months ended June 1985 (%)	3 months ended Sept 1985 (%)	12 months ended Sept 1985 (%)
Invested outside U.S. securities markets (see notes 2–5)	0.40	6.18	4.86	19.81	33.64
Indices					
Capital International Europe, Australia and Far East Index	5.14	9.63	6.69	14.97	41.42
Standard & Poor's Composite 500 Index	1.88	9.13	7.34	–4.05	14.50

* The Capital International Index for Europe, Australia, and the Far East is based on over 700 shares listed on the stock exchanges of all major European countries, Australia, and the Far East. It is adjusted to reflect foreign exchange fluctuations of the various currencies relative to the U.S. dollar. The returns include reinvested dividends.

The Standard & Poor's Composite Index of 500 Stocks includes reinvested dividends.

Exhibit 2 *Annual rates of return*

	1975 (%)	1976 (%)	1977 (%)	1978 (%)	1979 (%)	1980 (%)	1981 (%)	1982 (%)	1983 (%)	1984 (%)	10¾ years ended Sept 1985 (%)
Funds under management by AWIM											
Invested outside U.S. securities markets (see notes 2–5)	34.58	11.67	23.54	30.80	11.66	28.38	−3.86	−2.11	29.36	−2.69	16.60
Indices*											
Capital International Europe, Australia and Far East Index	37.22	3.71	19.22	33.93	6.03	24.36	−0.95	−0.54	24.89	8.18	16.07
Standard & Poor's Composite 500 Index	37.17	23.51	−7.38	6.49	18.27	32.47	−4.91	21.54	22.51	6.21	13.99

57

Ian H. Giddy

Case 7

Pharmacia: Facts or Fiction?

Raj Ramaya was a new financial analyst at Prudential-Bache Securities. Among his first tasks was to respond to a customer's request for information about a Swedish company, Pharmacia. The customer was a large U.S. pension fund manager. The client had heard that Swedish accounting practices differed in certain basic principles from U.S. "generally accepted accounting principles" (GAAP) and wanted a rundown on how to interpret these differences.

"Basically," the customer said, "I want to know this: is Pharmacia's performance better or worse than its annual report makes it appear?"

Raj had wisely begun his search for an answer by asking his boss, Ruth Rich, for advice on the differences between American and Scandinavian accounting practices.

Raj: First, what's this nonsense about "untaxed reserves"? Can they really reduce income for tax purposes by allocating some income to various reserve accounts?

Ruth: Sure. Swedish and Finnish companies, for example, may make transfers to various reserve accounts at the end of a statutory fiscal period. Such transfers reduce the company's current taxable income, thus increasing cash flow. Subject to certain limits, management may use their discretion to decide the amount of money to be transferred to untaxed reserve accounts in each year. Management may also reduce aggregate reserves, which under certain circumstances would increase reported net income or decrease net loss. The effect of these reserve accounts on the company is discussed in notes to consolidated financial statements. In analyzing results of operations, management gives greater weight to income (loss) before adjustments to untaxed reserves and income tax expense than to net income.

Raj: Wow! In the United States, generally accepted accounting principles would regard such adjustments as a distortion of reported income.

Ruth: Uh-huh. Also, Scandinavian businesses can use depreciation for tax purposes that is generally more rapid than straight-line depreciation. Swedes use depreciation in excess of straight-line expense, even including the use of a reserve for future investments, to write down fixed assets acquired. Of course this reduces the allowable depreciation of the assets in future fiscal periods. U.S. GAAP requires depreciation of equipment to be based upon the useful lives of the assets. Another thing. Inventories do not include overhead costs, which are expensed as incurred. U.S. GAAP requires that inventory costs include manufacturing overhead.

Raj: Anything else that might affect their earnings per share?

Ruth: I've noticed that local accounting practice allows certain land and buildings to be revalued to an amount in excess of cost. U.S. GAAP does not permit the revaluation of assets in the primary financial statements. Also, deferred income taxes are not provided for under Scandinavian accounting practice. U.S. GAAP requires comprehensive deferred tax allocation on all significant timing differences.

Raj, I'm sure that's not all. But somewhere in my files I've got a blurb from Pharmacia's annual report. They did an ADS issue in New York in 1981; then they found they had to explain their bizarre accounting rituals to Americans. See what they say about it. Then take a look at the 1982 P & L of Instrumentarium, a Finnish company. They've tried to show how U.S. accounting would change their earnings per share. I guess all this is about as clear as an Ingmar Bergman movie. Anyway, good luck.

Exhibit 1 Excerpts from Pharmacia Annual Report: Net income in Swedish accounting and financial analysis*

Swedish accounting practice results in concepts of income which do not show the income and profitability trend of companies. Ralph Hammar, Vice President — Finance, Fortia-Pharmacia, discusses a number of drawbacks of the present system and proposes a new structure for the Income Statement.

- If one chooses to study income before appropriations and taxes, the Company's earning capacity is over-valued. This easily leads — on completely incorrect grounds — to discussions about "excessive profits."
- In calculating important key data, deferred tax liability is often deducted, which does not take account of the Company's real tax expense.
- The Swedish mixture of performance and fiscal bookkeeping is not commonly used internationally and creates problems for companies whose shares are analyzed and handled in financial communities in other countries.
- In this Annual Report, Fortia-Pharmacia takes a first step towards providing more comprehensive financial information on Group income

During 1982, we at Fortia-Pharmacia, perhaps more than the majority of other Swedish companies, have been faced with the question of which yardstick of income best reflects the Company's earnings and profitability trend. After our U.S. stock issue at the end of 1981, we were exposed to an entirely new approach relative to the analysis of corporate profitability. In the United States, great importance is attached to net income and especially to income per share.

PROBLEM FORMULATION

During the past year, the disadvantages of the lack of a *relevant concept of net income in Swedish accounting practice* have become increasingly clear. Appropriations are the reason why the Swedish concept of net income does not reflect the actual income of companies.

In Sweden we have solved this problem by not focusing interest on net income, but instead analyzing an income level "higher up" in the Income Statement, commonly "income before appropriations and taxes." (Many consider that, in addition, one should ignore extraordinary items in judging the profitability of companies, but I shall not take up that discussion here.) From this concept of income is then derived "net income per share"

* *Moody's International, 1983.*

by first deducting a standard tax and then dividing the result by the number of outstanding shares.

In the United States, for example, the most common measure of profitability by far is net income per share. People are used to finding the net income on the last line of the Income Statement. Anything else seems strange to an American analyst, and is greeted with skepticism. The Swedish method of charging net income with a large number of tax appropriations is hard to understand and difficult to deal with in accordance with U.S. accounting standards.

DRAWBACKS OF THE CURRENT SYSTEM

Let me illustrate the line of reasoning given below with figures from Fortia-Pharmacia's Consolidated Income Statement for 1981 according to Swedish GAAP. The amounts are in millions of Swedish kronor.

Income before appropriations and taxes	116.1
Appropriations	−50.8
Income before taxes	65.3
Taxes	−20.2
Net income	45.1

The above mentioned method, used in Sweden for determining income, has great drawbacks. The principal yardstick of earnings currently used by Swedish companies is income before appropriations and taxes. This level of income greatly overvalues the company's earning capacity. A large and important item of expense — taxes — is omitted from the analysis. This leads, among other things, to discussions about excessive income and demands for compensation from various special-interest groups, occasionally on incorrect grounds.

The Swedish method of calculating net income per share is even more questionable. As previously stated one often starts from income before appropriations and taxes and deducts a tax charge calculated at a standard rate, often fixed at 50 percent. To analyze this method of calculation, we can examine the above figures. Income before appropriations and taxes is "used" in two ways. Of this amount, Skr 50.8 million is allocated to untaxed reserves. This allocation does not lead to an immediate tax consequence for the company, but theoretically one can assert that a deferred tax liability has arisen. Skr 65.3 million is left for purposes of taxation, resulting in a tax charge of Skr 20.2 million, or 31 percent. The Skr 65.3 million is definitely taxed and will not be subject to further tax.

If one now calculates net income with the help of a standard rate of tax of 50 percent, one obtains a theoretical tax of Skr 58.1 million. It is understandable if someone who says that it is correct to include deferred tax liability in the calculation, bases the tax calculation on the Skr 50.8 million allocated to untaxed reserves. But one cannot very well change the actual tax rate of 31 percent which arose on the income stated for actual taxation. The consequence of this method of calculation is therefore as follows:

Total standard tax	58.1
Actual tax	−20.2
Additional provision for deferred tax liability	37.9

One thus makes a provision of Skr 37.9 million for additional tax. This is, in its entirety, attributable to the Skr 50.8 million allocated to untaxed reserves. In Fortia-Pharmacia's case, the provision for future taxation is all of 75 percent, a figure which cannot arise, even theoretically.

In the U.S. one is more logical in calculating deferred tax liability when attempting to interpret Swedish accounting. One starts from the reported net income, reverses the appropriations made, but deducts a deferred tax liability which is calculated solely on the basis of the appropriations. The actual taxation is then left in the calculation.

DEFERRED TAX LIABILITY OR NOT?

A principal question is whether one should apply deferred tax liability at all to appropriations. Deferred tax liability is not booked in Swedish accounting, but the way in which appropriations are dealt with tempt one to deduct it for purposes of "external" financial analysis. The only tenable motive for doing this would be that *these allocations to untaxed reserves would, with great probability and within the near future, become subject to taxation and thereby lead to tax consequences.*

I can see various situations in which the untaxed reserves would be liquidated:

1. The company has tax losses. In this situation, liquidation of the untaxed reserves will not lead to any tax consequence.
2. In companies with declining or low profitability and growth, where the reported net income is not sufficient to cover the dividend to the shareholders. It does not seem probable that one would want to use liquidation of untaxed reserves as a basis for dividend.
3. The company is closed down. Again, it is difficult to see that liquidation of the reserves would lead to tax consequences, but this naturally depends on the financial position of the company when it is

liquidated. The argument is hardly relevant, however, since the analysis should not concern a "dismemberment value" for the company, but the company's situation as a going concern. This is the premise upon which shareholders invest in companies.

4. Companies which are exposed to marked cyclical functions. In these cases, inventory build-up may occur during slack business periods, leading to a reduction of the inventory reserve in good years. Depending on the nature of the tax situation, the effect of the fluctuating inventory may vary. If the company operates at a loss during poor years, the inventory reserve is probably liquidated without a tax consequence, and is then replenished when the company is again operating at a profit. The inventory reserve serves as a tool for equalizing the fluctuation of the taxable profit.

There are naturally other situations in which the untaxed reserves may be liquidated. They generally do not involve tax consequences. *As far as Fortia-Pharmacia is concerned, the following can be stated clearly: Our untaxed reserves have never, on the whole, been transferred to taxation and thereby caused the Group any tax expense.*

The need for allocating deferred tax liability to appropriations may also be evaluated on the basis of traditional risk analysis. Realization of the deferred tax liability can occur in a hypothetical future situation, which shall be judged on the basis of two criteria: the probability that the event will occur and the consequence if it occurs. The calculation of deferred tax liability is based only on the consequences, without taking any account of the probability that the event will occur. In Fortia-Pharmacia's case, one can say that the probability that the appropriated untaxed reserves will lead to a tax expense for the Company in the foreseeable future is minimal. The risk is so small that we consider that it in no way deserves to lead to reservations in a financial calculation.

If companies established reserves for potential costs which had a correspondingly low probability of occurring, one would have no profits at all to talk about. When, in addition, the calculation shown above for Fortia-Pharmacia means that one reserves a tax expense, which corresponds to 75 percent of the appropriated amount for a risk which, on the whole, can be judged to be non-existent, the analysis is, to say the least, of limited value.

It must also be pointed out that, in times of strong inflation, deferred tax liability overestimates the real tax expense. The current figure for a future tax payment is much lower than the nominal figure. An active discussion is in progress in the U.S., for example, on focusing more on cash base accounting than previously.

ACTUAL TAX EXPENSES PROVIDE MORE CORRECT INFORMATION

The method of deducting a standard rate of tax on the appropriated funds means that one must consider it irrelevant for the investor whether a company can make appropriations or not. A company of Fortia-Pharmacia's type — which is expanding rapidly and thus has sharp growth in inventory, large investments in fixed assets and intensive research activity — can make large allocations to various types of appropriations and utilize other tax deductions. If one compares such a company with a sales company — which perhaps leases its premises, has its inventory on consignment from its principals and conducts no research at all — the effective tax rate is entirely different. If these two companies have the same income before appropriations and taxes, it cannot be immaterial to the investor if the first-named company has an effective tax rate below 20 percent compared with a tax rate of more than 50 percent for the second company. The method of using deferred taxes does not show this difference.

CAN DEFERRED TAX LIABILITY BE DISREGARDED?

What happens if one disregards deferred tax liability? In the year that the untaxed reserves are transferred back to taxation, creating an actual tax charge, the expense will burden *that* year's calculation of net income per share. The advantage of this is that one then knows that there really will be a tax expense and it will thereby be relevant to make this charge. The tax expense has an impact during the year when the decision to tax the income is *taken,* instead of being charged against the year when the *appropriation* to untaxed reserves was made.

This effect can possibly be said to conflict with the general aim in accounting practice that income and expense which are related should be reported in the same year. For a research-intensive company like Fortia-Pharmacia, this is a dubious argument, however. We report approximately Skr 150 m. in research costs for which there is no corresponding income item until many years have elapsed. If the aim to show related costs and income in the same accounting period guided our accounting, all our research projects would be activated and not transferred to the Income Statement before they either failed and were discontinued or led to saleable products, in this latter case through a depreciation plan.

Since we already have such large deviations from this matching concept, we think it entirely incorrect to burden the calculation of our perhaps most important measure of profitability with a hypothetical cost for deferred tax liability which has slight or no probability of occurring during the foreseeable future, simply to attain this conformity requirement.

NEW STRUCTURE NEEDED FOR INCOME STATEMENT

Sweden is quite unique in mixing performance and fiscal accounting. To facilitate the assessment of Swedish companies by other countries, an international adjustment of the Swedish accounting rules must be carried out.

Swedish accounting needs a new and relevant net income concept for analyzing the profitability of companies. The "marked prudence" concept, which generally guides our accounting and the efforts of certain financial analysts to evaluate all companies in the same manner, should — in appropriate cases — yield to a different viewpoint. The aim of accounting should be to develop relevant key ratios and income data, making it possible for outsiders to evaluate the development of various companies in a correct manner.

In this year's accounts we have taken an initial step in this direction by introducing — as a supplement to the statutory Income Statement format — a more "operative" Income Statement. In the traditional Swedish annual accounts, all operating expenses, excluding depreciation and amortization, are shown on one line, while appropriations have been itemized on several lines. It is our view that appropriations, on the whole, do not belong to the Income Statement. They should be regarded as an appropriation of income. The following changes therefore appear in the new Income Statement:

1. Operating expenses have been broken down so that production, marketing and research costs appear separately. This is an adaptation both to the EEC's 4th directive and to practice in the English-speaking world.
2. Appropriations have been eliminated from the Income Statement. We have thereby created, for both Swedish and international analysts, a relevant concept of net income, which can be divided by the number of shares outstanding to show net income per share calculated in such a way that they may be regarded as a true measure of the Company's performance.

The net income arising in this way will be treated (transferred to the Balance Sheet) in the following way:

— An amount, whose size is determined by the rules applying to the calculation of appropriations, is being allocated to untaxed reserves.
— Remaining amounts are being allocated to retained earnings and are being made available for allocation by the Annual Meeting of Stockholders.

As a result of this, certain key ratios are shown, after deduction of actual tax. The ratios affected are the debt/equity ratio, return on equity, and net income per share.

The aim of these measures is to provide all our readers — irrespective of the "school" to which they belong — with a basis for analysis of a company's profitability trend.

We trust that the changes made in our Financial Statements, will be regarded as a step in the right direction in our efforts to provide correct and relevant financial information about our Group.

Exhibit 2 Notes to consolidated financial statements (Information as at and for the four months ended April 30, 1982 and 1983 is unaudited) The application of the above described accounting principles generally accepted in the United States would have had the following approximate effect on consolidated net income, shareholders' equity and financial position:

	Year ended December 31,				Four months ended April 30,		
	1980	1981	1982	1982	1982	1983	1983
	(In thousands, except per share data)						
Net income as reported in the Consolidated Statements of Income	FIM 8,941	FIM 28,975	FIM 26,821	$ 4,944	FIM 5,963	FIM 9,939	$1,832
Increase (decrease) for:							
Adjustments to untaxed reserves	28,540	35,213	20,494	3,777	7,580	5,133	946
Depreciation expense	8,295	(775)	(1,315)	(242)	(233)	(356)	(66)
Inventories	1,066	3,511	(276)	(51)	152	693	128
Capitalization of interest expense	553	—	1,954	361	195	1,585	292
Disposals of property and equipment			2,055	378			
Deferred income taxes	(22,688)	(22,390)	(13,518)	(2,491)	(4,539)	(4,162)	(767)
Income tax expense		(11,850)					
Net increase	15,766	3,709	9,394	1,732	3,155	2,893	533
Approximate net income in accordance with accounting principles generally accepted in the United States	FIM 24,707	FIM 32,684	FIM 36,215	$ 6,676	FIM 9,118	FIM 12,832	$2,365
Approximate net income per share in accordance with accounting principles generally accepted in the United States	FIM 12.48	FIM 16.51	FIM 15.56	$ 2.87	FIM 4.60	FIM 5.13	$ .95

	December 31,			April 30,	
	1981	1982	1982	1983	1983
	(In thousands)			(In thousands)	
Shareholders' equity as reported in the Consolidated Balance Sheets	FIM 104,211	FIM 134,834	$24,854	FIM 135,708	$25,015
Increase (decrease) for:					
Adjustments to untaxed reserves	139,981	121,555	22,406	128,561	23,698
Property and equipment, net	9,279	49,915	9,201	49,559	9,135
Inventories	5,393	5,117	943	5,810	1,071
Capitalization of interest	553	2,507	462	4,092	754
Disposal of property and equipment	—	2,055	378	2,055	378
Deferred income taxes	(91,572)	(106,878)	(19,700)	(112,145)	(20,671)
Revaluation of assets	(29,340)	(29,340)	(5,408)	(29,340)	(5,408)
Net increase	34,294	44,931	8,282	48,592	8,957
Approximate shareholders' equity in accordance with accounting principles generally accepted in the United States	FIM 138,505	FIM 179,765	$33,136	FIM 184,300	$33,972

Source: *Moody's International*, 1983.

Exhibit 3*

INSTRUMENTARIUM OY

History: Established in Finland in 1900.

Business: Co. operates through four divisions, Med Division, DPHM Division (Datex-Palomex-Merivaara), Metos Division and Optical Division. Co.'s divisions are engaged in hospital supplies and equipment, x-ray equipment and films, laboratory equipment, dental equipment, Datex electronics, dental x-ray equipment, x-ray film developing equipment, ophthalmic-optics, home health care products, electric sauna heaters, large scale catering equipment, marine catering equipment, Merivaara hospital furniture, professional electronics and Wang word and data processing machines.

Board of Directors

Matti Kavetvuo, Chairman, President
Bjorn Immonen
Jaakko Lassila
Seppo Oksanen
Antero Partanen

No. of Employees: Dec. 31, 1982, 2,065.

Head Office: P.O. Box 357, SF-00101 Helsinki 10, Finland. Tel.: (3580)711211. *Telex:* 124687 instr.

Consolidated Income Account, years ended Dec. 31 (in thousands of U.S. $):

	1981	1980
Net sales	130,397	112,443
Expenditures	107,360	93,387
Operating profit	23,037	19,056
Depreciation	2,603	4,843
Group reserve decr.	—	cr269
Other inc. & exp.	dr2,180	dr2,852
Change in res.	dr8,113	dr6,786
Interest exp.	1,947	1,712
Direct taxes	1,510	1,100
Minority int.	20	cr24
Net income	6,664	2,056

* Source: Moody's International, 1983.

Consolidated Balance Sheet, as of Dec. 31 (in thousands U.S. $):

Assets:	1981	1980
Cash & bank rec.	1,034	650
Sales rec.	20,131	19,492
Loans rec.	14,626	5,879
Advance pay	182	269
Accrued rec.	1,078	2,092
Other curr. assets	10,092	5,927
Total curr. assets	47,143	34,309
Inventories	31,209	29,023
Fixed assets	17,784	17,120
Stocks, shareholdings, other expend.	4,099	3,747
Group capital fds.	25	42
Adj. items	85	—
Total	100,345	84,250

Liabilities:		
Accounts pay.	7,188	6,624
Advance pay. rec.	476	1,655
Accrued liab.	5,891	3,235
Other short-term liab.	4,500	5,404
Total curr. liab.	18,055	16,918
Long-term debt	25,392	22,417
Reserves	32,866	24,790
Minority int.	64	49
Share capital	7,590	7,990
Equity reserves	16,378	12,486
Total	100,345	84,250

Note: U.S. dollar equivalents based on currency value of U.S. $1 = 4,348 Finn-marks.

Long Term Debt: Outstg., Dec. 31, 1982, $32,273,000 comprising of:
(1) $11,369,000 loans from financial institutions.
(2) $20,904,000 loans from pension funds..
Capital Stock: Instrumentarium Oy, share capital:
Outstg., Dec. 31, 1982, U.S.$9,464,000.

PHARMACIA AB

History: Established in Sweden in 1921 as AB Fortia, present name adopted June 1, 1983.

Control: HB Lundberg & Malmsten, a partnership of two individuals, owns 6.6% of total shares and 27.0% of total voting rights.

Business: Co. is principally engaged in the development, production and sale of medical science products — pharmaceuticals, diagnostics, separation products and techniques, and proprietary products.

Property: Co. operates facilities aggregating 1,819,000 sq. ft. located in Uppsala, Umea and Valinge, Sweden; Hillerod and Koge, Denmark; and Piscataway, N.J., U.S.A.

Kurt Mark, Chmn.
Gunnar Wessman, Pres.
Sven Boode, Exec. Vice-Pres.
Carl-Erik Sjoberg, Exec. Vice-Pres.
Ralph Hammar, Vice-Pres. — Fin.

Board of Directors

Kurt Mark	Erik Malmsten
Gunnar Wesman	⊤Ulf Mandren
⊤Einar Darberg	Bengt Samuelsson
Gunnar Hambraeus	Gosta Virding
Kurt Lanneberg	John Sjoquist

Deputy Directors

Sven Boode	⊤Ingvar Johansson
⊤Ake Hammarstrom	Carl-Erik Sjoberg
Ralph Hammar	

⊤Employee representative.
Auditors: Coopers & Lybrand AB.
Annual Meeting: In May.
No. of Shareholders: Dec. 31, 1982, 13,000.
No. of Employees: Dec. 31, 1981, 3,687.
Executive Office: Rapsgatan 7, Uppsala, Sweden. Tel.: (018)16 30 00. Telex: 76027.

Consolidated Income Account, years ended Dec. 31 (Skr. 000):

	1982	1981
Net sales	1,862,800	1,440,600
Other revenues	121,000	43,600
Total revenues	1,983,800	1,484,200
Cost of sales	610,200	496,400
Sell., gen. & adm. exp.	964,900	780,100
Deprec.	57,100	44,300
Interest exp.	56,900	56,200
Foreign exch. gains	23,600	6,500
Appropriations	188,900	50,800
Inc. bef. taxes	129,400	62,900
Inc. tax exp.	33,500	17,800

Minority interest	*cr*200	—
Net Income	96,100	45,100

Consolidated Balance Sheet, as of Dec. 31 (Skr. 000):

Assets:	**1982**	**1981**
Cash	374,000	342,600
Receivables	344,200	283,300
Inventories	417,800	303,600
Prepaid exps.	33,900	31,900
Total current	1,169,900	961,400
①Prop. & equip.	795,900	686,900
Other assets	126,700	31,300
Total	2,092,500	1,679,600

Liabilities:

Sh.-tm. debt	97,000	45,900
Curr. port. of lg.-tm. debt	16,200	24,200
Accts., etc., pay.	144,100	105,200
Accrued exps.	112,200	91,600
Taxes withheld	18,700	17,500
Accrued taxes	28,800	15,000
Other curr. liab.	23,400	18,800
Total current	440,400	318,200
Long-term debt	202,700	203,600
Pension liab.	131,100	110,800
Other liab.	1,500	100
Untaxed res.	548,300	360,700
Minority interest	600	—
Share capital	192,500	192,500
Legal res.	407,100	401,300
Retained earn.	168,300	92,400
Total	2,092,500	1,679,600
Net current assets	729,500	643,200
①Deprec.	282,900	218,900

Long Term Debt: Outstg., Dec. 31, 1982, (Parent Company), Skr. 218,900,000 comprising:

(1) Skr.10,600,000 7¼%–15½% mortgage and collateralized loans.

(2) Skr.3,000,000 3% other long-term loans.

Subsidiary Debt: Outstg., Dec. 31, 1982, Skr.109,000,000 6.5%–17.5% long-term loans.

Capital Stock: 1. Pharmacia AB share capital, class A; par Skr.10:

Outstg., Dec. 31, 1982, 3,122,375 shs. comprising: 2,259,750 restricted shs. and 592,625 non-restricted shs.; par Skr.10.

Par changed from Skr.50 to Skr.10 by 5-for-1 stock split in Sept., 1981.

As of Feb. 25, 1983, HB Lundberg & Malmston owned 6.6% of the outstanding shs.

Entitled to one vote per sh.

Has same rights of participation in assets and profits of Co. as Class B share capital.

Foreign ownership is restricted to 40% of entire capital and not more than 28% of the voting power of all shares. Shares which may be acquired only by Swedish persons are designated as "Restricted" and those which may be acquired by Swedish or foreign persons are designated as "Non-Restricted."

Dividends Paid (since 1977 — in Skr.):

On Skr.0.50 par shares:

1978 .... 0.58   1979 .... 0.73   1980 ... . 0.91
1981 .... 1.10   1982 .... 1.50

Listed: On Stockholm Stock Exchange.

2. *Pharmacia AB share capital Class B: per Skr.10:*

Outstg., Dec. 31, 1982 (Parent Company), 16,127,625 shs. comprising 9,906,450 restricted shs. and 6,281,175 non-restricted shs.: par Skr.10.

Par changed from Skr.50 to Skr.10 by 5-for-1 stk. split in Sept. 1981.

Entitled to one-tenth of a vote per sh.

Dividends and Other Provisions: Same as Class A share capital.

Listed: On Stockholm Stock Exchange.

American Depository Shares: On Nov. 19, 1981, Company offered 2,750,000 American Depository Shares representing 2,750,000 non-restricted Class B shares thru Morgan Stanley & Co. at $18.25 per ADS.

Dividends Paid (ADS): 1982 .... $0.161

Traded (ADS): OTC (NASDAQ Symbol: PHABY).

Financing Program — Rights Offerings: On August 21, 1981 Fortia announced a financing program which included a five-for-one stock split applicable of all of its capital stock, a 10% stock dividend and two rights offerings to non-United States stockholders. The stock dividend and rights offerings were based on post-split stock ownership. The subscription period for the rights offerings expired on November 13, 1981, trading in the rights having ended on November 6, 1981.

In one of the rights offerings, each stockholder was entitled to subscribe for shares of the same series and type (A Shares or B Shares, Restricted or Non-Restricted) as those held prior to the stock dividend on the basis of one additional such share for each ten such shares held. In the other rights issue, each stockholder was entitled to subscribe for one Non-Restricted B Share for each ten shares (regardless of type or series) held prior to the stock dividend.

The subscription prices in both rights offerings were Skr.65 ($11.62) per Non-Restricted Share and Skr.50 ($8.94) per Restricted Share.

Ian H. Giddy

Case 8

Consolidated Packaging Corporation

Mr. Richards, president of Consolidated Packaging Corporation (CPC), a growing aluminum and steel can manufacturing concern, is considering expanding production facilities in Europe for two reasons: 1) the company wishes to diversify its investments abroad, and 2) expanding overseas markets require local manufacturing facilities to avoid excessive transportation costs. The option available to CPC in Europe requires an investment of $100 million. If this amount were borrowed, it would be the equivalent of nearly 35 percent of the company's expanded assets.

In evaluating this proposal, company financial analysts have reduced cash flow projections to rates of return as a measure of comparison. Taking into account future uncertainties, three alternative scenerios are being considered for the existing domestic and proposed foreign ventures.

The analysts felt that the most probable outlook was a boom in Europe and slow growth in the United States, providing a 20 percent return from abroad and a 15 percent return on the domestic segment. They assigned a probability of 50 percent to this scenerio.

Least likely, with what CPC analysts felt was a 15 percent probability, was passage of very strict international trade regulations, causing a loss of 15 percent abroad while returning 20 percent domestically because of reduced foreign competition.

Finally, CPC analysts applied a 35 percent probability to cost increases for raw materials, which would result in a 7 percent loss for domestic production and a 10 percent return for international production.

Given these possibilities, Mr. Richards felt that the principles of portfolio management could assist in a risk-return analysis. He wondered whether foreign investment, like portfolio diversification, might improve the overall risk-return profile of the firm. The portfolio would be composed of the combined domestic and foreign operations and so, he reasoned, should be compared to the performance of the firm without any foreign investments.

Undertake the analysis referred to in the last paragraph. You may find it useful to review the concepts and techniques of evaluating risky investments covered in introductory finance textbooks. A measure of riskiness is variance; a measure of the joint riskiness of two projects requires covariances and correlations.

Gunter Dufey and Ian H. Giddy

Case 9

Roach Hotel Corporation
International Investment Sales

It is late afternoon on a quiet day. You are sitting on the trading desk, watching the screen absentmindedly, and chatting on the phone with Joe Dominick, who handles the investments for Roach Hotel Corporation International. Joe is very pleased with the $3 million worth of Dow Chemical Euroyen bonds you sold him in early December 1984, even though a slight rise in Japanese interest rates has caused the bonds to be quoted now at 97–98. However, Roach Hotel International bought the bonds on behalf of its Bermuda insurance company, which carried the liability risks for operating two hotels in Japan. Because of earthquake and fire danger in that country, the risks were considerable.

Suddenly Joe says, "Hey, look at Reuters news page!" There you see it on the screen: "After earlier providing indications that the withholding tax on domestic yen and Euroyen bond issues by Japanese companies would be removed, Japanese officials served notice today that they would submit legislation to extend the withholding tax to all yen bonds in order to regain effective control over the use of their currency worldwide." Joe barks on the phone, "What are we going to do now? Why did you sell me those bonds? Didn't you see this coming?"

What would you reply? Would you advise to sell, buy, or hedge?

Ian H. Giddy

Case 10

With a Little Help From Your FRNs

The fundamental relationships of yield structure analysis tell us that securities with high risks should bear high returns, and that securities with the same risks, taxability, and so forth should bear the same returns. When there is an obvious deviation from these, an opportunity for portfolio shifts, or swaps, exists. Let's see an application.

You have been transferred to London. You quickly realize that, in order to keep up with your FRNs (floating rate notes) you must look beyond the margin over LIBOR and figure the more useful measure of return, the Adjusted Total Margin, or ATM. This measure takes into account not only the spread over LIBOR, but also the short-term yield until the next refix date and the price at which the note is selling, relative to par. The ATM can be used as an index to identify the best values today for arbitrage and portfolio investors.

Look at Exhibit 1, a table of FRNs with semiannual refixings. Can you use ATM yield comparisons to identify swap opportunities to:

1) improve the ATM of an investor holding the Nova Scotia issue?
2) shorten the maturity of an investor holding the Nat West FRN?
3) reduce the risk of an investor holding the Standard Chartered (Hong Kong) issue of 1992?

Exhibit 1 Floating rate note spread analysis

Settlement Date = 5/13/84
Overnight LIBOR Rate = 15.375
1 Month = 14.875
2 Month = 14.625
3 Month = 14.500
4 Month = 14.500
5 Month = 14.500
6 Month = 14.375

Issue	Maturity	Min. Coupon	Current Coupon	Next Refix	Price	LIBOR Margin	ATM
Banque Francaise (BFCE)	10/1990	5.250	15.000	10/28	99.500	0.250	.2576
Bank of Nova Scotia	10/1990	5.250	15.125	10/29	99.625	0.125	.1304
Industrial Bank of Japan	10/1990	5.250	15.750	10/13	100.375	0.250	.2578
Credit Agricole	3/1992	5.250	15.438	9/24	99.500	0.250	.2611
Standard Chartered (H.K.)	3/1992	5.250	14.750	9/09	99.875	0.250	.2652
Standard Chartered (H.K.)	11/1993	5.250	13.313	5/18	99.000	0.125	.1555
Allied Irish Banks	4/1994	5.250	15.688	10/15	98.375	0.250	.2675
Midland International	7/1995	5.250	15.688	7/26	100.000	0.250	.2755
National Westminster	4/1996	5.250	15.938	10/14	100.125	0.250	.2583

Ian H. Giddy

Case 11

Thoughts While in a Sauna

Klaus Groenbarj, finance director of Wartsila, the Finnish company, was sweating in the sauna outside his family cottage on a birch-clad island in the Gulf of Finland, when suddenly he remembered that the next day, Monday, was when Wartsila USA would make an $80 million repayment of an intercompany loan. Groenbarj had insisted on this repayment because he felt that the U.S. subsidiary should be able to stand on its own two feet by now, and the money was needed for a forthcoming acquisition in Britain. The purchase price of £60 million would have to be paid to the British seller within one month.

What should we do with the money in the meantime? Groenbarj muttered to himself in Swedish. Hey! Maybe we could buy one of those floating rate notes that Arvo keeps telling me about. If we buy one that has a coupon-fixing date a month from now, and if nothing goes wrong, then we can sell it at par on the coupon refixing date and collect the coupon — a whole six months' worth.

Groenbarj thought for a minute. Then, leaping out of the sauna, he ran naked across the lawn and into the cottage. Ignoring his wife's guests, he rummaged in his briefcase where he found the latest *International Herald Tribune.* He rushed back into the sauna.

He tore out the section that lists floating rate notes and looked for a note whose next coupon date was around September 6th. Hmm, let's see. I wonder what my return would be if I bought one of these things? I guess we would have to pay the stated price plus accured interest. I'll assume we could sell the notes at par. Doesn't that make sense?

Course, he muttered in Swedish, its sterling we need. Maybe I should look for a sterling note, or perhaps a Eurodeposit. If I were to buy a dollar FRN we would have to hedge it into sterling. I wonder what the cost of hedging would be? Darn, he said in Swedish, I can't find the forward rates, only spot rates. Hey, here are some futures rates! We've never used those before, but Arvo keeps talking about them. Could that be a cheaper way to hedge? I'd better work out what it would cost compared to a forward contract.

Or how about a Eurodollar deposit hedged with futures? Or hedged with a forward contract? But no forward rates here! I know you're supposed to be able to work out what the forward rates are from the information given here . . . , but there seem to be a number of ways of doing this thing, and I don't have a pencil, and its too hot, anyway. I think I'll go for a swim. That new MBA recruit can work this out tomorrow. We'll see what they learn in that program.

Exhibit 1 **Currency rates** Late interbank rates on Aug. 8, excluding fees. Official fixings for Amsterdam, Brussels, Milan, Paris. New York rates at 2 P.M. EDT.

	$	£	D.M.	F.F.	It.L.	Gldr.	B.F.	S.F.	Yen
Amsterdam	3.286	4.29	112.735*	36.73*	0.1837	—	5.582*	133.835*	135.05y
Brussels (a)	58.80	76.715	20.1615	6.657	3.279*	17.893	—	23.944	24.115*
Frankfurt	2.911	3.815	—	32.57*	1.629x	88.71*	4.951*	118.60*	1.196*
London (b)	1.3105	—	3.8228	11.7283	2,345.14	4.3068	77.10	3.2183	319.225
Milan	1,790.50	2,337.50	614.00	200.17	—	544.88	30.384	728.30	7.329
New York (c)	—	1.313	2.9083	8.9225	1,785.00*	3.276	58.725	2.4507	243.725
Paris	8.9485	11.6935	306.90*	—	5.0015x	272.34*	5.195*	364.22*	3.6664*
Tokyo	244.80	320.385	83.84	27.35	13.67*	74.37	415.93*	99.33	—
Zurich	2.4538	3.2169	84.255*	27.435*	0.1373	74.785*	4.1823*	—	1.008*
1 ECU	0.7688	0.5885	2.2424	6.8808	1,376.82	2.5268	45.2833	1.8902	187.599
1 SDR	1.01282	0.77569	2.95531	9.06322	1,813.98	3.3281	59.6754	2.4874	248.455

Dollar Values

$ Equiv.	Currency	Per U.S.$
0.8352	Australian $	1.1973
0.0489	Austrian schilling	20.455
0.0168	Belgian fin. franc	59.425
0.768	Canadian $	1.3021
0.0943	Danish krone	10.605
0.1641	Finnish mark	6.095
0.0087	Greek drachma	115.05
0.1275	Hong Kong $	7.844

Currency	$ Equiv.	Per U.S.$
Irish £	1.055	0.9479
Israeli shekel	0.0034	293.50
Kuwaiti dinar	3.3546	0.2981
Malay. ringgit	0.4273	2.3405
Norw. krone	0.1197	8.3545
Phil. peso	0.0553	18.0695
Port. escudo	0.0066	151.075
Saudi riyal	0.2847	3.512

Currency	$ Equiv.	Per U.S.$
Singapore $	0.4643	2.154
S. African rand	0.621	1.6103
S. Korean won	0.0012	812.35
Span. peseta	0.0061	164.85
Swed. krona	0.119	8.4025
Taiwan $	0.0256	39.03
Thai baht	0.0435	22.975
U.A.E. dirham	0.2723	3.6727

£ Sterling: 1.2418 Irish £

(a) Commercial franc (b) Amounts needed to buy one pound (c) Amounts needed to buy one dollar (*) Units of 100 (x) Units of 1,000 (y) Units of 10,000

N.Q.: not quoted; N.A.: not available.

Source: *International Herald Tribune.*

Exhibit 2 Interest Rates

Eurocurrency Deposits (Aug. 8)

	Dollar	D-Mark	Swiss Franc	Sterling	French Franc	ECU	SDR
1M.	$11\frac{9}{16}-11\frac{13}{16}$	$5\frac{3}{8}-5\frac{1}{2}$	$4\frac{5}{16}-4\frac{7}{16}$	$11\frac{5}{8}-11\frac{3}{4}$	$11\frac{3}{8}-11\frac{7}{16}$	9.20– 9.35	$9\frac{3}{4}-10$
2M.	$11\frac{3}{4}-11\frac{7}{8}$	$5\frac{9}{16}-5\frac{11}{16}$	$4\frac{1}{2}-4\frac{5}{8}$	$11\frac{9}{16}-11\frac{11}{16}$	$11\frac{1}{2}-11\frac{5}{8}$	9.30– 9.45	$9\frac{7}{8}-10\frac{1}{8}$
3M.	$11\frac{13}{16}-11\frac{13}{16}$	$5\frac{3}{4}-5\frac{7}{8}$	$4\frac{11}{16}-4\frac{13}{16}$	$11\frac{1}{2}-11\frac{5}{8}$	$11\frac{13}{16}-11\frac{15}{16}$	9.45– 9.60	$10-10\frac{1}{4}$
6M.	$12\frac{1}{16}-12\frac{3}{16}$	$6\frac{3}{16}-6\frac{5}{16}$	$4\frac{7}{8}-5$	$11\frac{3}{8}-11\frac{1}{2}$	$12\frac{7}{16}-12\frac{9}{16}$	10 –10.12	$10\frac{1}{4}-10\frac{1}{2}$
1Y.	$12\frac{7}{16}-12\frac{9}{16}$	$6\frac{9}{16}-6\frac{11}{16}$	$4\frac{7}{8}-5$	$11\frac{3}{8}-11\frac{1}{2}$	$13\frac{1}{4}-13\frac{1}{2}$	$10\frac{1}{2}-10.65$	$10\frac{1}{2}-10\frac{3}{4}$

Rates applicable to interbank deposits of $1 million minimum (or equivalent).

Asian Dollar Rates Aug. 8

1 mo.	2 mos.	3 mos.	6 mos.	1 year
$11\frac{5}{8}-11\frac{3}{4}$	$11\frac{3}{4}-11\frac{7}{8}$	$11\frac{13}{16}-11\frac{15}{16}$	$12\frac{1}{16}-12\frac{3}{16}$	$12\frac{7}{16}-12\frac{9}{16}$

Key Money Rates

	Close	Prev.
United States		
Discount Rate	9	9
Federal Funds	$11\frac{1}{2}$	$11\frac{1}{2}$
Prime Rate	13	13
Broker Loan Rate	12.50	12.50
Comm. Paper, 30–179 days	11.15	11.15
3-month Treasury Bills	10.43	10.51
6-month Treasury Bills	10.55	10.61
CD's 30–59 days	10.75	10.75
CD's 60–89 days	10.875	10.98
Japan		
Discount Rate	5	5
Call Money	$6\frac{1}{8}$	$6\frac{5}{16}$
60-day Interbank	$6\frac{5}{16}$	$6\frac{5}{16}$
Britain		
Bank Base Rate	$11\frac{1}{2}$	12
Call Money	$12\frac{1}{8}$	$12\frac{1}{8}$
91-day Treasury Bill	$11\frac{1}{16}$	$11\frac{1}{4}$
3-month Interbank	$11\frac{9}{16}$	$11\frac{13}{16}$

West Germany

Lombard Rate	5.50
Overnight Rate	5.60
One Month Interbank	5.95
3-month Interbank	6.15
6-month Interbank	6.45

France

Intervention Rate	11¼	11¼
Call Money	11	11
One-month Interbank	11¼	11⅜
3-month Interbank	11¾	11⁹⁄₁₆
6-month Interbank	12½	17⅞

Sources: Commerzbank, Bank of Tokyo, Lloyds Bank.

Gold Prices

	A.M.	P.M.	Ch'ge		A.M.	P.M.	Ch'ge
Hong Kong	343.35	343.45	−3.00	Zurich	343.50	344.50	+1.625
Luxembourg	343.50	—	−3.25	London	343.90	344.50	+2.50
Paris (12.5 kilo)	343.81	344.10	−0.44	New York	344.40	—	+0.40

Official fixings for London, Paris and Luxembourg, opening and closing prices for Hong Kong and Zurich, New York Comex current contract.
All prices in U.S. $ per ounce.
Source: *International Herald Tribune.*

Exhibit 3 Exchange Rates

British Pound (1MM)

$ per pound— 1 point equals $0.0001

Season High	Season Low		Open	High	Low	Close	Chg.
1.5240	1.2965	Sep	1.3060	1.3175	1.3060	1.3135	+75
1.5100	1.2975	Dec	1.3085	1.3215	1.3085	1.3165	+85
1.5170	1.3005	Mar				1.3190	+85

Est. Sales 4,336   Prev. Sales 6,541
Prev. Day Open Int. 14,361 off 456

Canadian Dollar (1MM)

$ per dir— 1 point equals $0.0001

Season High	Season Low		Open	High	Low	Close	Chg.
.8147	.7471	Sep	.7666	.7677	.7645	.7649	−1
.8048	.7460	Dec	.7650	.7673	.7636	.7638	−1
.8050	.7446	Mar	.7633	.7633	.7633	.7633	−1
.7835	.7440	Jun	.7640	.7640	.7630	.7630	+2

Est. Sales 2,522   Prev. Sales 1,311
Prev. Day Open Int. 7,825 off 537

French Franc (1MM)

$ per franc— 1 point equals $0.00001

Season High	Season Low		Open	High	Low	Close	Chg.
.12380	.11180	Sep				.11180	
.12165	.11245	Dec				.11170	
.11905	.11200	Mar				.11150	

Est. Sales   Prev. Sales
Prev. Day Open Int.   286

German Mark (1MM)

$ per mark— 1 point equals $0.0001

.4037	.3435	Sep	.3453	.3477	.3447	.3462	+21
.4080	.3486	Dec	.3503	.3525	.3498	.3512	+21
.4110	.3552	Mar	.3555	.3571	.3548	.3561	+20
.3733	.3615	Jun	.3616	.3618	.3616	.3616	+17

Est. Sales 21,676   Prev. Sales 20,594
Prev. Day Open Int. 32,205 off 397

Japanese Yen (1MM)

$ per yen— 1 point equals $0.000001

.004615	.004068	Sep	.004126	.004143	.004121	.004128	+17
.004663	.004088	Dec	.004182	.004200	.004182	.004186	+17
.004695	.004208	Mar	.004244	.004253	.004243	.004247	+17
.004450	.004290	Jun				.004323	+18
		Dec				.004440	

Est. Sales 11,087   Prev. Sales 10,638
Prev. Day Open Int. 18,186 off 2,278

Swiss Franc (1MM)

$ per franc— 1 point equals $0.0001

.5020	.4065	Sep	.4100	.4134	.4099	.4117	+36
.5000	.4148	Dec	.4171	.4205	.4150	.4188	+37
.5035	.4228	Mar				.4258	+33
.5035	.4215	Jun	.4340	.4340	.4340	.4340	+40

Source: *International Herald Tribune.*

Exhibit 4 Floating rate notes Aug. 8

Dollar

Issuer/Min cpn/Mat.	Coupon	Next	Bid	Askd
Allied Irish $5\frac14$-95	$12\frac{5}{16}$	12-10	98.97	99.12
Allied Irish $5\frac14$-92	$11\frac14$	10-17	99.35	99.50
Allied Irish $5\frac14$-87	$13\frac18$	1-7	100.38	100.54
Arab Bkg Corp $5\frac14$-96	$10\frac{13}{16}$	9-17	98.80	98.95
Bca Naz. Lavoro $5\frac14$-91	$11\frac{7}{16}$	10-26	99.25	99.40
Bca de Roma 1990	$12\frac{5}{16}$	12-7	100.10	100.30
Bco Pinto $6\frac34$-85	$12\frac12$	11-19	99.25	100.25
BK Greece	$12\frac{3}{16}$	10-18	97.95	98.15
BK Ireland $5\frac14$-89	$12\frac{1}{16}$	8-31	100.03	100.18
BK Ireland $5\frac14$-92	13	1-25	99	99.50
BK Montreal $5\frac14$-90	$12\frac12$	12-20	100.25	100.45
BK Montreal 5-96	$12\frac{3}{16}$	10-26	100	100.15
BK Montreal $5\frac14$-91	$11\frac{3}{16}$	10-31	99.95	100.10
BK New York 1996	$12\frac14$	10-12	99.40	99.55
BK Nva Scotia $5\frac14$-88/93	$11\frac12$	10-31	99.96	100.11
BK Nova Scotia $5\frac14$-94	$13\frac18$	1-11	100.40	100.60
BK of Tokyo $5\frac12$-93	$11\frac{3}{16}$	10-24	100	100.17
BK of Tokyo $5\frac14$-89	$11\frac18$	10-29	100.30	100.50
BK of Tokyo 1987	$12\frac{13}{16}$	1-28	100.40	100.55
BK Tokyo $5\frac14$-Feb88/91	$12\frac38$	2-6	100.50	100.65
BK Tokyo $5\frac14$-Dec88/91	$12\frac12$	12-12	100.27	100.45
Bankers Trust $5\frac14$-94	$11\frac78$	9-24	100.07	100.23
Bankers Trust $5\frac14$-96	$12\frac{1}{16}$	11-13	100	100.07
BK Arabe Inv $5\frac12$-87/91	$11\frac{5}{16}$	9-28	$98\frac18$	$98\frac38$
BBL 5-95	$12\frac{11}{16}$	12-17	100.28	100.40
BBL 5-99	$11\frac{3}{16}$	10-11	99.20	99.35
BQ Indosuez $5\frac14$-89	$13\frac{3}{16}$	1-14	100.80	101
BQ Indosuez $5\frac14$-99	$11\frac{1}{16}$	9-21	99.88	100
BUE $5\frac14$-89	$11\frac78$	9-20	100.10	100.30
BFCE $5\frac14$-87	$12\frac34$	1-28	100.22	100.35
BFCE $6\frac38$-84	$10\frac{11}{16}$	8-23	99.90	100.40
BFCE $5\frac14$-Oct.88	$11\frac{5}{16}$	10-30	100.05	100.20
BFCE $5\frac14$-Jan.88	$12\frac{1}{16}$	1-22	100.30	100.45
BNP $5\frac14$-95	$12\frac38$	2-6	99.96	100.06
BNP $5\frac12$-Feb 91	$10\frac12$	8-22	100.15	100.30
BNP $5\frac14$-87	$11\frac{3}{16}$	9-24	99.75	—
BNP $5\frac12$-85/88	$12\frac78$	10-31	100.05	100.20
BNP $7\frac12$-84/96	$12\frac12$	12-13	99.72	99.87
BNP $5\frac14$-89	$11\frac{1}{16}$	11-9	99.70	99.85
BNP 1988/91	$10\frac34$	9-4	100.20	100.35
BNP $5\frac14$-1996	$12\frac{13}{16}$	1-22	100	100.20
BK Worms $5\frac34$-85	$12\frac{9}{16}$	12-19	99.85	100
BK Worms $5\frac14$-89/94	$12\frac38$	2-6	99.85	100.05
Barclays O'Seas 5-95	$12\frac14$	1-31	100.50	100.65

Dollar

Issuer/Min cpn/Mat.	Coupon	Next	Bid	Askd
Barclays O'Seas 5-90	$12\frac{11}{16}$	12-17	100.85	101
Barclays O'Seas 5-2004	$10\frac{9}{16}$	9-4	99.05	99.20
Bergen Bk $6\frac{1}{4}$-89	$12\frac{1}{16}$	8-31	100.20	100.33
Bergen Bk $5\frac{1}{2}$-88/91	$12\frac{3}{16}$	10-18	100.12	100.32
Belgium 5-04	$13\frac{1}{8}$	1-9	100.15	100.30
Belgium Perp	$12\frac{1}{2}$	2-11	99.70	99.80
CCCE $5\frac{1}{4}$-98	$12\frac{5}{8}$	2-11	100.35	100.50
CCCE $5\frac{1}{4}$-02	$12\frac{1}{16}$	9-14	100.45	100.60
CNCA $5\frac{1}{4}$-90/97	$11\frac{3}{8}$	9-24	100.12	100.27
CNCA $5\frac{1}{4}$-90/95	$12\frac{5}{16}$	12-7	100.20	100.35
CNT $5\frac{1}{4}$-90	$11\frac{1}{2}$	10-24	100.20	100.35
CNT $5\frac{1}{4}$-91	$11\frac{11}{16}$	11-8	100.20	100.35
CIBC $5\frac{1}{4}$-94	$12\frac{3}{16}$	1-18	100.18	100.33
Chase $5\frac{1}{4}$-93	$12\frac{3}{8}$	1-31	100.03	100.18
Chemical $5\frac{1}{4}$-94	$12\frac{1}{4}$	9-25	100.15	100.30
Christiana Bk $5\frac{1}{4}$-91	$12\frac{3}{16}$	11-9	100.33	100.53
Citicorp 6-94	$11\frac{13}{16}$	9-12	100.65	100.80
Citicorp undtd	$12\frac{1}{8}$	10-15	99.80	100.50
Commerzbank $5\frac{1}{4}$-89	$11\frac{13}{16}$	8-21	99.50	99.60
ComU. Montreal $5\frac{1}{4}$-91	$10\frac{11}{16}$	9-17	98.95	99.10
CCF $5\frac{1}{4}$-86/98	$11\frac{5}{16}$	9-26	100.05	100.20
CCF $5\frac{1}{4}$-90/95	$11\frac{9}{16}$	10-19	100.17	100.32
CCF $5\frac{3}{4}$-85	$11\frac{11}{16}$	11-9	99.95	—
CCF 1989/96	$12\frac{3}{4}$	11-30	100.35	100.50
CCF $5\frac{1}{4}$-Feb96	$10\frac{1}{16}$	8-22	99.90	100.05
CEPME $5\frac{1}{4}$-87/92	$12\frac{9}{16}$	12-12	100.20	100.35
CEPME $5\frac{1}{4}$-88	$11\frac{3}{4}$	9-6	100.28	100.38
Credit Nord $5\frac{1}{4}$-89/92	$12\frac{13}{16}$	12-27	99.85	100.05
Credit Fancier $5\frac{1}{4}$-88/93	$11\frac{1}{2}$	10-9	100.25	100.35
Credit Lyon $5\frac{1}{4}$-87	$11\frac{1}{16}$	9-21	99.80	100
Credit Lyon $5\frac{1}{4}$-90/97	$11\frac{5}{16}$	10-25	100.10	100.25
Credit Lyon $5\frac{1}{4}$-89/94	$13\frac{1}{8}$	1-7	100.52	100.67
Credit Lyon $5\frac{1}{4}$-91/95	$12\frac{11}{16}$	11-29	100.05	100.45
Cr. Lyon $5\frac{1}{4}$-Jan92/96	$12\frac{3}{4}$	1-18	99.95	100.10
Cr. Lyon $5\frac{1}{4}$-Jun92/96	$12\frac{11}{16}$	12-14	100.05	100.15
Credit Nat'l $5\frac{1}{4}$-88	$12\frac{3}{4}$	1-18	100.25	100.40
Credit Nat'l $5\frac{1}{4}$-90/94	$10\frac{11}{16}$	9-10	100.02	100.17
Creditanst 1994	$13\frac{1}{16}$	1-11	100.22	100.37
Creditanst $5\frac{1}{2}$-91/97	$11\frac{3}{4}$	9-18	100.50	100.70
Creditanst 1996	$10\frac{1}{2}$	8-23	100.28	100.43
Dai Ichi Kangyo $5\frac{1}{4}$-96	$12\frac{1}{8}$	11-13	99.50	99.65
Danske Oile $5\frac{1}{4}$-99	12	9-6	99.90	100.10
Den Norsk 6-Nov90	$12\frac{5}{16}$	11-9	100	100.50
Den Norsk 6-Dec90	$12\frac{1}{2}$	9-19	100	100.50
Denmark $5\frac{1}{4}$-Jan88/90	$13\frac{1}{4}$	1-9	100.50	100.65
Denmark $5\frac{1}{4}$-Oct88/90	$11\frac{5}{16}$	10-15	99.95	100.05

Exhibit 4 ***(Cont.)***

Dollar

Issuer/Min cpn/Mat.	Coupon	Next	Bid	Askd
Denmark 5¼-04	10⅜	8-17	99.60	99.70
Denmark 5¼ Perp.	12⅜	2-8	99.63	99.73
Die Ers.Oester 5¼-92/94	12¹¹⁄₁₆	1-28	99.20	99.35
Dresdner Bank 5¼-93	11³⁄₁₆	10-19	99.98	100.13
Dresdner Bank 5¼-89	11⅝	8-23	99.51	99.59
El Dorado Nucl. 5¼-89	10½	8-28	99.95	100.05
EdF 5¼-99	10⁹⁄₁₆	8-23	99.35	99.45
EdF 5¼-95	12½	2-11	100.25	100.40
Eurofima 5¼-89	11⅜	9-27	100	—
EAB 1993	12⅝	12-17	99.65	99.80
EAB 5¼-90	11⅜	9-26	99.80	99.95
EEC 5-88/90	13	1-7	100.33	100.38
Exterior Int'l 1996	12⁹⁄₁₆	12-21	99.28	99.43
Ferrovie 5¼-99	10¹¹⁄₁₆	8-31	99.80	99.95
First Chicago 5¼-94	11¹³⁄₁₆	8-21	100.05	100.20
First Interstate 5¼-95	11⁹⁄₁₆	9-6	99.45	99.60
Full 1994/96	12⅞	1-14	100.03	100.18
Genfinance 5¼-87	11⁹⁄₁₆	10-31	100	100.15
Genfinance 5¼-89/92	12¹⁵⁄₁₆	12-31	100.40	100.55
Genfinance 5-92/94	12⅞	1-22	100.09	100.24
GZB 5½-89	12¼	11-9	100.20	100.35
GZB 5¼-92	11⅝	9-10	100.20	100.35
GZB 5¼-96	12⁹⁄₁₆	11-29	99.93	100.08
Giro 5¼-91	12⁵⁄₁₆	9-25	100.20	100.35
Grindlays 5¼-92	11³⁄₁₆	9-28	100.22	100.37
Grindlays 5¼-94	12½	2-1	99.93	100.08
Great West. Fin 5¼-94	11	9-21	98.25	98.40
Hill Samuel 5¼-96	10½	8-24	99.85	100.05
Hispano Amer 5¼-95	11½	10-24	99.25	99.40
Hydro Quebec 5¼-94	12⅞	1-22	100.20	100.35
IC Industries 1991	10⁹⁄₁₆	7-15	98.85	99.35
Indonesia 1988/93	11½	10-9	98.95	99.15
IBJ 5½-85	12¹³⁄₁₆	12-5	100.35	100.55
IBJ 5¼-Oct 88	11⅜	10-15	100.25	100.40
IBJ 5¼-87	11⁵⁄₁₆	10-17	100.17	100.32
IBJ 5¼-Nov 88	12⅜	11-19	100.32	100.47
Ireland (Rep) 1994	13⅛	1-10	99.77	99.92
IHI 5¾-85	11⁵⁄₁₆	10-27	99.70	100.85
C. Itah 5¼-87	11⅛	9-21	100.10	100.30
J.P. Morgan 5¼-97	12³⁄₁₆	8-16	100.40	100.55
KOP Feb 1992	12½	2-1	99.85	100
KOP 5¼-May92	11¹¹⁄₁₆	11-9	100	100.20
Kleinwort Benson 5¾-91	12³⁄₁₆	8-17	99.75	99.90
Kleinwort Benson 5¼-96	—	—	99.85	100

Dollar

Issuer/Min cpn/Mat.	Coupon	Next	Bid	Askd
Korea Dev. Bk 7½-89	12¾	12-5	98⅛	98⅝
Korea Exchange 7½-88	11⁵⁄₁₆	10-5	99⅜	99⅞
Lloyds 5¼-93	11½	10-31	100.10	100.25
Lloyds 5¼-92	12⅜	10-6	100.25	100.40
Lloyds 2004	11³⁄₁₆	10-18	99	99.15
LTCB 5½-Jly 89	12¹⁵⁄₁₆	1-22	100.30	100.50
LTCB 5¼-85	12⁹⁄₁₆	11-14	100.30	100.50
LTCB 5½-Jun89	12⁹⁄₁₆	12-11	100.65	100.85
LTCB 5¼-86	12¹⁄₁₆	12-17	100.38	100.53
LTCB 5¼-92	12⅝	11-30	100.25	100.40
Malaysia 5¼-Apr89/92	11½	10-9	99.65	99.85
Malaysia 5¼-Dec89/92	12¾	12-5	99.60	99.85
Malaysia 5¼-88/93	10¹¹⁄₁₆	8-28	99.68	99.62
ManHan O'seas 5¼-94	11¹¹⁄₁₆	8-31	99.93	100.08
Marine Midland 5¼-94	12⅝	10-6	100	100.15
Midland 5½-93	12¹¹⁄₁₆	1-28	100.30	100.45
Midland 5-89	12⅝	12-24	100.38	100.53
Midland 5¼-92	12³⁄₁₆	12-7	100.27	100.42
Midland 9-91	11⁹⁄₁₆	10-31	100.16	100.26
Midland 5-99	10⁹⁄₁₆	9-6	99.20	99.35
Mitsui Fin 5¼-96	10⁹⁄₁₆	9-4	99.55	99.70
Morgan Grenfell 5-94	13¹⁄₁₆	1-11	99.90	100
Mortgage Den. 5¼-90/93	10¾	9-10	100.08	100.23
Mortgage Denm. 5¼-92	12⁹⁄₁₆	12-19	100.10	100.30
Natl Westmin 5¼-91	12¹³⁄₁₆	1-18	100.25	100.40
Natl Westmin 5½-90	12⅞	12-27	100.50	100.65
Natl Westmin 5¼-91	11⅜	10-16	100.05	100.20
Natl Westmin 5¼-92	11⁹⁄₁₆	10-25	100.20	100.35
Natl Westmin Perp	12³⁄₁₆	11-13	99.97	100.07
Neste Oy 5¼-94	10⁹⁄₁₆	8-23	99.60	99.80
New Zealand 5¼-87	11³⁄₁₆	10-9	100	100.20
N Zealand Steel 5¼-92	12⅝	12-24	100.25	100.50
Nippan Credit Bk 5¼-90	12⅜	2-11	100.20	100.35
Nippon Credit Bk 5¼-85	12⅞	12-28	100	100.50
Nippon Credit Bk 6½-86	13	1-16	100.22	100.37
Nordic Intl Fin 5½-91	11¹⁄₁₆	11-9	99.40	99.60
OKB 5¼-86	12⅜	11-19	100.30	100.45
OLB 5¼-94	12½	11-26	100.10	100.30
OLB 1995/99	11³⁄₁₆	10-11	98.75	98.85
Offshore Mining 5¼-91	12¹³⁄₁₆	12-4	100.30	100.50
Offshore Mining 1986	12¹³⁄₁₆	1-23	100.35	100.50
Pirelli 5¼-91/94	10¹¹⁄₁₆	8-23	95.50	96.50
PkBanken 5-88/91	12¹³⁄₁₆	9-19	100.18	100.38
Queensland 5¼-96	11⅝	11-9	100	100.10
Renfe 5¼-91	11³⁄₁₆	9-27	99.85	100
Royal Bk Scot. 5¼-86/94	12³⁄₁₆	10-16	100.20	100.35

Exhibit 4 (*Cont.*)

Dollar

Issuer/Min cpn/Mat.	Coupon	Next	Bid	Askd
Saitama 5¼-91/93	12¹¹⁄₁₆	12-5	100	100.15
Sanwa Int Fin 5¼-88	11¼	9-26	100.13	100.25
Sanwa Int Fin 5¼-92	10³⁄₁₆	8-16	99.30	99.45
Sanwa 2004	12⅞	1-28	100.05	100.15
Scand. Fin. 5¼-Apr93	11⅜	10-15	99.75	100⅛
Scand. Fin. 5¼-Dec93	12³⁄₁₆	12-21	98.60	98.75
Scot. Int Fin 5¼-92	11³⁄₁₆	9-24	99.85	100
SNCF 5¼-88	11¹¹⁄₁₆	10-30	99.70	99.85
SEAT 5¼-90/93	12⅝	12-24	98.95	99.10
Sté Fin Europ 5½-89	12¾	12-3	99.45	99.65
Sté Fin Europ 91	12³⁄₁₆	12-19	99.30	99.45
Sté Générale 5¼-90/95	10¾	9-4	100.32	100.47
Sté Générale 5¼-90	11¹¹⁄₁₆	11-9	100.15	100.30
Sté Générale 5¼-94	10¹³⁄₁₆	9-17	99.65	99.80
Spain (Kingd.) 5¼-92/97	10⁹⁄₁₆	8-23	99.15	99.30
Kingdom of Spain 5¼-93	10¹¹⁄₁₆	8-31	99.97	100.12
Stand & Chart 5½-90	10³⁄₁₆	8-16	100.25	100.45
Stand & Chart 5¼-94	13	1-7	100.05	100.20
Stand & Chart 5¼-91	12⅜	11-19	99.95	100.10
Stand Chart 5¼-Mar90	10¾	9-10	100.25	100.45
State Bk India 6¾-87	12¾	11-30	98.50	99
Sumitomo Fin 5½-88	12½	2-11	100.03	100.13
Sumitomo Heavy 5½-84	11¹³⁄₁₆	9-13	99.90	100.30
Sumitomo Trt 5¼-92/94	12³⁄₁₆	2-11	99.75	99.90
Sundsvallsbken 6-85	11⅜	10-11	99.90	—
Svenska Handels 5-87	12⅞	1-18	100.31	100.46
Sweden 9-91	12¹⁄₁₆	10-24	100.55	100.70
Sweden 5¼-87/89	10⅝	8-31	100.10	100.20
Sweden 5¼-93/03	12⁵⁄₁₆	11-19	100.26	100.31
Sweden 5¼-88/93	12⁹⁄₁₆	2-4	100.30	100.35
Sweden Perp	13¼	1-9	100.31	100.36
Taiyo Kobe 5¼-92/04	12⁷⁄₁₆	11-19	99.83	99.98
Takugin 5¼-92/94	10¾	9-17	99.45	99.60
Tokai Asia 5¼-94/99	12½	12-12	100.02	100.17
Toronto Dom 5¼-92	10³⁄₁₆	8-14	100	100.20
Toyo Trust 5¼-92/99	12⅝	12-14	100	100.10
TVO 5¼-94/04	11¹⁵⁄₁₆	9-6	98.40	98.80
Union Bk Norway 6-89	13³⁄₁₆	1-11	99.50	100
Union Bk Norway 5¼-99	10¼	8-21	96.50	97.50
United O'seas Bk 6-89	12½	9-28	100	100.25
Williams & Glyns 5¼-91	11	9-17	100.25	100.40
World Bank 1994	10.43	8-31	98.45	98.60
Yokohama 5¼-91/94	11	10-2	99.40	99.55
Zentralsparkasse 5¼-91	13¹⁄₁₆	1-14	100	100.20

Non Dollar

Issuer/min cpn/mat.	Coupon	Next	Bid	Askd
CEPME Stig 1996	$9\frac{5}{8}$	9-21	98.60	98.80
BOT Stig 1988/90	$9\frac{1}{2}$	8-21	99.80	—
Citicorp Stig 5¼-89/91	$9\frac{3}{8}$	8-15	99.03	99.18
Cred.Nat Stig 5½-91/95	$9\frac{1}{2}$	9-17	99.20	99.40
Denmark Stig 1993/98	$9\frac{3}{16}$	8-22	99.60	99.80
Kin. Belgium Stig 5-94	$10\frac{7}{8}$	1-6	98.75	98.95
Lloyds Eurof. Stig 8-90	$10\frac{7}{8}$	1-6	99.60	—
SNCF Stig 5½-90/93	$12\frac{9}{16}$	10-24	100.30	100.50
Yorkshire Stig 5¼-91/94	$9\frac{11}{16}$	9-25	99.05	99.25
Prv N Bruns.5¼-89/94	$11\frac{13}{16}$	8-17	99.40	99.70

Prices supplied by Credit Suisse-First Boston Ltd., London

Source: *International Herald Tribune.*

II

International Funding and Hedging Decisions

2.1

Foreign Exchange Risk Analysis and Management

Ian H. Giddy

Case 12

Le Serpent

Shortly after his arrival in Paris in late 1982, Jim Rogers was faced with a problem. He had recently joined the financial management staff of his company's French subsidiary. He now read a memo he had just received from the subsidiary's manager, Pierre Le Cheffe. As he read, he reflected that it was proving tough to gain the confidence of the subsidiary's management, who were naturally suspicious of a young American newcomer just out of le business school.

"Perhaps," he thought, "this memo will give me a chance to prove the value of a business school education. But what can I tell Le Cheffe?" He reread the memo carefully:

To: Jim Rogers
From: M. Le Cheffe

According to the financial press, France's weak export performance, high inflation, and dwindling reserves are leading people to believe that France might break out of the European "snake" limits and allow our currency to devalue (see attachment). I would value your opinion regarding the possible consequences of this. In particular, please give me a concise assessment of the effect of such an event on

1. cost and prices and the outlook for sales, and
2. interest rates, including the prospects for monetary policy following the exchange rate change.

What would your answer be?

Exhibit 1 *Rien ne va plus The bets are placed for France's next devaluation. The French government should speed it**

Every *huissier* at the Elysée palace is now staking his savings on the safest bet in Paris: that the French franc will soon again be devalued against the currencies of its partners in the European Monetary System (EMS). Ministers trotting out the customary denials, and the French government's decision to seek the familiar multibillion dollar standby credit from international banks, serve only to make the one-way bet still safer and stimulate hopes that the speculators will make their killing soon. For France's and Europe's sake, they better had.

The French currency has already floated to a new low against the dollar. The big rollers in the foreign exchange markets expect a surge into D-marks this autumn. They have stayed in francs so long only because of high French interest rates and because they guessed that the EMS governments would leave a decent interval after last June's realignments before realigning again. Their itch to dump the franc is not based only, or even mainly, on the socialist colours of the French government.

Despite the big switchback in France's economic policy last June, France's inflation rate will still run at 10% by the end of this year, versus 5% in West Germany and Holland, and France's overseas current account will remain in deep deficit. Longer term, the franc's most recent devaluation, in June, could help to reduce the deficit by increasing French competitiveness. But that will happen only if France's higher inflation is compensated

* Source: *The Economist,* September 18, 1982. Reprinted with permission.

for by faster-rising productivity. So far it has not been. It is French manufacturers who have suffered hangovers as wages have soared. Importers have made whoopee. In July, for the first time, France imported more cars than it exported, despite some of the world's tightest curbs against Japanese imports.

The chickens now coming home to roost are pretty tough old birds. When the Mitterrand government swaggered into office in May, 1981, the franc was already overvalued. France's inflation was already above the EEC average and its current account was already in the red. The Socialists then embarked on an intrepid experiment of reflation-in-one-country, determined to keep unemployment down rather than inflation. Public spending was pumped up and wages were allowed to soar. The predictable consequence in an open trading economy, surrounded by world recession, was a consumer-led import boom in France that rewarded not French companies but their West German and other foreign competitors.

All the suggested alternatives to another currency devaluation would make France's economic troubles worse. The import controls, touted by some, would institutionalise the loss of competitiveness. Higher interest rates, touted by others, would choke off private investment and send a lot of companies bankrupt. The big sin of the EMS (though there are big virtues to set against it) is that it has made currency depreciation seem an insult to French economic virility, in forcing the government to go cap in hand to its EEC colleagues. Fortunately, this confusion of currency management and patriotism has not reached the jingoistic extremes in France that it did in God-save-our-gracious-pound Britain in the first three quarters of the 1960s. Two sensible devaluations of the franc have been conceded by the Mitterrand government. A third ought to be on the way, and may not be the last.

The switch in French economic policy in June was fundamental. Prices and wages were frozen for four months, public spending hacked, the franc devalued. Although few figures for the months since July are yet available, impressionistic economic evidence suggests the freeze has been successfully enforced. According to the prime minister, Mr. Pierre Mauroy, the freeze will be replaced by a form of voluntary incomes policy when it expires at the end of October. France's biggest union group, the CGT, is sounding comfortingly co-operative. But, even though France's Socialists have eaten humble pie with reassuring gusto, the slowing of French inflation so far has served only to bring the country back into line with the rest of the OECD, not ahead of it.

Which is not good news for the EMS. The snake can stay healthy only so long as the economic policies of its principal members, France and West Germany, are roughly in line. With a switch in the West German coalition threatening to bring in an orthodox right-of-center government soon, the divide between the two countries is liable to widen. If France is as fond of the EMS as Mr. Jacques Delors (the finance minister) claims, then it will have to cut inflation more severely, or accept frequent devaluations, or both. By resisting the snake's medicine for too long, the French could kill it. The rattle in the snake's tail could then be nasty protectionism.

Exhibit 2 Rattling snake *

The European monetary system (EMS) will soon be reshuffled for the fourth time since September, 1981. Talk of an imminent devaluation of the French franc sent the French government into the markets this week to raise a $4 billion standby credit to stiffen its foreign exchange reserves, its first such borrowing since 1974. The credit, from a consortium of commercial banks, is for 10 years, but moneymen expect it to be exhausted within weeks.

Rumours of devaluation have sprung up quickly, but insistently. The French franc is still only at its mid-point in the EMS — each currency is allowed to float by 2.25% (except the lira, which is allowed 6%) against the others — and still has far to fall. The markets are jittery about the French government's chances of squeezing a voluntary pay policy out of the trade unions after October 31st, when the present wage and price freeze expires. But dealers also know nowadays how to make a fast buck (or fast mark) out of the EMS.

By guaranteeing short-term currency stability, the EMS has sent footloose cash chasing high nominal interest rates instead of strong currencies. After the last realignment in June, when the French franc was devalued by 10% against the D-mark, dealers rushed into Euro-francs because French interest rates were high and no new devaluation was likely for a while. Now this cash has begun to surge back.

The weakness of the D-mark could delay the reshuffle. Worries about Mr. Helmut Schmidt's coalition government have undermined the D-mark. But with French inflation still double West Germany's and France's current account deficit in 1982 likely to reach $8 billion (though a small proportion of gnp, see chart), a fresh run on the franc is expected soon.

The French franc is the currency most likely to force a realignment. This will release tensions from a stack of other currencies, all keen to devalue but not daring to call for a realignment alone. All are loth to allow the French a competitive advantage.

* Source: *The Economist*, September 18, 1982. Reprinted with permission.

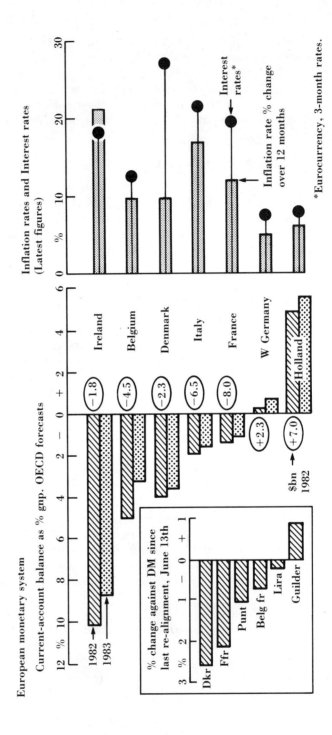

European monetary system

Current-account balance as % gnp. OECD forecasts

Inflation rates and Interest rates
(Latest figures)

*Eurocurrency, 3-month rates.

- The **Danish krone,** which followed France's devaluation in June, is weakened by huge foreign borrowing to finance the government's budget deficit, now 9% of gdp. Rumours are rife that the krone could be devalued by the new minority government when it takes office.
- The **Irish punt** remains surprisingly strong, despite an economy in an almighty mess. The punt has stayed high in the EMS because of high Irish interest rates and because it is scarcely traded on the Euromarkets.
- The **Italian lira,** beset by 15–20% inflation, is due for another of its regular devaluations. The last was in October, 1981.
- The **Belgian franc** will probably resist the temptation, just taking advantage of the revaluing D-mark and Dutch guilder. Belgium had its first formal devaluation since 1949 in February, and is loth to add to inflation.

Gunter Dufey and Thomas R. Hofstedt

Case 13

The Uncovered Transaction: Rolls Royce Australia

Assume that an Australian importer contracts to buy five Rolls Royce automobiles from a British company for £100,000. The contract is signed on February 1, the cars are shipped on May 1, and the account is settled on October 15 of that same year. The cars are sold on October 30 for A$250,000. Exchange rate movements over that time period are shown at the top of the next page. Show the accounting and cash flow implications for the Australian importer by completing the work sheet on the bottom of the next page.

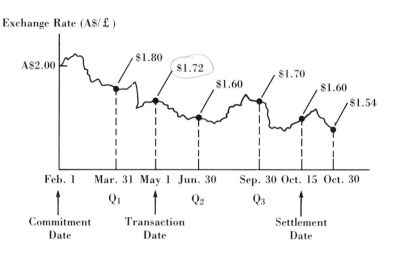

Exchange Rate (A$/£)

A$2.00 $1.80 $1.72 $1.60 $1.70 $1.60 $1.54

Feb. 1   Mar. 31   May 1   Jun. 30   Sep. 30   Oct. 15   Oct. 30
            Q₁   Q₂   Q₃

Commitment   Transaction   Settlement
Date   Date   Date

Worksheet for the uncovered transaction   *(Net positions)*

cash & inventory

stmt. Dates

	Balance sheet		Income statement
Date	Assets	Liabilities	Profit/Loss
Feb. 1	—	—	—
Mar. 31	—	—	—
May 1	A$ 172,000	A$ 172,000	—
June 30	A$ 172,000	A$ 160,000	A$ 12,000
Sept. 30	A$ 172,000	A$ 170,000	A$ 10,000
Oct. 15	A$ 12,000	0	A$ 12,000
Oct. 30	A$ 90,000	0	A$ 90,000

transaction gain → (not CF)
transaction loss (not CF)
transaction CF gain

Breakdown of revenues, costs and foreign exchange gains or losses

	A. Anticipated (economic) as of Feb. 1	B. Ex post (accounting) as of Oct. 30
Revenues	250,000	250,000
COGS (Expenses)	200,000	172,000
Operating Profit	50,000	78,000
FX G/L	0	12,000
Net Cash Inflows	50,000	90,000

using spot here, because don't have the forward rate.

Ian H. Giddy

Case 14

Imperial Power Corporation

In 1971, Imperial Power Corporation (IPC), a U.S.-based multinational firm, completed a new plant in Spain to manufacture fractional horse-power electric motors. These motors were sold to IPC subsidiaries in France and Germany, who assembled them into various end products that were then sold throughout Europe. Penetration of the Spanish market was, however, negligible. The plant site near Madrid had been chosen because of inducements from the Spanish government, the availability of a stable, suitably skilled labor force, and the expectation that presence in Spain would aid the marketing effort. To provide the required capital for the new subsidiary, Imperial Power of Spain, or IPS, IPC provided US $800,000 as a long-term loan in addition to equity capital. Chase Manhattan Bank in New York provided US $300,000 as an equipment mortgage guaranteed by IPC. In early 1982, the Madrid plant was operating at 70 percent of design capacity. The French and German subsidiaries were operating near full design capacity.

In late 1981, top management at IPC was concerned about the possibility of a devaluation of the Spanish peseta. Strong political unrest and an economy weakened by strikes led management to conclude that a devaluation of up to 20 percent was likely by the end of September 1982. Although the peseta/dollar exchange rate was technically floating, it was known that Spanish monetary authorities often intervened to keep the exchange rate within a narrow band. Therefore, the devaluation, if it happened, would be sudden rather than gradual. The current exchange rates (local currency per US$1) were:

DM	2.4127	SPta.	106.67
FF	6.27	£	0.5602

In addition to the debt incurred at the time of start-up, IPS had borrowed Pts. 7.5 million each from Banco Espanol de Credito and Chase Manhattan Bank (Madrid). The equipment mortgage, however, had been 50 percent repaid. Monthly reports received by IPC indicated that IPS had an average gross margin of 50 percent. Direct and indirect imported material accounted for 25 percent of the variable manufacturing cost, Spanish domestic material 15 percent, and the remainder was labor and overhead.

In an effort to reduce cash balances in anticipation of the devaluation, Imperial Power-Spain had purchased a $250,000 CD from Credit Lyonnais and bought Spanish treasury notes for Pts. 14 million. Payments due from the French and German subsidiaries totaled FF 250,000 and DM 200,000, respectively. IPS owed £32,000 to Essex Wire (UK), Ltd., and DM 125,000 to Ruhr Steel. The remainder of accounts payable was owed to local suppliers.

Exhibit 1 is the balance sheet for IPS as of March 31, 1982. Budgeted sales for the year ending March 31, 1983, were Pts. 280 million.

Exhibit 1 *Imperial Power Corporation Imperial Power of Spain, balance sheet as of March 31, 1982 (in thousands of pesetas)* [*]

Assets		
Cash	Pts.	6,300
Receivables & Securities		53,763
Inventories		41,000
New Plant & Equipment		75,100
Total	Pts.	176,163
Liabilities		
Accounts Payable	Pts.	32,620
Accrued Wages & Taxes		2,300
Long-Term Debt		116,336
	Pts.	151,256
Equity		24,907
	Pts.	176,163

[*] Foreign currency assets and liabilities translated at current exchange rates.

Questions

1. As Assistant Treasurer (International) for IPC in the United States, prepare an analysis of the exposure of the Spanish subsidiary:
   (a) using the current rate method,
   (b) using the monetary–nonmonetary method.
2. Then prepare an analysis of the economic (cash flow) effects on IPC of a possible devaluation of the peseta.
3. Finally, recommend a plan to present or minimize any losses.
4. Consider the company's transfer prices for sales between affiliates. What effect might alternative transfer pricing policies have on the gains or losses from exchange rate changes?

Gunter Dufey

Case 15

Kemp Corporation
Funding Multinational Operations

In 1975, Kemp Corp. U.S.A. decided to expand the production facilities of its French subsidiary, Kemp France SA. Located near Muhlheim, the plant was to serve the expanding markets for heavy construction machinery in the Middle East. These rapidly expanding markets were dominated by Caterpillar, Komatsu, and Terex. Kemp, while being in a very cyclical business, was well capitalized, had currently an AA bond rating, and Standard & Poor had given its credit subsidiary a commercial paper rating of P-1. Kemp, the parent, was never stingy with guarantees, but its treasury department demanded the same rates worldwide that it obtained at home.

As a banker to Kemp, you can offer the company the following funding options:

1. Commercial paper issued in the U.S. market, appropriately covered with a back-up line, at 8.5 percent for 180 days.

2. A U.S.$ term loan, priced at 10 percent, subject to renewal after twenty-four months.
3. A six-year revolving Eurodollar facility, currently priced at 9 percent for six months, or 10 percent for twenty-four months.
4. A six-year revolving Euro French franc facility at 13 percent for six months, or 14 percent for twenty-four months.
5. A domestic franc overdraft facility, 10 percent current cost.
6. A two-year term facility in domestic French francs at 11 percent, renewable at market rates.
7. A multicurrency facility consisting of UAE dinars, KDs and SRs, currently available at an all-in cost of 10 percent for ninety days, sourced out of the Bahrain OBU.

Issues:
A. What is the best French franc option Kemp can obtain, given the nature of its needs?
B. What is the least cost dollar option that you can provide to Kemp?
C. In which currency(s) should Kemp France be funded? Why?

Gunter Dufey

Case 16

General Electric's Yen Payables
or which exchange risk do you want to cover?

In January 1982 Bill Straub, finance manager of the Videotape Recorder Division of General Electric, was confronted with a nasty dilemma: What should he do with a big chunk of yen payables that his unit had accumulated in the course of its business?

Bill's division markets a line of videotape recorders under the General Electric label in the United States. Like all videotape recorders sold in the U.S. market, General Electric's were made in Japan by one of the four manufacturers that dominated the business and its associated technology. The four Japanese manufacturers sold machines under their own labels, but they also supplied U.S. marketers who sold them under their own names, and General Electric was one of them. Because the Japanese manufacturers had the field all to themselves, they invoiced their customers in yen, giving the customary ninety-day terms.

Bill Straub's dilemma was in part accentuated by the conditions on the distribution side of the videotape recorder business: There were about ten competitors active in the U.S. market, including the four captive marketing companies of the Japanese manufacturers. During the recession, demand for videotape recorders had slowed considerably as consumers' buying intentions weakened. As a result of soft demand and intense competition, margins were razor thin. In this environment, hedging costs began to matter. To make things worse, costs were at a record high: The yen had weakened a bit over the past months from Y242 per U.S. dollar to Y250. Ninety-day forwards at this time ran at Y246 per dollar, reflecting approximately a 6.5 percent premium when converted to an annual basis. The cost of U.S. dollar debt at the time was 15.5 percent, while rates for Euroyen (yen credits available from banks outside of Japan) were about 9 percent per annum.

In 1981, Bill's strategy of leaving the payables uncovered had turned out to be a brilliant tactical move. Not only had the dollar value of the yen decreased, but Bill's action had saved the division 6.5 percent hedging costs per annum — as he was careful to point out in his annual report. But now for 1982, what was he going to do as an encore? He recognized that the same superiors who patted him on the back for his success would sacrifice him without mercy if the yen turned the wrong way. As long as that currency would appreciate by no more than four yen for every ninety days, Bill could always argue that the hedging cost savings roughly equalled the translation losses. However, a glance at the historical evidence told him that the Japanese currency was given to abrupt swings, and Bill wondered whether this was a time when caution was the better part of valor.

Since any hedging strategy would represent a major change in financial policy for the division, Bill recognized that he had to convince people inside his company. In particular, senior management needed to know about the accounting and cash flow implications as well as about the various hedging alternatives.

Could you help Bill prepare his presentation?

Forwards cheaper than money market.
6.5 % vs. 15.5 %

Christine B. Hekman

Case 17

American Can Company — International Business Group

On August 19, 1976, Jim Berezin looked out over the lovely park surrounding American Can Company's headquarters in Connecticut's Hud-
son Valley. He knew that the two decisions facing him were important to
his company and to his career. Success would depend on both an accurate
analysis of ACC's foreign exchange exposure position and the persuasive-
ness of his presentation of his analysis and recommendations to the officers
on the treasurer's staff.

For several months Jim had agreed with the bankers he consulted.
They predicted that the Mexican peso would not devalue before December
1976, if it devalued at all. In the last week, however, several Mexican
sources suggested to him that peso devaluation was imminent. ACC's
Mexican subsidiary, Nueva Modelo, S.A., had a net exposed asset position

113

Exhibit 1 *American Can Company—International Business Group American Can Company and consolidated subsidiaries, balance sheets, 1974–75 ($000)*

	December 31, 1975	December 31, 1974
Assets		
Cash & Marketable Securities	142,951	83,967
Accounts and Notes Receivable	333,644	350,329
Inventories	431,931	522,937
Other Current Assets	24,853	26,970
TOTAL CURRENT ASSETS	933,379	984,203
Plant & Equipment	1,723,103	1,656,634
Less: Accumulated Depreciation	874,200	829,010
Net Plant & Equipment	848,903	827,624
Other Assets	72,998	91,903
TOTAL ASSETS	1,855,280	1,903,730
Liabilities		
Accounts Payable	140,952	166,264
Income Taxes Payable	42,104	61,280
Short-Term Debt	70,080	87,363
Accrued Expenses	163,340	181,464
Current Portion		
Long-Term Debt	15,559	12,403
Dividends Payable	10,548	14,039
Other Current Liabilities	24,934	23,118
TOTAL CURRENT LIABILITIES	467,517	545,931
Long-Term Debt	359,194	370,632
Special Reserves	136,924	141,050
Other Liabilities	101,387	91,062
Capital		
Share capital	282,388	282,351
Retained Earnings	507,870	472,704
TOTAL LIABILITIES AND CAPITAL	1,855,280	1,903,730

in pesos. A peso devaluation would result in reported losses when Nueva Modelo, S.A. was consolidated into ACC's financial statements.

Although Jim had to confront the immediate possibility of peso devaluation he knew that ACC's management also expected him to develop a program to deal with the persistent threat of loss due to changes in exchange rates. He knew he would need to compare the risk of exchange rate loss to the costs of the various alternatives available for eliminating the risk.

THE COMPANY AND ITS FOREIGN OPERATIONS

Founded by George Moore in 1901, American Can had grown into the second largest producer of consumer containers in the United States. ACC's consolidated financial statements are shown in Exhibits 1 and 2. Its pack-

Exhibit 2 American Can Company—International Business Group, *American Can Company and consolidated subsidiaries, income statements for years ending December 31, 1974 and 1975 ($000)*

	1975	1974
Net Sales	2,870,156	2,897,741
Cost of Goods Sold	2,382,628	2,391,824
Gross Profit	487,528	505,917
Selling and Administrative Expenses	303,818	285,217
	183,710	220,700
Other Income and Expense	(8,509)	620
	175,201	221,320
Interest Expense	34,657	32,520
Income before tax	140,544	188,800
Taxes	63,247	88,791
Income After Tax	77,297	100,009
Extraordinary Charge[1]	—	5,073
Net Income After Tax and Extraordinary Charge	77,297	94,936
Preferred Dividends	2,908	2,908
Common Dividends	39,223	42,597
Net Income Reinvested	35,166	49,431

[1] Costs relating to plant closing program.

aging business groups produced cans, cartons, wraps and plastic for food and beverage processors, and meat packagers. While packaging constituted the largest part of ACC's operations the company had diversified into the production of such consumer products as Dixie paper cups and plates, popular brands of tissue paper, toweling, and napkins, as well as Butterick and Vogue home sewing patterns. Smaller ACC business groups produced chemicals, plastics, and pharmaceuticals, and were engaged in publishing, printing, and solid waste recycling.

The American Can International Business Group supervised operations in Canada, Venezuela, the Dominican Republic, France, Germany, Japan, and Mexico. In 1975, international operations accounted for 15 percent of corporate sales and 25 percent of pretax earnings. The responsibility for planning and the control of foreign subsidiaries was vested in the Corporate Planning and Control groups, while the treasurer's office developed financial strategies for foreign operations. Jim was responsible for international cash management and corporate-wide banking relationships.

MANAGEMENT OF FOREIGN EXCHANGE EXPOSURE

Exposure reports were submitted quarterly by the financial staffs of ACC's foreign subsidiaries. The personnel of the subsidiaries were binational, and local personnel were frequently unacquainted with U.S. accounting conventions. To assure himself of accurate information, Jim had visited the financial directors of each subsidiary to explain the procedures for completing the report.

Each month Jim calculated the subsidiaries' exposure. He also gathered information on cash transactions between ACC and its foreign subsidiaries, such as dividend payments, which were scheduled for the near future. When he felt that exposure should be reduced he recommended action to the officers at ACC.

The company had a policy of avoiding speculation. "As a general principle we seek to finance our overseas operations in such a way as to minimize our exposure to loss from currency fluctuations and hence forgo speculative opportunities for windfall gains." One method of reducing such exposure is to match the currency denomination of assets and liabilities. Since most subsidiaries' assets were denominated in local currency, ACC could follow the strategy of denominating all debt in local currency. However, interest costs for borrowing foreign currency were often significantly higher than dollar interest rates. ACC evaluated this trade-off for each subsidiary. "With our foreign affiliates characteristically having substantial short-term assets in local currency, the amount of corresponding financing to be locally funded is a matter for management evaluation at both affiliate and corporate levels." While forward contracts could also be used to eliminate exposure, ACC had a policy for entering into such contracts only in protection of specific exposed cash flows such as projected dividend payments.

In Mexico, ACC's major debt was denominated in dollars. Since Mexican interest rates had been about 5–6 percent higher than U.S. rates for many years, this strategy had meant substantially reduced interest costs for ACC. Since the exchange rate had remained at MP 12.50 per U.S. dollar since 1954, ACC had accumulated these interest savings over many years. While the value of any debt denominated in pesos would decline with a peso devaluation, the accumulated interest gains from borrowing dollars had more than compensated ACC for this forgone opportunity. This strategy had proven successful over the many years of exchange rate stability, but Jim knew that it left Mexican assets exposed to exchange rate changes. In view of the increasing probability that the peso would devalue, the risk/cost trade-off that had existed for years was obsolete. It was time to re-evaluate ACC's peso position.

NUEVA MODELO, S.A.

American Can bought into Nueva Modelo in 1957. After a long history of operating losses, ACC revitalized the operation with an injection of management talent in the late sixties. The operations were turned around and began to show a profit in 1974. The company produced general purpose cans and food and beverage containers for the extremely competitive Mexican market. All products were sold in Mexico since it was uneconomical to transport such items as containers, which are bulky and have low value per unit. Nueva Modelo's financial statements for 1974 and 1975 are shown in Exhibits 3 and 4.

Competition was very lively. In addition to the Mexican subsidiary of another major U.S. container company, a Mexican-owned company competed aggressively for Nueva Modelo's customers.

Nueva Modelo's customers were segregated into two groups. About half of NMSA's containers were sold to large, food processing subsidiaries of U.S.-based corporations. One large, local food company and several smaller, local firms constituted the remaining half of their customer base. All of the trade credit extended by NMSA was denominated in pesos.

Tin plate was the major raw material used in container production. At the beginning of each year, NMSA's purchasing department presented its annual tin plate requirements to Altos Hornos de Mexico, a government-

Exhibit 3 **American Can Company—International Business Group** *Nueva Modelo, S.A. balance sheets, 1974–1975* ($000)

	Sept. 30, 1975			Sept. 30, 1974		
	Local currency	Exchange rate	U.S. dollar	Local currency	Exchange rate	U.S. dollar
ASSETS						
Cash & Marketable Securities	18,848	12.5	1,508	1,487	12.5	119
Accounts and Notes Receivable	34,646	12.5	2,772	46,437	12.5	3,715
Inventories	217,450	12.5	17,396	101,082	12.5	8,087
Other Current Assets	950	12.5	76	94	12.5	8
TOTAL CURRENT ASSETS	271,894		21,752	149,100		11,929
Gross Buildings and Equipment	113,914	12.0	9,459	108,564	12.0	9,030
Accumulated Depreciation	63,221	11.7	5,408	57,623	11.6	4,961
Net Building and Equipment	50,693		4,051	50,941		4,069
Land and Construction in Progress	13,563	12.5	1,085	13,811	12.5	1,105
NET FIXED ASSETS[1]	64,256		5,136	64,752		5,174
Other Assets	128	12.5	10	889	12.5	71
TOTAL ASSETS	336,278		26,898	214,741		17,174
LIABILITIES AND CAPITAL						
Accounts Payable	153,810	12.5	12,305	54,263	12.5	4,338
Income Taxes Payable	6,191	12.5	495	2,997	12.5	240
Current Portion Long-Term Debt[2]	547	12.5	44	547	12.5	44

TOTAL CURRENT LIABILITIES	160,548		12,844	57,807	4,622

TOTAL CURRENT LIABILITIES	160,548		12,844	57,807	4,622
Long-Term Debt[2]	113,172	12.5	9,054	113,720 12.5	9,098
Special Reserves	1,819		145	—	—
TOTAL LIABILITIES	275,538		22,043	171,527	13,720
Share Capital[3]	68,479	12.4	5,520	68,479 12.4	5,520
Retained Earnings	(7,740)		(665)	(25,265)	(2,066)
TOTAL CAPITAL	60,739		4,855	43,214	3,454
TOTAL LIABILITIES AND CAPITAL	336,277		26,898	214,741	17,174

[1] Fixed assets acquired at rates different from the prevailing rate of MP 12.5/$ have been fully depreciated.

[2] Long term debt includes the following obligations:

		1975	1974
—Notes payable in U.S. dollars to ACC at 6% per annum. Due Dec. 31, 1975, but to be renewed an additional year.	MP	$9,010,000	$9,010,000
—Debt to Banco Internacional Immobiliaria due in pesos. Short-term portion	MP	1,094,079	1,641,117
	MP	547,040	547,040
Remaining long-term portion	MP	547,039	1,094,077

[3] Share capital is translated at the exchange rates prevailing when capital was paid in.

These schedules reflect modifications of actual financial statements but are illustrative of Nueva Modelo's exposure position.

Exhibit 4 American Can Company—International Business Group Nueva Modelo, S.A. income statement for year ended Sept. 30, 1975 (000)

	Mexican peso	Exchange rate	U.S. dollars
NET SALES	285,486	12.5	22,839
Cost of Goods Sold	236,411	12.5	18,913
GROSS PROFIT	49,075		3,926
Selling and Administrative Expenses	11,886	12.5	951
GROSS OPERATING INCOME	37,189		2,975
Interest Expense	11,444	12.5	916
Other Income and Expense	3,562	12.5	285
Tax Expense	4,658	12.5	373
NET INCOME	17,525		1,401

These schedules reflect modifications of actual financial statements but are illustrative of Nueva Modelo's exposure position.

owned tin plate producer. Altos Hornos then scheduled a monthly quota of tin plate for NMSA. NMSA ordered additional tin plate from U.S.-based steel corporations to fill its needs.

THE HISTORY OF THE PESO

In April 1954, the Mexican peso was devalued from MP 8.65 to MP 12.50 per U.S. dollar and had remained fixed at that level since then. Throughout the 1960s, the stability of the peso, the availability of confidential bank accounts, and the stability of the Mexican political situation lured increasing numbers of foreign investors. In the face of the currency crises of the early 1970s the peso maintained its parity with the dollar. In fact, several times the International Monetary Fund used the peso, which was considered a very stable currency, to support other major currencies.

After economic slowdowns in 1971 and 1972, the Mexican government began expansionary efforts to improve economic growth. In 1973, the Foreign Investment Law was passed. This law reduced the freedom previously accorded to foreigners investing in Mexico. A slowdown in the rate of foreign investment and economic expansion followed. Prices continued to rise. From 1970 to the end of 1975, consumer prices rose 76 percent (see Exhibit

5 for price index history). Mexican inflation exceeded U.S. inflation by 28 percent. While the government attempted to pursue anti-inflationary policies, demands for wage increases generated substantial political unrest.

Inflationary pressure, political unrest, and the decline in foreign investment greatly reduced investor confidence in the peso. A pattern of "spring jitters" developed. Each spring rumors of devaluation prompted capital flight from Mexico. Government assurances that parity would be maintained reversed these periodic capital flights and reduced pressure on the peso. In the spring of 1976 there had been talk of a peso devaluation and the government had again promised to maintain parity. Most analysts felt that because of the relatively rapid inflation rate in Mexico, the peso would eventually be devalued; however, it was expected that the government would avoid devaluation until after the Presidential elections, which were scheduled for the fall.

The Financial Director of Nueva Modelo had just phoned to report that he thought the government would not wait until the fall but would de-

Exhibit 5 *American Can Company—International Business Group price index behavior*

| | Relative Prices | | Mexican Prices | |
| | Mexican/U.S. | | (1970 = 100) | |
	WPI	CPI	WPI	CPI
1958	.87	.95	74.5	70.7
1959	.88	.97	75.3	72.6
1960	.92	1.00	79.0	76.1
1961	.93	1.00	79.7	77.4
1962	.96	1.00	81.2	78.2
1963	.95	1.00	81.6	78.7
1964	.99	1.01	85.1	80.6
1965	.99	1.03	86.7	83.5
1966	.97	1.04	87.8	87.0
1967	1.00	1.04	90.3	89.6
1968	.99	1.02	92.0	91.6
1969	.98	1.01	94.4	95.1
1970	1.00	1.00	100.0	100.0
1971	1.00	1.01	103.7	105.7
1972	.99	1.03	106.7	111.0
1973	1.01	1.08	123.4	123.6
1974	1.04	1.19	151.2	151.3
1975	1.05	1.28	167.1	176.8

	Local currency	Exchange rate	U.S. dollar
ASSETS			
Cash & Marketable Securities[1]	5,551	12.5	444
Accounts and Notes Receivable[1]	60,889	12.5	4,871
Inventories[2]	121,956	12.5	9,756
Other Current Assets	1,794	12.5	145
TOTAL CURRENT ASSETS	190,190		15,216
Gross Buildings and Equipment	113,472	12.0	9,423
Accumulated Depreciation	66,179	11.7	5,644
Net Buildings and Equipment	47,293		3,779
Land and Construction in Progress	16,369	12.5	1,309
NET FIXED ASSETS	63,662		5,088
Other Assets	2,791	12.5	224
TOTAL ASSETS	256,643		20,528
LIABILITIES AND CAPITAL			
Accounts Payable	37,857	12.5	3,025
Mexican Income Taxes Payable	12,232	12.5	978
Short-Term Debt[3]	21,250	12.5	1,700
TOTAL CURRENT LIABILITIES	71,339		5,703
Long-Term Debt[4]	106,250		8,500
Special Reserves	3,752		301
TOTAL LIABILITIES	181,341		14,504
Share Capital	68,479	12.4	5,522
Retained Earnings	6,837		502
TOTAL CAPITAL	75,316		6,024
TOTAL LIABILITIES AND CAPITAL	256,657		20,528

1. All cash and marketable securities, receivables and payables were documented in pesos.
2. In July 1976, tin plate comprised 90% of inventories; work-in-progress and finished goods comprised 10%. Since much of Mexico's tin plate was imported, the market/replacement value (in pesos) of the raw materials portion of inventory would rise to exactly offset any devaluation. Within the inventory turnaround period, the market value of the finished goods inventories would not rise in response to a devaluation.
3. Bank debt of $1,700,000 is due to First National Bank of Maryland on September 25, 1976.
4. Long-term loan of $8,500,000 from the Bank of America. This loan is a refunding of part of the debt due ACC at the end of 1976. (See Note 2, Exhibit 3).

These schedules reflect modifications of actual financial statements but are illustrative of Nueva Modelo's exposure position.

value the peso much sooner. He felt a devaluation might be announced within the next several weeks. This reminded Jim of the warning that he had received while attending a meeting in Chicago in the spring. At that time, a Mexican banker had forecast that the devaluation would take place during the summer. In addition, Jim trusted the judgment of NMSA's Financial Director. In his words, "When Dave Wann doesn't sleep well, I don't sleep well."

THE DECISION

Jim knew that ACC's management would be concerned about the effect of a devaluation on the "bottom line." Under the FASB-8 accounting rules exchange losses would directly affect ACC's profit. As he headed back to his office Jim pulled NMSA's most recent financial statements (shown as Exhibits 6 and 7) from his files. He also gathered together information on peso forward rates and interest rates (see Exhibit 8). He planned to estimate the company's exposure and the loss ACC could expect if the peso devalued. He would also consider various hedging strategies and their costs. He could then recommend appropriate action to the Treasurer.

Exhibit 7 *American Can Company—International Business Group, Nueva Modelo, S.A. income statement for period covering October 1, 1975 through July 30, 1976 (000)*

	Mexican pesos	Exchange rate	U.S. dollars
SALES	317,645	12.5	25,412
Cost of Goods Sold	262,650	12.5	21,012
GROSS PROFIT	54,995		4,400
Selling and Administrative Expenses	14,005	12.5	1,120
GROSS OPERATING INCOME	40,990		3,280
Interest Expense	11,985	12.5	959
Other Income and Expense	2,210	12.5	177
Tax Expense	12,218	12.5	977
NET INCOME	14,577		1,167

These schedules reflect modifications of actual financial statements but are illustrative of Nueva Modelo's exposure position.

Exhibit 8 American Can Company—International Business Group

	Forward Rates[1]		Market Rates		Interest Rates	Eurodollar Rates[6]	
	Discount Percent Per Annum		Prime Rate		Guidance Rates to Subsidiaries[3,4,5] of U.S. Corporations	(percent per annum)	
			(percent per annum)		(percent per annum)		
	30 days	12 months	U.S.[2]	Mexico[3,4]		30 days	12 mos
1976							
JAN 30	8.10%	8.69%	6.75%	11.5%	12–11½%	5.07	6.75
FEB 27	6.38	10.39	6.75	12.0	13–12	5.19	6.94
MARCH 26	12.98	13.15	6.75	13.0	16–13	5.07	7.07
APRIL 30	29.89	24.55	6.75	not available	no market	5.19	6.75
MAY 28	12.30	20.70	6.75	no market	no market	5.81	7.69
JUNE 25	13.51	12.74	7.25	no market	no market	5.69	7.44
JULY 30	8.00	15.00	7.25	14.0	16–14	5.44	6.88

[1] Rates to sell pesos forward.
[2] Rates to borrow dollars.
[3] Rates to borrow pesos.
[4] Credit was rationed by the central bank so that credit may not have been available at stated rates.
[5] Rates on 6–12 month notes for subsidiaries of U.S. corporations, for credit in pesos; net of taxes.
[6] Average of bid and asked rates for dollar-denominated deposits in London banks.

Gunter Dufey

Case 18

Transmissions France S.A.
Protection Against the Effects of Devaluation

In 1962, an American automobile manufacturing company with large facilities abroad decided to expand its operations in the European Economic
Community, or Common Market. For efficiency, the company decided to
concentrate the total manufacturing of gear boxes in one plant. It was further decided to locate this plant near Strassbourg, France, because of the
well-placed location from a traffic standpoint and because of the considerable inducement the French government offered for industrial companies
that decided to invest in this particular part of the country. The company
had no other manufacturing facilities in France; however, it had very large
facilities in Germany and smaller ones in Holland. The plant in France
sold its entire output to these two plants, which assembled the vehicles and

then sold them throughout the Common Market and beyond, although the market share of the American company in France was nominal.

After certain political events during May 1968 in France, financial management at corporate headquarters in Detroit became rather concerned about the French currency situation and ordered its French subsidiary to keep working balances to the absolute minimum. Still, by year end management got more concerned about the situation. The value of the French plant was FF240 million at the end of 1968, and was entered at the official exchange rate with $60 million in the consolidated balance sheet of the parent.

In the beginning of 1969, the fundamental situation of the franc had not improved. Although the government of France had declined to devalue and had put severe restrictions on the outflow of Ffrs. — management in Detroit congratulated itself to have managed transfering its excess working balances just in time — a devaluation of the franc was still highly probable. With an expected magnitude of franc devaluation of up to 25 percent, management was concerned about a possible loss of anywhere between $5 to $27 million on the book value of its French operations. This caused some people in top management to suggest that the equivalent of FF240 million be hedged.

Don't hedge translation exposure (unless planning to sell plant)

Issues for Discussion

1. Analyze the situation and the attached balance sheet carefully, clearly stating your assumptions.
2. Analyze the potential sale of this operation to outside investors from the standpoint of the parent company: Specifically, would you anticipate to receive more or less, after the expectation of a devaluation of the French franc has become generally accepted?
3. Would refinancing the subsidiary's debt affect your evaluation? Note: interest cost of short-term liabilities in France is approximately twenty percentage points p.a. higher than those on U.S.-dollar denominated funds; on longer-term credits (three years plus), the difference is approximately ten percentage points p.a.
4. To what extent would freely floating exchange rates change the situation, if at all?
5. If you were the manager of the French operation, would you agree that the cost of forward cover should be charged to your results and your year-end bonus be reduced accordingly? Why or why not? What might be the arguments of the corporate controller?

Exhibit 1 *Projected balance sheets for Transmissions France S.A. December 31, 1969 (Figures in millions of FF or US $)*

Assets	I	II	III		
	FF	4FF = $1	5FF = $1		
			C	M	C/C
Cash and Current Receivables (FF)	FF 160	$ 40	$ 32	$ 32	$ 32
Inventories	40	10	8	10	8
Fixed Assets (Net of Depreciation)	400	100	100	100	80
	FF 600	$150	$140	$142	$120

Liabilities	I	II	III		
	FF	4FF = $1	5FF = $1		
			C	M	C/C
Current Liabilities (FF)	FF 60	$ 15	$ 12	$ 12	$ 12
Long Term Liabilities (FF)	—	—	—	—	—
Long Term Liabilities ($)	300	75	75	75	75
Capital and Retained Earnings (Net Worth)	240	60	53	55	33
	FF 600	$150	$140	$142	$120

Translation methods:

C: Current/noncurrent

M: Monetary/nonmonetary (Temporal method prescribed by FAS 8 yields equivalent results.)

C/C: Current/current (Reflects FAS 52 when inflation is less than 100 percent over past three years.)

Exhibit 2 **Projected balance sheets for Transmissions France S.A. December 31, 1969** (*Figures in millions of FF or US $*)

Assets	I	II	III		
	FF	4FF = $1	5FF = $1		
			C	M	C/C
Cash and Current Receivables (FF)	FF 160	$ 40	$ 32	$ 32	$ 32
Inventories	40	10	8	8	8
Fixed Assets (Net of Depreciation)	400	100	100	100	80
	FF 600	$150	$140	$142	$120

Liabilities	I	II	III		
	FF	4FF = $1	5FF = $1		
			C	M	C/C
Current Liabilities (FF)	FF 60	$ 15	$ 12	$ 12	$ 12
Long Term Liabilities (FF)	100	25	25	20	20
Long Term Liabilities ($)	200	50	50	50	50
Capital and Retained Earnings (Net Worth)	240	60	53	60	38
	FF 600	$150	$140	$142	$120

Translation methods:

C: Current/noncurrent

M: Monetary/nonmonetary (Temporal method prescribed by FAS 8 yields equivalent results.)

C/C: Current/current (Reflects FAS 52 when inflation is less than 100 percent over past three years.)

128

Exhibit 3 **Projected balance sheets for Transmissions France S.A. December 31, 1969** *(Figures in millions of FF or US $)*

| Assets | I | II | III | | |
| | FF | 4FF = $1 | 5FF = $1 | | |
			C	M	C/C
Cash and Current Receivables (FF)	FF 160	$ 40	$ 32	$ 32	$ 32
Inventories	40	10	8	10	8
Fixed Assets (Net of Depreciation)	400	100	100	100	80
	FF 600	$150	$140	$142	$120

| Liabilities | I | II | III | | |
| | FF | 4FF = $1 | 5FF = $1 | | |
			C	M	C/C
Current Liabilities	FF 60	$ 15	$ 12	$ 12	$ 12
Long Term Liabilities (FF)	300	75	75	60	60
Long Term Liabilities ($)	—	—	—	—	—
Capital and Retained Earnings (Net Worth)	240	60	53	70	48
	FF 600	$150	$140	$142	$120

Translation methods:

  C: Current/noncurrent

  M: Monetary/nonmonetary (Temporal method prescribed by FAS 8 yields equivalent results.)

  C/C: Current/current (Reflects FAS 52 when inflation is less than 100 percent over past three years.)

Gunter Dufey

Case 19

Gelenkwerke A. G. (Korea)
Coping with exchange fluctuations

Gelenkwerke A. G., headquartered in Düsseldorf, West Germany, had evolved over many years from a small tool and die shop in 1895 into a substantial enterprise employing more than twenty-five hundred people in three plants in Germany. It also had started a small plant in Belgium in 1958, which was its only foreign operation. However, the initial cost advantage proved transitory and the company did not expand that plant.

Like many other German companies, Gelenkwerke A. G. struggled throughout the 1970s with the problem of staying profitable in the face of relentlessly rising costs of labor and material, while import competition severely limited the ability of the company to achieve commensurate price increases for its output of large, complex machine tools.

The basic problem was not technological. Indeed, the firm's competitive advantage in terms of sophisticated production techniques permitted it to turn out products of superior quality. But the value of the deutsche mark, which had risen much faster than anyone expected and pushed costs out of sight, was a serious issue.

Like other companies, Gelenkwerke searched for a manufacturing base abroad with a better cost structure, and finally found one. After extensive studies during 1974 and 1975, it built a manufacturing plant in Korea (owned 100 percent by Gelenkwerke) through which it exploited the availability of relatively inexpensive, locally produced steel and, more important, a disciplined labor force that was able to acquire skills within a relatively short time. The capital-intensive plant came on stream in 1978, and soon its output, complex subassemblies, was shipped to Germany. There, the parts were put into drive assemblies and sold to large German customers.

While the technical people in top management of the company were quite pleased with the new venture, the finance director worried continually. Apart from the ever-present concern about the volatile political situation in that part of the world, the executive intensely disliked the associated foreign exchange and funding problems. He especially resented the constraints imposed by the Korean government as part of the 100 percent ownership deal: He felt he had too much equity capital tied up in the subsidiary and too large a proportion of the assets funded with deutsche mark denominated bank debt. Hedging alternatives were not present, as there was no forward market, although there was much talk about getting one started in the near future.

When the won devalued against the dollar in early 1980, the finance director made a determined effort to change the financing strategy of the firm. He obtained top management's agreement to make a comprehensive study of the foreign exchange risk and the funding alternatives of the firm. Particularly, he obtained agreement within the group of executives, in principle, to pay the high Korean interest rates* because, fundamentally, the company was extremely profitable.

---

*Interest rates on local currency loans were 21 percent higher than similar DM facilities, and some foreign banks active in Korea offered won loans which were only 17 percent higher if the parent company provided an unconditional guarantee.

Exhibit 1 **US$ and won relative to DM, 1970–1980** *(Quarterly averages – 1970 = 100)*

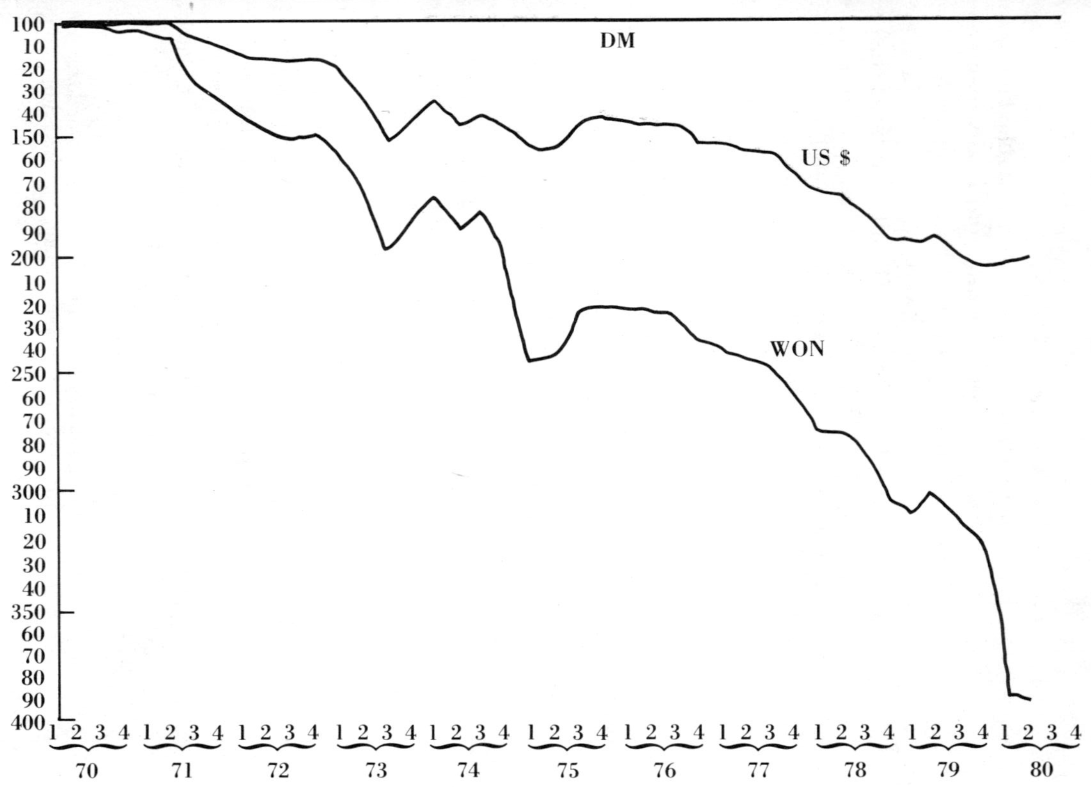

132

Exhibit 2 February 1980: Projected balance sheet for Gelenkwerke (Korea) December 31, 1980 (Figures in millions, won or DM, respectively)

Assets	I	II	III		
	Won	W330 = 1DM	W412.5 = 1DM		
	Won	DM	C	M	C/C
			DM	DM	DM
Fixed Assets (net of depreciation)	33,000	100	100	100	80
Inventories	3,300	10	8	10	8
Cash and Current Receivables	13,200	40	32	32	32
	49,500	150	140	142	120

Liabilities	I	II	III		
	Won	W330 = 1DM	W412.5 = 1DM		
	Won	DM	C	M	C/C
			DM	DM	DM
Capital and Retained Earnings (net worth)	19,800	60	53	55	33
Long Term Liabilities (DM)	24,750	75	75	75	75
Long Term Liabilities (Won)	—	—	—	—	—
Current Liabilities	4,950	15	12	12	12
	49,500	150	140	142	120

Translation methods:

C: Current/noncurrent

M: Monetary/nonmonetary (Temporal method prescribed by FASB #8 yields equivalent results.)

C/C: Current/current

Exhibit 3 February 1980: Projected balance sheet for Gelenkwerke (Korea) December 31, 1980 (Figures in millions, won or DM, respectively)

Assets	I	II	III		
	Won	W330 = 1DM	W412.5 = 1DM		
			C	M	C/C
	Won	DM	DM	DM	DM
Fixed Assets (net of depreciation)	33,000	100	100	100	80
Inventories	3,300	10	8	10	8
Cash and Current Receivables	13,200	40	32	32	32
	49,500	150	140	142	120

Liabilities	I	II	III		
	Won	W330 = 1DM	W412.5 = 1DM		
			C	M	C/C
	Won	DM	DM	DM	DM
Capital and Retained Earnings (net worth)	19,800	60	53	60	38
Long Term Liabilities (DM)	16,500	50	50	50	50
Long Term Liabilities (Won)	8,250	25	25	20	20
Current Liabilities	4,950	15	12	12	12
	49,500	150	140	142	120

Translation methods:

C: Current/noncurrent

M: Monetary/nonmonetary (Temporal method prescribed by FASB #8 yields equivalent results.)

C/C: Current/current

Exhibit 4 February 1980: Projected balance sheet for Gelenkwerke (Korea) December 31, 1980 (Figures in millions, won or DM, respectively)

Assets	I	II	III		
	Won	W330 = 1DM	W412.5 = 1DM		
			C	M	C/C
	Won	DM	DM	DM	DM
Fixed Assets (net of depreciation)	33,000	100	100	100	80
Inventories	3,300	10	8	10	8
Cash and Current Receivables	13,200	40	32	32	32
	49,500	150	140	142	120

Liabilities	I	II	III		
	Won	W330 = 1DM	W412.5 = 1DM		
			C	M	C/C
	Won	DM	DM	DM	DM
Capital and Retained Earnings (net worth)	19,800	60	53	70	48
Long Term Liabilities (DM)	—	—	—	—	—
Long Term Liabilities (Won)	24,750	75	75	60	60
Current Liabilities	4,950	15	12	12	12
	49,500	150	140	142	120

Translation methods:

C: Current/noncurrent

M: Monetary/nonmonetary (Temporal method prescribed by FASB #8 yields equivalent results.)

C/C: Current/current

135

Gunter Dufey

Case 20

The Rhode Island Golfball Manufacturing Company (RIGBMC)
or Foreign Exchange Trials and Tribulations

At the end of 1981, the Rhode Island Golfball Manufacturing Company was considering where to locate a new warehouse for its international business. Essentially this business focused on one market, Japan, where the company had built — more by accident than by strategic design — a very profitable market for its "High Stability" ® homing golf balls. Fifty percent of RIGBMC's output went to that market. The product had achieved a loyal following among Japanese executives, giving it a 3 percent market share at the upper end of the prestige/price scale.

The options were simple: The warehouse could be located near headquarters and ship to Japan using air freight via Flying Tigers, who served Tokyo out of Boston's Logan Airport three times a week. Others in the International Division argued the warehouse should be located near the superhighway between Narita and Tokyo. Consultants' studies had proved inconclusive; the advantage of slightly better service and lower transportation cost was virtually offset by the tremendous land values in Japan. However, the International Division Manager argued that the analysis had not considered the lower interest cost of yen financing, which ran approximately 8 percent per annum versus a U.S. dollar mortgage loan of 13 percent per annum.

You are one of the financial managers of RIGBMC. Analyze the accounting, risk, and cost-of-funds aspects of this decision.

Richard Moxon

Case 21

The Mexican Peso
or *Recuerdos Tristes de un Pasado Alegre*

The decision by the Mexican government to float the peso caught David Louis, Assistant International Treasurer for Fibrex Corporation, at a particularly inconvenient time. The announcement on August 31, 1976, cut short his Labor Day weekend of backpacking so that he could spend time preparing for a meeting of the Fibrex International Executive Committee. The meeting had been called to review the impact of the peso float on the company, and to decide on a plan of action to deal with the consequences of the float. He knew that both the International Controller and the President of Fibrex de Mexico would be there to report on the impact of the float, which at least at first glance appeared to have caused some serious problems for the company. As the person responsible for following international currency developments, Louis felt sure that he would be asked why the float had caught the company off guard, and what the future of the peso was now. He decided to begin by reviewing the material in his file of news clippings on the Mexican peso.

Although the last devaluation of the peso had occurred in 1954, concern over the possibility of a devaluation had existed for years. This concern intensified in 1976, but most observers had not expected a devaluation until at least after the inauguration of Mexico's new president in December. And, some analysts felt that the discovery of significant oil reserves might improve Mexico's balance of payments to such an extent that a devaluation would not be necessary. Exhibits 1 and 2 are representative of expert opinion in mid-1976.

Mr. Louis was, therefore, not the only one caught off guard by the peso float, and most observers were surprised by the extent to which the government allowed the peso to fall. When the Mexican Central Bank opened on Thursday, September 2, after a one day holiday, it began quoting pesos at about 20.5 per dollar as compared to the previous value of 12.5 pesos per dollar. By Friday opinions had become sharply divided on how far the peso might fall. Some felt that the market had already overreacted, while others saw no end in sight to the peso's decline. Observers also disagreed on whether the float would be successful in curing Mexico's balance of payments difficulties. A representative assessment of the situation is given in Exhibit 3.

In making his assessments of a currency's strength, Louis had always supplemented the opinions of others (including that of the foreign exchange trader at his bank) with his own analysis of the country's balance of payments and other economic indicators. He decided that for preparation for the meeting, he had better review this information one more time. Exhibits 4 through 9 summarize the material he had in his file.

Exhibit 1 . What is in store for the Mexican peso: A corporate assessment*

Amidst widespread rumors of an impending devaluation of the Mexican peso, BIMR editors have interviewed a number of financial officers of firms with extensive Mexican operations to determine how companies feel about the peso devaluation and what they are doing about their exposure in that currency. The responses vary markedly. Some firms are extremely concerned and are preparing for a devaluation in the next few months. Others do not anticipate any adjustment before next year at the earliest — i.e., after the new Lopez Portillo administration takes office — and are monitoring the situation closely but taking no specific protective actions.

*Article in *Business International Money Report*, March 4, 1976 (Reprinted with permission of the publisher, Business International Corporation)

Although the Mexican peso has maintained the same MP12.50/$1 parity with the US dollar for over twenty years, this is not the first time that rumors of a devaluation have surfaced: such rumors have cropped up periodically for years, especially around the spring season. But this time, apprehension seems particularly prevalent. Mexico's growing trade deficits — close to $3.6 billion in 1975 and estimated to be $4 billion this year — plus an inflation rate at least twice that of the United States (the latter takes about 60 percent of Mexican trade) have prompted a number of treasurers and bankers to conclude that an adjustment of the peso is inevitable.

Other financial officers believe that Mexico's ongoing success in obtaining large amounts of overseas funds to enhance its huge current account deficits indicates that Mexico can indeed defend the present exchange rate of the peso. In January, for example, Mexican state-backed borrowings on the Euromarket alone amounted to over $360 million, a pace which continued unabated last month.

Whether or not they are deeply concerned about a devaluation, many firms have been looking at protective measures but have not found them always attractive. Hedging on the forward market is very expensive, and cover is often difficult to obtain. In a thin market, quotes run as high as 12 percent p.a. for one-year forwards, just slightly less for shorter terms. Since few buyers appear in the market, only forward contracts for three months or shorter are readily filled, and companies wishing to sell pesos as far out as a year are having little success.

Another alternative would be to step up borrowing locally, although the cost is also considered high; for instance, short-term credit rates are presently around 14–16 percent p.a., but other charges make the effective expense substantially higher. Whether these or other options represent feasible protection against the currency risk is contingent on each firm's assessment of its own exposure.

THE CORPORATE REACTION

Below, a representative sampling of corporate responses to the present peso uncertainty:

Company A, a consumer products manufacturer, fears that the Mexican situation may be comparable to that of Argentina, where a currency adjustment was delayed from mid-1972 to March 1975 and, when it came, was wholly inadequate. This firm notes that both local borrowings and forward contracts are quite expensive, while the tax cost of speeding up remittances to the parent is almost prohibitive. (Dividends paid to foreign parents are subject to a withholding tax ranging from 15 percent to 20 percent depending on the amount.) Nevertheless, Company A is trying to improve its debt-to-equity ratio in Mexico and is planning to acquire about 60 percent of its financing there in pesos. Meanwhile, it is considering hedging up to the remainder of its exposure.

Company B, a capital goods producer, said that it has been advised to secure forward cover for 25 percent of its peso exposure, if cover can be attained at a reasonable cost, which is not presently the case in this firm's opinion. Stressing that it is looking for cover, not actively chasing it, Company B reported that it also is seeking local borrowings, as well as having its Mexican affiliate accelerate its payments on intra-company purchases.

Company C, in the communications field, feels that having peso loans cover 100 percent of its exposure would be desirable, but, because of cost and availability, has managed to obtain less than half of its borrowings in pesos. Company C emphasizes that it is not altering its investment strategy in Mexico because of the peso situation and that it would only resort to the use of leads and lags in the expectation of an immediate devaluation. This firm's general exposure strategy is to hedge only specific transactions, such as large dividend payments by foreign subsidiaries.

Company D, also a consumer goods manufacturer, stated that in response to the current uneasiness it has secured some peso loans at the relatively low cost of 12.5 percent; these loans will be used for paying intra-company obligations. To complete its cover, Company D, for the first time, has entered through its bank into forward contracts, which it has been able to obtain at a rate of about 10 percent p.a.

Company E, a major chemical concern, does not feel that a devaluation is likely in the near future and is presently taking no extraordinary measures to cover its peso exposure. The firm maintains that the costs associated with such efforts are not at this time justified by the risks.

Exhibit 2 *Prospects to June 1977**

Over the next twelve months the development of the Mexican economy will be assisted by a generally more favorable international background. Most of the main industrialised countries are now experiencing an economic recovery and the United States, the country whose economic development has the most direct effect on that of Mexico, is expected to experience real GNP growth of around 6.5 percent in 1976. Also relevant are Japan, where a growth rate of some 5 percent seems likely, and West

*Excerpts from the Economist Intelligence Unit's *Quarterly Economic Review for Mexico*, July 30, 1976. (Reprinted with the permission of the Economist Intelligence Unit Limited)

Germany, where the probable growth rate is put at about 4.5 percent. Based on these and other forecasts it is expected that the import volumes of OECD member countries will rise by about 7–8 percent in 1976 over 1975, following a fall of 9.5 percent in 1975. U.S. imports alone are forecast to rise by over 10 percent. In general terms, these expansionary trends are expected to continue into the first half of 1977.

These trends point to reasonably buoyant growth for Mexican exports, which showed no growth in 1975. Unofficial estimates of the growth of exports in the first five months of 1976 support this view and exports are estimated to have increased by nearly 17 percent in these months compared with the same period of 1975. One of the most buoyant sectors of exports is likely to be that related to petroleum. By early May Pemex reported that production was averaging 895,000 b/d compared with an average of 806,000 b/d in 1975. Production is, therefore, well on target towards the level of 1 mn b/d which is expected to be reached towards the end of the year. Based on this production forecast, Pemex expects exports of crude and refined products to be averaging 200,000 b/d and this points to an export total for the year in excess of $500 mn compared with $435 mn in 1975 and a mere $38 mn in 1974.

Particular emphasis is being placed on the development of higher-value exports of refined petroleum products, which should be helped by recent increases in refinery capacity. Some of these products will be included in the total for manufactured items and, bearing in mind this and the increase in demand from the United States, this category of exports is expected to increase by about 25 percent. As regards the other categories of exports — notably agriculture and mining, which jointly account for about one-third of the total — export values are expected to increase significantly as a result of both higher volumes and better prices. The sum of these forecasts suggests an export total of $3,380 mn in 1976, an increase of 18 percent on the 1975 level, and this forecast is the same as was given in the last review (QER No. 2 — 1976, page 20).

Nor does there seem any reason to change the forecast of imports given in the last review, which showed a fall of some 4 percent to $6,320 mn for 1976 imports. In fact, unofficial estimates of imports in the first five months of 1976 put the fall at 5.1 percent. Behind this will lie a fall in the value of imports of cereals to around $500 mn, compared with $640 mn in 1975, as a result of an improvement in domestic cereals production. Import restrictions, and a growing shortage of domestic credit, are likely to reduce imports of consumer durable goods. As regards nondurable production goods, further import substitution projects, notably in the plastics, papers, fertiliser, and steel products sectors, should also reduce imports.

On the basis of these forecasts the trade deficit should be reduced in 1976 to $2,940 mn compared with $3,721 mn in 1975, a fall of 21 percent.

After allowing for an increase in the net outflow on other items, especially debt servicing on the current account of the balance of payments, this points to a current account deficit of about $3.0 bn in 1976 compared with $3.6 bn in 1975. Despite the increase in overseas indebtedness, which has now surpassed $20 bn, the government will have no problems in financing a deficit of this order. There is no sign that international public and private financial institutions are likely to regard Mexico as anything other than a reasonable credit risk.

The improvement in the balance of payments, which will become increasingly apparent as 1976 progresses, should ease the pressure on the peso. However, speculation as to a possible devaluation is likely to continue, not least because of the change in president. Some calculations suggest that as a result of a high rate of domestic inflation over the last three years, the peso is anything up to 40 percent overvalued. There may be some truth in the belief that the peso is overvalued but it is difficult to see what could be gained by a devaluation of this order. Unless substantial capacity is available in manufacturing industry, which it is not, exports of manufactured exports would not increase in volume in response to a devaluation, while the servicing of foreign debt would become even more costly. At the same time the cost of importing necessary capital goods imports and foodstuffs would be increased.

On balance, a major devaluation of the order of 40 percent as suggested in some quarters seems unlikely, but the probability of a smaller devaluation is much more likely, if only to end speculation. The timing of this is unlikely to be before the change of president in December. Much more probable is a shift of the peso:dollar rate in the first half of 1976 when it can still be blamed on the Echeverria administration.

These developments in the balance of payments and exchange rate will be taking place against the background of an expanding economy. Real GDP grew by 3.8–4.2 percent in 1975 and growth of 5.5–6.0 percent is forecast for 1976, with expansion of this order continuing in the first half of 1977. To some extent this growth will be export-led, with both the manufacturing and mining sectors benefiting from higher overseas demand. Agriculture is also forecast to have a better year than in 1975, when an increase of around 4 percent in output was recorded. On the demand side, apart from the growth of exports, public sector investment and consumption expenditure should be adequate to support GDP growth of the order indicated above, but private sector investment is likely to remain weak until export demand feeds through the system. Here, some improvement may follow the change of president if the new president can boost business confidence. Private consumption, although benefiting from wage increases in 1976, is unlikely to be a buoyant force in the economy this year.

Exhibit 3 *Mexican peso float: inflation will determine the appropriate level**

Mexico's decision to float, i.e., devalue, the peso after twenty-two years of solidarity with the dollar has left observers — from the most sophisticated international treasurer or banker to the small private investor — pondering the currency's future.

For the short term, difficulties will continue, if not multiply, but the country's longer-term outlook remains promising. Market analysts had almost all agreed that the peso was overvalued in dollar terms, and companies had generally attempted to cover their exposure. But the timing of the move nevertheless caught many off guard. Adding to the confusion, the decision was made on the eve of a holiday, leaving question marks as to what the new rate will be.

The initial market reaction has been dramatic indeed. When Mexican banks opened their doors on Thursday following Wednesday's holiday, they found the central bank quoting a rate for the peso of MP20.4–20.6/$1,

*Article From *Business International Money Report.* September 3, 1976 (Reprinted with permission of the publisher, Business International Corp.)

Exhibit 4 *Mexico's balance of payments, 1956–1975*

Balance of payments		1956	1957	1958	1959	1960	1961	1962	1963
Mexico		Millions of US dollars				Minus sign indicates debt			
Goods and Services	77a.d	−114	−296	−265	−161	−333	−228	−167	−201
Trade Balance, cif	77acd	−228	−420	−391	−271	−428	−317	−225	−263
Exports, fob	77bad	—	—	—	—	—	—	930	985
Imports, cif	77ccd	—	—	—	—	—	—	1,155	1,248
Travel	771dd	224	230	242	248	260	269	275	307
Investment Income	77gdd	−143	−134	−143	−169	−191	−204	−237	−266
Other Services	77r.d	33	28	27	31	26	24	20	21
Transfers: Private	77tad	−3	1	—	−3	−7	−14	−17	−16
Government	77tgd	1	2	1	2	2	1	2	−1
Capital, n.i.e.: Private	78add	218	189	149	100	166	277	267	215
Central Govt	78k.d	−24	−3	48	8	−46	−34	−13	75
Deposit Money Banks: Assets	78pad	—	—	−60	19	55	−24	−29	−35
Liabilities	78pbd	35	12	56	25	8	56	−31	26
Allocation of SDRs	78w.d	—	—	—	—	—	—	—	—
Monetary Authorities	79a.d	−73	32	80	−60	23	33	−2	−125
Monetary Gold	79bad	−25	−13	37	1	6	24	18	−44
SDR Holdings	79bbd	—	—	—	—	—	—	—	—
IMF General Account	79bcd	—	—	—	−22	—	45	−45	—
Other Assets	79rad	−47	49	43	−41	10	−40	13	−76
Other Liabilities (Net)	79rld	−1	−4	—	3	7	4	12	−5
Net Errors and Omissions	79w.d	−40	63	−9	70	132	−67	−10	62

Source: *International Financial Statistics,* August, 1976.

60 percent below the former rate of MP12.5. Undoubtedly, the authorities felt that such a low peso rate would discourage outflows, since most peso holders would be unwilling to absorb that great an exchange loss. This strategy has apparently been at least somewhat successful, since no mad rush to buy dollars has occurred. The 60 percent drop seems, however, to represent an overcorrection that will be partially reversed. Most estimates had put the overvaluation of the peso in the range of 30–40 percent, with expectations that the adjustment would roughly match this amount. But some experts believe that even a 50 percent devaluation would be justified, and a new rate settling somewhere in the range of MP18–19:$1 cannot be ruled out.

The key determinant of an appropriate level for the peso will be the extent of the inflationary impact of the adjustment. The step comes at a time when inflation was again spiraling (WPI is rising at an annual 16 percent rate). Helping to dampen the effects, however, will be a strengthening of price controls covering a wide range of basic consumer and industrial goods. But the expected wage increases, to be applied retroactively September 1, will add fuel to the inflationary fires. And if the fires get too hot, the downward adjustment of the peso will have to be even larger to maintain the competitive advantage of the devaluation.

1964	1965	1966	1967	1968	1969	1970	1971	1972	1973	1974	1975
−412	−398	−391	−635	−757	−609	−1,123	−895	−980	−1,489	−2,989	−4,183
−445	−431	−420	−618	−710	−633	−923	−759	−864	−1,428	−2,650	−3,169
1,054	1,146	1,244	1,209	1,258	1,458	1,437	1,520	1,882	2,419	3,443	3,445
1,499	1,577	1,664	1,827	1,968	2,091	2,360	2,279	2,746	3,847	6,093	6,613
327	361	396	441	501	528	416	533	623	839	902	810
−324	−333	−394	−473	−559	−617	−695	−738	−700	−907	−1,447	−1,856
30	11	27	15	11	113	79	70	−39	97	206	33
−9	−5	−5	5	13	17	48	50	54	66	100	114
−2	—	4	2	—	—	7	7	10	8	13	12
536	142	334	467	390	701	466	791	907	1,478	2,023	3,719
7	17	49	96	106	76	177	14	37	119	590	854
−4	−29	91	−76	−160	112	−47	−27	−85	−179	210	−68
93	−11	84	140	−54	−89	89	−35	73	49	473	304
—	—	—	—	—	—	45	40	42	—	—	—
−46	66	27	−68	−83	62	−87	−180	−221	−99	−38	−170
−30	11	49	−57	1	−4	−8	−8	12	13	41	—
—	—	—	—	—	—	−48	−40	−42	—	−1	52
—	−10	−32	−9	−38	21	−23	37	—	—	—	—
−12	60	−19	−11	−57	36	4	−171	−190	−154	−78	−222
−4	5	29	9	11	9	−12	2	−1	42	—	—
−163	218	−195	69	545	−270	425	234	164	46	−381	−582

THE ANTIDEVALUATION CAMPAIGN

The timing of the move came as a surprise given President Luis Echeverria's strong stance on maintaining the peso's fixed parity. The government's claims that the country lacked the productive capacity to capitalize on a lower exchange rate, that it could not cut down on the 80 percent of its imports categorized as economic essentials, and that it would suffer heavily by a revaluation of the foreign debt — now totaling, both public and private, a whopping $22 billion — seemingly had attracted some converts. This improved climate had spurred a steady narrowing of the discounts on forward pesos since mid-June.

Naturally, the authorities now play down these problems. Finance Minister Mario Raymond Beteta claims that Mexico does have sufficient unused industrial capacity to take advantage of the new exchange rate, that the higher peso cost of imports will encourage investment in domestic replacements and that foreign debt is paid and serviced from current account income, which should benefit from the float.

Whether or not the anticipated merits of the downward float can be transferred into economic reality, however, has not yet been determined. In the short run, the advantages to the export and tourism sectors may be more than offset by the drawbacks of an unavoidable new wave of inflation and increased costs, in many cases not immediately recoverable through increased prices. Unquestionably, the economy will be facing a thorny adjustment period in the coming months.

The government has also taken a chance regarding foreign investment in Mexico. Although international companies will experience many problems, the investment atmosphere will not be greatly altered, and the country's international credit standing may even improve. But the small individual investors, primarily those located in the United States, will be severely affected. Investments in the Financieras (savings and loans), from the United States alone, now amount to an estimated $6 billion, roughly equivalent to the total foreign fixed investment to the nation. Some experts feel that following the last peso devaluation in 1954, it took Mexico nearly ten years to regain the confidence of private investors.

Exhibit 5 *Mexico's international reserves, 1970–1975 (End of year figures in millions of U.S. dollars)*

	1970	1971	1972	1973	1974	1975
Gold	176	200	188	195	157	150
SDRs	48	96	139	154	158	101
Reserve Position in IMF	135	106	106	118	120	114
Foreign Exchange	385	550	731	888	960	1,168
TOTAL	744	952	1,164	1,355	1,395	1,533
IMF Quota	370	402	402	466	453	433
Net Drawings (+) or Sales (−) with IMF	−41	−4	−4	−5	−5	−5

Source: *International Financial Statistics*, May, 1976.

Exhibit 6 *Selected economic indicators for Mexico*

	1970	1971	1972	1973	1974	1975
Gross Domestic Product (current prices in billion pesos)	418.7	452.4	512.3	619.6	812.9	982.5
Money Supply (billion pesos)	53.8	57.9	68.2	83.5	100.8	

Source: *International Financial Statistics*, May, 1976.

Exhibit 7 *Mexican Peso Forward Exchange Rates in 1976*

Date	Forward Discount (%/year) vs. U.S. $			Date	Forward Discount (%/year) vs. U.S. $		
	3 months	6 months	1 year		3 months	6 months	1 year
1/8/76	− 6.61	− 7.10		4/29/76	−18.63	−20.29	−18.10
1/15	− 7.54	− 7.82		5/6	−18.63	−20.29	−18.10
1/22	− 7.54	− 7.25		5/14	−18.10	−20.47	−18.10
1/29	−13.91	− 8.44	− 7.82	5/21	−18.63	−20.29	−18.10
2/5	−13.91	− 8.44		5/28	−20.00	−24.05	−18.08
2/12	−13.91	− 8.44		6/4	−20.00	−24.05	−18.08
2/19	−13.91	− 8.44		6/10	−20.00	−20.90	−19.92
2/26	−10.60	− 8.58		6/18	−20.00	−20.90	−19.92
3/4	−10.60	− 8.58		6/24	−12.71	−13.58	−17.83
3/11	−10.60	− 8.58		7/1	−12.71	−13.58	−17.83
3/18	−10.60	− 8.58		7/9	−12.49	−13.77	−16.09
3/25	−11.21	−10.76	−11.42	7/16	−11.21	−10.76	−12.66
4/1	−12.11	−12.88	−12.96	7/23	−11.21	−12.18	−12.66
4/8	−21.23	−17.66	−16.17	7/30	−11.21	−12.18	−12.66
4/15	−18.63	−18.99	−16.17	8/6	− 8.77	−10.76	−12.96
4/22	−12.71	−16.32	−15.32	8/13	− 8.16	− 9.31	−12.66
				8/20	− 8.16	− 9.31	−12.66
				8/27	− 9.08	−10.76	−13.56

Source: *Business International Money Report*, weekly issues for 1976.

Exhibit 8 *Selected U.S. and Mexican Interest Rates*

	Commercial Bank Deposit Rates (end of month)		Commercial Bank Lending Rates to Prime Borrowers[*]	
	U.S.	Mexico	U.S.	Mexico
December, 1973	9.25	9.50	9.75	13.50
December, 1974	9.25	9.50	10.25	14.00
December, 1975	5.50	9.50	7.25	14.00
February, 1976	5.13	9.50	6.75	14.50
March, 1976	5.20	9.50	6.75	14.50
April, 1976	5.05	9.50	6.75	14.50
May, 1976	5.90	9.50	7.00	14.50
June, 1976	5.75	9.50	7.25	14.50
July, 1976	5.38	9.50	7.00	14.50
August, 1976	5.25	9.50	7.00	14.50

[*] In Mexico the requirement of about a 20% compensating balance raised the effective interest rate.

Source: Morgan Guaranty, *World Financial Markets,* September, 1976.

Exhibit 9 *Price Indexes for the United States and Mexico (1970 = 100)*

	United States		Mexico	
	Wholesale Prices	Consumer Prices	Wholesale Prices	Consumer Prices
1954	79.3	69.2	57.4	49.3
1955	79.5	69.0	65.2	57.2
1960	86.0	76.3	79.0	76.1
1965	87.5	81.2	86.7	83.5
1970	100.0	100.0	100.0	100.0
1975	158.4	138.6	167.1	176.8

Source: *International Financial Statistics,* May, 1976.

Ian H. Giddy

Case 22

Morris De Minas

It was August 1984 in New Jersey and the management of Morris Mini Mainframe Computer Company was looking for the most desirable alternative to finance the working capital needs of its Brazilian affiliate, Morris de Minas Ltda. The total need was for 82,650 million cruzeiros, or US$39,320,000 at the then-prevailing exchange rate of 2,102 cruzeiros per United States dollar.[1] The funds were required to meet competition by

Prepared by Geraldo Valente and Ian Giddy. © 1985 Ian H. Giddy, New York University.

[1] The cruzeiro (Cr$) is the Brazilian currency. Its exchange value was set in relation to the US dollar, and exchange rates against other currencies were determined from their rate relative to the US dollar. For instance, while the Cruzeiro/US dollar exchange rate remained fixed until it was adjusted, the Cruzeiro/Deutsche mark exchange rate varied daily, according to the free-market fluctuations of the Deutsche mark/US dollar exchange rate. Under the minidevaluation system that had been prevailing in Brazil since 1968, the cruzeiro was continually devalued by small amounts at frequent intervals in order to take account of the chronically higher inflation rate

providing installment credit for increased sales forecast for the first half of Morris de Minas' fiscal year (Exhibit 1); this was a level of sales that the company felt it could sustain in the future.

BACKGROUND

Morris was a manufacturer of "supermini" computers based in Hacketts-town, New Jersey. It had gone international a long time ago and by 1983 about two-thirds of its revenues were earned outside the United States. Morris (USA) entered the Brazilian market in 1971 by assembling and distributing computers in Belo Horizonte, in the state of Minas Gerais. Late in the 1970s, after it became known for the high quality of its products, Morris (USA) expanded its operations in Brazil to manufacture and distribute a line of superminis, which included a full line of disk drives, printers, and other peripherals. Sales in Brazil focused on medium-sized enterprises, foreign and domestic, and were made on a revolving and installment credit basis. Such sales had amounted (excluding financial charges) to 36,246 million cruzeiros (Cr$) in fiscal year 1982, 86,593 million cruzeiros in 1983, and 158,916 million cruzeiros in 1984 (Exhibit 1). Morris was beginning to feel the pinch of competition from the North American minicomputer manufacturers, who, having been excluded from the Brazilian market in their principal products by severe import controls, had moved aggressively into the one segment, halfway between minis and mainframes, that remained the principal domain of foreign producers.

Past experience in several countries, including the United States, had shown that the availability of credit was fundamental to maintaining a market position. This aspect was even more important in Brazil, where

---

in Brazil than in most of its trading partners. Prior to the introduction of the minidevaluation policy, the cruzeiro came to be overvalued as a consequence of prolonged high inflation periods without adjustments in the exchange rate. Expectations of large devaluations were built up, encouraging the delay of exports, anticipation of imports, and, more important, eroding the competitive position of Brazilian goods in international markets. On the other hand, to the extent that the magnitude of the smaller and periodical devaluations reasonably matched inflation, this policy of minidevaluations avoided the occurrence of destabilizing speculation, especially in the form of capital outflows. Furthermore, it guaranteed the competitive advantage of the Brazilian exports. At least on two occasions, however, the Brazilian government had failed to adjust the cruzeiro exchange rate adequately by minidevaluations. Thus in December 1979 and in February 1983 two minidevaluations of 30 percent (each) had broken the continuity of the minidevaluation policy, raising, as a consequence, some doubts about the credibility of this exchange rate system. *Sources:* Financing Foreign Operations (FFO), "Domestic Financing: Brazil," June 1984. Peat, Marwick, Mitchell & Co., "Banking in Brazil," 1982.

Exhibit 1 *Morris de Minas selected financial data (Cr$ Million)*

	Fiscal (August 31)		Forecast for first 6 months of fiscal	
	1982	1983	1984	1985
Total Sales	36,246	86,593	158,916	166,194
Time Sales	30,954	75,865	142,548	152,063
Ending Balance Time Sales Receivables	18,525	49,236	92,484	175,134
Net Earnings Before Foreign Exchange Loss	4,952	6,321	14,927	15,964
Return on Net Worth Before Foreign Exchange Loss	13%	8%	11%	
Return on Investment After Foreign Exchange Loss	3%	1%	5%	

Working Capital Needs: Cr$ 82,650 Million
　　　　　　　　　　　　US$ 39,320 Thousand (Cr$2,102/US$1)

Equity: Cr$16,530 million 　　*Debt:* Cr$66,120 million
　　　　　US$ 7,864 thousand 　　　　　　US$31,456 thousand

companies frequently incurred indebtedness in the hope of benefiting from the chronically high inflation rate. Therefore, to assure sales, Morris de Minas would need to extend its investment in receivables from time sales for the foreseeable future.

Until recently, Morris (USA) had followed a policy of financing its growth almost entirely from its own cash flow without resort to external borrowing. For subsidiaries operating in countries with high inflation rates and soft currencies, that policy had sometimes led to heavy foreign exchange losses, as reflected in Morris de Minas' profitability in years 1982 and 1983, when equity was by far the most significant source of the affiliate's funds (Exhibits 1 and 2). However, during the fall of 1983, in a move aimed at limiting exposure to exchange losses, Morris (USA) management had set new equity participation limits for all subsidiaries potentially subject to high foreign exchange risk. According to the new policy the parent company would commit equity capital to its Brazilian affiliate only to the extent of 20 percent of its present working capital needs. The implication was that Morris de Minas would have to obtain Cr$66,120 million from outside sources in this instance.

David Albuquerque, the vice-president of finance for the Latin Ameri-

Exhibit 2 *Morris de Minas balance sheets (CR$ Million)*

	Fiscal (August 31)		
	1982	1983	1984
Assets			
Cash and Marketable Securities	2,658	3,597	7,086
Accounts Receivable	4,282	6,046	14,513
Time Sales Receivable	18,525	49,236	92,484
Inventory	7,947	16,319	29,486
Total Current Assets	33,412	75,198	143,569
Net Fixed Assets	16,452	43,341	121,485
Total Assets	49,864	118,539	265,054
Liabilities			
Accounts Payable	4,795	16,286	59,239
Accrued Taxes	1,846	5,211	13,180
Other Liabilities	3,652	9,142	45,236
Total Current Liabilities	10,293	30,639	117,655
Notes Payable	2,311	5,341	16,462
Capital Stock	29,325	70,986	111,469
Retained Earnings	3,149	5,135	9,152
Reserves	4,786	6,456	10,316
Total Liabilities	49,864	118,539	265,054

can Division, was in charge of exploring possible financing arrangements and preparing a financing plan. Albuquerque realized that both the Brazilian expected inflation rate and tax legislation, as well as the future behavior of the exchange rate, would play major roles in his analysis. These were difficult to predict; nevertheless he regarded this as a good opportunity to stack up the company's financing choices against one another in a systematic fashion and perhaps also to give some thought to the total financial structure of the Brazilian subsidiary.

BRAZIL'S ECONOMIC ENVIRONMENT[2]

Brazil's rate of economic growth had been impressive for most of the past twenty years, up to 1980, except in the beginning of the 1960s when the

[2] Most of this synthesis is based on material from: Financing Foreign Operations (FFO), "Domestic Financing: Brazil," June 1984. The Economist Intelligence Unit

Exhibit 3 *Morris de Minas, Brazil's gross domestic product*

	1979	1980	1981	1982	1983
Total (CR$ billions)					
At Current Prices	6,239	13,104	26,833	53,150	130,805
Real Increase (%)	6.8	7.9	−1.9	1.4	−3.3
Per Capita (CR$ thousands)					
At Current Prices	54	110	220	425	1,021
Real Increase (%)	4.2	5.4	−4.1	−0.8	−5.4

Source: *International Monetary Fund*

GDP (Gross Domestic Product) growth rate fell to 1.6 percent, mainly due to a marked slowdown in the manufacturing sector. However the recovery occurred rapidly, and from 1968 through 1973 the economy expanded at impressive rates averaging over 10 percent per annum. Following this period of "economic miracle" GDP increased at a rate above 5 percent per annum between 1974 and 1980, except for 1978.

However, in order to support its massive program of development, Brazil had incurred an extremely high level of indebtedness. Brazil's foreign debt had reached US$100 billion in 1984. High interest rates on dollar funds and the unwillingness of foreign lenders to advance additional loans provoked a deep economic recession. The initial effect of the severe reduction in the pace of economic growth was felt through a fall in GDP of 1.9 percent and a decline in per capita income of 4.1 percent in 1981 (Exhibit 3). In 1982 there was a recovery in the rate of growth of the GDP that registered 1.4 percent. Nevertheless, this improvement was short-lived; in 1983 Brazil returned to a negative rate of economic expansion, with the GDP falling by 3.3 percent. 1983 showed an even more pronounced decrease in per capita income of 5.4 percent, in contrast with 0.8 percent in 1982. Adding to this, an unfavorable export performance had affected Brazil's capacity to meet the financial obligations pertinent to its huge foreign debt, since Brazil had lost a critical amount of foreign reserves. As a consequence the Brazilian government, whose basic goal was the stabilization of the balance of payments, had to ask the International Monetary Fund (IMF) for funds, which involved submitting to a rigid program of economic austerity developed by the Fund and the country's main private creditor banks.

While in 1984 there was an expectation of small but positive GDP

(EIU), "Quarterly Economic Review of Brazil: Annual Supplement," 1983. The Economist Intelligence Unit (EIU), "Quarterly Economic Review of Brazil," No. 3, 1984. Peat, Marwick, Mitchell & Co., "Banking in Brazil," 1982.

growth, due mainly to an impressive export performance, the outlook for 1985 was more uncertain because it was believed that the inflation rate would remain high, at least for the first half of the year.

Public expenditure had been among the most prominent causes of Brazil's lack of financial stability for a long time. Brazil had three separate, unconsolidated budgets: the fiscal budget, the monetary budget, and the budget for state-owned firms. In recent years it had proved to be politically impossible to finance the public deficits by noninflationary means. While fiscal budget surpluses had been achieved every single year since 1976, it was not until 1983 that the monetary budget introduced a liquidity squeeze, reduced credit subsidies, cut the public enterprise budget, and effected a transfer of funds from the fiscal to the monetary budget. 1983 also marked the beginning of an attempt to control the spending and borrowing activities of the nearly six hundred public sector companies in foreign markets. This was part of a greater effort directed towards the reduction of the public sector financing needs from 17 percent of GDP in 1983 to 5 percent in 1984 and 4 percent in 1985. The state companies were still expected to register deficits in 1984, but limits had been set in order to keep the deficit under control.

The rate of growth of the money supply (M1) had increased from 36.8 percent in 1974 to 87.6 percent in 1983 (Exhibit 4); current policy for 1984 was to keep monetary growth under 50 percent. In the early months of the year, however, the money supply growth rate was far beyond the desired

Exhibit 4 **Morris de Minas, money supply and inflation in Brazil**

| | Percentage Change Over Previous Year | |
	Money Supply (M1)*	General Price Index**
1974	36.8	34.6
1975	35.6	29.4
1976	42.3	46.2
1977	37.0	38.8
1978	40.9	40.8
1979	53.2	77.2
1980	76.4	110.3
1981	65.1	95.1
1982	75.4	99.7
1983	87.6	211.0

*Source: International Monetary Fund
**Source: Getulio Vargas Foundation, Rio de Janeiro, Brazil

level, which made more strict measures seem inevitable. Monetary expansion in the first seven months of 1984 alone had risen to over 139 percent.

The pace of inflation had similarly accelerated over the last decade. In every year but three since 1974, the inflation rate had increased, reaching 211 percent in 1983. Frequently cited causes for this included strong internal demand, unchecked monetary expansion, acute increases in prices in world markets (especially for petroleum), and some food supply related problems. In addition, recent salary increases above the amount permitted by the wage legislation, price adjustments allowed to industry and commerce who in turn passed them on to consumers, and the reduction of subsidies for oil, sugar and wheat had made it certain that the inflationary wave would continue. By the end of August 1984 the annual rate of inflation stood at 219.3 percent, and higher industrial costs were expected to cause a further rise in the overall price level of the economy. Moreover, the funding crisis facing the government was having an impact on industry's costs by means of very high interest rates. Therefore it was very unlikely that Brazil would come into 1985 with less than 230 percent inflation. Both inflation and monetary expansion were expected to stay high, up to the time when a combination of growth and structural changes could relieve the pressure caused by the financing of the nearly US$25 billion internal debt from domestic financial markets.

The exchange rate of the cruzeiro had weakened from 7.44 cruzeiros to the U.S. dollar in the end of 1974 to 252.67 at the end of 1982 (Exhibit 5). On February 18, 1983 the government devalued the cruzeiro by 30 percent, partly influenced by the negotiations with the IMF concerning the debt

Exhibit 5 *Morris de Minas, exchange rate and monetary correction in Brazil*

End of period	CR$/US$	O.R.T.N. (CR$)
1974	7.44	105.41
1975	9.07	130.93
1976	12.35	179.63
1977	16.05	233.74
1978	20.92	318.44
1979	42.53	468.71
1980	65.50	706.70
1981	127.80	1,382.09
1982	252.67	2,733.27
1983	984.00	7,012.99
1984 (August)	2,102.00	14,619.90

Source: Central Bank of Brazil.

rescheduling program. Prior to the maxidevaluation the cruzeiro had stood at 292.5 to the U.S. dollar; afterward it stood at 380.5. The minidevaluation policy since then, in line with inflation, brought the rate to 984 cruzeiros to the U.S. dollar by late 1983, and 2,102 to the U.S. dollar by the end of August of 1984. Given the usually much higher rate of inflation in Brazil relative to that of its trading partners, the country would become increasingly uncompetitive in world markets if there were no adequate adjustment in the cruzeiro exchange rate. Thus, in order to diminish its reliance on external savings, Brazil — under the terms of the IMF stabilization agreement — had adopted an aggressive exchange rate policy: it would devalue the cruzeiro fifteen days after each quarter at a rate equal to "general price inflation without accidental factors" during the preceding three months. For purposes of this policy, accidental factors were defined to include the reduction of subsidies, rises in international prices, poor crops, and similar events.

In 1983 and in the first half of 1984 Brazil had had no difficulty in complying with its commitment. Furthermore, since the U.S. dollar had been rising in relation to other currencies, the government was inclined to accelerate the pace of devaluation in order to back up the competitiveness of Brazil's exports in European and Asian markets. While prices for Brazilian goods in the United States rose only 2.6 percent from the middle of 1983 through the middle of 1984, prices for such goods rose 12.7 percent in West Germany, 15.1 percent in France, and 17.1 percent in Italy.

The Brazilian financial system was reasonably well equipped to handle a full range of banking activities, especially in the large cities. However, by virtue of government regulations, lines of credit were not always easy to obtain. In particular, foreign companies' affiliates frequently had to struggle for funds, using newly developed financing methods. While several factors might be held responsible for high interest rates in Brazil, the most direct was probably expectation of high inflation, as reflected in the periodic adjustment of the price index. Another related major factor that contributed to high interest rates was the frequent "squeeze" of the price index. In Brazil, indexing or monetary correction[3] might be safely regarded as the fundamental interest rate factor in the economy, since it accounted

---

[3] The index of monetary correction was given by the percent change in the par value of the Obrigacoes Reajustaveis do Tesouro Nacional (National Treasury Indexed Bonds), ORTNs, and was set by the government on a monthly basis. The ORTNs were created in October 1964 with an initial par value of CR$10. They had been issued since then by the Bank of Brazil for the Treasury, and the month-to-month index change was used in a wide variety of contracts in Brazil, notably in financial instruments. For example, the par value of one ORTN was Cr$7,012.99 in December 1983 and Cr$14,619.90 in August 1984. Thus the indexing or monetary correction for the first eight months of 1984 was 108.5 percent (14,619.90/7,012.99). The monetary correction rate for the last 12 months stood at 200.2 percent.

for the major part of the cost of a bank loan, of the yield on a certificate of deposit (CD), of the return on a savings account, and of a typical cruzeiro devaluation, and thus of the cost of a loan denominated in foreign currency (Exhibit 5). It also provided guidelines for overnight transactions in the money market. As may be seen from Exhibits 4 and 5, however, the monetary correction factor did not always equal the inflation or devaluation rate, perhaps as a result of the Bank of Brazil's effort to bring down inflation. Therefore, when investors believed that the monetary correction might be lagging or underestimated the high inflation, they attempted to compensate for this by requiring very high interest rates over monetary correction, which caused a further increase in the cost of bank funding and, in turn, bank lending rates.

Finally, there was the strain put on the financial system by excessive government borrowing in the money market. The sale of new government bonds exhausted bank reserves and drove up the overnight rate on open-market transactions, which in turn pushed up the bank's marginal cost of funding and therefore the lending rates.

Externally, the cruzeiro was not convertible. There was no active forward market for the cruzeiro and cover was usually not obtainable. Foreign currency could officially be obtained only for transactions specifically sanctioned by the government, from institutions authorized to operate with foreign exchange. All transactions had to be supported with appropriate, and often onerous, documentation and were closely monitored by the Central Bank, which performed a daily inspection of transactions made through each registered broker.

There was also an illegal but highly organized parallel market for U.S. dollars (mostly cash in the form of U.S. one-hundred dollar bills), but companies were advised not to participate in it since transactions in this market were not endorsed by the Brazilian government. Nevertheless the daily black market rate was quoted prominently in the major newspapers. In late August the parallel market rate stood at Cr$2,445 per U.S.$1.

THE FINANCING ALTERNATIVES

After a few phone calls to Brazil and discussions with financial officers of other multinational corporations operating under similar conditions, several options to meet the financing needs of Morris de Minas had emerged. In order to make his task easier, Albuquerque divided the alternatives into those not involving exchange risk and those doing so. Two options, a Euro-dollar loan to Morris de Minas and the establishment of a financing subsidiary, fell into the latter category, while another, a back-to-back loan, bore only partial exchange risk. Albuquerque thought he should begin with two widely used financing techniques that involved no foreign exchange risk.

1. DISCOUNTING OF RECEIVABLES AT BRAZILIAN COMMERCIAL BANKS

Traditionally, the most prevalent form of short-term financing for a company such as Morris was to discount receivables, with recourse, at Brazilian commercial banks.

The normal range of terms on trade bill discounts was 30 to 120 days, although occasional 180-day operations were observed. The range of nominal rates was 9 to 11 percent per month, including a 0.125 percent tax on financial transactions, all of which would be tax deductible. However, with the prevailing practice of charging upfront commitment fees and requiring compensating balances of 25 to 35 percent, the effective rate was approximately 395 percent per annum. Given the fact that firms need some balances to back up their day-to-day operations, the effective rate of interest would be less because the actual required compensating balance was not quite as high as it seemed to be.

The major drawback with this method, however, was that local banks did not have an abundant supply of cruzeiros. Because of the tight monetary policy of the Brazilian government, both in the form of a 35 percent reserve requirement and other restrictions on the use of demand deposit funds, commercial banks often had a limited amount of funds they could make available to a client for the discounting of receivables. Compounding the problem was the fact that foreign-owned subsidiaries in Brazil faced official restrictions on lending, since the Brazilian government reserved 75 percent of commercial bank loan portfolios for privately owned local firms, which forced foreign-owned companies to compete with state agencies for the remaining 25 percent of the domestic credit supply. As a result, firms with large sales volumes and large working capital needs, as in the Morris de Minas case, would find it extremely difficult, if not impossible, to set up such large discount lines, even considering the use of a large number of banks. Adding to this, Albuquerque felt that the local subsidiary should not enter into discount agreements with more than twenty local banks because of the complications that almost certainly would arise from this expedient. In consequence, he felt that the firm should not count on raising more than half the required amount in this manner.

It was also possible to discount Morris' receivables with recourse at local private finance companies, which were the normal sources of credit to consumers, and which were somewhat less constrained by government regulations.

Albuquerque's assistant had computed the cost of discounting the receivables to be, on the average, approximately equal to 494 percent per annum. All of this cost would be deductible in computing profits subject to Brazilian corporate taxes, which for Morris de Minas would be approximately 45 percent.

2. LOAN FROM LOCAL INVESTMENT BANKS

As another alternative without currency risk, the Brazilian subsidiary would borrow its cruzeiro requirement from local investment banks. The six-month investment bank loan rate was regarded as the Brazilian prime rate and was related to the banks' CD rate, which had a minimum term of six months, according to Central Bank regulations.

A legal rate control imposed by the Central Bank of Brazil prevented large banks from charging more than 20 percent per annum over monetary correction on a six-month loan. Taking into account semiannual compounding, this came to 9.54 percent for six months. For small banks, the limit was 24 percent per annum. But as in other high-inflation countries, it was very difficult, if not impossible, to control interest rates in Brazil. Bankers were accustomed to living with interest rate controls and had quickly developed a number of ingenious ways to circumvent them on both CDs and term loans, such as discounts for CDs and commitment fees and/or compensating balances for loans. Thus the old trick of charging a commitment fee up front had became general practice in recent years. Although fees varied, the most common charge was 5 percent for a six-month loan. There was also an upfront financial transactions tax of 0.125 percent per month on principal plus interest. Therefore, in order to obtain 100 cruzeiros, for example, one would have to borrow approximately 106 cruzeiros. Albuquerque's assistant calculated this as follows:

$$\begin{aligned}
\text{Borrowing requirement for CR\$100} &= \frac{100}{1\text{-Upfront fee (\%)} - \text{Upfront taxes (\%)}} \\[2mm]
&= \frac{100}{1\text{-Upfront fee (\%)} - (\text{Prin.} + \text{Interest}) \times \text{F.T. tax}} \\[2mm]
&= \frac{100}{1 - .05 - (1 + .0954) \times 6 \times .125/100} \\[2mm]
&= 106.18
\end{aligned}$$

From this, the effective loan rate, before indexing, could be calculated by figuring that for each Cr\$100 obtained, Morris would have to pay the 9.54 percent interest rate on Cr\$106.18. This effective interest charge, plus the ORTN monetary correction, would be fully deductible in computing profits subject to Brazilian corporate taxes.

However, because of current tight local credit conditions, Morris might have to use a large number of banks, perhaps ten, to meet its working capital needs in full.

3. RESOLUTION 63 EURODOLLAR LOAN[4]

The first of the alternatives bearing currency risk would be a Eurodollar loan under Resolution 63 of the Central Bank of Brazil. In general, the cost of a six-month Resolution 63 loan included the six-month LIBOR (London Interbank Offered Rate), which in late August was quoted at 12.25 percent per annum, plus a spread of 2.25 percent per annum over LIBOR, plus an upfront local commission of 7 percent per annum, and plus an upfront tax (Financial Transactions Tax) of 0.25 percent on principal plus financial charges. The remittance of interest on foreign loans was subject to an effective withholding tax of 20 percent of the sum of LIBOR plus any spread. Financial charges (including any foreign exchange losses) on Morris de Minas borrowing, however, were deductible in computing profits subject to the Brazilian corporate profits tax.

4. BACK-TO-BACK LOAN[5]

A second alternative involving minimal exchange risk was a back-to-back loan, also known as a cash-collateralized loan. The back-to-back loan was a financial arrangement between the Bank of Brazil and the United States parent company. Morris (USA) would make a dollar deposit equal to Morris de Minas' funds needs in the New York Branch of the Bank of Brazil. In return, the Brazilian bank would lend the countervalue in cruzeiros, at the prevailing exchange rate, to Morris de Minas.

At the maturity of the loan, the parent company's dollar funds would

---

[4] Resolution 63 loans were medium to long-term foreign currency credits extended by a foreign bank to a Brazilian bank, which passed them on to local borrowers, in cruzeiros, as foreign currency-denominated loans. As for all incoming foreign loans, the term and rate structure of Resolution 63 loans were regulated by the Central Bank of Brazil. In August 1984 these repass loans had a minimum term of three months, whereas the minimum term of credits granted by a foreign bank was eight years. While the Brazilian bank was liable for the foreign credit and bore the credit risk when it passed the funds on, the ultimate borrower, among other costs, assumed the foreign bank's credit charges and the exchange risk as well. The Central Bank of Brazil, however, assured that exchange was available when needed for paying off the loan.

[5] This exchange financing technique is generally used, when possible, to extend financing to a company's affiliates in countries that have high interest rates and/or restricted capital markets.

be returned simultaneously with the repayment of the loan in cruzeiros by the Brazilian subsidiary. The exchange risk would be borne by the Bank of Brazil, because the exchange rate of cruzeiros for dollars would remain the same both when the parent currency is converted for local lending and when it is returned to the parent at maturity.

The parent company's dollar deposit in New York would earn interest at the prevailing market rate of 11 percent per annum. On the other hand, the Bank of Brazil would charge an interest rate equivalent to 20 percent p.a. over indexing on the loan in cruzeiros. Interest and monetary correction on this cruzeiro loan to Morris de Minas would be tax deductible.

It was the Morris (USA) policy to charge 13 percent p.a. payable in dollars in all loans made to its subsidiaries. Since the back-to-back loan would tie up Morris dollar funds, a 13 percent interest charge per year, payable in dollars, would be required of Morris de Minas on the dollars deposited in New York. However, since the parent company would receive interest of 11 percent p.a. on its dollar deposit with the Bank of Brazil, the Brazilian affiliate would only be charged for the remaining 2 percent p.a. interest. This interest payment would not be tax deductible in Brazil because the dollar deposit was not loaned directly to Morris de Minas. In addition, it would be subject to a 20 percent withholding tax applied to all interest remittances on foreign loans.

Another alternative, possibly cheaper, would be a direct loan from the parent company, Morris (USA). In recent months Morris (USA) had made similar dollar-denominated loans to foreign subsidiaries at an interest rate of 13 percent p.a. However, Brazilian regulations stipulated a minimum term of eighteen months on such foreign loans made directly by foreign companies to its affiliates in Brazil, and there was no assurance that the foreign exchange would be available to repay the loan, or at what price. For this reason Albuquerque felt that a surcharge of perhaps 2 percent would have to be added to the rate normally charged for subsidiary loans.

5. A WINDOW: RESOLUTION 63 LOAN WITH NO EXCHANGE RISK[6]

Yet another alternative was a variation on the Resolution 63 loan. In this type of financing, the Circular 767 of the Central Bank of Brazil allowed the lending bank to charge a fixed rate for the expected devaluation of the cruzeiro against the U.S. dollar as a part of the loan's cost. In practice this meant that the bank would charge a sort of "currency premium" in addi-

---

[6] Financing Foreign Operations (FFO), "Brazil: Financial Update Bulletin", October 1984.

tion to monetary correction. Because the bank would substitute a fixed charge for the actual devaluation of the cruzeiro over the term of the loan, the foreign exchange risk was shifted away from the borrower towards the lending bank. Furthermore, reflecting the aggressive Brazilian foreign exchange policy of devaluating the cruzeiro at the same rate as inflation, which made unnecessary a one-shot maxidevaluation, the effective cost, including the premium, over monetary correction was as low as 20 percent per annum, compared with common cruzeiro denominated loans costing 35.3 percent per annum over monetary correction.

However, this window might not continue open for long because banks were getting increasingly concerned about the government policy towards inflation, devaluation, and monetary correction after the January 1985 presidential election. To use it, the firm would have to move quickly.

6. ESTABLISHING A FINANCE COMPANY IN BRAZIL[7]

The final alternative consisted of establishing a finance company (financeira) in Brazil to assure consumer sales financing. There were four types of finance companies operating in Brazil: financeiras pertaining to financial conglomerates, financeiras related to industrial groups, financeiras linked to retail groups, and independent financeiras. All of them were subject to the same government regulations, which were fairly loose. They differed basically in terms of the market segment they attended. Funding was obtained through the issuance and sale of "letras de cambio"[8] in the money

---

[7] Authorization for the establishment of finance companies in Brazil was granted by the federal government, through the Central Bank, via the issuance of a "carta patente" (registration certificate). Since no new cartas patente had been issued for a number of years, the market value of an existing registration certificate was very high. Assuming that Morris de Minas could find a registration certificate for sale in the Brazilian financial market, it would have to pay about US$3 million for it. Furthermore, because the foreign ownership of financial institutions was restricted and carefully supervised in Brazil, Morris de Minas would still have to get the necessary Central Bank approval of the purchase, what should only be expected if it could convince the Brazilian authorities that its entry would bring very expressive benefits to the financial market in general. The Central Bank's manner of thinking towards this issue could be inferred from its manifest preference to intervene in failed institutions, assuming their losses, but keeping their control in hands of nationals, or even to liquidate the institution rather than authorizing the transfer of their control to foreigners. Nevertheless, if the purchase of the registration certificate by Morris de Minas were carried out successfully, all of the US$3 million investment (plus capital gains if any, from the resale of the carta patente) would be repatriated when the finance company was eventually collapsed always assuming that the authorities would continue to allow such funds to be remitted.

[8] A letra de cambio was a form of draft. It was an instrument in which the finance company promised to pay a certain sum of money to the bearer at a definite future time. In August 1984, the minimum term of a letra de cambio was six months. In general, letras de cambio were sold at a discount.

markets. However, contrary to the common practice, financing would have to be extended to consumers prior to the sale of the drafts in the market.

In a typical consumer sales financing transaction, the customer signs promissory notes and a credit contract with the finance company, which would pay cash directly to the seller. The finance company, then, would issue letras de cambio which would be sold to investors on the Brazilian money market, where such drafts were actively traded. Presently, six-month letras de cambio were being discounted at a rate equivalent to 295 percent per annum in Belo Horizonte.

Despite the minimum required investment of approximately U.S.$3 million in the proposed finance company, which would issue and guarantee the letras de cambio, it was felt that Morris might not be able to obtain the total amount of funds to attend its immediate working capital needs due to factors such as timing, and most important, legal constraints on the ratio "outstanding loans (and consequently, outstanding letras de cambio) to equity" of finance companies in Brazil. Since the company would exist on paper only, Albuquerque felt that the cost of running it would be minimal, apart from start-up legal expenses.

As usual, Morris de Minas would have to pay 13 percent p.a. to its U.S. parent for the investment in the finance company which would tie Morris (USA) funds. In addition, Morris de Minas would incur the cost related to the discounting of the letras de cambio. All these costs were assumed to be tax deductible, since the funds would be advanced to Brazilian corporations. As before, the remittance of interest on foreign loans would be subject to a withholding tax of 20 percent.

FINAL REMARKS

Having gathered all the background information needed to properly evaluate the various financing methods that had been identified, David Albuquerque began to work on his plan. He knew that anticipations about Brazilian inflation and its effects on the behavior of exchange rates would be the key variables in the choice of the appropriate financing strategy. But overall he wanted to make a recommendation that would meet the company's needs, enable Morris to overcome government and monetary regulations, and minimize costs and risks while leaving the door open to future Morris visits to the Brazilian money markets.

Ian H. Giddy

Case 23

Gulp (Canada)

The assistant international treasurer of Gulp Oil Company had a problem. The company had a large investment in Canada to extract, refine and sell oil in that country. Because the Canadian company was not quite profitable, Gulp (USA) expected to have to make intercompany loans of $10 million in six and twelve months' time. As it was, they had already loaned over $1.2 billion to Gulp (Canada).

The problem was how to hedge the exchange risk involved. The corporate controller suggested that the firm's FAS 52 exposure be hedged since Canada was a U.S. dollar functional currency subsidiary. However, the new MBA on the team suggested they hedge the future Canadian dollar sales revenues of C$124 thousand per quarter, and Canadian dollar tax payments of about C$ 50 thousand per annum.

Exhibit 1 Gulp (Canada)

Assets (C$ millions)		Liabilities (C$ millions)	
Cash	10	C$ Payables	218
Receivables	115	Taxes	3
Inventory	143	Intercompany loan	1613
P & E	1480	Capital	− 86
	1748		1748

Exchange rate C$1.22 per US$

The date was January 11, 1983. Gulp Canada's preliminary balance sheet as of December 31, 1982 is shown above.

What is Gulp's exposure? the assistant treasurer wondered. What should she do to hedge it fully? What if they were forced to divest 50 percent by 1986, as the new Canadian law dictated?

2.2

Funding and Capital Structure

Ian H. Giddy

Case 24

Bookwell's Financing Choices

It was 9:30 on a cold Wednesday morning, and John Ackton had a problem. At 10:30 A.M. the company's financial staff had a meeting and John was expected to make recommendations on how to finance the firm's expanding working capital.

John Ackton was Assistant Treasurer of Bookwell's Ltd., a newly acquired British subsidiary of Bookrite, the New York publishing firm. Based in Oxford, Bookwell's was a publisher and distributor of academic books; at the time, their market was primarily in the United Kingdom. In their last budget, Ackton and his colleagues had estimated additional working capital needs of £2 million for the next six months.

John Ackton's inclination was to take out a £2 million, six-month sterling loan from Barclay's Bank in London, with whom the company had done business for years. He was keen to make a good show, however, of evaluating all possibilities, so he had posed himself three questions.

First, should Bookwell's borrow in England, as in the past, or should it borrow in the Euromarket? What was the risk of the latter?

© Ian H. Giddy, New York University.

John had been able to obtain the following information about six-month interest rates:

Deposit rates (per annum)		*Loan rates* (per annum)	
Domestic bank deposits	10.56%	Domestic bank loan	13.00%
Eurosterling deposits	11.06%	Eurosterling loan	11.92%

Second, should the company obtain short-term or longer-term debts? John knew he could borrow at fixed rates for one to twelve months, and although he had not yet obtained quotes for all maturities, his Reuters screen revealed the following Eurodeposit rates:

Eurosterling deposits	
3 months	10.94%
6 months	11.06%

John had a feeling that U.K. interest rates might be brought down a bit, so he wondered whether it might be advisable to take the shortest possible maturity in hope of rolling it over at a lower cost.

Third, and most important, was the question of in which currency to borrow. John knew that the Eurodollar market had the greatest availability of funds and lower interest rates than the sterling market, but he feared the exchange risk involved in borrowing in dollars. According to forecasts, sterling could rise if U.S. interest rates came down. One possibility worth considering was to borrow abroad and hedge the exchange risk in the forward market. But how to evaluate these choices? He had only the following information (for six-month loans):

Eurodollar loan rate	10.50%
Eurosterling loan rate	11.92%
S/£ forward premium (cost of cover)	2.39%

Exchange rates	**Dollars per pound**	**Pounds per dollar**
Spot rate today	$1.71	£ .585
6-month forward rate	$1.69	£ .592
Forecast of $/£ spot in 6 months	$1.72	£ .581

(Note: The "pounds per dollar" is simply the inverse of the "dollars per pound," e.g., .585 = 1/1.71)

Can you help John Ackton make recommendations on these three decisions? Consider carefully the principles behind each choice.

H. Lee Remmers

Case 25

Standard Electronics International

On 29 December, 1978, Charles Duvalier, the Treasurer of Standard Electronics International (SEI), began to review a loan request just received from the firm's German affiliate (Exhibit 1). The loan was for DM 2.5 million and intended to be used for financing working capital needs.

SEI was a medium-size manufacturer of computer peripheral equipment based in Sunnyvale, California (forty miles south of San Francisco). It had grown rapidly during the past ten years and sales were forecast to reach $250 million in 1979. About 40 percent of its revenues were earned outside of the United States, mostly in Europe. Manufacturing affiliates were located in Sunnyvale, Munich, and Singapore. Eleven sales affiliates were located throughout Europe, Japan, and the United States.

Exhibit 1 *Working capital loan request*

To: Charles Duvalier, Corporate Treasurer, SEI, Sunnyvale
From: Fritz Schmidt, Director of Finance, SEI, Munich
Subject: Request for Approval of Working Capital Loan

As you have instructed, we have set out below the required information concerning our request for a loan to finance working capital needs over the next 3 months.

1. *Amount of Loan:* DM 2,500,000 (or foreign currency equivalent)
2. *Period for which loan is required:* 3 months
3. *Loan Options*

	Nominal interest rate 12 month basis
a) Deutschemarks	6.200%
b) Eurodollar	11.75%
c) EuroSterling	14.125%
d) EuroSwiss francs	0.8125%
e) Intra-company (as indicated in your telex of 22/12/78)	12.00%

4. *Exchange Rates:* Please note that foreign currency loans can be covered for the period of the loan by a forward contract to buy the foreign currency forward in the amount of the loan principal and interest.

	DM per $	SFR per $	$ per £
Spot rate (28/12/78)	1.90500	1.69175	1.97160
Forward rate (contract maturity 28/3/79)	1.87055	1.64625	1.96325

5. *Tax Rates:* We assume that the present policy of remitting all earnings after tax will continue. On this basis, corporation and municipal taxes will be 43.70%. To this, another 15% withholding tax on dividends should be added. Total taxes will therefore be 52.145% on these assumptions. We also expect that foreign exchange gains will be added to, and losses can be deducted from taxable income. This applies equally to gains and losses on interest, principal, and forward contracts. All interest expense, including that on intra-company loans, can be deducted from taxable income.
6. *Earnings:* Earnings *before* interest on the above loan and before taxes are expected to be DM 4,000,000 during the next 3 months.
7. We would be grateful if you would telex your reply as soon as possible.

Exhibit 2 *Standard Electronics International selected financial data*

	SEI Germany pro forma balance sheet 31 December 1978	
	Deutschemarks (thousands)	Dollars** (thousands)
1. *Assets*		
Plant and Equipment	8,500	4,461.94
Inventories	5,000	2,624.67
Accounts Receivable	4,000	2,099.74
Cash	3,000	1,574.80
	20,500	10,761.15
Capital and Liabilities		
Owners equity	12,000	6,299.21
Loans*	6,000	3,149.61
Accounts payable	2,500	1,312.34
	20,500	10,761.15

  * includes the DM 2,500,000 loan requested.
** DM amounts translated into dollars at DM 1.905 PER $.

2. As one of the loan options, SEI Sunnvale would lend dollars to SEI Germany at a 12% rate of interest. This would be financed by borrowing dollars in the U.S. domestic money market at 11.25%.
3. Earnings of SEI as a whole before taxes and exclusive of any foreign income received from SEI Germany or expenses connected with financing the DM 2,500,000 loan were expected to be $6,000,000 during the first three months of 1979.
4. The tax rate applicable to U.S. domestic earnings is 48%. A maximum of 48% on foreign source income (dividends, interest, royalties, etc.) could be charged, but this may be changed if excess foreign tax credits are available.

SEI maintained excellent relations with its banks and had been able to obtain financing on favorable terms in the countries where it operated as well as on the Eurocurrency markets. The affiliates commonly borrowed or temporarily placed on deposit funds in a number of major currencies including U.S. dollars, UK sterling, Swiss francs, Deutschemarks, French francs and yen. It had been SEI practice, until recently, to allow the foreign affiliate management considerable discretion to negotiate the terms and currency of these arrangements providing that the overall amounts had been included in the budget and approved at corporate headquarters.

However, the continuing volatility of the foreign exchange markets had convinced Duvalier that the effective cost (return) of many loans (time deposits) was turning out to be substantially different from that originally thought when the terms were agreed upon and the decision taken. He strongly believed that the cost of borrowing (or return from a time deposit) had to be measured in terms of the effect on after-tax parent consolidated profits; he was concerned that these could be seriously affected by movements in the exchange rates, by the tax treatment of certain costs and earnings at both the level of the affiliate and the parent company, and by the accounting rules used to translate the financial statements of foreign affiliates in preparing the consolidated accounts of the corporation.

For these various reasons, Duvalier had instructed the affiliates to begin to submit to his office for approval all requests to borrow or place funds on deposit. He realized, however, that to make a detailed analysis of each request would add considerably to the administrative burden of his office as well as perhaps create some resentment in the affiliates by reducing their autonomy.

Therefore, in reviewing the request just submitted by the German affiliate, he hoped also to be able to come up with a simple approach that would allow such decisions to be taken from the point of view of maximizing parent consolidated after-tax earnings, and yet be easily delegated to the affiliate management. To be effective, Duvalier believed that any such approach would have to be simple and easily understood, and require a minimum amount of data and computation.

Arthur I. Stonehill

Case 26

Tektronix, Inc.

In June 1974 Ken Knox, Assistant Treasurer, Tektronix, Inc., was trying to arrive at a rational policy for determining the most desirable financial structure for Tektronix UK, a British manufacturing subsidiary of Tektronix, Inc., U.S. In particular he wanted to determine how much debt, if any, Tektronix UK should carry, and in what currency the debt ought to be denominated. He realized that the policy decision on Tektronix UK might serve as a new guideline for the desired financial structures of the other foreign subsidiaries of Tektronix, Inc. The policy also needed to be consistent with recent corporate decisions to refund existing corporate short-term debt either in the United States or abroad, and to reduce exposure to foreign exchange losses.

BACKGROUND

Tektronix is the world's leading producer of oscilloscopes. It was founded in January 1946 by Howard Vollum and Jack Murdock. Howard Vollum had worked with radar in the military during World War II and recognized the need for a better oscilloscope. Jack Murdock was also a veteran with a similar belief and good skills in business administration. During the first year the founders developed an oscilloscope for use in the electronics industry that was technically superior in reliability and performance to any on the market at the time. The firm occupied an 11,000 square foot building in Portland, Oregon, in March 1947. In May 1947 the first oscilloscope was delivered. Its technical superiority and low price soon created an outstanding reputation for Tektronix and the problem soon became producing enough oscilloscopes to meet demand. The product line was also broadened to include additional types of oscilloscopes and related instruments.

Sales grew dramatically from $257,000 in 1948 to $4,022,000 in 1951. Production facilities were moved to the new 20,000 square foot Sunset plant west of Portland in 1951. Sales and profits continued to expand. Production facilities were expanded greatly by the purchase of a 300-acre farm near Beaverton, Oregon, and its conversion to a model industrial park. The product line continued to be broadened in oscilloscopes, and in the late 1960's into related technologies such as information display equipment (graphic computer terminals). Sales and profits continued to grow unabated as shown in Exhibit 1. During the fiscal year ending May 25, 1974, net sales reached $271 million. The main customers continued to be the manufacturers of electronic equipment, electrical equipment, and computers. Other customers were government agencies, research laboratories, educational institutions, and the broadcast and TV industry.

INTERNATIONAL ACTIVITIES

In the early years Tektronix marketed oscilloscopes through existing distributors and commission agents in the United States and abroad. It soon became apparent, however, that the technical nature of the product required a closer relationship with the customer and greater attention to quality control and servicing. Therefore Tektronix developed its own direct selling organization in the United States starting in 1950. Its first non-U.S. direct selling sales office was started in Canada in 1957. Wholly owned marketing subsidiaries were established in Switzerland in 1961, United Kingdom and Australia in 1963, France in 1966, Denmark in 1969, The Netherlands and Sweden in 1970, and Belgium in 1971.

Exhibit 1 Tektronix consolidated financial statistics (Dollars, shares and square feet in thousands)

Fiscal year ending in May	1965	1966	1967	1968	1969	1970	1971	1972	1973	1974
NET SALES	81,364	102,162	129,961	135,021	151,011	168,939	149,442	167,482	202,855	271,428
EARNINGS	7,347	11,111	13,620	13,810	14,572	15,005	9,904	11,764	16,739	21,353
Per Share	$0.88	$1.33	$1.64	$1.64	$1.72	$1.75	$1.16	$1.37	$1.94	$2.47
% of Sales	9.0%	10.9%	10.5%	10.2%	9.7%	8.9%	6.6%	7.0%	8.3%	7.9%
% of Beginning-of-Year Shareowners' Equity	19.1%	25.1%	24.8%	20.3%	17.4%	15.0%	8.6%	9.3%	12.1%	13.7%
INCOME BEFORE INCOME TAXES	13,608	19,703	25,611	25,825	26,379	26,398	16,806	21,008	30,479	38,497
% of Sales	16.7%	19.3%	19.7%	19.5%	17.5%	15.6%	11.2%	12.5%	15.0%	14.2%
Income Tax Rate	46.0%	43.6%	46.6%	46.0%	44.6%	43.2%	41.1%	44.0%	45.1%	44.5%
PAYROLL BEFORE PROFIT SHARE	26,111	32,605	38,413	41,625	49,214	60,281	56,338	58,609	70,949	94,258
EMPLOYEE PROFIT SHARE	7,553	10,810	13,744	13,542	13,360	13,144	8,275	10,462	14,875	18,706
Facilities in Use at Year End (in Square Feet)	1,203	1,441	1,596	1,711	1,813	2,111	2,329	2,429	2,612	2,940
COST OF FACILITIES	30,893	35,986	41,447	47,638	59,256	76,146	81,381	84,947	89,681	111,302
INVESTED IN FACILITIES (during year)	3,915	5,728	5,889	6,644	12,269	17,289	6,047	4,915	7,075	23,530
FACILITIES DEPRECIATION (mostly accelerated)	2,358	2,470	3,008	3,470	3,870	4,904	5,898	6,394	6,834	7,525

ACCUMULATED DEPRECIATION	49,947	43,514	37,726	32,140	26,789	22,348	18,955	15,929	13,197	11,323
TOTAL ASSETS	251,061	206,599	173,743	157,808	155,619	127,813	107,552	93,348	76,459	59,402
ACCOUNTS RECEIVABLE NET	55,230	44,417	32,833	27,113	29,165	27,428	22,873	21,675	17,111	12,701
INVENTORY (including supplies)	97,230	72,904	56,066	63,085	59,252	41,599	35,289	34,305	28,537	19,727
CURRENT ASSETS	176,405	151,033	120,539	101,991	101,506	86,728	74,840	63,375	52,975	39,180
CURRENT LIABILITIES	68,484	46,644	31,802	28,963	38,674	27,042	22,183	23,480	20,935	14,513
WORKING CAPITAL	107,921	104,389	88,737	73,028	62,832	54,686	52,657	39,895	32,040	24,667
LONG-TERM INDEBTEDNESS (including current portion)	973	1,100	1,288	1,930	429	501	988	2,134	610	583
Common Shares Outstanding at Year End	8,651	8,651	8,602	8,588	8,572	8,555	8,456	8,323	8,336	8,360
SHAREOWNERS' EQUITY	175,488	155,630	138,488	126,338	115,841	100,297	83,824	67,897	54,938	44,335
COMMON-SHARE CAPITAL	12,213	12,158	9,357	8,889	8,325	7,774	7,507	6,009	6,009	6,009
REINVESTED EARNINGS	163,966	144,140	129,186	117,467	107,532	92,546	78,320	64,511	50,892	39,781
Number of Employees at Year End	12,693	10,580	8,334	9,091	9,957	8,813	7,892	7,302	6,500	4,992

Foreign manufacturing facilities were established in 1958 on the Isle of Guernsey in order to serve customers in the European Free Trade Association without having to surmount restrictive trade barriers and tariffs. This operation also received British Commonwealth preference treatment. The Isle of Guernsey uses the pound sterling as its normal currency and for all practical purposes is treated as if it is part of the British Isles for monetary purposes. Guernsey residents must abide by the same regulations set by the Bank of England as other British residents.

A secondary manufacturing operation was started at Heerenveen, The Netherlands, in 1961. This served the Common Market countries from within the common external tariff barrier. In 1965 Tektronix established a fifty-fifty joint venture with Sony Corporation to serve the Japanese market. In 1970 the marketing subsidiary in the United Kingdom was merged with an independent oscilloscope manufacturer (acquired in 1967) to form Tektronix UK.

In addition to avoiding tariff barriers, Tektronix preferred to compete on the home markets of potential competitors to insure that the competitors did not have an easy base from which to compete in the United States and other markets.

International operations played an important role in the spectacular growth of sales and earnings. In 1974 non-U.S. sales were $116 million or approximately 40 percent of consolidated sales. The corresponding figure for foreign net earnings was $9 million, or about 50 percent of total net earnings.

International activities received all the attention they deserved since many of the key corporate officers had come up through the "international group." This included Tektronix's President and several of the Vice-Presidents. Les Stevens, Group Vice-President — Finance, had been International Finance Manager before becoming the chief financial officer. Ken Knox had assisted him on the international headquarters staff prior to being appointed Assistant Treasurer.

FINANCIAL STRUCTURE

Tektronix followed a policy of trying to finance its growth almost entirely from its own cash flow without resort to external long-term borrowing. As a result, with the exception of the period 1961–64, there were insignificant amounts of long-term debt in the financial structure. Current liabilities were also modest compared to current assets and the overall debt ratio (total debt/total assets) was usually under 30 percent from 1965 until 1974.

The rate of growth of Tektronix was not constrained significantly by its reliance on internal cash flow. Instead, growth was directly related to its market opportunities in the test and measurement field and later in the information display field as well. It had been corporate policy not to stray outside of their area of technological expertise. No attempt was made to diversify as a means of reducing business risk. The steady growth of the oscilloscope field, and Tektronix's very strong market position as leader in the field, combined to establish a relatively stable return on assets and equity. The general feeling was that potential risk reduction from diversification outside of the industry would have been less than the added risk from a managerial and expertise viewpoint.

The low debt–low diversification policies also reduced the perceived need for Tektronix to calculate what an upper limit might be on its debt ratio. The financial executives did not worry about finding an optimal debt ratio which might theoretically minimize its cost of capital although they were quite familiar with the theory. In fact management had not been overly concerned about the level of fluctuations in market price of Tektronix's common stock. It was publicly traded starting in 1963 and soon listed on the New York Stock Exchange. They were very concerned, however, about return on sales, and growth in earnings.

One factor that favored the above goals was that almost from the start Tektronix had a very generous profit-sharing plan. Typically the employees received 35 percent of consolidated profit before income taxes and charitable deductions. Profit sharing was an important part of each employee's total compensation package. In the early years, prior to going public, an employee common stock ownership plan was in effect. As much as 12 percent of the common stock became employee-owned. Stock options continued to be granted in later years but employee ownership as a proportion of the total did not grow substantially.

In June 1974 Tektronix decided to modify its traditional no-debt finance structure policy. It was motivated by a belief that the tight credit conditions of the previous years might continue for several more years. A brief easing of credit conditions and interest rates, because of the Federal Reserve Board's desire to stimulate the lagging U.S. economy, convinced management that the time was ripe to borrow long term as insurance against the day when they might need the funds and not be able to borrow them easily. This had not occurred in the past but the frightening degree of inflation worldwide had increased the need for working capital just to maintain the same pace. Furthermore, both domestic and foreign sales continued to climb dramatically. With the prospect of further high rates of real and inflation-induced growth, management felt that it was now opportune to consider $20–40 million in long-term debt which would refund existing short term borrowings of $23 million. Long-term debt was less than $1 million at the May 1974 year end.

FINANCIAL STRUCTURE OF FOREIGN SUBSIDIARIES

Tektronix followed a policy of starting new foreign subsidiaries with intercompany credit from sister subsidiaries or the parent firm. Typically, equity would be extremely small but the debt would be entirely accounts payable to related companies. This arose from importing the initial inventory on extended payment terms or direct loans from affiliates. As a result the apparent debt ratio of the new subsidiary appeared quite high relative to local norms but was almost riskless since the debt was internal to Tektronix. Thus, the entire original capital could be considered equivalent to equity from the viewpoint of an outside creditor or supplier. Because of the rapid rate of growth in earnings, each of the Tektronix subsidiaries soon were able to repay the original debt out of cash flow, thus acquiring more normal balance sheet ratios.

The decision to borrow locally for working capital needs was made by corporate headquarters rather than local managers. Tektronix believed that leads and lags in the intercompany trade accounts was the optimal method of local financing considering its flexibility, high local interest rate costs, and effective local income tax rates. In addition, control by headquarters permitted better coordination of exposure to foreign exchange losses.

The cost of local debt varied widely among countries of concern to Tektronix. Exhibit 2 shows key interest rate indicators. Generally Tektronix could borrow locally on a short-term basis at rates close to money market rates. Medium- and long-term borrowing for Tektronix, however, would probably cost approximately 2–4 percent over the host country government bond rate to reflect the normal risk differential between public and comparable risk private borrowing.

The after-tax cost of debt also varied widely due to differing effective corporate income tax rates and qualifications for deductibility of interest. Effective corporate income tax rates for Tektronix in the United States were 50 percent, in the United Kingdom 48 percent, in the Netherlands 48 percent, and the Isle of Guernsey 20 percent. In the United Kingdom, however, interest paid to related companies could not be deducted for tax purposes. Thus, interest paid by Tektronix UK to Tektronix, Inc. or other affiliates could not be deducted for tax purposes. On the other hand inter-

Exhibit 2 Interest rates

Central Bank Discount Rates
(End of period quotations in percent per annum)[1]

	1962	1963	1964	1965	1966	1967	1968	1969	1970	1971	1972	1973 II	1973 III	1973 IV	1974 Jan	1974 Feb	1974 Mar	1974 Apr	1974 May
United States	3.00	3.50	4.00	4.50	4.50	4.50	5.50	6.00	5.50	4.50	4.50	6.50	7.50	7.50			7.50	8.00	8.00
United Kingdom	4.50	4.00	7.00	6.00	7.00	8.00	7.00	8.00	7.00	5.00	9.00	7.50	11.50	13.00	12.75	12.50	12.50	12.00	12.00
Industrial Europe																			
Austria	5.00	4.50				3.75		4.75	5.00	5.00	5.50								6.50
Belgium	3.50	4.25	4.75		5.25	4.00	4.50	7.50	6.50	5.50	5.00	5.50	6.50	7.75		8.75			8.75
Denmark	6.50	5.50			7.50	6.00	9.00	9.00	7.50	6.50	7.00	7.00	8.00	9.00	10.00				10.00
France	3.50	4.00		3.50			6.00	8.00	7.00	6.50	7.50	7.50	11.00						11.00
Germany	3.00			3.50	5.00	3.00		6.00	6.00	4.00	4.50	7.00							7.00
Italy	3.50						3.75	3.75	5.50	4.50	4.00		6.50						6.50
Netherlands	4.00	3.50	4.50		5.00	4.50	5.00	6.00	5.50	5.00	4.00	5.00	6.50	8.00					8.00
Norway	3.50							4.50	4.50	4.50							5.50		5.50
Sweden	4.00		5.00	5.50	6.00		5.00	7.00		5.00									6.00
Switzerland	2.00		2.50		3.50	3.00		3.75		3.75					5.50				5.50
Canada	3.24	4.00	4.25	4.75	4.75	6.00	6.50	8.00	6.00	4.75	4.75	6.25	7.25	7.25				8.25	8.75
Japan	7.30	5.84	5.84	6.57	5.48	5.48	5.84	6.25	6.00	4.75	4.25	5.50	7.00	9.00	9.00				9.00

[1] See country pages for changes within each year or quarter.

Exhibit 2 (*Cont.*)

Money market and Euro dollar rates
(In percent per annum)

	1962	1963	1964	1965	1966	1967	1968	1969	1970	1971	1972	1973			1974				
												II	III	IV	Jan	Feb	Mar	Apr	May
United States[1]	2.78	3.16	3.55	3.95	4.88	4.33	5.35	6.69	6.44	4.34	4.07	6.61	8.39	7.46	7.76	7.06	7.96	8.33	—
United Kingdom[1]	4.18	3.66	4.61	5.91	6.10	5.82	7.09	7.64	7.01	5.57	5.54	7.36	10.24	11.62	12.09	11.92	11.96	11.51	11.35
Industrial Europe																			
Belgium[2]	2.13	2.29	3.35	3.17	3.88	3.19	2.84	5.40	6.25	3.70	2.46	3.19	5.77	7.10	8.52	7.94	8.96	9.21	9.52
France[2]	3.61	3.98	4.70	4.17	4.79	4.80	6.15	8.95	8.68	5.84	4.95	7.61	9.26	11.27	13.53	12.48	12.15	11.83	12.91
Germany[2]	2.66	2.99	3.29	4.11	5.34	3.35	2.58	4.81	8.67	6.05	4.30	11.05	12.06	11.25	10.40	9.13	11.63	5.33	8.36
Netherlands[2]	2.51	2.82	3.75	3.73	6.42	5.67	5.19	7.76	7.96	5.20	1.93	2.93	9.04	12.29	11.82	10.86	9.07	9.86	9.10
Canada[1]	4.00	3.56	3.75	3.99	4.99	4.64	6.27	7.19	5.99	3.56	3.56	5.19	6.14	6.44	6.22	6.07	—		
Japan[2]	10.31	7.54	10.03	6.97	5.84	6.39	7.88	7.70	8.29	6.42	4.72	6.13	7.88	9.44	11.65	12.10	12.48	12.04	12.00
Euro Dollar London[3]		3.95	4.32	4.81	6.12	5.46	6.36	9.76	8.52	6.58	5.46	8.47	10.99	10.13	9.37	8.50	9.23	10.53	11.67

[1] Average tender rate for three-month Treasury Bills.
[2] Average of daily or weekly Call Money rates.
[3] Average of daily quotations for three month deposits.

182

Central Government Bond Yields

(Average yields to maturity on issues with at least 12 years' life in percent per annum.)

	1962	1963	1964	1965	1966	1967	1968	1969	1970	1971	1972	1973			1974				
												II	III	IV	Jan	Feb	Mar	Apr	May
United States	3.95	4.00	4.15	4.21	4.66	4.85	5.26	6.12	6.58	5.74	5.63	6.22	6.59	6.31	6.56	6.54	6.81	7.04	—
United Kingdom	5.90	5.43	5.98	6.56	6.94	6.80	7.55	9.04	9.22	8.90	8.91	10.03	11.16	11.93	12.89	13.50	13.68	14.21	13.80
Industrial Europe																			
Belgium	5.24	4.98	6.41	6.44	6.62	6.70	6.54	7.20	7.81	7.35	7.04	7.32	7.46	7.69	7.92	8.14	8.22	8.36	8.71
France	5.02	4.97	5.08	5.27	5.40	5.66	5.86	7.64	8.06	7.74	7.35	7.99	8.47	8.80	9.32	9.73	9.98	—	10.31
Germany[1]	5.9	6.1	6.2	7.1	8.1	7.0	6.5	6.8	8.83	8.0	7.9	9.3	9.8	9.6	9.6	9.9	10.4	10.4	10.6
Italy	5.78	6.10	7.41	6.94	6.54	6.61	6.70	6.85	9.01	8.34	7.47	7.41	7.41	7.46	7.43	7.49	7.80	8.27	—
Netherlands	4.21	4.22	4.92	5.50	6.59	6.18	6.49	7.51	8.22	7.35	6.88	7.33	8.33	8.33	9.17	9.19	9.74	10.08	—
Sweden	4.89	4.93	5.64	6.18	6.57	6.06	6.31	6.98	7.39	7.23	7.29	7.39	7.41	7.39	7.30	7.27	7.15	7.73	7.83
Switzerland	3.13	3.25	3.97	3.95	4.16	4.61	4.37	4.90	5.82	5.27	4.97	5.38	5.60	6.07	6.41	6.72	7.09	7.27	7.30
Canada	5.09	5.09	5.19	5.21	5.69	5.94	6.75	7.58	7.91	6.95	7.23	7.62	7.76	7.65	7.75	7.74	—	—	—
Other Countries																			
Australia	4.92	4.58	4.72	5.21	5.25	5.25	5.21	5.81	6.75	6.92	6.03	6.63	7.50	8.50	8.50	8.50	8.50	8.50	8.50
India	4.36	4.68	4.73	5.32	5.54	5.52	5.07	5.00	5.00	5.00	5.00	5.00	5.00	5.00	5.00	5.00	5.00	5.00	5.00
New Zealand	5.25	5.15	5.06	5.10	5.28	5.51	5.53	5.54	5.51	5.52	5.52	5.59	6.01	6.05	6.06	6.04	6.04	6.05	—

[1] Bonds of local authorities.

Exhibit 2 (Cont.)

End of Month Forward Rates

Three-months rates of the currencies shown against the US dollar

Expressed as a premium or discount (−) on the spot rate, in percent per annum

	Mar	Apr	May	June	July	Aug	Sept	Oct	Nov	Dec	Jan	Feb	Mar	Apr	May
						1973							1974		
Pound sterling	−2.78	−2.41	−1.54	−1.91	−3.10	−4.39	−4.51	−4.35	−5.50	−6.54	−10.54	−9.20	−9.36	−5.10	−3.06
Belgian franc	5.99	3.17	2.33	2.44	3.57	3.77	7.37	1.74	1.72	2.61	−2.83	−6.54	−6.88	−3.41	−7.66
French franc	.70	.17	.63	.29	1.94	1.85	−1.60	−2.63	−1.25	−2.04	−5.02	−4.90	−3.36	−2.36	−2.36
Deutsche mark	8.17	4.65	5.86	2.80	2.04	1.62	1.65	.65	−2.14	−1.04	−2.01	−2.25	−.48	2.12	−2.06
Netherlands guilder	8.15	4.86	3.95	1.07	2.15	.89	.16	−.31	−.43	−3.40	−3.16	−1.29	—	.92	1.21
Swiss franc	4.82	5.06	6.20	11.62	10.47	5.94	4.50	3.75	−1.75	1.11	4.13	−1.54	−1.07	.82	2.69
Canadian dollar	2.48	1.63	1.05	1.60	2.52	2.55	1.43	−.08	.36	.32	−.12	.37	.74	—	—

Source: International Monetary Fund, *International Financial Statistics*, July 1974, page 26.

est income from affiliates was taxable in all countries of concern to Tektronix.

DIVIDEND POLICY FOR FOREIGN SUBSIDIARIES

The European subsidiaries of Tektronix were owned by a Swiss subsidiary which was in turn wholly owned by Tektronix, Inc. Dividends passed through the Swiss subsidiary and were subject to various national dividend withholding taxes depending on the particular bilateral tax treaties. The average withholding tax was 15 percent, but the net cost to Tektronix, Inc. was negligible because these dividend withholding taxes could be used as tax credits against U.S. income taxes on foreign earnings repatriated by Tektronix, Inc. There were no significant dividend restrictions except for the normal limitation of not paying dividends greater than historical retained earnings. Dividend decisions were made by corporate headquarters in Beaverton, Oregon.

FOREIGN EXCHANGE MANAGEMENT

Starting with the currency crisis of August–December 1971, and the official devaluation of the dollar by 8.6 percent in December 1971, the problem of foreign exchange management became more acute. Under the subsequent "managed float" system, exchange rate movements were much more volatile than under the fixed rate system established in 1944 at Bretton Woods. Exhibit 3 shows movements in major currencies since 1971. Exchange rate movements of the British pound sterling and the Dutch guilder were particularly important to Tektronix because of the locations of its manufacturing plants. Between 1971 and June 1974 the pound had declined from $2.4442 to $2.3902 and looked to be heading further downward. On the other hand, the Dutch guilder had appreciated from $.28650 to $.37747 in the same time span.

As a result of floating exchange rates, Tektronix's income was actually increased by $56,644 in 1971; $1,151,315 in 1972; and $606,008 in 1973. However, it was decreased by $1,015,161 in fiscal 1974. Typically a foreign exchange gain or loss was made by foreign subsidiaries changing their local currencies into dollars to pay the Tektronix manufacturing subsidiaries for products the importing subsidiaries had previously purchased. Foreign exchange gains or losses also resulted from translation of the foreign subsidiaries' local currency accounts into dollars in order to present a consolidated worldwide Tektronix financial statement. Tektronix used the

Exhibit 3   *Foreign exchange rates (In cents per unit of foreign currency)*

Period	France (franc)	Germany (Deutsche mark)	Japan (yen)	Netherlands (guilder)	Switzerland (franc)	United Kingdom (pound)
1971	18.148	28.768	.28779	28.650	24.325	244.42
1972	19.825	31.364	.32995	31.153	26.193	250.08
1973	22.536	37.758	.36915	35.977	31.700	245.10
1974–June	20.805	39.603	.35340	37.757	33.449	239.02

Source: Board of Governors of the Federal Reserve System, *Federal Reserve Bulletin,* July 1975, page 75.

monetary-nonmonetary method for translating its subsidiary statements. In particular, the strength of the Dutch guilder resulted in translation gains when the Dutch manufacturing operation was consolidated on the parent's dollar books.

As a result of the fiscal 1974 foreign exchange loss, Les Stevens, Group Vice-President — Finance, initiated a review of Tektronix's international financial policies. He recognized that methods proven to be successful in the 1960s may not be the best approach in the future. This review would include start-up capitalization, working capital financing, long-term debt, dividends, and the currency and inflation problems now impacting those policies. Based on long experience in the international finance function, Les Stevens knew of the poor results most companies and banks, as well as advisory services, had achieved in forecasting the timing and magnitude of currency movements. He was aware of the increased attention Wall Street analysts were giving publicly held international companies and the impact on earnings caused by their currency exposure. This belief caused a strong bias for a policy of neutral currency exposure. This would mean balancing exposed assets and liabilities wherever feasible so that Tektronix would be basically indifferent to shifting currency values. This fit well with overall corporate philosophy, which favored conservative accounting methods and frowned on speculative financial practices. Les Stevens assigned Ken Knox, Assistant Treasurer, to review the financial structure of each subsidiary in light of these policy issues.

TEKTRONIX UK

Ken Knox's first priority was to examine the financing of Tektronix UK because he believed the United Kingdom economy, and its currency, were fundamentally weak. He felt that an analysis and solution of the Tektronix

UK situation would provide him a chance to determine reasonable financial policy guidelines for the other foreign subsidiaries as well.

Tektronix originally entered the United Kingdom market through an independent distributor. However, in accordance with corporate policy of selling direct, Tektronix bought out the distributor's interest in June 1963 and formed Tektronix UK as a 100 percent owned marketing subsidiary. As was its custom, Tektronix provided a minute amount of equity capital but financed the import of inventory on extended terms from its manufacturing plants in the United States and on the Isle of Guernsey. An additional reason for the low equity base was a capital tax which was levied on equity in the United Kingdom. In any case, the small size and lack of outside stockholders in Tektronix UK made its financial structure invisible to the outside world, and no local credit was being requested.

In 1969 one of the United Kingdom's many currency crises caused the Bank of England to impose a 50 percent import deposit requirement for six months on goods bought from outside the United Kingdom. In order to avoid the import deposit it was necessary to manufacture within the United Kingdom. In 1970 a merger was consummated between Tektronix UK and Telequipment Ltd., a previously acquired U.K. manufacturer of oscilloscopes. It was agreed that the surviving name would be Tektronix UK.

As a result of the floating exchange rates after 1971, and the corresponding weakness of the pound, Tektronix UK generated a considerable foreign exchange loss during the next few years, as did the sterling subsidiaries on the Isle of Guernsey. In early 1974 a "minimum distribution" dividend was paid by Tektronix UK to the parent firm in order to establish the foreign exchange losses for tax purposes. A mere translation loss would not result in any tax savings although it appears in statements prepared for financial reporting purposes.

The imposition of the import deposit scheme and the growth in the U.K. manufacturing operations had caused severe strain on Tektronix UK's working capital. The intercompany accounts and loans from Tektronix Guernsey had been used extensively to finance the U.K. operations. Exhibit 4 shows the balance sheets of the European manufacturing subsidiaries of Tektronix as of May 31, 1974. Exhibit 5 shows the income statements for the fiscal year ending May 31, 1974, for the same subsidiaries.

In determining financial policy for Tektronix UK, and ultimately the other foreign subsidiaries, Ken Knox knew that he must justify his recommendation to the Corporate Finance Committee in Tektronix, Inc., the outside directors of the subsidiaries, and perhaps the host country monetary authorities. In so doing he needed logical answers to several problems. One problem was how to coordinate foreign borrowing, if any, with the probable need for Tektronix as a whole to raise external debt of some sort,

Exhibit 4. Balance sheets as of March 31, 1974, for the European manufacturing subsidiaries of Tektronix, Inc. (in thousands)[1]

	TEK United Kingdom		TEK Guernsey		TEK Netherlands	
	pounds sterling	dollars included	pounds sterling	dollars included	guilders	dollars included
Cash and short-term investments	£ 100		£ 100		FL12,500	$4,000
Accts. receivable: non-affiliates	4,000		200	$ 480	8,000	3,016
Accts. receivable: affiliates	100		1,200	2,880	8,000	3,016
Inventory	3,300		3,000		12,500	
Total current assets	£ 7,500		£ 4,500		FL41,000	
Net plant and equipment	1,300		800		6,900	
Long-term notes of affiliates	—		3,800[2]		1,300[3]	
Total assets	£ 8,800		£ 9,100		F 49,200	
Accts. payable: non-affiliates	£ 900		£ 200		FL 800	
Accts. payable: affiliates	1,000	$1,000	300	$ 720	4,800	$1,810
Notes payable	—		100		300	
Other current	700		—		2,400	
Total current liabilities	£ 2,600		£ 600		FL 8,300	
Long-term notes to non-affiliates	—		—		800	
Long-term notes to affiliates	3,200[2]		—		—	
Capital stock	500		1,500		7,000	
Retained earnings	2,500		7,000		33,100	
Total liabilities and net worth	£ 8,800		£ 9,100		F 49,200	

[1] TEK UK and TEK Guernsey are shown in pounds sterling. TEK Netherlands is shown in guilders. Figures in the "dollars included" column show portions of the total balance which are actually denominated in U.S. dollars. For example, TEK UK owes other affiliates the equivalent of £1,000,000. This amount includes $1,000,000 denominated in dollars; the remainder is denominated in sterling. The pound sterling is translated at $2.40 and the guilder at $0.377. Actual numbers are disguised.

[2] TEK UK owes TEK Guernsey £ 3,200,000, mostly for inventory. The debt has an indefinite maturity and no interest charge.

[3] Scandinavian affiliates owe TEK Netherlands 1,300,000 guilders.

Exhibit 5 *Income statements for fiscal year ending May 31, 1974, for the European manufacturing subsidiaries of Tektronix, Inc. (in thousands)**

	TEK UK	TEK Guernsey	TEK Netherlands
	(pound)	(pound)	(guilder)
Sales	£ 15,000	£ 10,000	FL 53,000
less cost of sales	−12,000	−7,000	−40,000
Gross Profit	3,000	3,000	13,000
less operating expenses	− 2,000	− 600	− 5,300
Income Before Profit Share	1,000	2,400	7,700
less profit share	− 300	− 700	− 2,700
Income After Profit Share	700	1,700	5,000
less non-operating expense (income)			
Interest Income	—	(300)	(1,300)
Interest Expense	—	—	—
Foreign Exchange Loss (Gain)	200	100	(2,700)
Other	100	100	5,300
Income Before Taxes	400	1,800	3,700
less income taxes	− 200	− 400	− 1,800
Income After Taxes	200	1,400	1,900

*Not actual numbers.

whether in the U.S. capital market, host country capital markets, or the Eurodollar market. He knew the Board of Directors were considering adding corporate debt in the $20–40 million range.

A second problem was to coordinate any foreign borrowing with the recently adopted program to reduce exposure to foreign exchange rate fluctuations. In this respect local borrowing was only one alternative to reduce exposure. For example, another alternative would be to purchase hedging contracts (see Exhibit 2 for forward exchange rates). Considering the costs of local borrowing or hedging, however, it was unclear to Ken Knox if the benefits of reducing foreign exchange losses alone were worth the costs to accomplish it. Furthermore, any program that was only designed to reduce translation or transaction exposure could have an impact on underlying economic exposure. He was unsure how to measure economic exposure but felt it should not be neglected.

In the event that he recommended some borrowing by Tektronix UK, it would be necessary to specify where the funds would be raised and in what currency. Tektronix UK could borrow dollars internally from Tektronix, Inc., or other currencies from sister subsidiaries, either as a direct loan or through changing the payment terms of accounts receivable and/or payable. It could also borrow pounds or Eurodollars in the U.K. from the London branch of one of the major U.S. banks or from Tektronix's British banks. However, at this time resident sterling was under extreme credit restrictions imposed on both U.S. and British banks by the Bank of England. The Bank of England would have to approve any nonsterling loan to Tektronix UK whether from a Tektronix affiliate or from the Euro-markets.

All U.K. residents, including Tektronix UK and Tektronix Guernsey, could not purchase nonsterling securities with resident sterling. A separate kind of pound sterling held in the so-called investment pool could be used to purchase nonsterling securities, but this "investment sterling" sold at a premium of 10–40 percent above resident sterling, depending on supply and demand conditions, and was currently at a 25 percent premium. For example, Tektronix UK could borrow resident sterling and convert it into dollar-denominated time certificates of deposit by first purchasing investment sterling at a premium. If Tektronix UK then wished to convert back from these dollar CD's to sterling, it would be allowed to sell 75 percent of the dollars for investment sterling, thereby recapturing a premium, but the remaining 25 percent of the dollars would need to be sold for resident sterling without any premium. Thus the cost to Tektronix UK of raising dollars would be increased by the need to use more sterling (investment sterling at a premium) for a given number of dollars than would be needed for a normal trade transaction (resident sterling). Furthermore, 25 percent of this premium paid for investment sterling would be lost on conversion from dollars back to sterling. The remaining 75 percent of the premium might or might not be recaptured on conversion of dollars to sterling, depending on whether the premium had changed in the meantime due to supply and demand conditions in the investment sterling market.

Extensive external borrowing by Tektronix UK might raise some eyebrows in London. Although the firm had been virtually invisible to the British financial community this borrowing might increase its visibility slightly. A very high debt ratio for Tektronix UK would cause its debt ratio to stand apart from British firms in the same industry. On the other hand, Ken Knox was not overly familiar with British finance structure norms and was of the opinion that the British might be indifferent to what finance structure Tektronix UK carried as long as it promptly paid its obligations. This attitude might or might not prevail elsewhere, but just in case country norms were important, he had Exhibit 6 prepared. It shows what typical debt ratios might be in the countries where Tektronix and its manufactur-

Exhibit 6 *Average corporate debt ratios in selected countries and years**

Country	1966	Year 1970	1972
U.K.			
Electronics Industry	47%	33%	27%
All Manufacturing	45	35	35
The Netherlands			
Electronics Industry	45	53	55
All Manufacturing	49	56	59
The U.S.			
Electronics Industry	43	46	48
All Manufacturing	42	46	47
Japan			
Electronics Industry	63	63	61
All Manufacturing	69%	69%	69%

* Total debt as a percent of total assets at book value. Each company is weighted equally.

ing subsidiaries are located. It excludes Guernsey because of its size and the fact that it would probably be using U.K. norms.

Ken Knox would like to have had time to analyze and forecast the future exchange rate prospects for various currencies, but he needed to make a recommendation within two weeks in order to contribute to the overall corporate decision on borrowing externally. For what it was worth, the financial press was full of speculation that the dollar was really undervalued in June 1974, but this did not seem to show up in the spot or forward exchange markets. In any case, his recommendation had to include policy for all foreign subsidiaries, whether or not they normally dealt in dollars.

Gunter Dufey

Case 27

Desperately Seeking L/C
Turning to Japan for Cut-Rate Loans

Japan's fears of losing control over its currency have virtually barred overseas borrowers in recent years from the country's capital markets, where the prime rate is 6.75 percent for short-term money and 8.9 percent for long-term. But a few U.S. airlines have zeroed in on a financing scheme that has opened the yen-lending window — at least for the moment. Unless the Japanese government changes the rules, the new device — called a deferred-purchase agreement — seems sure to spread. It could offer cut-rate financing for oil rigs, ships, and other costly equipment, as well as airplanes.

Moreover, Japan is considering opening a second cheap-money win-

Source: Reprinted from the November 23, 1981 issue of *Business Week* by special permission, © 1981 by McGraw-Hill, Inc. Adapted for case discussion by Gunter Dufey, The University of Michigan, 1981.

Desperately Seeking L/C **193**

dow by resurrecting the dollar-denominated "Samurai lease." That was a 1978 ploy to cut Japan's trade surplus with the United States and dump excess dollars.

Trying for more. Only two of the new deferred-purchase agreements have been struck so far: the first by Continental Airlines, Inc. in May and the second by PSA Inc. in August. In both cases, a group of Japanese trading companies led by Marubeni Corp. bought airplanes, which Continental and PSA had on order, from U.S. manufacturers. The airlines then bought the planes from the trading companies on ten-year, yen-denominated credit with 20 percent down. The Japanese required the carriers to buy letters of credit from U.S. banks guaranteeing repayment. After all costs and a lending spread for the Japanese companies, Continental is paying a fixed rate of 11.2 percent on its $58 million in yen debt, and PSA is paying 10.5 percent on $78 million. The carriers would be paying 17 percent or more for U.S. financing.

Continental is so ecstatic about its deal that, although it has no more planes on order, it is negotiating to refinance $40 million of its existing planes in Japan. That would cut $2.5 million from 1982 interest costs, figures the airline's financial vice-president, Roy M. Rawls. Flying Tiger Line Inc., a big freight airline, hopes to sign a yen refinancing deal reportedly valued at $80 million in a few weeks. Hawaii's Aloha Airlines Inc. is negotiating a $27 million deal.

The debts must be repaid in yen, so the risk is that the costs of repayment could soar if the yen surges against the dollar. Because Continental and Flying Tiger generate ample yen revenue from flying Pacific routes, they need not worry much about exchange rates. PSA is another story. The West Coast airline receives only modest yen revenue, so it must buy the bulk of its semiannual debt payment of 1.4 billion yen (about $6.2 million at current exchange rates) in the open market. PSA does not plan to hedge in the futures market because the company believes the cost would cancel the interest rate advantage. Its vulnerability to exchange rates prompted Bank of America and Crocker National Bank to refuse to issue PSA the required letter of credit. On its third try, PSA got one from a group of four banks led by First National Bank of Chicago. "PSA is betting the company," chides one banker, noting that the airline yen debt equals 54 percent of its $145 million net worth.

PSA insists it is not taking undue risks. Its president, Paul C. Barkley, accepts the general belief that the yen will strengthen against the dollar. But even under the airline's worst-case assumption — a dollar worth only 160 yen, versus 228 yen at present — Barkley figures the company's yen-borrowing costs should not exceed the cost of borrowing in dollars. If they threaten to do so, PSA might yet hedge in yen futures. The cheap financing, meanwhile, would mean savings of about $5 million a year at current rates — a welcome economy for a carrier that has been operating at a loss.

Another source? Meanwhile, Japan's Finance Ministry is mulling the reintroduction of the "Samurai lease." Under a short-lived program in 1978, Japanese trading companies bought U.S. airplanes with dollars borrowed cheaply from the Japanese government. That qualified the planes as U.S. exports to Japan, cutting Japan's trade surplus. Then the Japanese companies leased them at cut rates to European, Canadian, and Asian airlines for payment in dollars. Many U.S. airlines asked for Samurai leases, but Japan decided that importing U.S. planes, then exporting them to the U.S., would be little more than a statistical mirage.

The Finance Ministry — prodded by the Ministry of International Trade and Industry — is considering resurrecting these leases and offering them to U.S. companies. Opinion is split on whether the leases will resurface. However, Aloha Airlines, for one, is postponing signing its deferred purchase deal in the hope of getting a Samurai lease instead.

U.S. equipment buyers hope Japan at least continues to allow deferred purchases. U.S. bankers say there is no reason the device could not be used to finance any capital equipment, including factories, although movable goods are preferred in case of defaults. One hindrance is a Financial Accounting Standards Board rule requiring companies to change the reported value of foreign-denominated debt as exchange rates fluctuate. If the yen strengthens, PSA and Continental must take currency translation write-offs on their entire yen debt, which hurts profits. The FASB is expected to revise the rule by year end, however, and it may limit write-offs to current portions of foreign debt.

The main worry is that Japan's Finance Ministry might ban deferred purchases if they become too widespread. It came close to killing the device in May when Continental Airlines announced that it had secured a "loan" from "three Japanese lenders." Marubeni argued successfully that the deal was not a loan and hence did not fall under the ministry's jurisdiction. Says Continental's Rawls: "As far as I'm concerned, you can call it a 'deferred pig in a poke' as long as the rate is 11 percent."

The article had been passed around and the meeting of senior credit officers at Metrobank's Airlines Division was drawing to a close. Decisions had now to be made on providing letters of credit (L/Cs) to the three U.S. carriers mentioned in the article. All three were seeking L/Cs to back up their forthcoming "deferred-purchase agreements" which apparently provided low-cost yen financing.

"None of these is a top-notch credit," said the first banker, "and a letter of credit has just as much credit risk as a loan, and the Fed is about to apply capital requirements against our L/Cs. I don't like it. On the other hand Coastbank has turned PSA down, which probably means it's a strong credit."

"I know what a letter of credit is," said the second banker. "The point is that we can get a decent fee for once and this financing reduces these airlines' costs. My only concern is about the exchange risk when an American airline borrows yen, especially in Japan where passenger fares are controlled."

"But isn't that just a paper exposure based on currency transaction? And won't that all change when the FASB revises its rules and replaces FAS 8 with FAS 52?" asked the third banker.

There was a moment's silence. Then the rookie credit officer blurted out: "This may be a dumb question, but what routes do these airlines fly, and who is their competition?"

The first banker replied, "Continental Airlines flies routes between Tokyo and Guam, Samoa, and other U.S. possessions, carrying primarily Japanese tourists in competition with Air Nippon. It also flies between Denver, Houston, and Washington, D.C. Flying Tigers carries live cattle from the western U.S. to Japan (the sukiyaki run), while returning with Japanese consumer electronics and similar cargo. It is in competition with NWO, UAL, PANAM, JAL, KAL, and THAI.

"PSA flies primarily between SFO and LAX, and other points on the West Coast. On these routes it carries a goodly number of Japanese businessmen who like the smiling faces on the planes and the friendly flight attendants.

"Let me summarize the issues. First, given that the creditworthiness of all three airlines seems equally precarious, to which of these three airlines — Continental, PSA, or Flying Tiger — should we grant an L/C? Do any of them really face exchange risk, and if so, why? Is there any crucial additional information that we need?

"Second, what do you think of Barkley's argument that he can always hedge his company's yen debt with futures?

"Finally, why are these American carriers so excited about yen financing? Is there some apparent market imperfection or arbitrage opportunity?"

Gunter Dufey

Case 28

Kent Consolidated Overseas

Kent Consolidated Overseas Manufacturing Company (KCO) was a highly integrated manufacturer of trucks for both commercial and industrial applications. More than 90 percent of its business was in the manufacture of industrial trucks, axles, transmissions, and related components. Rental of its products and sale of replacement parts were also important phases of the company's operations. KCO had some eleven manufacturing plants in the United States and manufacturing and sales subsidiaries in England, France, and Germany as well as Canada and several South American countries. Sales in 1974 were $987 million, with net income of $36.1 million. Of this, overseas sales (excluding $95 million in exports from

© by The University of Michigan Graduate School of Business Administration, 1975. Revised 1985. This case was prepared by Jeffrey R. Williams under the supervision of Professor Gunter Dufey as a basis for class discussion and not to illustrate either effective or ineffective handling of an administrative situation.

the United States) were $209 million, of which $151.7 million (72.6 percent) were accounted for by subsidiaries in England, France, and Germany.

KCO operations worldwide had experienced substantial growth in recent years and overall company volume had doubled since 1970. Management felt that the addition of much-needed plant and equipment was necessary for the continued success of the company; thus, production capacity was scheduled to increase by 22 percent during 1975. KCO's projected capital expenditures companywide for 1975 were $64.8 million (as compared to $51.8 million in 1974). Partially because of the scale of the expansion program, KCO had recently secured additional financing: $72 million were raised through an offering of debentures and notes, and revolving credit agreements with seven major banks were increased to $109 million (up from $35 million in 1973).

Kent Consolidated also controlled Kent Credit Corporation (KCC), a wholly owned, nonconsolidated domestic finance subsidiary of the company, which financed retail time sales of Kent products through Kent's independent dealers and retail branches. Kent subsidiaries in England, France, and Germany also had wholly owned subsidiaries which assisted in financing their sales. These non-U.S. finance subsidiaries were combined with Kent Credit for administrative and reporting purposes, and the combined financial statements of Kent Credit were reported separately from KCO's operations (but the income of Kent Credit was included in the consolidated income of the company). In 1974, Kent Credit raised an additional $36 million in capital with an offer of five-year debentures, and another $18 million in the form of a five-year subordinated bank note.

COMPANY DEBT POSITION

At year-end 1973, Kent Consolidated's total debt was $130.2 million; by year-end 1974 it had risen to $196.4 million, an increase of $67.7 million. The company's treasury department was kept busy during the year financing this growth and estimates were that by year-end 1975, total company debt would reach approximately $303 million. Although the company had received an "A" rating by both Moody's and Standard & Poor's, both investment services indicated that this was despite Kent's coverage of its fixed charges (earnings coverage of interest expenses), which had been declining.[1] By the end of the year, Kent's net tangible assets were expected to be only 1.21 times long-term debt compared with Standard & Poor's mini-

---

[1] Standard & Poor's minimum coverage guideline for an "A" bond rating was five times before taxes and two to three times after taxes.

Exhibit 1 *Kent consolidated overseas balance sheet ($000)*

	1973	1974
Assets		
Current Assets:		
Cash	$ 19,983	$ 28,820
Accounts & Notes		
Receivable	54,769	96,324
Inventories	268,952	334,145
Prepaid Expenses	6,242	9,623
Total Current Assets	349,946	468,912
Rental Equipment:	41,312	39,373
Investments & Advances		
Finance Subsidiaries	57,319	53,691
Minority-owned Companies	13,244	15,109
Property, Plant, & Equipment	110,998	147,069
	$572,819	$724,154
Liabilities		
Current Liabilities:		
Notes Payable	$ 24,484	$ 54,534
Accounts Payable	70,696	88,060
Accrued Payrolls	16,215	19,102
Accrued Other	12,452	16,848
Installment Obligations	10,954	12,827
Taxes on Income	12,166	1,889
Current Installment on Debt	3,269	11,518
Total Current Liabilities	150,236	204,778
Long-Term Debt:		
Borrowings	100,160	170,771
Installment Obligations	29,995	25,613
Accrued/Deferred Items:		
Accrued Items	6,403	7,305
Rentals	16,556	20,491
Income Taxes	14,240	19,755
Shareholders' Equity:		
Common Stock	106,554	106,901
Retained Earnings	148,675	168,540
Total Equity	255,229	275,441
	$572,819	$723,652

mum guideline of 2.25 times. Working capital would be equal to 76 percent of long-term debt compared with Standard & Poor's minimum guideline of 80%. (See Exhibit 1 for Kent Consolidated's 1973–1974 assets and liabilities.)

Kent's average borrowings, interest expense and average cost of funds from 1972 through 1974 for the parent and the subsidiaries as a group were as follows:

	Average borrowings ($000)	Interest expenses ($000)	Average cost of funds (%)
Parent:			
1972	$30,096	$1,440	4.90
1973	$41,472	$3,024	6.62
1974	$83,016	$7,992	9.36
Subsidiaries:			
1972	$54,792	$5,040	9.20
1973	$63,576	$6,984	11.04
1974	$94,464	$14,040	14.83

Kent Credit and its subsidiaries had a long-term debt position at year-end 1974 of $169.5 million in senior and senior-subordinated securities. United States lines of short-term credit were $150 million, with $41.5 million outstanding. Canadian lines of short-term credit were $26.6 million, with $21.5 million outstanding, while Eurodollar Revolving Credit agreements amounted to $23.8 million, with no outstanding balance. Overseas finance subsidiaries had additional short-term bank lines of credit in the amount of $62.1 million, of which $19.7 million was unused. At year end, the average interest rate on outstanding short-term bank borrowings was 11.21 percent, and 10.36 percent on commercial paper.

BORROWING LIMITATIONS

In February 1972, the Board of Directors of Kent Consolidated adopted a policy of borrowing limitations for the parent company and for its subsidiaries. This policy placed certain ratio limitations on the borrowing of Kent, the parent, and other ratio limitations on the consolidated subsidiaries as a group. For the parent these were: (1) working capital not less than $57 million, (2) working capital must exceed funded indebtedness, and (3) a current ratio of not less than 2.00. For the subsidiaries as a group the limitations were: (1) a minimum working capital of $18 million,

(2) working capital not less than funded indebtedness, and (3) a current ratio not less than 1.5.

A large portion of the debt of Kent's subsidiaries was guaranteed by the parent. By year-end 1975, Kent's (the parent) funded indebtedness was expected to exceed working capital by $23 to $69 million, with the difference accounted for by whether the debt of Kent's subsidiaries as a group was borrowed long-term and guaranteed, or borrowed short-term — where the guarantee would not be considered as a debt of Kent, the parent. If the debt was guaranteed, the total guarantees to subsidiaries by year-end would be an estimated $78 million. Kent's financial executives believed, after lengthy discussions with Kent lenders around the world, that if the company established most of its consolidated subsidiaries on a viable financial basis, guarantees of the indebtedness of these subsidiaries could be eliminated. If this were done, by year end the company's violation in its working capital guidelines would be considerably less than $69 million, which was the estimated shortfall should the continued guarantee route be followed.

Under terms of loan agreements with private lenders (insurance companies), any loans with a maturity of more than one year and guaranteed by Kent were considered indebtedness of the parent. For Kent's financial managers this meant that the ability of the parent to leverage its own balance sheet was dependent upon the maximum amount of funds that could be obtained for the subsidiaries based upon their own financial statements. Lenders in nearly all countries had indicated that they would be willing to lend to the company's subsidiaries in their respective country without a Kent guarantee, provided the subsidiary committed itself to maintain senior liabilities not greater than two times the equity of the subsidiary plus subordinated debt.[2] Subsidiaries would also be required to maintain a current ratio of at least 1.5.

Kent would also be required to agree to do one of the following should nonperformance arise: (1) cause the subsidiary to repay its loans, (2) guarantee the subsidiary's loans, or (3) cause the subsidiary to reestablish the ratios. This requirement was imposed by the banks because it was their view that Kent, since it was the sole shareholder, could take action that could cause a default, leaving the banks with a debtor that was insolvent. From Kent's standpoint, this arrangement did not constitute a guarantee, because Kent had the option of taking action prior to any default that

---

[2] Lenders generally wished to include as senior liability for this ratio 10% of the indebtedness of any finance subsidiary, 10% of any discounted obligations for which the subsidiary might be liable, and 100% of any guarantees made by the subsidiaries of the indebtedness of third parties.

would prevent the subsidiary from going into default. In Kent's view, this action could take many forms besides having Kent increase its investment in the subsidiary and, as one example, management cited the option of liquidating some of the assets of the company. Management felt that the overall "debt transfer" approach might be beneficial, as this would permit the parent to leverage the balance sheets of each of its subsidiaries with a minimum effect on the borrowing capacity of the parent.

Kent's foreign subsidiaries were subject to numerous laws and regulations of foreign governments relating to investments, operations, currency restrictions, and revaluations and fluctuations of currencies.[3] On the question of how to finance projected capital increases in foreign subsidiaries, management was concerned with three issues: (1) Where to source the required capital and in what form, (2) the optimum manner in which to transfer the funds through the firm, and (3) in what form the monies should be put into the affiliates where they would be ultimately used. Additionally, worldwide economic factors led management to expect a high degree of uncertainty in financial markets, which made contingency planning for the company's funding activities all the more important. With these issues in mind, Kent financial management turned to financing the projected requirements of its three biggest subsidiaries: Kent Limited (England), Kent–France, and Kent–Germany. (See Appendix 1 for an abstract of the 1974–1975 international financial environment and Appendix 2 for a description of Kent's business strategy.)

KENT LIMITED (UNITED KINGDOM)

For the period 1970 through 1974, Kent Limited lost $15.3 million on a legal basis, and although capital was increased by $7.7 million in 1972, by year-end 1974 the subsidiary had a deficit net worth position of $7.2 million. Kent Limited had been financed primarily by intercompany loans, first from Kent Consolidated and then from Kent Credit. Kent and its operating subsidiaries had advances to Kent Limited totaling $3.6 million, and Kent Limited had bank lines totaling £3.0 million (US$7.0 million), with £1.44 million (US$3.38 million) outstanding. In 1969, Kent Limited had borrowed £4.3 million (US$10.4 million) from three mutual funds in the United Kingdom on a "back-to-back" basis, while another Kent subsidiary had lent these same mutual funds the $10.4 million. Kent Limited loans from private lenders were guaranteed by the parent at an interest

---

[3] Foreign currency losses which resulted in deductions from KCO's income were $2.3 million in 1973 and $1.9 million in 1974.

rate of 6 percent to 8 percent per annum. Kent Limited's other loans had an interest rate of 5 percent to 7 percent, about 1 percent below the interest rate on pound sterling loans.

The Bank of England required that foreign-owned British companies have equity plus funds borrowed outside the United Kingdom equal to at least 7 percent of their fixed assets. Because of Kent Limited's losses, Kent was required to finance 70 percent of these losses from funds outside the United Kingdom. For a British company to borrow outside the country it was required to obtain permission from the Bank of England, which was usually given, provided the loan was for a term of not less than two years. In order for Kent Limited to get back into compliance with the fixed asset ratio imposed by the Bank of England, the subsidiary would have to borrow, outside the United Kingdom, $3.2 million at the beginning of the year and $11.0 million by year-end 1975, based on company projections (see Exhibit 2 for the three subsidiaries' 1974 and estimated 1975 assets and liabilities).

In August 1974, Kent Consolidated's Board of Directors authorized an increase in its capital in Kent Limited by £3.6 million (US$8.3 million) in order to eliminate the subsidiary's deficit net worth position and reduce interest expenses.[4] The effect of this capital increase would be to transfer the debt that Kent Limited had under its lines of credit to the debt of the parent, which would put the interest expense for these borrowings in KCO, where they would be tax deductible. Because of Kent Limited's past losses there was no possibility of having the subsidiary borrow on its own financial structure, and KCO management felt the subsidiary's balance sheet ratios were meaningless. With respect to operational needs, if assumptions based on historic inventory turnover were considered, the subsidiary's projected requirement was $2.88 million. If both historic inventory and earnings performance ratios were applied, cash requirements for the year would be $8.7 million. On this basis, the total need for direct KCO loans and guarantees for the year would be $17.0 million.

United Kingdom tax law permitted 100 percent depreciation on new capital assets in the year of acquisition. The tax deferral aspects of this provision had substantial cash flow value to a profitable company, but were without value to a subsidiary such as Kent Limited, which paid no U.K. taxes. Consequently, long-term leasing of fixed assets had grown substantially in recent years since it shifted the depreciation advantage to a leasing company, which then passed most of this advantage on to the lessee in the form of a lower effective interest rate. Fixed asset leasing had an ad-

---

[4] In the Spring of 1975, KCO was still awaiting approval from the Bank of England for this investment.

Exhibit 2 *Kent consolidated overseas subsidiary balance sheets: 1974, 1975 (est.)*
England, France, Germany (U.S. dollars, amounts in thousands)[1]

	England		France		Germany	
	1974	1975 (est.)	1974	1975 (est.)	1974	1975 (est.)
Assumptions						
Sales	$33,500	$57,537	$48,989	$82,110	$69,254	$94,398
Net income	$(4,600)	$(6,330)	$(2,066)	$(2,053)	$ 2,079	$ 1,889
Return on sales	(13.7)%	(11.0)%	(4.2)%	(2.5)%	3.0%	2.0%
Capital appropriations	$ 785	$ 1,148	$ 1,018	$ 2,277	$ 1,785	$ 5,806
Capital expenditures	$ 462	$ 1,346	$ 706	$ 1,161	$ 1,856	$ 3,564
Inventory turnover to sales	2.4X	3.0X	3.0X	3.9X	2.8X	3.3X
Comparative Balance Sheets						
Inventories	$17,003	$21,501	$19,567	$24,790	$29,040	$34,014
Other current assets	3,852	2,897	20,607	26,726	4,812	4,963
Total current assets	20,855	24,398	40,174	51,516	33,852	38,977
Rental Equipment	1,838	4,680	1,728	2,616	4,110	5,421
Investments and advances	1,720	2,472	1,124	4,149	3,135	4,724
Net properties	1,237	2,220	3,259	3,665	8,660	11,315
Total assets	$25,650	$33,770	$46,285	$61,946	$49,757	$60,437

Exhibit 2 (Cont.)

	England		France		Germany	
	1974	1975 (est.)	1974	1975 (est.)	1974	1975 (est.)
Short-term debt (*)	$ 8,163	$ 3,765	$26,153	$24,378	$ 128	$ 2,252
Other current liabilities	8,685	8,130	13,031	12,230	11,440	14,067
Total current liabilities	16,848	11,895	39,184	36,608	11,568	16,319
Long-term borrowings (*)	13,603	13,971	4,564	1,464	24,983	18,549
Rental equipment obligations	2,452	5,015	—	2,617	5,014	6,546
Accrued items and deferred credits	—	—	—	—	—	—
Capital stock	8,094	16,446	6,178	6,178	7,723	7,723
Retained earnings	(15,347)	(22,239)	(3,641)	(4,144)	469	1,313
Total shareholders' equity	(7,253)	(5,793)	2,537	2,034	8,192	9,036
Additional funds required (*)	—	8,682	—	19,223	—	9,987
Total liabilities	$25,650	$33,770	$46,285	$61,946	$49,757	$60,437
Total debt (*)	$21,766	$26,418	$30,720	$45,065	$25,111	$30,788

1. Financial statements of subsidiaries operating outside the United States were translated into U.S. dollar equivalents at (1) current exchange rates for net current assets, except inventories and long term debt, (2) exchange rates applicable at the time of acquisition of inventories and properties, and (3) average exchange rates for the year for income and expense amounts, except depreciation. Translation gains and losses were included in current income. Inventories of foreign subsidiaries were valued at the lower of cost or market on the first-in, first-out method.

ditional advantage for foreign-owned companies in the United Kingdom, since leased assets were excluded from the Bank of England's requirement that foreign-owned companies finance a minimum percentage of their fixed assets through either equity or foreign borrowings. In the case of Kent Limited, the leasing of new fixed asset acquisitions under a Kent guarantee would mean significant interest savings and a reduction in the extent to which Kent Limited would have to be supported by direct intercompany loans or equity investments.

The British prime rate was 8.5 percent at the end of 1972, 14 percent at the end of 1973, and 13 percent by the end of 1974. The rate was expected to average 11.25 percent during 1975. Kent Limited's average borrowings, interest expense, and average cost of funds for the last three years were as follows:

	Avg. borrowings	Interest exp.	Avg. cost[5] of funds
1972	$10.6 million	$0.86 million	8.30%
1973	$10.7 million	$0.65 million	5.91%
1974	$13.1 million	$1.37 million	10.69%

The subsidiary's total debt was projected to increase to $26.4 million by year-end, assuming the £3.6 million capital increase would be effected during the year, in which case changes in total debt would be the net of the capital increase. For KCO financial planners, the question was to what extent the funds requirements should be financed through a combination of local borrowing and leasing of facilities, and to what extent they should be met through (foreign currency) intercompany borrowings. If the new funds, in addition to the capital increase, could be obtained in the U.K. they would probably have to be guaranteed by the parent. Funds obtained in other currencies would be at a lower interest cost but with consequent foreign exchange risk.

KENT FRANCE

Kent France was financed primarily with local borrowings within France on a short-term basis from French banks and the French branches of some of Kent's U.S. banks. Of $26.2 million short-term debt on its balance sheet (not including discounted receivables), $7.3 million were loans denomi-

[5] Because the subsidiary paid no U.K. income taxes, after tax cost of borrowings was the same as before tax cost.

nated in U.S. dollars, of which $1.44 million had been borrowed from Kent's U.S. finance subsidiary. The French Central Bank annually reviewed the credit files of large borrowers for the purpose of authorizing access to its relatively low-cost trade note discounting program. Comments by the bank on financial conditions of borrowers carried great weight in French domestic financial markets, as most of the major banks were nationalized. Although French financial authorities were generally not permitting banks to accept new guarantees from outside of the country in support of domestic credit facilities, to date, French leaders had been willing to extend credit to Kent France based on outside guarantees. Kent management felt this arrangement was not acceptable on a long-term basis, particularly since in its most recent review of Kent France, the French Central Bank indicated the subsidiary was in need of an immediate increase in its capital position.

Borrowing requirements of Kent France had grown substantially as a result of the expansion of French retail distribution activities for truck products, French government restrictions on the ability of Kent France's finance subsidiary to factor receivables, and unprofitable operations on a legal entity basis. As a result, the company's year-end borrowings of FF81.8 million (US$18.4 million) were extremely high in relation to the subsidiary's capital base. Management felt this debt-ratio problem could be solved by the increase in Kent France's capital position to FF36 million (US$8.1 million).

Depending on whether the restrictions on the growth of the finance company were lifted during the year, the subordination of intercompany loans (including those already outstanding) of an additional FF36 million might be necessary. If restrictions were eased, the need for subordinated borrowings at year end could drop to an estimated FF14.4 million (US$3.2 million). In order for Kent France to borrow without a Kent guarantee, it was felt that KCO or one of its subsidiaries should subordinate existing intercompany debt and extend subordinated intercompany loans to Kent France up to a total of FF43.2 million (US$9.6 million).

Kent France's total debt was $30.7 million at year-end 1974 and was expected to total $45.1 million at year-end 1975, based on sales projections. Bank lines totaled FF113.8 million (US$25.6 million) and borrowings outstanding under these bank lines were FF109.4 million. Long-term borrowings totaled $4.6 million (FF20.7 million), virtually all of which matured in 1976. These funds had been borrowed under a term loan guaranteed by KCO with Bank of America and a French bank.

The French prime rate was 9.15 percent at the end of 1972, rose to 12.45 percent by the end of 1973, and was approximately 14.45 percent during 1974. In 1975 the rate was expected to average 13.75 percent. Kent

France's average borrowings, interest expense, and average cost of funds was as follows:

	Avg. borrowings	Interest exp.	Avg. cost of funds
1972	$5.9 million	$0.43 million	7.32%
1973	$6.2 million	$0.86 million	14.45%
1974	$18.4 million	$2.88 million	15.87%

Kent France's total liabilities were 12.07 times Kent's investment and were expected to increase by year-end 1975 to 29.44 times investment, based upon company projections and the assumption that Kent would not increase its investment in the subsidiary, and including intercompay loans as liabilities. Kent France's current ratio was 1.06 and at year-end 1975 was expected to be 1.4, assuming additional funds were borrowed on a long-term basis.

For Kent France's capital structure to be put on a sound footing from a credit standpoint, Kent would have to increase its investment in Kent France by $13 to $15 million, provided Kent subordinated its $1.44 million of intercompany loans to Kent France. The alternative to this would be for Kent to guarantee the debt of Kent France, which would mean that $39.9 to $45.0 million of Kent parent's domestic borrowing capacity would be used up on these guarantees. If the guarantee route was followed, Kent would still be forced to increase its investment in Kent France, but by a much smaller amount, and the guarantee approach would not solve the potential problems of Kent France being required to borrow more funds outside of France (although these foreign loans could be guaranteed just as well as borrowings inside of France).

KENT GERMANY

Until 1970 Kent Germany was financed primarily with intercompany loans from Kent Credit and secondarily with short-term bank borrowings within Germany. In 1970 the Germans established regulations requiring noninterest-bearing deposits (bardepot) to be placed with their central bank by any German entity that borrowed from lenders outside of Germany. Originally this deposit was 25 percent of the foreign loans, but was eventually raised to 100 percent.[6] To avoid these deposits, Kent financed

---

[6] The bardepot was still in effect by the end of 1974.

Kent Germany with borrowings from German banks and the German branches of the company's U.S. banks. In order that these borrowings would be classified as long-term debt on the balance sheet and to assure availability of the money, the company set up revolving credit agreements.

Kent Germany had revolved credit agreements guaranteed by KCO with nine banks, totalling DM114.0 million (US$47.3 million), of which about DM56 million (US$23.3 million) had been borrowed. The interest rate on these borrowings fluctuated with the German prime bank rate. At the end of 1972 the prime rate was 8.50 percent, in 1973 it rose to 14 percent and subsequently dropped to 11 percent by the end of 1974, where it was expected to remain during most of 1975. Kent Germany's average borrowings, interest expense, and average cost of funds were as follows:

	Avg. borrowings	Interest exp.	Avg. cost of funds
1972	$8.2 million	$0.50 million	6.01%
1973	$12.9 million	$1.22 million	9.59%
1974	$20.7 million	$2.74 million	13.24%

Kent Germany's liabilities (including intercompany loans) were projected to grow from 3.2 times KCO's investment to 4.6 to 5.7 times by year's end, depending on operating results. If Kent Germany's balance sheet was to be put on a sound credit basis so that its total liabilities did not exceed twice KCO's investment, Kent would have to increase its investment in its subsidiary by $9.4 to $13.0 million. This would, in the opinion of management, allow Kent to eliminate its guarantee of Kent Germany's debt. Kent was considering authorizing the parent or one of its subsidiaries to increase the investment in Kent Germany to DM21.6 million (US$9.0 million) through either (1) an increase in capital stock, (2) subordinated company loans, (3) guaranteed third party loans, or some combination of these. Additionally, authorization might be required for new subordinated intercompany loans of up to DM8.6 million (US$3.5 million) that might be needed to support the subsidiary's projected 1975 growth. The subsidiary's current ratio was projected at 1.73 by year-end, which was above the "rule of thumb" minimum because Kent Germany's borrowings were classified as long-term. Management felt, however, that any lender to the subsidiary would be satisfied as far as the company's liquidity was concerned even without a guarantee of the loans by the parent.

Appendix One

Kent Consolidated Overseas

FINANCIAL ENVIRONMENT

In late 1974, government policies became expansive in the United States, the United Kingdom, Germany, and elsewhere, and were expected to become even more so in 1975. A major element introducing uncertainty was the trend in wages, the most important element in the cost of doing business. If wages were to continue to rise in line with the rise in demand for output brought about by stimulative government policy, the result would be higher rates of inflation. As far as the general financial outlook was concerned, Kent management felt developments pointed to lower interest rates and continued availability of short-term funds, particularly as governments were inclined to pursue expansive policies. Continued high rates of inflation, however, were expected to make markets for long-term funds for corporations difficult and expensive worldwide. These difficulties were expected to be reinforced by the investment behavior of the oil exporting countries and the high demands of increased deficit financing by public borrowers.

THE UNITED KINGDOM

Retail prices increased by 19 percent during 1974 and real output amounted to 1 percent less than in the year earlier. Governmental attempts at restraint through fiscal and monetary policies resulted in higher interest rates, while controls were in effect over price increases allowed by business firms. At the same time, wage levels rose 26 percent. This led to severe liquidity problems in the business sector and to a general decrease in investment. The country's balance of payments deteriorated during the year to a $10 billion deficit on current account. The British pound weakened in foreign exchange markets against other European currencies, and the weakness would have been more pronounced were it not for capital inflows. High nominal interest rates, aggressive borrowing by the British government, and large investments by some oil exporting countries in combination with the prospects for North Sea oil kept Sterling stronger on foreign exchanges than underlying conditions would otherwise warrant. In November, British economic policy became mildly expansionary, but what the resulting effects would be was uncertain.

FRANCE

The French economy had experienced relatively good growth beginning in 1974, supported by expansive economic policies and favorable underlying long-term growth conditions. Subsequently, consumer prices rose by 15 percent and the balance of payments current account deteriorated. As a consequence, the government switched to restrictive policies in terms of monetary aggregates, credit ceilings, and special tax measures, resulting in reduced corporate profits, construction slowdowns, and rising unemployment (2.3 percent). The French franc appreciated slightly relative to other currencies on a trade-weighted basis, due primarily to capital inflows. Projections were that credit conditions would remain tight with little change into 1975, after which a forecasted shift in monetary policy might ease conditions somewhat.

GERMANY

Although the German economy was relatively weak in 1974 (real output up only 1 percent, and unemployment at 3.7 percent, an eighteen-year high), management felt it represented one of the few bright areas worldwide. German authorities were the first to switch to a policy of fiscal and monetary restraint in early 1973. These policies were followed rather thoroughly and sustained. The result was a rate of inflation that went from 7.9 percent to 6.5 percent during the year. With domestic demand curtailed, especially in the automotive, construction, and textile industries, the combination of domestic slack and strong foreign demand for capital goods resulted in a German export boom. Together with reduced rates of inflation and high interest rates, the Deutsche mark strengthened in 1974. In the latter part of the year, monetary policy became more expansive and interest rates declined. This was coupled with a fiscal policy that provided an effective tax cut for lower income groups and an investment tax credit for business.

Appendix Two

Business Strategy and Market Characteristics of Worldwide Operations

KCO had essentially two product lines: Industrial trucks (lift trucks) and heavy-duty axles, transmissions for off-highway vehicles, and similar engineering products. Accordingly, the company's activities were divided into two product groups, "Materials Handling" and "General Products," each directed by a Group Vice-President who reported directly to the CEO.

Worldwide sales of the Materials Handling Group in 1974 were $647 million. General Products accounted for $545 million in worldwide sales; however, $205 million of this amount was accounted for by sales to the Materials Handling Group. The remaining $340 million in sales went to unrelated manufacturers of construction machinery. In this industry segment KCO had a strong market position because of the quality and high technological standards of its power-trains.

While KCO's operations in Latin America were quasi-self-sufficient because of local content regulations, KCO's activities in North America and Europe were highly integrated. Large trucks were manufactured in the U.S. plants and then shipped to Europe (and elsewhere) as needed. In this line, KCO's trucks were the leaders in the field, because of product quality and excellent after-sales service. All of these trucks were powered by gasoline engines that the company purchased under long-term contract from a U.S. supplier.

Only about 15 percent of KCO's output of large trucks was shipped to Europe, because customers in that market preferred smaller sizes, with either diesel or electric engines. Thus, the European plants specialized in small lift trucks, whereby diesel-powered units were produced in Germany and electric trucks were built in the United Kingdom. Sixty percent of all the power-trains needed came from the United States; the remainder were built in the German plant by the General Products Group. Approximately 70 percent of the output of the United Kingdom plant was sold in the domestic market, where occupational safety rules mandated the use of electric trucks in warehouses. The problem with the United Kingdom market was not only its small volume, but KCO had to fight for the market with two domestic competitors, who had 50 percent and 20 percent of the market respectively. The lack of economies of scale and continuing labor problems caused nothing but grief for the Vice-President of the Materials Handling Group.

Germany was a somewhat different story: it was KCO's largest operation in Europe. Fifty percent of its output of trucks was sold domestically, 35 percent went to France and the remainder was sold in the smaller European countries and elsewhere. Only 5 percent was shipped to the United States.

In Germany the company had a strong market position; it faced three medium-sized domestic competitors and was only occasionally bothered by Japanese imports. The big problem was the French market, which was wide open to imports and where a domestic competitor was dominant. KCO's marketing operation in France was a big headache, but management felt it could not abandon the market since its German plants would lose so much production volume that it too would become unprofitable.

KCO's production facilities in France were under the General Products Group. They were the results of a somewhat misguided acquisition in the late 1960s. The plant produced construction machinery, transmission, and axles, but not the type used in trucks. Most of the output (60 percent) was sold in France, but 40 percent was exported to the Middle East and French-speaking Africa, where the company had carved out a respectable and rapidly growing market share in direct competition with United States and Japanese competitors.

H. Lee Remmers

Case 29

Novo Industri A/S

In early October 1978, Kare B. Dullum and Mads Øvlisen, Executive
Vice-Presidents for Corporate Finance and Corporate Affairs of NOVO
Industri A/S (NOVO), and William Hopper and Richard Webb, Directors
of Morgan Grenfell & Co. Ltd., the lead bank, met with the co-managers,
namely the Deutsche Bank, the Swiss Bank Corporation (Overseas), and
the Copenhagen Handelsbank to agree on the final terms for the company's $20 million convertible Eurobond issue. Most of the features of the
issue had been worked out in the previous four months between NOVO
and the managing syndicate. The Board of Directors and Corporate Management of NOVO had earlier agreed to the issue's main features; indeed,
the convertible loan represented a major and carefully prepared element of
the company's strategy for international growth and development. The

July 1979, H. Lee Remmers, Professor of Finance, INSEAD, Fontainebleau, France.

principal points remaining to be settled between NOVO and the banks included the coupon rate, the "conversion premium" (i.e., the premium over the price of the B shares current at the time of issue at which conversion could take place), and the offering price.

The issue had been announced on the 19th of September, and all of the other terms of the issue had been set out in the *Preliminary Prospectus* published on that day. Market uncertainty had greatly increased during the previous few months due to the weakness of the dollar and its resulting impact on the dollar segment of the international bond market. During the previous four weeks, the dollar had depreciated by almost 5 percent against the Danish Kroner (Dkr.), and by similar or greater amounts against other currencies. In these circumstances, there was more than a negligible chance that the issue might have to be postponed or the final terms be drastically altered from the target figures that had been negotiated: a coupon rate of around 7 percent; the issue price at 100 percent of principal amount; a conversion premium of under 15 percent. A third possibility, although rather unlikely, was to abandon the idea of a convertible in favour of a 'straight' bond issue or a variable rate note, denominated in dollars or Deutschemarks. This would delay the issue, however, for new arrangements would have to be made by the managers to place a non-convertible dollar loan. A Deutschemark loan would, in addition, require a reorganization of the issuing syndicate with a German lead bank.

COMPANY HISTORY

NOVO is the parent company of an international group of companies based in Denmark which specializes in the manufacture and sale of insulin, enzymes, and certain other pharmaceutical and biochemical products.

Incorporated in 1940, the origins of the company date back to the 1920s when two brothers, Harald and Thorvald Pedersen, developed an industrial process to extract insulin from the pancreas gland of animals for use in the treatment of diabetes. The business developed slowly during its early years, but by the end of the 1930s NOVO was exporting insulin to over twenty countries, and had set up research laboratories to improve its insulin preparations and to broaden its range of products. During the next thirty years, this research led to development of a superior type of insulin, a range of industrial enzymes, as well as a number of other products. Moreover, this effort was essential to the perfection of its technical know-how which is critical in the extraction and fermentation manufacturing processes in this business. In 1964, a NOVO enzyme began to be used in the production of "biological" detergents. Sales of enzymes rose sharply from Dkr. 15 million in 1965 to Dkr. 386 million by 1969, with total group sales growing from Dkr. 103 million to Dkr. 518 million during the same period. This growth was short-lived, however, for sales of enzymes for use in detergents collapsed in late 1969 and early 1970, due to concern over consumer safety following adverse publicity about the hazards to workers engaged in the production of enzyme-enriched detergents.

Although an investigation sponsored by the U.S. Food and Drug Administration established that this concern was largely unfounded, the effect on NOVO's total sales was dramatic, falling to Dkr. 264 million in 1971. This led to a drastic reorganization and a restructuring of the company and its management into its present form. Among the most important of its new products since then has been a greatly improved form of insulin which was introduced in 1973, and an enzyme trilogy used to convert corn starch into high-fructose corn syrup which was put on the market in 1975. The NOVO Group's success has been reflected in the steady growth of sales, which were expected to reach about Dkr. 950 million for 1978, with pre-tax profits expected to be between Dkr. 105 and 115 million.

COMPANY ORGANIZATION

NOVO is organized into two product divisions, for pharmaceuticals and enzymes, and into divisions which cover corporate research; quality control and regulatory affairs; corporate finance; corporate affairs; and engineering and maintenance.

The following table analyzes the Group's sales by product division for the five years and six months ended 30th June 1978:

Years ended 31st December
(in Dkr. million)

	1973	1974	1975	1976	1977	6 months ended 30th June, 1978
Pharmaceuticals	218	256	298	325	401	228
Enzymes	163	217	261	359	445	220
	381	473	559	684	846	448
Other revenue	6	9	13	14	18	7
Total	387	482	572	698	864	455

The following table gives a geographical analysis of Group sales of pharmaceuticals and enzymes for the year ended 31st December 1977:

**Sales
(in Dkr. million)**

	Pharmaceuticals	Enzymes	Total	%
Denmark	28	6	34	4
North and South America	37	188	225	27
E.E.C. (excluding Denmark)	136	133	269	32
Rest of Europe	127	88	215	25
Asia and Australasia	52	21	73	9
Other	21	9	30	3
	401	445	846	100

At the present time, one-quarter of these sales are in Danish kroner, about the same amount in U.S. dollars, with the remainder in other foreign currencies. The Group employs close to 2900 people of whom about 2400 are in Denmark.

PRODUCT-MARKET DATA

Pharmaceuticals: NOVO's manufacture of pharmaceuticals is based mainly on the process of extraction, but the processes of fermentation and synthesis are also used. The most important products of this division are the range of insulin preparations of which NOVO is the second largest producer (Eli Lilly in the United States is the largest).

A major part of NOVO's research efforts has been directed towards producing highly purified insulin preparations which have a number of advantages in the treatment of diabetes; in this respect, its preparations are considered to be superior to others in the market. Other pharmaceutical products include compounds used in the treatment of cardiovascular disorders, penicillin, various antibiotics, diagnostic aids for clinical use, and veterinary products. Typical for this type of business, most of NOVO's pharmaceutical products are sold under prescription only; and product introduction, marketing, and prices are subject to control by the public authorities in its various national markets.

Enzymes: Enzymes are proteins which act as catalysts in biochemical processes and have a variety of industrial uses. They are produced by extraction from animal or vegetable tissues or by fermentation of microorganisms; this latter process is used almost exclusively by NOVO in its manufacture of industrial enzymes. The company is the largest single producer of industrial enzymes accounting for about 50 percent of total free market sales. About three-fourths of NOVO's enzyme sales are made to the detergent and starch industries. Many are large companies, although none represents more than 15 percent of total enzymes sales. Close links are maintained with these customers to develop new enzymatic processes on an industrial scale.

Research: Spending on research and development, including quality control and various technological services, has run over 10 percent of annual group sales for the past eight years. These activities are considered essential to maintaining NOVO's position as a specialized manufacturer of pharmaceuticals and biochemicals and include basic research, development of new products, and the monitoring of drug performance and drug and enzyme safety. About 550 or one-fourth of NOVO's employees in Denmark work in its laboratories located near Copenhagen. Additional research and technical support is carried out in smaller laboratories in the United States, in Switzerland and in Japan. NOVO's policy is to obtain patent protection in its major markets, although management does not consider its business to be dependent upon any single patent or group of patents. What is important, however, is the technical know-how developed by NOVO for its manufacturing processes, and these are closely guarded secrets.

Production: The NOVO Group operates three large production plants in Denmark, and five smaller plants in France, Switzerland, South Africa, and Denmark. In 1978, construction was begun on a new enzyme manufacturing plant in North Carolina and an insulin filling plant in Denmark; both were expected to come on stream in early 1979. The company also acquired an enzyme manufacturing plant in Switzerland (from Ciba-Geigy) during 1978. In value, over three-fourths of these assets were located in Denmark.

Between 1973 and the end of 1977, capital expenditures amounted to Danish kroner 317 million. Expenditures in 1977 were Dkr. 74 million and were expected to total Dkr. 170 million in 1978. In addition, the company spends heavily on plant maintenance: Dkr. 40 million in 1977 and over Dkr. 42 million expected in 1978. This is necessary to keep the plants at high levels of efficiency and cleanliness to ensure the quality and safety of its products.

FINANCIAL DATA

Issued Capital: The company's share capital is in the form of A and B shares, both classes having a nominal value of Dkr. 100 per share or multiples thereof. At the time of the convertible bond issue, the aggregate nominal value of the A share capital was Dkr. 61,875,000 with that of the B share capital being Dkr. 222,229,000. Each Dkr. 100 nominal of A share capital is entitled to ten votes whereas each Dkr. 100 nominal of B share capital has only one vote. All of the A share capital and Dkr. 5.9 million nominal amount of the B share capital were held by the NOVO Foundation, a non-profit-making institution set up by the NOVO founders in 1951 and whose main purpose is to aid scientific, humanitarian or social endeavours, and to maintain NOVO's independence. The Foundation is not involved in the management of NOVO.

Prior to the convertible issue, the Foundation's holdings in NOVO gave it 74.3 percent of the total voting rights. This would fall to around 70–71 percent as a result of the convertible issue, assuming full conversion and no other changes in the share capital. The NOVO Foundation considered it important that its voting rights did not fall below two-thirds of the total outstanding.

The B shares were first listed on the Copenhagen Stock Exchange in 1974. Up to then, all the share capital of the company had been held by the NOVO Foundation and the Pedersen family. The offering price was Dkr. 150 per Dkr. 100 nominal of B share capital. Since then, the effect of two bonus issues, two rights issues, and two issues to employees at a discount from market price has been to reduce the original offering price of Dkr. 150 to an adjusted price of Dkr. 89. The table below sets out the closing bid prices for the B shares quoted on the Copenhagen Stock Exchange from May 17, 1974 when the B shares were first listed. The prices have been adjusted as explained above.

During the past two years, NOVO B shares have been among the most actively traded securities on the Copenhagen Stock Exchange which listed 313 stocks of 249 companies at the end of 1977. Officially recorded transactions in 1977 of the B shares amounted to only 2.5 percent of the total outstanding; but as is traditional in Denmark, a much larger volume of the B shares (14.3 percent) were traded outside of the Stock Exchange and not recorded in the published data.

	Years ended 31st December									
	1974		1975		1976		1977		1978	
Quarter ended	Low	High	Low	High	Low	High	Low	High	Low	High
31st March			86 – 101		164 – 180		227 – 249		248 – 266	
30th June	86 – 89		102 – 148		166 – 180		234 – 248		240 – 263	
30th September	86 – 88		132 – 146		175 – 213		234 – 252		234 – 244	
31st December	86 – 89		143 – 180		205 – 232		240 – 257			

On 31 July 1978 the B shares were distributed among 2909 shareholders as set out below:

Holdings of B share capital Dkr. of nominal	Number of shareholders	% of total B share capital
500– 1,000	503	0.2
1,001– 5,000	1,036	1.6
5,001– 25,000	1,121	4.8
25,001–100,000	154	3.5
100,001–250,000	30	2.0
over 250,000	65	87.9
	2,909	100.0

Of these, less than 5 percent were held by members of the Board of Directors and their families with about another 3 percent held by the NOVO Foundation.

Financing: From 1973 until the end of June 1978, NOVO invested close to Dkr. 400 million in fixed assets and another Dkr. 243 million in working capital. A bit less than 60 percent of this had been financed by the cash flow from operations and the remainder from loans and the sale of new shares. Another Dkr. 70–80 million was already planned to be spent for plant and equipment during the remainder of 1978 and further increases in working capital could be expected during this time.

Among the problems faced by a rapidly growing company with such large and probably continuing demands for capital funds is not only the need to maintain a reasonably healthy financial position, but also — and perhaps this is the more critical issue — to be always assured that it can obtain the necessary funds when and where they are needed. Therefore, although Mr. Dullum believed it important to try to minimise the firm's cost of funds, he also believed that this must often be subordinated to the strategically more essential consideration of *availability* of capital, especially in view of the uncertainties of the markets for 1979 and beyond.

Based in a small country like Denmark, where domestic capital is relatively scarce and expensive, the appetite for funds of a firm like NOVO can quickly outstrip the ability of the local market to provide them. With returns of 15 percent or more available from fixed interest securities, it is very difficult for companies to sell equities (the dividend yield on NOVO B shares at the time the issue was being planned was a bit less than 4 percent). The rights issue in 1977 for slightly over Dkr. 50 million was about as large an issue as was possible on the Danish market and alone represented some 25 percent of the total raised in new issues in Denmark that year. The amount of new finance needed by NOVO was well over twice that amount.

Secondly, reflecting Denmark's chronic balance of payments problems, the central bank of Denmark was insisting that all or most foreign investments be financed abroad in order not to put further strain on its foreign currency reserves. This would certainly apply to NOVO, in spite of its large foreign exchange earnings (over 95 percent of its sales are outside of Denmark); in the future, the bulk of its foreign investments would have to be financed offshore. This was not without its difficulties, for at the time the convertible issue was being planned, NOVO was not very well known in financial centres outside of Denmark. Since its shares had not been traded outside of Denmark, NOVO would have to rely for some time to come on debt and its cash flow to finance its foreign operations. Given the situation, NOVO set about to strengthen its capital base and to become better known outside Denmark. The rights issue in 1977 had, as a major objective, the improvement of the group's capital base. As a result of this operation, and NOVO's increased profitability, total group indebtedness (total liabilities as a percent of the total assets) decreased from over 53 percent in 1976 to about 47 percent in 1977. Although this level of indebtedness was considerably below that typical for Danish or other Scandanavian industry in its business-risk category, it would nonetheless be considered relatively high by the international financial community.

With the company's capital base strengthened by the increase in capital, NOVO's management believed they were in a position to tap successfully the foreign or international capital markets for the relatively large amounts of funds they would need to carry out their current investment plans, while at the same time get the international acceptability so important for their longer term future development outside of Denmark.

The questions were several: Should they plan for a straight debt issue or for a convertible? A private placement in Europe or in the United States, or a public Eurobond issue? If a private placement, should it be a fixed rate or variable rate loan? In what currency should the issue be denominated?

THE CONVERTIBLE BOND

From NOVO's standpoint there were a number of attractive features to be obtained from a convertible: it would be less burdensome than a straight debt issue, for the interest rate could be expected to be between 2 percent and 3 percent lower; if it were successful, that is, if the price of the shares increased as expected, the bonds would be converted, thus further broadening the capital and shareholder base to provide NOVO the flexibility needed for future financing; finally, a convertible could normally be sold with a longer maturity than a non-convertible loan under the market conditions expected to prevail at the time of the issue.

There are at least two main areas of uncertainty affecting the convertible issue. One was related to the probable reaction of the Danish stock market to the announcement of the issue; the other was related to the probable response from the international investors.

In the Danish capital market, domestic convertible bonds are issued at their nominal value — usually Dkr. 1000 per bond — and generally are convertible into an equal nominal amount of share capital. Conversion can take place only after a specified period, normally five years. Existing shareholders are given preemptive rights (which can be sold during a limited period) to purchase the convertible bonds. Thus in many ways, such an issue in the Danish market can be considered a sort of delayed rights issue. A convertible NOVO Eurobond issue would be sold mainly to *other* than existing shareholders at nominal value ($1000 per bond), but with a conversion price in excess of the share's *market* price at the time of issue. Existing shareholders would not have preemptive rights to subscribe to the Eurobond convertible. Although from most points of view, the Eurobond convertible appeared attractive to the company, there was some risk that the existing shareholders might object that their interests were not being adequately taken into account since the terms of the bond gave them no advantage over new shareholders. On the other hand, given the condition of the Danish capital market where equities were depressed by high yielding government bonds, to raise over Dkr. 100 million, the equivalent of $20 million, in new share capital was deemed next to impossible, and to try could seriously depress the price of NOVO shares.

From the point of view of the international bankers, since the bond would be denominated in dollars, but convertible into Danish Kroner securities at some future date, potential investors might find it difficult to assess what they were buying. As a fixed interest security, they would be at least assured of a yield based on the nominal interest rate and the issuing price if they held the bond to maturity. And if the bond were called prior to maturity, they would realize slightly more. However, as an equity, the value of the convertible would be influenced by the performance of the company and of the Danish Stock Exchange which jointly would affect the price of the shares. It would also be affected by dollar/kroner exchange rates and dollar interest rates. With so many variables having a potential impact on the value of the convertible, there was a considerable risk that the issue would fall flat and be left with the underwriters.

In spite of these concerns, the NOVO management decided to proceed with the preparations for a Eurodollar convertible bond public issue in the

international bond market as their first choice, with a private placement of
either a fixed interest bond or a roll-over variable interest rate loan as a
fall-back alternative. A fixed interest public issue was considered to be impractical, the size of issue probably being too small to interest the market
sufficiently being one factor, the relatively small size of NOVO and the fact
that much of its existing debt consisted of mortgage loans being others.

In the fall of 1977, Morgan Grenfell had been called in to act as the
main advisor. This relationship arose from an earlier meeting between
NOVO and Morgan Guaranty Trust in New York where financing possibilities of the American plant were discussed. Morgan Guaranty believed
NOVO's requirements would be better met by a Eurobond issue than by
dollar debt raised in New York, and arranged for an introduction to Morgan Grenfell in London.

Having Morgan Grenfell as advisor also reflected NOVO's preference
for a dollar issue. Although they were aware that a dollar loan would carry
at least a 3 percent or 4 percent higher coupon rate of interest than either a
Deutschemark or Swiss franc loan, NOVO management preferred dollar
debt. This was for two reasons: First of all, they expected the dollar to
either weaken or, at worst, to move in parallel in relation to the Danish
kroner. Secondly, even if this did not happen, the company was expecting
an important development of their American business, and the dollar cash
inflows would easily offset any exposure resulting from the loan. Whichever
direction the currencies moved, NOVO management believed a dollar
denominated loan reduced their risk to foreign exchange loss compared
with loans expressed in Swiss francs or Deutschemarks.

As part of their decision to proceed with a convertible loan, the NOVO
management took steps to obtain a listing of the B shares on a stock exchange outside of Denmark. Of the two main possibilities, London or Luxembourg, the London Stock Exchange was chosen as probably being more
suitable for satisfying one of NOVO's major objectives in the issue — that
of increasing its visibility in, and acceptance by, the international financial
markets. The press coverage in London would reach a larger potential investor group than would whatever coverage it could hope for in Luxembourg; and in the international financial community, a London listing was
considered to be more "respectable." Arrangements were made with the
London brokerage house Cazenove & Co. to begin dealing in the B shares
shortly after the convertible issue was made.

The listing of B shares in London was an essential element in the attempt to broaden internationally the NOVO shareholder base, and
thereby permit it to tap the markets for the large amounts of funds it would
need in the future. Since NOVO was a Danish company with the bulk of
the trading in its shares on the Copenhagen market, there was the danger

that few, if any, shares would be traded in London; some inducement had to be offered to potential new investors to prevent a "flowback" of B shares to Copenhagen.

Since potential investors in Eurobonds prefer, indeed require, the anonymity provided by a security issued in bearer form, it was decided to transform the existing B shares into bearer form as well. The hope was that upon conversion, the original international investors would hold on to the B shares or sell them to investors *outside* of Denmark. Another advantage of switching the B shares to bearer form was that they could be brought into the Euroclear quotation system, important for assuring ease of trading and their acceptability on the secondary market outside of Denmark.

TERMS OF ISSUE

Most of the provisions covering the bonds were typical for an issue of this type. The bonds would be issued in bearer form in denominations of $1000 each. Interest would be paid annually free of tax on January 15 of each year. The final redemption would be in 1989 unless previously redeemed, converted or purchased as explained below. The company would have the option to redeem all or part of the bonds during the twelve months following January 15 of each respective year at the following percentages of their principal amount:

1980 — 104	1983 — 102.5	1986 — 101
1981 — 103.5	1984 — 102	1987 — 100.5
1982 — 103	1985 — 101.5	

At least thirty days notice of redemption (generally published in the Financial Times) to the bondholders would have to be given and, in the case of partial redemption, the bonds to be redeemed would be selected by lot in a drawing. The company could also redeem the bonds under certain circumstances where changes in the tax treatment of repayments of principal would have a material effect on the company's financial charges.

The bonds would be convertible into B shares of the company beginning 15 April 1979 up to and including 30 December 1988, at the conversion price. For purposes of conversion, the Danish kroner value of the (dollar) bonds would be based on the actual exchange rate at the time of issue and remain fixed throughout the life of the bonds. The conversion price would be adjusted for any further issue of securities that would have a dilution effect such as bonus issues, rights issues, or convertibles. However, no adjustment would be made for B shares sold to employees at less than market prices. No withholding tax would be required to be deducted on payment of interest, on premiums (in case of redemption), or on repayment of principal.

SETTING THE FINAL TERMS

The key variables that remained to be agreed between the banks and NOVO were the coupon rate, the conversion price, and the issue price. Of major concern to the banks, as the target date for the issue approached, was the increasing pressure on the dollar in the exchange markets. The dollar's weakness, which had persisted during the first half of 1978, began to accelerate with alarming speed during late summer, the final weeks of September and into early October. The market for fixed interest dollar issues was in a turmoil, both in respect to interest rates and to their successful placement.

A convertible issue of the type planned by NOVO was also exposed to these uncertainties. First of all, the wisdom of buying dollar securities was becoming more and more doubtful in the opinion of the market. Secondly, since the exchange rate for translating the dollar value of the bonds into Danish kroner would be fixed at the time of the issue, the rapidly changing value of the dollar was having a direct impact on the value of the convertible bond. In such conditions, the success of the issue was far from clear. This problem could be partly compensated by reducing the conversion premium, by increasing the coupon rate, by reducing the issue price, or by a combination of all of these. Obviously, neither Morgan Grenfell nor NOVO was anxious to have to resort to such expedients. Finally, the possibility of substituting a fixed interest public issue in dollars or in another currency was effectively ruled out for reasons indicated above.

It was with these issues to resolve that Dullum and Hopper met to decide what they should do.

Gunter Dufey

Case 30

K Mart Australia
Part A

INTRODUCTION

In early 1972 management of S. S. Kresge (Kresge), a leading U.S. retailer headquartered in Troy, Michigan, was reviewing future strategy in respect to its venture in Australia. It was the company's first — and so far only — major foreign operation outside of North America.

The venture had been started only four years earlier. Its purpose was to conduct a self-service discount department store business in Australia, employing essentially the same "K mart" merchandising concept that had been so successfully developed and applied by Kresge in the United States.

A preliminary review showed quickly that there was every reason to be satisfied with the basic arrangement. The "K mart" concept seemed to work successfully in Australia, and the cooperation with the Australian partner went very smoothly. The current problem was one of financing, as the subsidiary's ambitious expansion plans were threatened unless sufficient long-term funds could be secured.

In the United States, Kresge leases its stores. The same policy was established for the Australian venture. This was found to be particularly attractive because payments under true leases can be deducted for Australian tax purposes, whereas depreciation of land and buildings is not a tax-deductible expense. Still, it was precisely in this area where K mart (Australia) was experiencing difficulties. One company executive put the basic problem as follows: "It got tough to find developers and financing in Australia, which has a booming economy, not too much native capital, and a tight network of foreign exchange controls. Each 'K Mart' project costs $2 to $3 million to develop, and that is a pretty sizeable investment for an Australian lender to make."

COMPANY HISTORY

K mart (Australia) Ltd. was incorporated in the state of Victoria in Australia in 1967 as a joint venture of Kresge and G. J. Coles and Coy Ltd. of Australia ("Coles"). Its registered office and main office of business is in Melbourne, Australia. The combined capital contribution of Kresge and Coles was A$4.5 million, comprised of 4.5 million fully paid shares of A$1 par value. A majority of 51 percent of the shares is held by Kresge and the remaining 49 percent by Coles.

The partners in the joint venture, Kresge and Coles, have very similar corporate backgrounds. Each initially operated a variety store business. Each has diversified and expanded its business so that Kresge's "K mart" stores are the leading discount department store chain in the United States, and Coles's New World Supermarkets are a leading retail food chain in Australia. The managements of Kresge and Coles have cooperated in the exchange of retail information for many years, and the K mart Australia venture represented an opportunity for both companies to combine their retailing abilities and experience.

The operations of Kresge and Coles, as well as summaries of their financial statements, are outlined in Appendix One.

Under a thirty-year agreement, dated January 1968, Coles provides management, services, and certain facilities on a year-to-year basis for the operation of "K mart" stores for a service fee, and Kresge provides its knowledge of self-service discount department store design and operations.

"K mart" stores located in Australia are one-level structures of approximately 100,000 square feet, typically located along major streets in suburban locations. "K mart" stores are intended to be very convenient for their suburban clientele. Generally each store provides parking areas for at least five hundred automobiles, and all stores contain a fast-food restaurant and auto servicing facilities. In addition, each "K mart" contains a supermarket licensed to and operated by Coles.

As in the United States, "K mart" stores emphasize discount pricing of department store selections of popular consumer merchandise such as apparel, sporting goods, fabrics, footwear, lawn and garden care items, toys, electronic home entertainment goods, and such convenience items as health and beauty aids.

The first Australian "K mart" was opened in 1969, and a total of ten stores were operating by 1972 in five of the six Australian states. These stores employed about sixteen hundred people. Five additional stores were planned for opening by the end of 1973.

"K mart" stores presently operated and planned are set forth in the table below:

Major city and state	Suburban location	Date opened or planned
Melbourne, Victoria	Burwood East	April 1969
Sydney, New South Wales	Blacktown	October 1969
Adelaide, South Australia	Ingle Farm	October 1969
Perth, Western Australia	Morley	November 1969
Adelaide, South Australia	Kurralta Park	November 1969
Geelong, Victoria	Belmot	August 1970
Newcastle, New South Wales	Waratah	October 1970
Adelaide, South Australia	Firle	November 1970
Wollongong, New South Wales	Warrawong	April 1971
Brisbane, Queensland	Chermside	August 1971
Sydney, New South Wales	Merrylands West	November 1972
Hobart, Tasmania	New Town	October 1973
Brisbane, Queensland	Cannon Hill	October 1973
Melbourne, Victoria	Campellfield	October 1973
Sydney, New South Wales	Fairfield West	October 1973

Expenses incident to the heavy initial opening schedule above resulted in operating losses to K mart (Australia) in 1969 and 1970 and additional capital contributions were made by Kresge and Coles. Kresge's additional advances as of December 31, 1971 were about A\$3.2 million. Operations became profitable in 1971, and K mart (Australia) had no long-term debt. Appendixes One, Two, and Three provide background information on the joint venture partners, Australian financial markets, and U.S. capital control programs respectively.

Appendix One

S.S. Kresge Company

S.S. Kresge Company is engaged in the retail sale of a wide range of general merchandise through the operations of a chain of "K Mart" promotional or discount department stores, "Kresge" variety stores, and "Jupiter" limited-line small discount stores. Operations are conducted throughout the United States, Canada, Puerto Rico, and Australia. Since the commencement of the "K mart" program in 1962, Kresge has experienced substantial growth. During the period 1962–1971 Kresge opened 486 "K mart" stores, nearly quadrupled its retail selling space, and increased sales from approximately $480 million to approximately $3.1 billion. In addition since 1961 Kresge has undertaken a critical reevaluation of its existing stores, resulting in the closing or modernization of certain "Kresge" stores and the conversion of other "Kresge" stores to "Jupiter" stores.

Kresge was incorporated under the laws of the State of Michigan in 1916 as the successor to a business developed by its founder, S.S. Kresge, who opened his first store in Detroit in 1899. The registered and main office of business of Kresge is located at 3100 West Big Beaver Road, Troy, Michigan in a new international headquarters building.

The majority of Kresge's net sales are made in the United States. The balance of sales outside the United States is made principally in Canada. S. S. Kresge Company Ltd., a wholly owned subsidiary, operates a chain of "K mart," "Kresge," and "Jupiter" stores throughout Canada, managed along organization lines similar to the parent company.

The following table sets forth the number of stores in operation at the end of each fiscal year last ended January 26, 1972.

Stores in operation	1967	1968	1969	1970	1971
K mart	216	273	338	411	486
Kresge	614	593	566	539	520
Jupiter	113	116	118	123	116
Total	943	982	1,022	1,073	1,122

The aggregate selling area for all stores increased from approximately 22 million square feet at the end of 1967 to about 40 million square feet at the end of 1971.

Kresge presently employs approximately ninety-four thousand people.

"K MART" STORES

Kresge has a continuing program of opening from seventy to seventy-five "K mart" stores each year. During 1971, seventy-five "K mart" stores were opened, and Kresge expects to open at least ninety stores during 1972. Sales of "K mart" stores, excluding licenses, were approximately $1.6 billion in 1969, $2.0 billion in 1970, and $2.6 billion in 1971. In the opinion of Kresge, suitable sites are available to sustain the current rate of the "K mart" expansion program. However, the rate of the program and form of the financing arrangements will be subject to the terms of available long-term financing.

A "K mart" provides a full department store range of first grade merchandise with over sixty thousand items. It differs from the conventional department store in its approach to merchandising in that lower selling prices are achieved by rapid inventory turnover, the elimination of limited-appeal or fringe items, and the use of self-service, central check-out operations. The "K mart" stores are one-floor, generally freestanding units, located in high-traffic suburban areas of major cities and medium-sized cities, and provide parking space for approximately nine hundred cars. These stores generally range in size from 75,000 to 95,000 square feet of gross area (exclusive of supermarkets), of which approximately 78 percent is selling area. To date, most "K mart" stores have been located in the midwestern, southern, and western regions of the United States. Commencing in 1971 Kresge began locating "K mart" stores in the Middle Atlantic and New England areas.

In addition to conventional department store lines, including a limited-menu cafeteria, substantially all "K mart" stores contain an auto accessory and service department for the sale of tires, batteries, and accessory merchandise, usually located under the same roof but sometimes in a separate eight- to ten-bay garage. Normally supermarkets averaging 20,000 to 22,000 square feet are located under the same roof but with separate checkouts. Most supermarkets are operated by subtenants or are under other agreements by licensees, as are several of the general merchandise departments. Currently, approximately 87 percent of all sales in "K mart" stores, exclusive of supermarkets, are made by Kresge.

"KRESGE" STORES

Until 1961, all of Kresge's sales were derived from "Kresge" variety stores, which were primarily concentrated in the northeastern and midwestern sections of the United States and Canada. The reduction in the number of "Kresge" stores has resulted from the normal expiration of leases, from conversions to "Jupiter" stores, and from a critical review and disposition of operating units prior to lease termination dates where an adequate return was not being achieved. Kresge has no plans to open new "Kresge" stores during 1972. "Kresge" stores stock approximately sixteen thousand items of variety store merchandise. Selling area generally ranges from 5,000 to 40,000 square feet and averages approximately 14,000 square feet. Most of the stores contain a fountain or snack bar and operate on a self-service basis with central service checkouts.

Sales of "Kresge" stores were approximately $474 million in 1969, $470 million in 1970, and $468 million in 1971.

"JUPITER" STORES

In 1961, Kresge began its "Jupiter" conversion program by renovating six unprofitable "Kresge" stores and reopening them under the "Jupiter" name. These stores generally range in size from 4,000 to 10,000 square feet of selling area. "Jupiter" stores offer from twenty-five hundred to five thousand items, consisting basically of variety merchandise with emphasis on high turnover lines, promotional activity, and discounted prices. The "Jupiter" conversion program has related primarily to stores in neighborhood areas of central cities and smaller city "main street" locations.

Sales of "Jupiter" stores were approximately $72 million in 1969, $74 million in 1970, and $77 million in 1971.

G. J. COLES AND COY LIMITED

G. J. Coles and Coy Limited is engaged in the retail distribution of a wide variety of general merchandise principally through "Coles" Variety Stores and of food through "New World" Supermarkets and other food stores. Coles also owns varying interests in nine shopping centers in which its stores are located. Both general merchandise and food operations are conducted throughout Australia. Since the acquisition of its first grocery store in 1958, Coles has pursued a policy of major development in supermarket food retailing, and 162 supermarkets were opened during the ten years ended June, 1972. Total sales increased from A$195 million to A$504 million over the same period. Coles has a program of constantly evaluating its retail stores, which has resulted in the closing of a number of smaller food shops and some variety stores, and the modernization and enlarging of a number of others.

Coles was incorporated under the laws of the State of Victoria in 1921 as the successor to a retailing proprietorship developed by its founder, G. J. Coles and his brother, A. W. Coles, in 1914. The following table sets forth the number of stores in operation at the end of each of the five fiscal years last ended at June 24, 1972.

Stores in operation:	1968	1969	1970	1971	1972
Variety and general merchandise	278	273	267	264	261
Supermarkets	94	109	125	150	167
Food markets	193	177	167	153	137
Total	565	559	559	567	565

Aggregate selling area for all stores (excluding "K mart" stores) at the end of fiscal 1972 approximated 4.4 million square feet.

Coles currently employs approximately twenty-eight thousand people.

FINANCIAL STATEMENTS

The following is a summary of the capitalizations of Kresge and Coles as of the end of their latest fiscal years.

	Kresge (At January 26, 1972 United States Dollars)	Coles (At June 24, 1972 Australian Dollars)
	Audited	Unaudited
Short-term debt	$ 31,404,000	A$ 13,098,000
Long-term debt:		
Mortgage notes	$ 1,164,000	A$ 11,348,000
Debentures	—	23,000,000
Promissory notes	23,685,000	—
Convertible subordinated debentures	125,000,000	—
	149,849,000	34,348,000

	Kresge (At January 26, 1972 United States Dollars)	Coles (At June 24, 1972 Australian Dollars)
Shareholders' equity:		
Preferred stock	—	300,000
Common stock, surplus & reserves	548,469,000	112,107,000
	$698,318,000	A$146,755,000
Shares of Capital Stock:		
Preferred		
Authorized	10,000,000 shs.	150,000 shs.
Issued	—	150,000 shs.
Common		
Authorized	250,000,000 shs*	159,400,000 shs.
Issued	109,679,091 shs*	118,522,930 shs.

* Adjusted for a three-for-one stock split and an increased number of authorized shares approved by shareholders on June 21, 1972.

The following tables summarize the audited sales and income data of Kresge and Coles for the past ten years.

Kresge*									
1962	1963	1964	1965	1966	1967	1968	1969	1970	1971
(Millions, in United States Dollars)									
Sale $483	$544	$689	$851	$1,090	$1,386	$1,732	$2,185	$2,559	$3,100
Net Income 8**	11	17	23**	29	35	48	54	67	96

* Kresge's fiscal years ended in December through 1966 and thereafter in January commencing with the year ended January 31, 1968. Results of operations for the transitional one-month period ended January 31, 1967 are excluded from the foregoing table because of immateriality.
** Includes an extraordinary charge of $1,020,000 in 1962 and an extraordinary credit of $1,316,000 in 1965.

Coles is the third largest retailer in Australia by volume of sales. It competes actively with other retailers at all of its trade locations.

For the six months ended July 26, 1972, Kresge reported sales of $1,635,600,-000 and net income of $41,700,000 as compared to sales of $1,365,200,000 and net income of $36,600,000 for the corresponding six months of 1971. With respect to such comparative interim financial data, which is unaudited, the management of Kresge is of the opinion that all adjustments (consisting of normal recurring accruals) necessary to a fair statement of the results for such interim periods have been included.

	Coles*									
	1962	1963	1964	1965	1966	1967	1968	1969	1970	1971
	(Millions, in Australian Dollars)									
Sales	A$195	A$197	A$211	A$230	A$251	A$279	A$318	A$346	A$383	A$428
Net profit**	6.7	7.5	7.6	8.2	8.3	8.9	9.7	10.4	10.6	10.9

* Coles's fiscal years end in late June.
** Before extraordinary items.

For the fiscal year ended June 24, 1972, Coles reported sales of A$503,970,-
038 and net profit of A$12,321,572. The financial statements from which such
figures are derived are subject to audit, which will be distributed to shareholders
for approval at their annual meeting in October, 1972.

Kresge and Coles lease most of their properties. Minimum annual rentals
under the relevant leases aggregated approximately $120,658,000 for Kresge at
January 26, 1972 and A$6,068,000 for Coles at June 26, 1971.

Appendix Two

Australia — Financial Markets in 1972

Taking into account that it is a country with a GNP of only $28.2 billion and a population of 13 million, Australia has reasonably well-developed financial and capital markets. Particularly with the emergence of numerous merchant banks in the late 1960s, even long-term financing had become easier to obtain. In addition, the Reserve Bank had shifted away from direct controls on bank lending to monetary measures that operated more widely throughout the market. This spurred increased competition among commercial banks. Most importantly, easy access to the Euromarkets enabled subsidiaries of foreign companies to circumvent any problem with or limitation on local long-term borrowing.

This was significant because since 1965 the government had limited local borrowing by foreign-owned companies. In September 1969 these discriminatory regulations were generally revised and made more stringent.

This summary is largely based on information found in Business International Corporation, *Financing Foreign Operations*, Part III — Domestic Financing, Australia, pp. 531–47.

The guidelines in force during 1970–1972 on local borrowing, which affected companies with foreign equity participation in excess of 25 percent, applied to new borrowings of more than A$100,000 annually. The borrowing capacity of a foreign owned firm varied with (a) the percentage of local and foreign equity, (b) the length of time in country, and (c) the amount of funds sought.

Subsidiaries which were between 25 percent to 100 percent foreign-owned could borrow not only according to the above guidelines but also additional amounts based on 4:3 ratio of local equity against additional local borrowing capacity, that is, 30 percent local equity = $40 local borrowing of additional funds. Convertible bonds or notes were considered equity at a rate of 50 percent of their value.

The regulations grouped wholly owned subsidiaries into two categories. Those in the country over four years as of June 30, 1967 could borrow locally up to 10 percent of any desired increase in investment; those under four years could borrow 2.5 percent for each year on a cumulative basis up to 10 percent.

In practice there had been significant exceptions granted since the 1969 guidelines came into effect. Alcoa of Australia Ltd., 51 percent owned by Alcoa of the US, was granted permission by the Reserve Bank to borrow up to A$83.5 million to finance expansion of alumina production for export to Japan. Of this total, A$36 million was borrowed locally from a syndicate of Australian commercial banks and the Australian Resources Development Bank, which is refinancing the transaction. The remainder was obtained from foreign sources — the US Alcoa group and the Eurodollar market. (Under the guidelines Alcoa could have borrowed up to A$54 million locally.)

As of 1972 there had been no limits on borrowing from abroad. However, the Reserve Bank required financial institutions to report amounts of A$250,000 or more to identify intended uses. Eurocurrency borrowings were frequent and were facilitated by a change of policy in the taxing of interest.

Interest payments to nonresidents were subject to a 10 percent withholding tax. On May 25, 1971 this tax was waived on interest paid on funds borrowed abroad by an Australian-owned venture or for investment in an Australian-owned venture (that is, 60 percent or more locally owned). The withholding tax has also been waived on funds raised through public offerings abroad.

Foreign-owned firms especially turned to the Eurocurrency market for funds. For example, Queensland Alumina Ltd. — owned by Kaiser Aluminum and Chemical Corporation (38.5 percent), Pechiney (20 percent), and Rio Tinto Zinc Corporation (15.1 percent) — in 1972 borrowed the equivalent of A$50 million through a Deutsche mark loan for the expansion of its Gladstone bauxite refinery. Earlier, it had raised US$20 million in Eurobonds at 9 percent due in 1982.

Partnership Pacific Ltd. — and consequently a number of competing institutions — established a financial service whereby future exchange convertibility for repayment of loans from abroad was guaranteed. Fees for this service varied widely. Australian authorities never provided this guarantee, although remittances were never obstructed. In principle, all foreign exchange transactions were subject to exchange controls that were administered by the Reserve Bank on behalf of the government. Considerable discretionary powers were delegated to the commercial banks authorized to handle foreign exchange transactions. Controls appeared strict, but in practice were not a problem. Overseas capital could enter freely, but for equity investments from outside the sterling area, the authorities required payment in a currency deemed appropriate for the nonresident, for example, a U.S. resident would be required to transfer U.S. dollars in payment for the equity. Nonresidents must also have approval, which was normally given, to repatriate capital.

Residents had to obtain prior approval before borrowing foreign funds, whether from inside or outside the sterling area. Residents also were required to obtain permission to transfer capital abroad and had to report ownership of foreign securities.

All current income due to firms or individuals from investments in or loans to Australian companies, although subject to exchange controls, could be freely remitted abroad.

Suppliers of long-term funds in Australia were few. Sources included the following specialized institutions: the Commonwealth Development Bank, some finance companies, some development finance companies, the Australia Resources Development Bank (ARDB), and the Australian Industry Development Corp. However, foreign-owned firms were not generally recipients of these funds.

Long-term loans, meaning over eight years, were available from the Commonwealth Development Bank, ARDB, and the Australian Industrial Development Corp. Industrial borrowings from the Commonwealth Development Bank ranged from 6.75 to 7.25 percent. However, loans from commercial banks that were refinanced by the ARDB were most costly — 8 to 10.25 percent for ten years. Some long-term notes were also available from trading banks under overdraft arrangements when finance was sought for a specific expenditure.

Mortgage loans to corporate borrowers were almost entirely the province of the life insurance companies. Such loans competed with leaseback arrangements, which were comparatively popular in Australia. Mortgage loans ran twenty-five years or longer, costing at the time 8 to 8.75 percent. Prepayment was usually permitted without penalty.

Leaseback was introduced about fifteen years ago and by 1972 was developing rapidly. The life insurance companies were the major functionaries in this area. This method of financing had been used for metropolitan office blocks, retail stores, shopping centers, and industrial buildings. Generally, single-purpose industrial buildings were shunned.

A key factor in the leaseback of commercial properties was that risk was shifted from the life insurance company to the lessee, who became the head tenant in a block of premises. The lessee assumed the risk of vacancies and problems of administration. If the lessee was successful in attracting tenants, he found the rental collections virtually matched his lease obligations; therefore, his space cost little or nothing.

Rental costs included the following components: basic rental, which was related to current mortgage rates, ranging from 8 to 8.75 percent annually; stamp duty, which was based on the total rent paid during the period of the lease and varied from .375 to .50 cents per A$100; and amortization costs, which were from over 3 percent to under 1 percent depending on the type of property leased. Usually industrial sites were charged the higher rate and office blocks the lower.

Some leases contained provisions that permitted adjustment of rental rates on a fixed schedule, or the lessor could demand an equity kicker to participate in the earnings of the company.

Common lease lengths were fifty to sixty years for office buildings, thirty to forty-five years for shopping centers, and twenty to thirty years for industrial buildings. It was difficult to arrange shorter leases, particularly for existing industrial structures.

Options for repurchase could be negotiated, but they were not common due to tax complications. Under a straight lease the rental cost was an allowable deduction for tax purposes, but it may not have been if there was a purchase option in the contract.

Private placement of bonds with institutional investors was another source of long-term funds. There was a cost saving when compared to a public issue, but like all fixed-interest borrowings, private placements by foreign-owned firms were subject to government approval. Thus only a few foreign-owned companies had raised funds by this method.

In May 1970 Comalco Ltd., a 50–50 aluminum joint venture of Conzinc Rio Tinto, in which Rio Tinto Zinc of the U.K. has a significant holding, and Kaiser Aluminum of the U.S., raised A$31.5 million by a private placement of unsecured notes at rates ranging from 8 percent for ten-year notes to 8.5 percent for twenty-five year notes. The offer gave buyers the option to make payment in installments by the end of December 1972. Furthermore, institutions subscribing to the note issue were given the opportunity to subscribe to shares at a rate of A$100 in shares for A$500 of notes.

Private placement of equity was rather rare. In the recent past, however, two new venture capital funds had been formed. Technology Resource Development (TRD) and International Venture Corp. (IVC) could develop into sources of Australian equity financing. They were as yet untested by foreign firms, but they might have been used by a firm seeking local equity funds.

There was considerable speculative activity in the public stock and bond markets, but the primary markets were very limited sources of funds for established companies. Official figures for the year ending December 1971 revealed that companies listed on Australian stock exchanges raised A$954.5 million in fresh capital, compared to A$1 billion in the previous year. Of the 1971 total, 45 percent was in equities compared to 47 percent in 1970. The balance was in fixed-interest borrowings.

The outlook for equity financing in 1972–1973 did not appear to be particularly bright. Although ordinary share prices were high as of May 1972, trading volume was at its lowest level since 1968. This was an election year, which increased uncertainty. Additionally, the crash of Mineral Securities, a A$100 million investment company, destroyed some confidence in the market. External factors affecting the stock market included Japan's economic slowdown and the subsequent decline in purchases of Australian raw materials. This depressed the value of mineral shares.

On the other hand, some brokers were forecasting an upturn in private-sector securities due to easy money conditions and a high rate of inflation. Also, there was an obvious widening of share ownership among Australians in the past decade, especially for smaller investors, due primarily to the sales efforts of the brokers.

At the time, Australia had no overall legislation governing the issuing and trading of securities beyond the Uniform Companies Law and the Securities Industries Act. The effects of the above were limited; however, stricter legislation, brought about by the collapse of Mineral Securities, was expected. Each state had its own legislation regulating its stock exchange, with New South Wales having the most rigid code. It is worth noting that government controls did not allow the listing of foreign parent stock on Australian exchanges; however, foreign-owned companies could list their own securities.

Placement of a public issue usually took place through members of the Stock Exchange or development finance companies.

Underwriting costs began at 1.25 percent and ranged upward, depending on the firm placing the issue. Normally, older firms paid a lower percentage than newer companies. Broad distribution, which was necessary if the issue was to be listed, was accomplished through the subunderwriting services of pension funds, life offices, and smaller brokers.

Costs of advertising and of issuing the prospectus were also calculated by the issuing company to obtain a total cost of issue.

Finance companies were the most active borrowers of funds in the bond market. The variety of maturities offered ranged from three months to ten years, and rates tended to vary with the market.

A tight money policy since the spring of 1970 drove the coupon rate upward to between 8.25 percent and 9 percent on bonds of eight- to ten-year maturity.

In general, industrial borrowers had to exceed the official long-term bond rate, which was 7 percent, by at least two points.

In the past very few foreign owned firms attempted to raise funds via the issuing of equity. Comalco, owned principally by Conzinc Rio Tinto, was one of the exceptions. Comalco made a public offering of 13 million shares at A$2.75 (10 percent of total equity). A dividend yield of 1 percent to investors was offset by a strong market position, which included one of the largest bauxite deposits in the world, a refinery under construction, and substantial forward sales.

Appendix Three

U.S. Capital Control Measures

THE INTEREST EQUALIZATION TAX*

In July of 1963, the so-called Interest Equalization Tax on the acquisition of foreign securities was enacted by the United States Congress. The law provides for the imposition of a tax upon the purchase of the common stock issued by a foreign corporation, or the debt obligation of foreign obligators with a remaining life in excess of one year, by a U.S. resident from a foreign resident.

Canadian securities and those issued by public entities of recognized less-developed countries, as well as a limited amount of new securities issued by Japanese entities that carry the guarantee of the Japanese government, are exempt from the tax.

The tax rate is currently 10 percent on the value of common stocks, and the equivalent adjusted for maturity, for fixed-interest instruments. The tax rate

*Source: Tax Research Institute of America, Inc. *Tax Coordinator*, Vol. 6, pps. 124–92
Tax Research Institute of America, Inc., *Tax Coordinator*, Vol. 5, 0-9300.

may be increased up to 22.5 percent and decreased to zero by Executive Order. Rates have been adjusted several times since the tax was enacted to keep yield differentials to approximately 1 to 1½ percent above international interest rates.

Thus, the object of the legislation was not to raise revenue but rather to prevent U.S. residents from acquiring additional foreign securities. This is accomplished by making the yields of foreign securities noncompetitive with U.S. securities, or alternatively, by raising the yield cost to foreign borrowers sufficiently to make the U.S. capital market unattractive for raising funds through securities issued.

THE VOLUNTARY FOREIGN CREDIT RESTRAINT (VFCR) PROGRAM**

The VFCR Program is embodied in a set of Guidelines that were issued by the Federal Reserve Board in 1965 to limit capital outflows by banks and nonbank financial institutions. Since its inception, the program has been revised and amended several times, the last major revision dating from November 1971.

The key feature of the program is that it puts a ceiling on increases of each bank's and nonbank financial institution's foreign claims. Originally, the ceilings were set for each bank at 105 percent of the amount of foreign assets outstanding at the end of 1964. As of November 1971, the Guidelines permit each bank the option to compute a new ceiling as the highest of (a) 85 percent of its General Ceiling as of September 30, 1971; (b) its General Ceiling less any export credits thereunder on September 30, 1971; or (c) 2 percent of its total assets at the end of 1970. Export credits were generally exempted from any ceilings; so are claims on Canadian borrowers since 1968.

Loans to the residents of the developed countries of continental Western Europe, however, have been made subject to special constraints on the grounds that these countries have particularly strong balance-of-payments positions and relatively well-developed capital markets.

Guidelines applicable to the nonbank financial institutions such as insurance companies, pension funds, and the trust departments of commercial banks are similar to those for banks, although the range of categories of foreign assets under the VFCR Program is somewhat narrower than that for the commercial banks.

Agencies and branches of foreign banks in the United States had been asked previously to act in accordance with the spirit of the VFCR Program, although they were never directly subject to the tight control that is exercised by the Federal Reserve Banks over U.S.-based institutions.

**Source: Brimmer, Andrew F. "Commercial Bank Lending Abroad and the U.S. Balance of Payments." Address before a Symposium on the International Monetary System in Transition, Sponsored by the Federal Reserve Bank of Chicago, March 16, 1972. Federal Reserve Board, *Bulletin,* January 1971, pps. 9–20.

FOREIGN DIRECT INVESTMENT
REGULATIONS (FDIR)*

(OFDI Restrictions)

In January 1968, mandatory restrictions were imposed on foreign direct investment by U.S.-based corporations. The regulations are issued and administered by the Office of Foreign Direct Investment, a unit of the U.S. Department of Commerce, on the basis of an Executive Order by the President.

The regulations were preceded by a program of voluntary guidelines dating from 1965 whereby a limited number of U.S. corporations with substantial overseas business were asked to improve their individual contributions to U.S. balance-of-payments performance. This was to be achieved by whatever means the company chose: increasing exports, reducing the level of direct investment activities in developed countries, increased foreign financing, and the like. In addition, the firms were requested to reduce their short-term investments held abroad. Thus there were certain precedents to the FDIR provisions.

The 1968 mandatory program, in principle, severely limits the amount of additional direct investment that U.S.-based investors can make in their affiliated foreign enterprises through net transfer of capital and/or reinvested earnings.

The amounts of net positive direct investment, called "allowables," that each direct investor is permitted to make are limited to $2 million per year on a worldwide basis, with an additional $4 million for investment in less-developed countries only.

Alternatively, a direct investor may elect to compute his allowables as a percentage of his average annual direct investment during 1965–66. These percentages are 35 percent for so-called Schedule C countries, which comprise the developed countries of Western Europe; they are 65 percent for Schedule B countries, which include the United Kingdom, Japan, and a number of partially industrialized countries; finally, 110 percent for less-developed countries, which are included in Schedule A. Investment in Canada is exempt from the regulations.

As a third alternative, the "earnings allowable" permits a direct investor to make an annual amount of positive direct investment in each scheduled area, based upon 40 percent of its share of the previous year's earnings of its foreign affiliates in the respective scheduled area.

While some additional provisions provide some flexibility, the foreign direct investment regulations would have a crippling effect on new foreign direct investment, were it not for the provision that the proceeds of long-term foreign

---

Sources: U.S. Department of Commerce, Office of Foreign Direct Investments, *General Bulletin — Interpretative Explanation and Analysis of the Foreign Direct Investment Regulations.* U.S. Government Printing Office, Washington, D.C. 1970; U.S. Department of Commerce, Office of Foreign Direct Investment. Summary of the Foreign Direct Investment Regulations. U.S. Government Printing Office, Washington, D.C., February 11, 1971; and John L. Ellicott, "United States Controls on Foreign Direct Investment: The 1969 Program," *Law and Contemporary Problems,* Winter, 1969, pp. 47–63.

borrowing are deducted in calculating foreign direct investment, and a charge against a direct investor's "allowables" is made only upon repayment of the borrowing.

Alternatively, of course, a transfer of capital from a foreign affiliate to the parent reduces the direct investor's investment during the year in which it occurs, even if this transfer may be only temporary, that is, for the duration of the annual or quarterly reporting dates, to be revised immediately afterwards.

In addition, the regulations limit the liquid balances that a direct investor may hold abroad. Generally, the amount of such balances that a direct investor may hold at the end of each month cannot exceed the greater of US$100,000 — or the average month-end amount of liquid foreign balances held by the direct investor during 1965–66.

From an economic point of view it is clear that the Foreign Direct Investment program is concerned with the sources of financing, that is, it is directed at new outflows of funds from the United States and the use of reinvested earnings; its aim is not to curb plant and equipment expenditures per se.

It is worth noting that the affiliates of foreign enterprises in the United States are effectively exempt from the restrictions.

Gunter Dufey

Case 30

K Mart Australia
Part B

On September 6, 1972, a US $22,500,000 Eurobond issue was announced on behalf of K mart Australia. Goldman, Sachs and Co. was the lead manager of the underwriting group. The initial market reception for the issue indicated strong investor interest; the issue was double over-subscribed. Moody's Investors Service rated it "A."

The details of the offering, as put forward in the Prospectus*, are reproduced here.

*The following material is directly taken from the Prospectus. A few passages not relevant for the purpose of this case have been excluded. See *Prospectus,* K mart (Australia) Properties Finance Limited, U.S. $22,500,000 Trust Debentures, Goldman, Sachs and Co., Representatives of the Underwriters, September 6, 1972.

$22,500,000
K MART (AUSTRALIA) PROPERTIES
FINANCE LIMITED
7¾ percent trust debentures
S. S. KRESGE COMPANY
and
G. J. COLES & COY LIMITED

have unconditionally and jointly and severally guaranteed lease payments and other funds sufficient to provide for payment of principal, premium, if any, and interest on the Debentures.

All proceeds of the offering will be used to purchase or construct eight "K mart" discount department stores in Australia (the "Properties"), which will be leased to a joint venture of Kresge and Coles. All shares of the owner and lessor of the Properties will be held in trust for the benefit of the debentureholders.

On September 15, 1984, holders of the Debentures may either allow the Debentures to mature on December 15, 1984, or elect, subject to certain conditions, to extend the maturity of the Debentures to September 15, 2002. The Debentures as extended on December 15, 1984, will pay interest equal to a rate of 10.486 percent on the principal amount thereof and will be payable at maturity in an amount not to exceed the then realizable value of the Properties.

The Debentures are entitled to an annual sinking fund from 1973 through 1984 which will retire at least 17.27 percent of the issue. The Debentures may not otherwise be redeemed prior to September 15, 1984, except in the event of imposition of certain withholding taxes by the Commonwealth of Australia, Bermuda, the Cayman Islands, or the United States of America, or the imposition of certain taxes by the Commonwealth of Australia upon the lessor of the Properties.

Principal and interest on the Debentures will be paid in United States dollars without reduction for taxes imposed by the Commonwealth of Australia, Bermuda, the Cayman Islands, or the United States of America to the extent set forth herein. Interest will be payable on each September 15, commencing in 1973, in New York City, Amsterdam, Brussels, Frankfurt/Main, London, Luxembourg, Milan, and Paris.

Application has been made to list the Debentures on the Luxembourg Stock Exchange.

Offering Price 99¾ percent and Accrued Interest from September 15, 1972.

The Debentures have not been registered under the United States Securities Act of 1933 and are not being offered in, or to persons who are nationals or residents of, the United States of America or its territories or possessions, or to residents of the Commonwealth of Australia or Bermuda, or to Canadian persons.

The Debentures are offered by the several Underwriters named herein, when, as and if issued, and accepted by the Underwriters, subject to their right to reject orders in whole or in part. It is expected that delivery of the Debentures will be made at the office of First National City Bank, Citibank House, 336 Strand, London, W.C. 2, England, on or about September 21, 1972.

Goldman, Sachs & Co.
Representatives of the Underwriters
The date of this offering Circular is September 6, 1972.
No person is authorized to give any information or to make any representation not contained in this Offering Circular, and any information or representation not contained herein must not be relied upon as having been authorized by K mart (Australia) Properties Finance Limited, Kurralta Properties Pty. Limited, K mart (Australia) Limited, S. S. Kresge Company, G. J. Coles & Coy Limited or any Underwriter. Neither the delivery of this Offering Circular nor any sale made hereunder shall, under any circumstances, create any implication that there has been any change in the affairs of such corporations since the date hereof or that the information herein is correct as of any time subsequent to the date as of which such information is set forth.

This Offering Circular does not constitute an offer or solicitation by anyone in any jurisdiction in which such offer or solicitation is not authorized or to any person to whom it is unlawful to make such offer or solicitations. See "Underwriting."

TABLE OF CONTENTS

The Lease
The Lease Guaranty
The Debenture Purchase Agreement
Underwriting
Experts
Legal Opinions

In connection with this offering, the Underwriters may overallot or effect transactions which stabilize or maintain the market price of the Debentures offered hereby at levels above those which might otherwise prevail in the open market. Such transactions may be affected on any securities exchange on which any such securities are listed for trading, in the over-the-counter market or otherwise. Such stabilizing, if commenced, may be discounted at any time.

Unless otherwise indicated, currency amounts referred to herein are stated in United States dollars. Financial data with respect to G. J. Coles & Coy Limited and certain other amounts, where indicated, are stated in Australian dollars. At the official parity rate established under the Articles of Agreements of the International Monetary Fund, one Australian dollar equals 1.216 United States dollars. On September 1, 1972, the cable buying rate in New York City for freely convertible Australian dollars was US $1.194 for A$1.00.

INTRODUCTION

K mart (Australia) Properties Finance Limited (the "Company"), a Bermuda company, has been organized for the express purpose of obtaining funds to be used to purchase four "K mart" discount department stores together with their underlying land, to purchase four additional sites and to construct four new "K mart" stores on those sites (the "Properties"). All of the Properties are located in Australia and are to be leased and operated by K mart (Australia) Limited, henceforth referred to as "K mart Australia."

The Company is a wholly-owned finance subsidiary of Kurralta Properties Pty. Limited (the "Leasor") which is a company organized in the Australian Capital Territory for the express purpose of owning the Properties and leasing them to K mart Australia pursuant to a lease agreement described herein (the "Lease"). All shares of the Lessor will be held in trust (the "Stock Trust") for the benefit of the debentureholders. See "The Debentures–Debentureholders as Stock Trust Beneficiaries."

The 7¾ percent Trust Debentures offered hereby (the "Debentures") are obligations of the Company which will receive funds sufficient to make mandatory sinking fund and interest payments on the Debentures from lease payments made by K mart Australia to the Lessor. Such lease payments, in Australian dollars, are unconditionally guaranteed, jointly and severally, by Kresge and Coles (the "Guarantors"). The amount of such lease payments will be at least equal to that amount which would amortize the $22,500,000 principal of the Debentures and pay interest at the rate set forth on the cover page hereof in level annual payments over the thirty-year period to September 15, 2002. All expenses of operating and maintaining the stores will be the obligation of K mart Australia under the Lease, the performance of which is likewise guaranteed by Kresge and Coles. Prior to September 15, 1984, the Debentures may be redeemed in part only through operation of the sinking fund and in whole only in the event of imposition of withholding taxes by Australia, Bermuda, the Cayman Islands or the United States or the imposition of certain taxes by Australia upon the Lessor. See "The Debentures," "The Lease" and "The Lease Guaranty."

The Guarantors have unconditionally and jointly and severally guaranteed to provide sufficient funds, in US dollars, to redeem all the then outstanding Debentures and to assume beneficial ownership of the shares of the Lessor in the event that the debentureholders allow the Debentures to mature on December 15, 1984. However, on or before October 15, 1984 holders of not less than 50 percent of the outstanding Debentures may elect to extend the maturity date of the Debentures to September 15, 2002, provided they deposit sufficient funds with the Trustee to purchase all the Debentures held by those who do not so elect. In such event the electing debentureholders shall receive Trust Debentures (As Extended) due 2002 (the "Extended Term Debentures") in a principal amount equal to the Debentures they hold and have purchased from disapproving debentureholders.

The Memorandum of Association, By-Laws and annual audited financial statements of the Company will be available at the Luxembourg office of the paying agent. On September 13, 1972, the Company's Memorandum of Association and on September 8, 1972 legal notice required for Luxembourg Stock-Exchange listing will be published in the Memorial Journal Officiel du Grand-Duchy de Luxembourg — Recueil Special des Societés et Associations.

KURRALTA PROPERTIES PTY. LIMITED

Kurralta Properties Pty. Limited was incorporated in the Australian Capital Territory for an unlimited duration on May 16, 1972 with an authorized capital of A$20,000. Its only intended activity relates to the ownership of all the shares in the Company, the acquisition and ownership of the Properties to be financed hereby, the leasing of such Properties to K mart Australia and other activities related to this financing.

The Directors of Lessor are John C. Morgan and Keith McKenzie of the Royal Bank Trust Company (Cayman) Limited, Roger E. Davis of Kresge, and J. D. Button of the law firm, Davies, Bailey, and Carter. The Lessor maintains its registered office and main office of business at 159/173 London Circuit, Canberra City, Australian Capital Territory. Price Waterhouse & Co. are its auditors.

At the date of this Offering Circular the long-term debt and capital of the Lessor will consist of its debt to the Company equal to the amount of Debentures offered hereby and A$15,000 of share capital, comprised of 15,000 fully-paid shares, A$1 par value, owned and held under the Stock Trust.

The Memorandum and Articles of Association and annual audited financial statements of the Lessor will be available at the Luxembourg office of the paying agent.

USE OF PROCEEDS

The proceeds from the sale of the Debentures will be lent by the Company to the Lessor. Of the net proceeds, after underwriting commissions and expenses (estimated at $21,400,000), approximately $10,700,000 will be used by Lessor to purchase four existing "K mart" stores and four store development sites. The balance of the net proceeds, will be applied to the construction of four additional "K mart" stores on the sites purchased. Such balance (approximately $10,700,000), pending its use for construction purposes, will be used by K mart Australia for general corporate purposes and may be temporarily invested in short-term securities. The locations of the "K mart" stores to be purchased and constructed as well as a description of all properties leased and planned by K mart Australia are set forth under "K mart (Australia) Limited." To the extent that the balance of the proceeds is insufficient to complete construction of the additional "K mart" stores, the Guarantors have guaranteed the performance of K mart Australia in undertaking to contribute such amount as may be necessary to complete such construction. If the balance of the proceeds exceeds the completed cost of constructing the four additional "K mart" stores, such excess may be applied at the direction of K mart Australia to retire Debentures by means of optional sinking fund payments.

K MART (AUSTRALIA) LIMITED

K mart (Australia) was incorporated in the State of Victoria in Australia in 1967 as a joint venture of S.S. Kresge Company and G.J. Coles & Coy Limited. Its registered office and main office of business is 236 Bourke Street, Melbourne, Australia. The combined capital contribution of Kresge and Coles is A$4,500,000, comprised of 4,500,000 fully paid shares, A$1 par value, owned 51 percent by Kresge and 49 percent by Coles, with additional advances from Kresge as of December 31, 1971 of about A$3,210,000. K mart Australia has no long-term debt. Price Waterhouse & Co. are its auditors. Annual audited financial statements including the year ended December 31, 1971 will be available at the Luxembourg office of the paying agent.

Under a thirty-year agreement, dated January, 1968, relating to the Guarantor's ownership of K mart Australia, Coles provides management, services, and certain facilities on a year to year basis for this operation of "K mart" stores for a service fee, and Kresge provides its knowledge of self-service discount department store design and operations. K mart Australia has leased property from Coles and rents fixtures from an affiliate of Kresge.

["K mart" stores presently operated and planned are set forth in Part A, Introduction.]

All of the "K mart" stores and sites to be purchased or constructed by the Lessor with the proceeds of this offering, except the Fairfield West site, will be purchased at cost from Coles, which has been leasing stores to and carrying sites for K mart Australia on an interim basis by arrangement between Coles and Kresge. The site for the Fairfield West "K mart" was purchased by Coles in 1961 and was originally intended for use in Coles operations. Coles and Kresge subsequently determined that the site would be used for a "K mart" store, and the property will be sold by Coles to Lessor at a price, which is greater than Coles' cost, determined to compensate Coles for carrying the property since purchase, but not greater than current fair market value.

THE GUARANTORS

(For a detailed review of the guarantors' operations see Part A, Appendix Two of this case.)

Annual audited financial statements of Kresge and Coles will be available at the Luxembourg office of the paying agent. There is no material litigation pending against either Kresge or Coles.

THE DEBENTURES

The Debentures will be limited to US $22,500,000 aggregate principal amount and are to be issued by the Company under an Indenture, dated as of September 15, 1972 (the "Indenture"), between the Company and The Royal Bank of Canada Trust Company of New York, New York (the "Trustee"). Issuance of the Debentures was authorized by the board of directors of the Company on August 31, 1972. Certain of the following statements are brief summaries of particular provisions contained in the Indenture, including the Form of Debenture set forth therein. Such summaries do not purport to be complete, and reference is made to the Indenture. Copies of the Indenture will be available for inspection from the Trustee and the paying agent.

The Debentures and the Indenture will be governed by and construed in accordance with the laws of the State of New York. The Debentures will be issued as coupon bearer Debentures in $1,000 denominations only, and title will pass by delivery.

Application has been made to list the Debentures on the Luxembourg Stock Exchange.

PAYMENT OF INTEREST

The Debentures are to bear interest from September 15, 1972 at the interest rate set forth on the cover page of this Offering Circular payable annually on September 15 beginning September 15, 1973.

The Debentures and the coupons appertaining thereto may be presented for payment in United States dollars at the main offices of the First National City Bank in New York City and, subject to any applicable laws and regulations, in London (city office), Paris, Frankfurt/Main, Amsterdam, Milan, Luxembourg, and Brussels. Payment at offices outside New York City will be made by a US dollar check drawn on a bank in New York City or by a transfer to a US dollar account maintained by the payee with a bank in New York City. The Company has the right at any time to terminate the designation of any paying agent and to designate other paying agents, but will maintain an office for payment in New York City and London as long as Debentures remain outstanding and, as long as the Debentures are listed on the Luxembourg Stock Exchange, in Luxembourg. The Company will not appoint a paying agent in Australia.

EVENT OF MATURITY

The debentureholders may either allow the Debentures to mature on December 15, 1984, or elect to extend the maturity of the Debentures to September 15, 2002. As more fully set forth in the Form of Debentures and the Form of September 15, 1984 Coupon, the coupon bearing the interest payment date of September 15, 1984 provides that a holder may vote for extension if he deposits with the Trustee an amount equal to the principal amount of his Debenture to which such coupon is affixed plus interest thereon from September 15 to December 15. If no vote or deposit is made by October 15, 1984, the holder of the Debenture will be deemed to have voted not to extend.

The election to extend the maturity of the Debentures requires approval by holders of not less than 50 percent in the aggregate principal amount of the then outstanding Debentures. On December 15, 1984, in the event extension is approved, the deposit with the Trustee will be applied to purchase all the Debentures of the disapproving debentureholders at a price equal to 100 percent of their principal amount plus accrued interest from September 15, 1984 and the Debentures so purchased together with any excess funds on deposit (and interest thereon) will be allocated by the Trustee on a pro rata basis to each approving debentureholder. On December 15, 1984 such approving debentureholder will then receive at the office of the paying agent Extended Term Debentures in an amount equal to the sum of the principal amount of the debentureholders. The Extended Term Debentures, as extended, will be subject to certain provisions and terms as described herein under "The Extended Term Debentures."

The Company and the Guarantors have agreed to endeavor to effect any registration with any governmental authority under any Federal or State law of the United States that may be required before the Extended Term Debentures may be lawfully distributed.

In the event that less than 50 percent in aggregate principal amount of the outstanding Debentures are voted in favor of the maturity extension, on December 15, 1984 the funds deposited by approving debentureholders will be returned (together with interest thereon) and all outstanding Debentures may be presented to the Trustee or paying agent for payment. In accordance with the Debenture Purchase Agreement, Kresge and Coles are jointly and severally and unconditionally obligated to purchase in United States dollars all Debentures then outstanding at a price equal to 100 percent of their principal amount plus accrued interest from September 15, 1984.

On August 10, 1972, the Reserve Bank of Australia authorized the borrowing by Lessor from the Company of the principal amount of $22,500,000 and has approved Coles entering into the Debenture Purchase Agreement. All payments by the Lessor to the Company, including payments utilized to pay the principal of, premium, if any, and interest on the Debentures, and any payment by Coles under the purchase commitment will require further Reserve Bank authorization which cannot be obtained in advance. The current Australian exchange control policy is to approve applications for such authorizations to the extent required to make payments on authorized external borrowings.

In case any Event of Default occurs prior to December 15, 1984 as a result of the imposition of foreign exchange control restrictions by Australia on payments of principal, premium, if any, or interest by the Lessor to the Company, Kresge and Coles shall, at the option of the debentureholders, purchase all the Debentures then outstanding in United States dollars at 100 percent of their principal amount together with accrued interest thereon to the date of purchase if such restrictions continue for a period of 365 days from the date of their imposition by Australia.

DEBENTUREHOLDERS AS STOCK TRUST BENEFICIARIES

In accordance with the terms and provisions of the Kurralta Properties Stock Trust, a trust created under the laws of the Cayman Islands (the "Stock Trust"), the holders of the Debentures at any particular time are designated the sole and exclusive beneficiaries of the Stock Trust and, accordingly, are the owners of the entire beneficial interest in the corpus of the Stock Trust consisting of all the issued shares of the Lessor, the owner of the properties. An undivided beneficial interest in the shares of the Lessor held in the Stock Trust is transferable only upon the transfer of a Debenture of the Company. The Stock Trust provides that, so long as the Debentures are outstanding in the hands of the debentureholders, the trustee thereof, Royal Bank Trust Company (Cayman) Limited (the "Stock Trustee"), shall not sell the shares of the Lessor or permit them to become encumbered. The Stock Trustee shall vote the shares held in the Stock Trust on behalf and in the interest of the debentureholders so as to give effect to the terms of the Indenture, but shall not vote such shares so as to cause the sale of any of the Properties during the term of the Debentures except in the case of condemnation or casualty or of optional redemption prior to maturity as set forth below. The debentureholders' undivided beneficial interest in the Stock Trust shall terminate if Kresge and Coles purchase the debentures (i) on December 15, 1984 unless the debentureholders shall elect to extend the debentures, or (ii) in the event of redemption of the Debentures in whole.

At least thirty days prior to September 15, 1984 and each year thereafter if the Debentures are extended, the Stock Trustee shall make available to the debentureholders the number of Properties then under lease and such other information with respect to the Properties and the Lease as in its sole judgment the Stock Trustee believes may be useful to the debenture-holders.

REDEMPTION

THE SINKING FUND — The Debentures will be subject to redemption through operation of a sinking fund on September 15, 1973 and on each September 15 thereafter to and including September 15, 1984, at a price equal to 100 percent of their principal amount. The amounts of the sinking fund payments have been determined in accordance with the principal amortization schedule (rounded to the nearest $1,000) of a $22,500,000 loan to be retired by September 15, 2002 on the basis of level debt service payments at the interest rate of the Debentures. Such amounts follow:

September 15	Principal Amount of Debentures	September 15	Principal Amount of Debentures
1973	$207,000	1979	$325,000
1974	224,000	1980	351,000
1975	242,000	1981	378,000
1976	260,000	1982	407,000
1977	280,000	1983	438,000
1978	302,000	1984	473,000

The sinking fund will retire a total of at least 17.27 percent of the Debentures. In addition, if the proceeds to Lessor from the sale of the Debentures exceed the costs required to purchase and construct the Properties, or funds are received by K mart Australia as a result of the condemnation or casualty of any of the Properties under the Lease, K mart Australia may cause the Company to make an optional sinking fund payment in any year at a price equal to 100 percent of principal amount in an amount not to exceed the amount of the mandatory sinking fund payment for such a year. The right to make such optional sinking fund payments is not cumulative, and any such payment may not be substituted for future mandatory sinking fund payments.

K mart Australia will be further entitled, at its option, to direct that any sinking fund payment may be satisfied by crediting Debentures acquired otherwise than through a sinking fund payment at their principal amounts. Amounts representing the difference between the purchase price thereof and the principal amount shall be applied to reduce rental payments.

CONDEMNATION AND DESTRUCTION OF PROPERTIES   — If during the term of the Debentures, the lease with respect to any of the Properties is terminated due to destruction or condemnation of such property, K mart Australia shall continue to pay to Lessor annual amounts equivalent to the rent applicable to such property. Such payments will continue to and until September 15, 1984, the final interest and sinking fund payment date on the Debentures, at which time an amount equal to the gross cost of the property condemned or destroyed, reduced as set forth under "The Lease—Abandonment, Condemnation and Destruction," will be payable by K mart Australia to Lessor to be applied on September 15, 1984 to redeem Debentures at 100 percent of their principal amount. K mart Australia shall have the option to apply any such amounts prior to September 15, 1984 to optional sinking fund payments as specified above.

OPTIONAL REDEMPTION   — If (i) direct or indirect taxes, assessments, or other governmental charges are imposed by Australia on Lessor, its property, or its income (other than those direct taxes, assessments, or other governmental charges imposed on the same basis and at the same rate on other Australian real estate leasing companies wholly owned, directly or indirectly, by residents of Australia or on the property of such companies) and such taxes, assessments, or other governmental charges would require K mart Australia to make additional rental payments under the Lease in any fiscal year ending September 15 in excess of one percent of the principal amount of the Debentures outstanding, (ii) taxes, assessments, or other governmental charges are imposed through withholding or deduction by Australia on the payment of principal, premium, if any, or interest by the Lessor to the Company, or (iii) the Company is required to make additional payments of interest in the circumstances described under "Taxation," and such taxes, assessments or other governmental charges, and/or additional payments of interest result from any change in, or amendment to the laws or treaties of Bermuda, the Cayman Islands, the Commonwealth of Australia, or the United States of America or any political subdivision or taxing authority of any thereof or therein affecting taxation, or any change in the official application or judicial interpretation becomes effective on or after the delivery date of the Debentures, then in such event K mart Australia shall have the right to purchase all the Properties at a price sufficient to redeem the Debentures, and the Company shall, if K mart Australia exercises such right, use the proceeds therefrom to redeem the Debentures forthwith, in whole, but not in part, upon not less than thirty days notice to the debentureholders, at a price equal to the principal amount thereof plus a premium (expressed as a percentage of the principal amount) determined as follows: If redeemed during the twelve-month period beginning after September 15 in each of the following years:

Year	Redemption Premium	Year	Redemption Premium
1972	1%	1976	1/25%
1973	7/8%	1977	3/8%
1974	3/4%	1978	1/4%
1975	5/8%	1979	1/8%

and thereafter without premium, together in each case with accrued interest, if any, to the date fixed for redemption. Whether such additional rental payments from K mart Australia would be required shall be determined by K mart Australia on the basis of the evidence which shall be in the possession of K mart Australia and on the basis of the laws and treaties in effect on the date of such determination or (if K mart Australia so elects) those to become effective on or before the next succeeding rental payment date.

TAXATION

The Company will pay as additional interest such additional amounts as may be necessary so that the net payment of the principal of and premium, if any, and interest on a Debenture to a holder thereof or of any coupon appertaining thereto who, as to Bermuda, Australia, the Cayman Islands, and the United States (including, for the purposes hereof, the United States of America, its territories, its possessions and all areas subject to its jurisdiction) is a nonresident alien individual, a nonresident alien fiduciary of a foreign estate or trust, or a foreign corporation, after withholding or deduction from such payment for any tax, assessment or governmental charge imposed by withholding or deduction with respect to such payment to such holder will not be less than the amount provided in such Debenture or in such coupon to be due and payable; provided, however, that the foregoing shall not apply to any tax, assessment, or governmental charges which —

(A) is imposed by reason of one or more of the following: (i) such holder (or a settlor or beneficiary of, or a person holding a power over, or interest in an estate or trust administered by a fiduciary holder or a shareholder considered as controlling a corporate holder) being considered as having engaged in a trade or business or having had a permanent establishment, or having been physically present, in Bermuda, the Cayman Islands, Australia, or the United States, (ii) such holder's status as a personal holding company with respect to the United States, (iii) any other relationship or former relationship between such holder (or a settlor or beneficiary of, or a person holding a power over, of interest in an estate or trust administered by a fiduciary holder or a shareholder considered as controlling a corporate holder) and Bermuda, the Cayman Islands, Australia, or the United States (including, without limitation, such person's status as a citizen, former citizen, domiciliary, former domiciliary, resident, or former resident thereof); (iv) such holder is a corporation incorporated outside Bermuda, the Cayman Islands, and Australia, and either has its central management and control in, or is controlled by shareholders who are residents of any of said jurisdictions; or

(B) is an estate, inheritance, gift, transfer or personal property tax similar thereto; or

(C) would not have been so imposed but for the presentation of any debenture or coupon by such holder for payment on a date more than ten days after such payment becomes due or is provided for, whichever is later.

The Company shall not be required to make any payment with respect to or on account of any tax, assessment, or other governmental charge which (i) is not specifically provided in the preceding paragraph, (ii) is payable otherwise than by withholding or deduction from payments of principal of and premium, if any, and interest on the Debenture, or (iii) is imposed by any government other than Bermuda, the Cayman Islands, Australia, or the United States or any political subdivision or taxing authority thereof or therein.

INTEREST EQUALIZATION TAX

United States persons (as defined in the Interest Equalization Tax Act, including persons who elect to be treated as such) will be required to report and pay interest equalization tax imposed by the United States with respect to acquisition of the Debentures from the Company or other non–United States persons, except where a specific statutory exemption is available. The Company makes no representations as to the availability of any such statutory exemption.

APPLICATION OF LEASE RENTALS

It is contemplated that amounts equivalent to the annual rental payments made with respect to the Properties and certain other amounts specified in the Lease will be deposited to the account of the Trustee or the paying agent by K mart Australia in an amount sufficient to pay interest and to make sinking fund payments pursuant to letters of direction from the Company to the Lessor and from the Lessor to K mart Australia.

COVENANTS OF LESSOR

So long as any Debentures are outstanding, the Lessor may not sell, lease, convey, mortgage, or encumber the Properties, except as provided in the Indenture and the Lease.

So long as any of the Debentures are outstanding, the Stock Trustee will enforce all rights of the Lessor under the Lease for the benefit of the holders of the Debentures.

EVENTS OF DEFAULT

The Indenture provides that the following constitute Events of Default: (i) Default in the payment of principal of or premium, if any, on any of the Debentures; (ii) default for a period of thirty days in the payment of interest on any of the Debentures; (iii) default in the deposit of any sinking fund payment with respect to the Debentures; (iv) any event constituting an Event of Default under the Lease, and (v) default after thirty days notice (which may be extended, in certain circumstances by the Trustee) in the performance of any other covenant in the Debentures or in the Indenture.

In case an Event of Default shall have occurred and be continuing, the Trustee or the holders of not less than 25 percent of the aggregate principal amount of the Debentures then outstanding may declare the principal of all the Debentures to be due and payable immediately, but upon certain conditions such declaration may be annulled and past defaults may be waived by the holders of a majority in aggregate principal amount of the Debentures then outstanding. If such Event of Default occurs as a result of the imposition of foreign exchange control restrictions by Australia and such restrictions have continued for a consecutive period of at least 365 days or as a result of certain defaults under the Lease including bankruptcy of or default of any material obligation by either Kresge or Coles, the Trustee or the holders of not less than 25 percent of the aggregate principal amount of Debentures then outstanding may require the Guarantors to purchase all Debentures then outstanding in United States dollars pursuant to the Debenture Purchase Agreement.

MODIFICATION OF THE INDENTURE

The Indenture contains provisions permitting the company and the Trustee, with the consent of the Guarantors and the holders of not less than 50 percent in principal amount of the Debentures at the time outstanding, to modify the Indenture or any supplemental indenture or the rights of the holders thereof; provided, that no such modification shall, except as otherwise provided therein, (i) extend the fixed maturity of any Debenture or reduce the principal amount thereof, or reduce the rate or extend the time of payment of interest thereon, or reduce any premium upon the redemption thereof, or make the principal thereof or premium, if any, or interest thereon payable in any coin or currency other than as provided therein without the consent of the holder of each Debenture so affected, (ii) have the effect of modifying or affecting in any manner adverse to the holders of the Debentures the obligations of K mart Australia under the Lease to make rental payments in respect of the due and punctual payment of the principal of premium, if any, and interest on the Debentures or the sinking fund payments without the consent of the holder so affected, (iii) separate the ownership of the Debentures from the beneficial interest of the holders thereof in the Stock Trust prior to the date that the Debentures are redeemed or cancelled, (iv) reduce the aforesaid percentages of Debentures, the consent of the holders of which is required for any such supplemental indenture, without the consent of the holders of each Debenture so affected, or (v) provide that principal and interest moneys be payable otherwise than to the bearer of the Debenture.

A meeting of debentureholders may be called at any time by the Trustee, the Company, or holders of at least 10 percent of the outstanding Debentures for purposes specified in the Indenture.

NOTICES

Notices to debentureholders will be given by publication in a newspaper in New York City and London and, so long as the Debentures or Extended Term Debentures are listed on the Luxembourg Stock Exchange, in Luxembourg. It is expected that such publication will appear in the London *Financial Times*.

THE EXTENDED TERM DEBENTURES

The Extended Term Debentures will be dated September 15, 1972 and will be issued under the Indenture. They will be limited to $18,613,000 aggregate principal amount, and will be held by the Trustee until December 15, 1984 at which time they will be substituted for the Debentures if holders of not less than 50 percent of the Debentures elect to extend the Debenture maturity. The terms and provisions of the Extended Term Debentures shall be the same as those of the Debentures except as set forth in the Indenture, and the Lease and the Stock Trust shall continue to apply to the Extended Term Debentures. The following statements are brief summaries of certain of those provisions of the Indenture, including the form of Extended Term Debenture set forth therein. Such summaries do not purport to be complete. Copies of the Indenture will be available from the Trustee and the paying agent.

It is expected that prior to December 15, 1984 application will be made with a recognized exchange for listing the Extended Term Debentures.

PAYMENT OF PRINCIPAL AND INTEREST

The Extended Term Debentures shall bear interest from September 15, 1984, payable annually on each September 15 beginning September 15, 1985. The amount of such interest will equal 10.486 percent annual yield on the principal amount of the Extended Term Debentures outstanding as of December 15, 1984, and such amount will be reduced thereafter in the event of partial *pro rata* redemption of the Extended Term Debentures as set forth below.

There will be no mandatory sinking fund established with respect to the Extended Term Debentures. The principal amount of the Extended Term Debentures will become due and payable on September 15, 2002, and payment of the principal amount will be effected through a sale of the Properties for cash at their realizable value. K mart Australia shall have a right of first refusal to purchase the Properties. The proceeds from such sale, after payment of all commissions, taxes, if any, and other related expenses, shall be applied to redeem the Extended Term Debentures. In the event the net proceeds from the sale of the Properties exceeds the principal amount of the Extended Term Debentures outstanding at maturity, the excess, if any, shall be distributed by the Lessor to the Stock Trustee as a dividend or liquidating distribution for the benefit of the debentureholders. In the event the net proceeds from the sale of the Properties are less than the aggregate principal amount of the outstanding Extended Term Debentures, such proceeds shall be applied *pro rata* to redeem and cancel all Extended Term Debentures.

K mart Australia shall have the option to extend the term of its lease on the Properties for five years from September 15, 2002. The Properties will be sold at the maturity of the Extended Term Debentures subject to the lease, if extended.

REDEMPTION

The holders of not less than 50 percent of the Extended Term Debentures may elect to have all the Extended Term Debentures redeemed on September 15, 1994, which election must be made in accordance with instructions printed on the interest coupon due on September 15, 1993 and at the time such coupon is presented for payment. All the Extended Term Debentures shall be redeemed on the next interest payment date following the abandonment, condemnation, or destruction of *all* the Properties or at any time in the event of the termination of the Lease by K mart Australia as a result of the imposition of those taxes which permit redemption of the Debentures. The amount paid to holders of the Extended Term Debentures upon any such redemption shall be the then net realizable value of the Properties, but shall not be less than the Minimum Redemption Price (defined in the Lease as the "Formula Purchase Price"). The Minimum Redemption Price is computed on the basis of the principal amortization schedule of a thirty-year level debt payment, 7¾ percent loan dated September 15, 1972 in an amount equal to the Debentures originally issued less any subsequent partial redemptions of the Debentures or Extended Term Debentures (other than mandatory sinking fund payments.)

Each of the Extended Term Debentures shall be redeemed in part on a *pro rata* basis prior to maturity, effective as of the next interest payment date, in the event that the Lease is terminated with respect to *less* than all of the Properties because of abandonment, condemnation or destruction of any such Properties. The aggregate amount paid to holders upon such event shall be the net realizable value of any such Properties, but shall not be less than the Minimum Redemption Price multiplied by a fraction, the numerator of which is the cost of such Properties abandoned, condemned, or destroyed, and the denominator of which is the cost of all the Properties. The amount of interest payable on the Extended Term Debentures after any such partial redemption shall be reduced proportionately by the same fraction. The cost of the Properties shall be the initial gross cost thereof to the Lessor ("Formula Price" in the Lease) less any subsequent partial redemptions (other than mandatory sinking fund payments).

If the amount paid upon any partial or total redemption of the Extended Term Debentures with respect to any property or Properties sold exceeds the cost of such property or Properties, less any prior partial redemptions (including sinking fund payments), the excess shall be distributed *pro rata* to the Extended Term debentureholders as beneficiaries of the Stock Trust.

Beginning September 15, 1985 and on September 15 of each year thereafter, the Trustee shall publish the Minimum Redemption Price and the interest payable on September 15 of the following year with respect to each $1,000 principal amount of Extended Term Debentures as adjusted for any partial redemptions.

EXTENDED TERM DEBENTUREHOLDERS AS STOCK TRUST BENEFICIARIES

The Stock Trust provides that the Stock Trustee shall not cause the sale of the Properties unless the Extended Term Debentures are redeemed in the circumstances described above under "Redemption." In all events, and without being instructed to do so by the Extended Term debentureholders, the Trustee is required to cause the sale of the Properties (directly or by sale of the shares of the Lessor) at maturity in 2002.

TAXATION

The discussion under the caption "Taxation" and "Interest Equalization Tax" applies equally to the Extended Term Debentures.

THE LEASE

The Lease, entered into as of September 15, 1972 between Lessor and K mart Australia, consists of a master lease agreement and individual leases applicable to each of the Properties. Certain of the statements made below are brief summaries of particular provisions contained in the Lease. Copies of the Lease will be available from the Trustee and the paying agent.

NET LEASE

The Lease is a "net lease" under which K mart Australia will pay all expenses incurred in connection with the Properties, including without limitation all costs of insurance, operation, repair, maintenance, rebuilding and any other charges related to use and occupancy of the Properties; the cost of operation of the Lessor and the Company; all obligations, claims, liens, and levies against the Properties; all direct and indirect taxes, duties, assessments, and other governmental charges levied against the Properties, the Lessor, and the Company (except for certain taxes and assessments levied in connection with a sale of the Properties); and all fees of trustees and paying agents.

TERMS AND RENTALS

The Lease will become effective as of the date of the delivery of the Debentures as set forth on the cover page of this Offering Circular and the leasehold estate created thereby shall then begin and, subject to the provisions for earlier termination contained in the Lease, will expire on September 15, 2002, unless K mart Australia exercises its option to renew the Lease for an additional period of five years.

K mart Australia agrees to pay all expenses and to pay as rent for the Properties at least one business day prior to each annual interest payment date (commencing with September 14, 1973) amounts which in the aggregate will equal the interest on the outstanding Debentures or Extended Term Debentures, as the case may be, and the mandatory sinking fund payments on the Debentures. If at any interest date the amount deposited with the Trustee or paying agent under the Indenture is insufficient to make such required payments of principal and interest, K mart Australia shall be required to pay such deficiency as additional rent to the Lessor.

The obligations of K mart Australia to make the payments required under the Lease, and to perform and observe the other agreements on its part contained in the Lease (which obligations constitute general obligations of K mart Australia) are absolute and unconditional and shall not be subject to diminution by set-off, counterclaim, abatement, recoupment, or otherwise.

INSURANCE AND MAINTENANCE

K mart Australia is required to keep the Properties insured during the term of the Lease at their replacement value to the extent obtainable. If such insurance is not obtainable, the Properties will be self insured by K mart Australia at fair market value. K mart Australia is also required to carry insurance covering public liability in amounts of not less than A$250,000.

K mart Australia agrees to maintain the Properties in good repair and operating condition and to make all necessary repairs and replacements.

ABANDONMENT, CONDEMNATION, AND DESTRUCTION

If, during the respective terms of either the Debentures or the Extended Term Debentures (i) the Properties (or any part thereof) are damaged by fire or casualty or (ii) title to, or the temporary use of, the Properties (or any part thereof) is taken under the exercise of the power of eminent domain, then in either of such events, the Lease may be terminated with respect to the property damaged or condemned. If the Lease is not terminated K mart Australia shall continue to be obligated to pay the rental and other payments due under the Lease.

During the term of the Debentures, K mart Australia may not terminate the Lease with respect to any of the Properties if it has become uneconomic and unsuitable for K mart Australia's continued use and occupancy. During the term of the Extended Term Debentures, however, K mart Australia may elect to terminate a lease if any property has become uneconomic and unsuitable for K mart Australia's purposes.

In the event K mart Australia elects to terminate the Lease with respect to any of the Properties in the circumstances described in the preceding paragraphs, the Lessor shall have the right, for six months, either to require K mart Australia to purchase the property, or to sell the property to a third person subject to K mart Australia's right of first refusal.

During the term of the Debentures the purchase price to be paid for the property will be the greater of (i) its then realizable value or (ii) an amount equal to the gross cost of the property to Lessor reduced by certain amounts specified in the Lease including that portion of mandatory sinking fund payments allocable to such property ("Formula Purchase Price" under the Lease). The proceeds from a sale of the property will be lent by the Lessor to K mart Australia and the terms of such loan will provide that annual debt service payments, including interest and principal, will be an amount equal to the rent previously payable with respect to the property sold. That portion of such loan equal to (ii), as reduced by annual payments of principal, will become due and payable on September 14, 1984 but may be reduced or retired prior to such date to the extent K mart Australia exercises its option to cause Lessor to make optional sinking fund payments. If the proceeds of such sale exceed an amount equal to (ii), the excess shall be repaid to Lessor for distribution on September 15, 1985 to the Extended Term debentureholders, as beneficiaries of the Stock Trust, if the maturity date of the Debentures has been extended.

During the term of the Extended Term Debentures, the proceeds from the sale of the property shall be applied by Lessor to effect a *pro rata* partial redemption of each Extended Term Debenture in the amount and manner described under "The Extended Term Debentures — Redemption."

If any of the Properties are damaged and K mart Australia elects not to terminate the lease, K mart Australia shall at its expense, repair, rebuild or restore the property damages to substantially the same condition as existed prior to the event causing such damage. K mart Australia shall be reimbursed for its expenses, to the extent available, from insurance proceeds.

Similarly, in the event any of the Properties are condemned and K mart Australia elects not to terminate a lease, K mart Australia shall, at its expense, repair, rebuild, or restore the property as nearly as possible to its prior condition or acquire other improvements suitable for K mart Australia's operations on or adjacent to the property, or portion thereof, condemned. K mart Australia shall be reimbursed for its expenses, to the extent funds are available therefrom, from any condemnation award.

SUBLETTING OF PROPERTIES

K mart Australia may sublet or license the properties, but such subletting or licensing will not operate to relieve K mart Australia of its primary liability under the Lease.

DEFAULTS

The Lease provides that the happening of one or more of the following events will constitute an "Event of Default":

(1) Failure of K mart Australia to pay any sums when due under the Lease;

(2) Failure of K mart Australia for a period of thirty days to observe and perform any other of its covenants, conditions, or agreements under the Lease;

(3) Certain events of bankruptcy, dissolution, liquidation, or reorganization in bankruptcy by K mart Australia or the Guarantors; or

(4) Default by either of the Guarantors under any indenture, mortgage or similar agreement which default substantially impairs their obligation under the Guaranty.

MODIFICATIONS AND AMENDMENTS

No amendment to the provisions of the Lease is permissible without the consent of the Trustee and the Guarantors. Pursuant to the provisions of the Indenture the consent of the holders of not less than 50 percent of the principal amount of all Debentures or Extended Term Debentures then outstanding is also required, except for amendments, changes, or modifications (i) required by the provisions of the Lease and the Indenture, (ii) in connection with the curing of ambiguities or formal defects or omissions, (iii) further describing and identifying the Properties, or (iv) which in the judgment of the Trustee do not prejudice the Trustee or the debentureholders.

THE LEASE GUARANTY

Certain of the following statements are brief summaries of particular provisions contained in the Lease Guaranty, dated as of September 15, 1972 by Kresge and Coles in favor of Lessor. Copies of the Lease Guaranty will be available from the Trustee and the paying agent. The Lease Guaranty was authorized by the directors of Kresge and Coles on August 22, 1972 and September 5, 1972, respectively.

Kresge and Coles jointly and severally and unconditionally guaranty the full and prompt payment in Australian dollars in Australia when due and at all times thereafter of each and all the rents and other sums to be paid by K mart Australia to the Lessor under the terms of the Lease and the full and prompt performance and observance by K mart Australia of each and all of the covenants and agreements required to be performed and observed by K mart Australia under the terms of the Lease. The Guaranty shall be a continuing, absolute, and unconditional guaranty and shall remain in full force and effect until K mart Australia shall have fully and satisfactorily discharged all of its obligations to the Lessor under the Lease.

THE DEBENTURE PURCHASE AGREEMENT

Certain of the following statements are brief summaries of particular provisions contained in the Debenture Purchase Agreement, dated as of September 15, 1972, between Coles, Kresge, the Company and the Trustee. Copies of such agreement will be available from the Trustee and the paying agent.

Kresge and Coles are obligated, jointly and severally and unconditionally, to purchase from the Company in United States dollars all the Debentures outstanding at a price equal to 100 percent of their principal amount plus accrued interest, (i) on December 15, 1984, if the maturity date of Debentures is not extended to September 15, 2002; (ii) at any time if the Trustee or debentureholders have declared the principal amount of the Debentures to be due and payable because of any default in the payment of principal, premium, if any, or interest by the Company resulting from the imposition by the Commonwealth of Australia of restrictions which remain in effect for a continuous period of at least 365 days and which have the effect of preventing the lawful conversion of Australian dollars into United States dollars or the lawful remittance outside of Australia of such converted Australian dollars; or (iii) at any time in certain other events including bankruptcy of or default of any material obligation by either Kresge or Coles.

There is no obligation on the part of Kresge and Coles to purchase the Extended Term Debentures.

In the event of the imposition of those taxes which permit the redemption of the Debentures or Extended Term Debentures, Kresge and Coles may at their option purchase all the outstanding Debentures or Extended Term Debentures by providing funds to the Trustee in an amount equal to the amount required for distribution to the debentureholders upon such redemption.

UNDERWRITING

Subject to the terms and conditions set forth in the Underwriting Agreement, the Company has agreed to sell to each of the Underwriters named below, and the Underwriters, for whom Goldman, Sachs & Co. are acting as representatives, have severally agreed to purchase, at a price of 99¾ percent and accrued interest from September 15, 1972, an aggregate of $22,-500,000 principal amount of Debentures:

GOLDMAN, SACHS & CO.

Bahamas

Cisapline Overseas Limited

Gutzwiller, Kurz, Bungener Securities Limited

Credit Suisse (Bahamas) Limited

Swiss Bank Corporation (Overseas) Limited

Belgium

Banque de Bruxelles S.A.
Continental Bank S.A.

Kredietbank N.V.
Societe Generale de Banque S.A.

Bermuda

Union Bank of Switzerland (underwriters) Limited

Denmark

Privatbanken i Kjobenhavn

France

Banco di Roma (France)

Banque de Paris et des Pays-Bas

Banque National De Paris

Banque de Suez et de l'Union des Mines

Banque de Neuflize, Schlumberger, Mallet

Morgan & Cie International S.A.

Germany

Commerzbank Aktiengesell-
chaft
Deutsche Bank Aktienge-
sellchaft
Deutsche Girozentrale-
Deutsche Kommunalbank

C. G. Trinkaus & Burk-
hardt
Vereinsbank in Hamburg

Kuwait

Kuwait Investment Co.
S.A.K.

The Netherlands

Amsterdam-Rotterdam
Bank N.V.

Sweden

Skandinaviska Enskilda
Banken

United Kingdom

Banque Belge Limited

Cazenove & Co.
Kleinwort, Benson Limited

Manufacturers Hanover
Limited

N.M. Rothschild & Sons
Limited
Joseph Sebag & Co.
S.G. Warburg & Co. Lim-
ited
White, Weld & Co. Limited

United States

Baer Securities Corporation

The Daiwa Securities Co.
America, Inc.

Lehman Brothers Incor-
porated
Merrill Lynch, Pierce, Fen-
ner & Smith Securities Underwriter Ltd.

Under the terms and conditions of the Underwriting Agreement, the Underwriters are committed to take and to pay for all of the Debentures offered hereby, if any are taken. The Company will pay to the Underwriters at the time of delivery of the Debentures a commission equal to 2½ percent of the aggregate principal amount of the Debentures and an amount not to exceed $50,000 to reimburse the Underwriters for certain expenses. The Guarantors have agreed to indemnify the Underwriters and certain other persons against certain liabilities.

Subject to the provisions described in the following paragraphs, the Underwriters propose to offer Debentures in part directly to retail purchasers at the initial public offering price set forth on the cover page of this Offering Circular, and in part to certain dealers at such price less a concession of 1½ percent of the principal amount, and any Underwriter may offer Debentures to certain brokers or dealers who are either a parent or a subsidiary of such Underwriter at not less than such price to dealers. The Underwriters may allow, and such dealers or brokers may reallow, a discount not in excess of ½ percent of the principal amount to certain dealers. After the Debentures are released for sale to the public, the offering price and other selling terms may from time to time be varied by the representatives.

Each Underwriter has agreed that it will not offer or sell Debentures in the United States of America, its territories or its possessions, in Australia or to nationals or residents thereof, except in transactions with other Underwriters and certain dealers. Each dealer will agree not to offer or sell Debentures in the United States of America, its territories or its possessions, in Australia or to nationals or residents thereof.

Each Underwriter has also agreed that it will not directly or indirectly sell any Debentures to Canadian persons except for (i) sales to Underwriters or securities dealers who are such persons but who agree that they are purchasing Debentures as principals for resale to persons who are not Canadian persons and (ii) sales to agents or fiduciaries who are Canadian persons but who are acting for the benefit of persons who are not Canadian persons. For the purpose of this paragraph, a "Canadian person" includes an individual who is a resident of Canada, a corporation or other entity (other than a bank) organized under the laws of Canada, or any political subdivision thereof, and any branch or office within Canada of any of the following: any bank or trust company organized under the banking laws of Canada or any province thereof, or any private bank or banker subject to supervision and examination under the banking laws of Canada or any province thereof.

Each Underwriter has also agreed, and each dealer will agree, that it will not directly or indirectly sell any Debentures to residents of Bermuda (including corporations organized under the laws thereof) who do not have a specific permit to purchase such Debentures or external account status under the Bermuda foreign exchange control regulations.

The Company will pay a fee of $112,500 to Goldman, Sachs International Corporation as compensation for services rendered in the development and preparation of the financing contemplated hereby.

EXPERTS

The audited financial statements included in this Offering Circular have been examined by Price Waterhouse & Co., independent certified public accountants and chartered accountants of Kresge and Coles, respectively, as indicated in their reports with respect thereto, and are included in this Offering Circular in reliance upon their opinions and on their authority as experts in accounting and auditing matters in the United States of America and Australia, respectively.

LEGAL OPINIONS

Legal matters in connection with the offering described herein will be passed upon for Kresge by Dickinson, Wright, McKean & Cudlip, Detroit, Michigan; for K mart Australia and for Coles by Moule, Hamilton & Derham, Melbourne, Australia; for the Lessor by Davies, Bailey & Cater, Canberra City, Australia; and for the Underwriters by Baker & McKenzie, Chicago, Illinois. All such counsel shall rely, with respect to Bermuda law, upon the opinion of Conyers, Dill & Pearman, Hamilton, Bermuda, and with respect to other matters of local law, upon the opinions of other counsel resident in the relevant jurisdictions.

Ian H. Giddy

Case 31

ECUs for Intel

You have been invited to a meeting with Arvind Sodhani, Assistant Treasurer (International) of Intel, to present and discuss ideas with Intel's Treasurer, Harold Hughes, on the possible use of the European currency unit as a financing vehicle.

Intel has already experimented with foreign currency borrowing and hedging techniques to match its international exposure. Headquartered in Santa Clara, California, the firm has manufacturing facilities located in Swindon, England, in Manila, the Philippines, in Penang, Malaysia, in Singapore, and in Tsukuba, Japan, as well as in a number of locations in the West Indies and the United States. Its international sales, about 29 percent of 1984's total sales of $1.6 billion, are concentrated in Western Europe and Japan. Although Intel is known by many as the producer of the "brains" of the IBM PC, it also supplies semiconductor integrated circuits used in other computers and in communications, industrial automation, military and other electronic equipment, and even computer systems.

Intel has foreign exchange problems in a number of areas: it has foreign assets in the manufacturing operations mentioned above, sales subsidiaries in all the major industrial countries, and millions of dollars of sales revenues monthly. For example, the U.S. plants, including that in Puerto Rico, produce substantially all the semiconductors sold in West Germany. These are first sold to the U.K. subsidiary at very low prices for resale to the German subsidiary at near-market prices. Intel also borrows heavily in the countries in which it does business, for working capital purposes. In January 1985 Intel was one of the first U.S. companies to tap the yen Euro-bond market. Its seven-year, 12.5 billion yen issue bore a coupon of 6⅝ percent and was lead managed by Citicorp's Capital Markets Group. Apart from this bond and working capital borrowings, Intel had no foreign currency debt. During the first three months of 1985, $12 million of the bonds were repurchased. In May 1985 the company issued a $215 million zero coupon bond with warrants that were valid for ten years. The latter bore a strike price of $40 at a time when the company's shares were trading at about $30. The funds raised from the full exercise of the warrants would be sufficient to cover the balloon payment of the bonds in 1995. The units consisting of notes plus warrants were priced at 43.55 percent, providing an effective interest rate of 8.5 percent.

Intel recognizes that it has economic exposures that are not strictly quantifiable. These "intangible" exposures, according to Sodhani, cannot be handled with traditional forex hedging tools: "Suppose you have a major market share in Germany, and you intend to be there for a number of years. You are going to sell your products and earn Deutsche marks. You don't know the size of that exposure, so you can do very little about it. If you do something, it will have a P&L impact that won't be offset."

Longer-term price, cost of sales, and competitive exposures — Sodhani's "intangible" subcategories — are closely related. To illustrate this, Sodhani elaborated on his description of Intel's position in Germany. "We compete with the Japanese in the German market, selling products manufactured in the United States. That gives us a cost exposure vis-a-vis our Japanese competitors. They have a yen cost of sales, and we have a dollar cost of sales. If the yen and Deutsche mark move in such a way that we become totally noncompetitive in the market, we have a massive exposure." Even if the Deutsche mark/dollar rate were to remain stable over the next ten years, Intel would still suffer if the yen devalued against the Deutsche mark.

One solution to the problem lies in pricing. To remain competitive, Intel needs the flexibility to adjust its prices. This requires a strategic decision, not just a forex management decision. "Treasury has a considerable input into this decision-making process, but it isn't made entirely on a currency basis;" Sodhani explained. "On the other hand, currency considerations are intrinsic to the strategic decision-making process."

In the German example, if the yen/Deutsche mark rate moved against Intel, the firm might consider manufacturing its products in Japan for export to Germany in order to achieve cost-of-sales parity with its strongest competitors. But many other factors enter into the sourcing decision. For instance, language barriers, time zone differences, and high Japanese tax rates might make manufacturing in Japan impractical. In that case, Intel would have to look at other ways to maintain its competitive edge, such as instituting more efficient production techniques to reduce the dollar cost of sales or launching marketing campaigns to justify selling its product at a premium. In the end, if all else failed, Intel might simply be forced to trim its margins.

More information about Intel can be found in the attached Appendixes.

Your focus for the meeting will be on financing to meet Intel's domestic expansion plans and to deal with the firm's foreign exchange problems. Arvind has noted that one issue is the volatility of the company's sales abroad (and at home!). The semiconductor business is one in which big orders, placed well in advance, can be cancelled if the prices of chips drop. Conversely, when demand is strong and prices pick up, the industry is well known for its tendency to renege on commitments. When demand outstrips production, an "allocation" system is instituted. Intel is regarded in the industry as being a fair allocator, even to competitors of its foster parent, IBM.

Sodhani and Hughes want you to discuss the pros and cons of an ECU issue, denominated in the European community's basket of currencies. (For more details on ECU bonds see the Appendix.) The alternatives under consideration are:

a ECU bond issue at 8.56 percent;
a Euro DM bond issue at 7.70 percent;
a Eurodollar bond issue at 10.50 percent;
a three currency (equal weight of dollars, Deutsche marks, and yen) at 8.28 percent; or
a Samurai bond at 6.75 percent

Study Questions

What are the advantages and disadvantages of the ECU bond, from the point of view of Intel and from the investors' viewpoint? What about the alternatives? What would you recommend?

Appendix One

The Semiconductor Industry

The semiconductor industry is experiencing hard times. Since July of 1984, new orders have fallen by some 30 percent. Employment in Santa Clara County, which includes Silicon Valley and hence a high concentration of electronics firms, fell at an annual rate of 3.6 percent between May and July. This contrasts with average annual employment growth of just under four percent through the first half of the decade. In addition, August's 6.0 percent unemployment rate in Santa Clara County was much higher than the 4.3 percent rate that prevailed last December.

Another indicator of hard times in the semiconductor industry is the "book-to-bill" ratio which compares the value of new orders with the value of products shipped. A book-to-bill ratio of 1.1 is required to maintain the industry's average annual 20 percent increase in nominal sales. The ratio has not been above 1.0 since August 1984; it was stagnant at 0.72 from May through July of this year, and rose only to 0.74 in August. While the industry has always

Source: Federal Reserve Bank of San Francisco, *Weekly Letter,* October 18, 1985.

followed a boom–bust cycle, the severity and persistence of the current problems are causing some to question the long-run viability of the U.S. semiconductor industry.

Despite its problems, the semiconductor industry continues to show signs of vitality. Even in Santa Clara County, for example, employment in July remained 1.4 percent above its level at the same time last year, and the August unemployment rate of 6.0 percent was well below the national rate of 7.0 percent. Indeed, there are several reasons to expect that the current downturn is a short-run rather than long-run problem. This *Letter* argues that the U.S. semiconductor industry is likely to resume its long-run growth trend. However, the direction in which change seems to be headed suggests that, in the future, domestic jobs in the semiconductor industry will consist almost entirely of positions requiring highly sophisticated technical skills.

LONG-RUN TRENDS

Historically, the semiconductor industry has grown rapidly. New uses for semiconductors and innovations that have reduced the cost of making them have combined to produce average annual growth of 20 percent in nominal sales.

As the chart shows, orders of electronic components (which include but are not limited to semiconductors) have until recently grown more rapidly than orders of other manufactured products. This increase in volume has been accompanied by profound changes in the industry. The most obvious change has been technological. As chips have become more powerful and cheaper to produce, their uses have become more varied, prices have fallen, and sales have risen. The increased variety of products has, in turn, led to greater specialization in production. For example, Japanese producers now dominate the market for 64K and 256K memory chips, while U.S. producers dominate the market for custom chips and those with telecommunications and military applications.

In addition, the industry is becoming more international. More and more, U.S. producers are establishing factories overseas to reduce labor costs and improve access to foreign markets. At the same time, Japanese firms, concerned about possible U.S. retaliatory trade measures, are establishing production facilities in the U.S. Thus, firms and production facilities are increasingly dispersed throughout the world. Moreover, firm headquarters and production facilities are more likely than ever to be located in different countries.

SOURCES OF CURRENT WEAKNESS

The stage for the current downturn was being set in 1983 when 60 percent growth in the number of personal computers sold left semiconductor producers unable to supply enough chips. Existing U.S. producers responded by investing in plant and equipment to expand their capacity to produce. Meanwhile, overseas producers, particularly from Japan, took advantage of the shortfall in U.S.

production capacity by expanding their U.S. market share. Japanese producers, by dominating the memory chip market, expanded their share of the total U.S. market by three percentage points in 1984, to 16 percent.

Shortly after the industry developed the ability to meet chip demand, the fastest growing component of demand, the personal computer market weakened. There are two main explanations for this slowdown. First, some analysts argue that business users of personal computers are learning how to operate the systems they have before making additional purchases. Although limited uses for *home* computers may prevent that segment of the personal computer market from recovering its previous strength, only a fraction of personal computers — most likely less than 20 percent of sales — are sold for household use. The alternative explanation emphasizes the slowdown in the national economy, which has reduced business investments across the board. By either explanation, the current slowdown is but a temporary deviation from a long-run growth trend and not a secular slowdown.

Even a short-term slowdown can have enormous consequences. Estimates of the 1985 change in the number of personal computers sold range from a decrease of more than 30 percent to an increase of 30 percent. However, even 30 percent growth would present hardship for some firms since some capital investments were based on euphoric projections (made in 1983) of 100 percent annual sales growth.

The consequences for semiconductor manufacturers have been swift and severe. In the middle of 1984, semiconductor orders began falling until, by the end of 1984, chip inventories had built up to as much as $1.5 billion. Enormous price reductions and, ultimately, production slowdowns and losses followed. To the extent that the problem is simply excess inventory accumulation, the current downturn is no different from previous boom–bust cycles in the electronics and semiconductor industries.

However, several other factors have exacerbated what probably would have been a relatively severe bust anyway. In particular, the fast pace of technological innovation, which is the backbone of the industry, ironically compromises the industry's ability to adapt to changing market forces. Costs are especially difficult to cut because research and development as well as capital expenditures must continue to receive priority even during a downturn if firms are to emerge strong in a future upswing. Moreover, increasingly specialized technological innovations limit producers' abilities to switch from the production of one kind of chip to another as demand changes.

Another factor hurting the U.S. industry is Japan's growing prominence as a major competitor. The most recent boom provided an opportunity for Japanese firms to reap the benefits of their heavy investments in producing low-cost chips. By making certain products at lower cost than their American counterparts, the Japanese have forced U.S. firms to establish smaller market niches, reduce costs, or both. The high value of the dollar exacerbates the threat posed by low-cost Japanese firms. As in other U.S. industries that compete with foreign producers, the high value of the dollar makes U.S. products more expensive than foreign products and therefore hurts sales of products made in the U.S.

THE OUTLOOK

The outlook for the U.S. semiconductor industry depends on several factors. The most important are growth in product demand and competitive position relative to other producers. Competitive position in turn depends on technological innovation, costs relative to those of other producers, and the extent and character of market segmentation.

Semiconductor demand will continue to grow as long as the technological innovation that expands uses and reduces costs continues to stimulate increased demand. Household items such as television sets and military uses such as surveillance would be greatly improved by the expanded capacity of smaller chips. Factories could be monitored by robots that can see, and the ability of machines to recognize voices could make offices more efficient. Although the pace of expansion will eventually slow as new uses are exhausted, most agree that the potential for further growth remains substantial.

Manufacturing Orders, 1980–1985

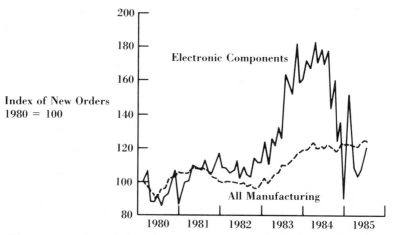

The pattern of specialization in the industry has actually cushioned U.S. producers somewhat from the current downswing. Since personal computers are a major source of demand for the memory chips in which Japanese producers hold a 70 to 90 percent market share, Japanese firms that export chips to the U.S. were far more devastated than U.S. producers when personal computer demand slowed. One analyst, who in late July anticipated a 20 percent reduction in total U.S. semiconductor sales for 1985, expected a decrease of 65 percent in the sales of memory chips. By concentrating on custom chips and other products with more stable demand, U.S. producers can continue to insulate themselves from the more excessive ups and downs of the industry.

Traditionally, U.S. firms have enjoyed technological superiority over their foreign rivals. Their greater innovativeness is generally attributed to the relatively unstructured environment at many U.S. firms. This environment is claimed to foster creativity while the American cultural and economic system encourages risk-taking. Furthermore, venture capital, which is more readily available in the U.S. than elsewhere, facilitates innovative research and risky investment projects. If this pattern continues, U.S. producers should be able to retain their technological advantage in innovative and custom chips.

Intel Corporation Second Quarter Report

LETTER TO SHAREHOLDERS

Market demand for semiconductor devices remains depressed. Intel's new orders in the quarter again fell well below current shipping levels and prices continued to deteriorate. No real signs of recovery are yet visible. The softness extends quite generally across the computer-related industry reflecting lower market growth than had been expected earlier. It is taking longer than we originally anticipated for the industry's excesses to be corrected. As discussed below, we are taking several actions to assure that Intel is in the strongest possible position when the correction runs its course and growth resumes.

Quarterly revenue dropped to $360 million, 12% below the equivalent period last year and down 4% from the immediately preceding quarter. Earnings dropped to $.08 per share, down 83% from a year ago, and we experienced an operating pretax loss of $8 million. Consistent with reduced expectations for 1985 results, the provision for income tax taken in the first quarter was reversed in Q2.

For the first six months net income was $20 million or $.17 per share, down 81% from the prior year's first half.

The difficult business environment caused us to take a number of actions in June. We announced plans to lay off about 950 people, we said U.S. employees would take seven days off without pay in the third quarter, and we postponed merit increases for all employees.

We also announced plans to close our oldest and smallest wafer fabrication plant, located in Santa Clara, California, by the end of this year. It is no longer large enough to be cost-effective. Fewer than 100 of the plant's employees will eventually be part of the 950 laid off in June; most will be switched to other Intel plants in Santa Clara. Expenses associated with the layoff and plant closing are included in second quarter results.

Along with others, we supported the Semiconductor Industry Association's filing with the Federal Government charging unfair trade practices by Japanese manufacturers. America's share of the Japanese semiconductor market has been a virtually constant 10% over the past 15 years. Meanwhile we have watched Japanese manufacturers carve out an 18% share of our free market. The time has come to stop predatory action in our market and to achieve a meaningful opening of the Japanese semiconductor market to U.S. companies.

Appendix Three

Intel Corporation Second Quarter Report
Consolidated Earnings Financial Statements

Income	Three months ended June 29 1985	Three months ended June 30 1984	Six months ended June 29 1985	Six months ended June 30 1984
Net Revenues	**$360,046**	**$410,087**	**$ 735,295**	**$ 781,657**
Cost of sales	240,977	204,089	488,920	390,131
Research & development	49,623	44,271	98,365	86,527
Marketing, general & administrative	77,042	79,692	150,376	149,535
	367,642	328,052	737,661	626,193
Operating income (loss)	**(7,596)**	**82,035**	**(2,366)**	**155,464**
Interest and other	12,203	10,654	22,437	22,441
Income before income taxes	**4,607**	**92,689**	**20,071**	**177,905**
Income taxes	(4,640)	38,003	—	72,941
Net income	**$ 9,247**	**$ 54,686**	**$ 20,071**	**$ 104,964**
Earnings per share	**$ .08**	**$ .47**	**$ .17**	**$ .90**
Capital shares & equivalents	117,540	116,616	117,525	116,597

Balance Sheet	At June 29	At June 30
	1985	1984
Current Assets		
Cash and short-term investments	$ 325,596	$ 304,019
Accounts receivable	323,032	346,511
Inventories	192,191	209,551
Prepaid taxes and other assets	135,659	107,378
Total current assets	**976,478**	**967,459**
Property, plant, and equipment, net	**840,789**	**613,144**
Long-term investments	**291,411**	**223,621**
Other assets	**22,774**	**30,244**
Total assets	**$2,131,452**	**$1,834,468**
Current Liabilities		
Short-term debt	$ 60,878	$ 41,870
Accounts payable and accrued liabilities	157,387	203,971
Deferred income on shipments to distributors	68,187	81,344
Income taxes payable	—	7,624
Total current liabilities	**286,452**	**334,809**
Long-term debt	**263,528**	**133,768**
Deferred taxes on income	**153,997**	**119,348**
Shareholders' equity		
Capital stock	730,818	663,182
Retained earnings	696,657	583,361
Total shareholders' equity	**1,427,475**	**1,246,543**
Total liabilities and shareholders' equity	**$2,131,452**	**$1,834,468**

Price range of capital stock, Intel's Capital Stock, without par value, is traded on the NASDAQ/National Market System under the symbol INTC. The following table sets forth the closing prices on the NASDAQ/National Market System for the Capital Stock for the quarters indicated. The prices in the table are adjusted to reflect a 2-for-1 stock split effected June 30, 1983.

Calendar Year	High	Low
1983:		
First quarter	$24.13	$18.69
Second quarter	37.94	21.81
Third quarter	45.13	36.13
Fourth quarter	43.38	35.38
1984:		
First quarter	$42.88	$31.50
Second quarter	37.75	28.50
Third quarter	37.25	26.25
Fourth quarter	31.50	25.25
1985:		
First quarter	$32.00	$24.50
Second quarter (through May 10, 1985)	29.25	25.50

On May 10, 1985, the closing price of the Capital Stock on the NASDAQ/National Market System was $28.25.

Dividend Policy

Intel has never declared or paid cash dividends and has no present plans to do so.

Capitalization of Intel, The unaudited consolidated capitalization of Intel at March 30, 1985, and as adjusted to give effect to the offering made hereby (assuming no exercise of the Underwriters' over-allowment option), is set forth below:

	Outstanding	As adjusted
	(thousands)	
Long-term debt:		
8% Industrial Revenue Bonds due 2013(1)	$ 80,000	$ 80,000
7.95% Industrial Revenue Bonds due 2013(1)	30,000	30,000
6⅜% Yen Guaranteed Bonds due 1992(2)	37,124	37,124
Zero Coupon Notes due May 15, 1995(3)	—	68,746
Other	37,658	37,658
Total long-term debt	184,782	253,528

	Outstanding	As adjusted
	(thousands)	
Shareholders' equity:		
Capital Stock, without par value:		
200,000,000 shares authorized;		
114,660,584 shares issued and outstanding	700,076	700,076
Warrants to purchase 5,375,000 shares of Capital Stock	—	24,886
Retained earnings	687,410	687,410
Total shareholders' equity	1,387,486	1,412,372
Total capitalization	$1,572,268	$1,665,900

(1) Adjustable and redeemable (at the option of either Intel or the bondholder) every five years beginning 1988 through 2008.

(2) Based on an exchange rate of ¥255.9 = $1.00.

(3) Represents the principal amount of the Notes at maturity, less the original issue discount (estimated to be $680.25 for each $1,000 principal amount of Notes at maturity), of which $115.75 is attributable to the value of the Warrants included in the Units.

DESCRIPTION OF THE ECU

INTRODUCTION

The ECU is a composite currency, consisting of specified amounts of currencies of each of the ten Member States of the EEC. Although the ECU's primary role initially related to the European Monetary System (the "EMS") and the operations of the EEC institutions, commercial use of the ECU by other governmental bodies and private entities has developed rapidly over the past several years. Because the ECU is a composite currency, its exchange rate tends to be more stable than those of its component currencies, since changes in the latter may offset each other in the ECU exchange rate. Interest rates on ECU denominated debt have tended to reflect the weighted average interest rates of borrowing in each of the component currencies.

The ECU Within the European Banking System. Although there is no central bank which issues ECU bank notes, the ECU is increasingly recognized in the international financial markets as a freely convertible foreign currency. To facilitate the growth of the ECU for private commercial transactions, certain European banks have established a clearing mechanism for the ECU, thus enabling the transfer of ECU without necessarily having to make separate transactions in each of the component currencies. Banks are also able to cover open ECU positions by undertaking transactions in the component currencies.

Many financial institutions, primarily in the Benelux countries, Britain, France, Denmark and Italy, make both spot and forward markets in the ECU against the U.S. dollar and other currencies. These exchange rates are published in most European daily financial publications and through several news services.

There is also an ECU market for overnight investments and investments with maturities of up to one year.

The Use of the ECU for Denominating International Debt Issues. The first ECU denominated debt issue was underwritten early in 1981. The ECU is now a significant currency for denominating international debt issues in the Eurobond markets. At October 31, 1984, there were at least 5.7 billion principal amount of outstanding public ECU denominated securities issued in the Eurobond markets. In addition, a substantial amount of ECU denominated securities have been placed privately.

The following table sets forth the statistical compilations of the Commission of the European Communities (the "Commission") of the number and aggregate principal amount (in millions of ECU) of public ECU bond issues in the Eurobond markets for each of the calendar years 1981 through 1983 and for the ten months ended October 31, 1984:

	1981	1982	1983	Oct. 31, 1984
ECU borrowings by the European Communities, their institutions and public and private issuers in the Member States	150	572	1,330	1,522
ECU borrowings by public and private issuers in non-Member States, the World Bank and others	40	150	605	1,294
Total	190	722	1,935	2,816
Number of issues	5	17	33	53

Such compilations of public debt issues show that during the first ten months of 1984 the ECU has been the third most utilized currency for issuance of bonds on the Eurobond markets (after the U.S. dollar and the German mark), as determined by amount of the indebtedness raised.

There is a well developed secondary market for ECU denominated public issues in Europe, and most issues trade on a daily basis in the Eurobond market.

The Use of the ECU for Other Commercial Transactions. The ECU is increasingly used for pricing, invoicing and settling commercial transactions within the EEC and with other European countries.

DEFINITION AND COMPOSITION

Following the Resolution of December 5, 1978, of the Council of the European Communities (the "Council"), concerning the establishment of the EMS and the rôle of the ECU in the EMS, the ECU was defined by the Council Regulation of December 18, 1978, as the sum of specified amounts of the currencies of the Member States. The ECU's composition, and thus its value, were identical to those of the European Unit of Account ("EUA"), which had been used in the EEC's accounts since 1975. Following adoption of the ECU in the EMS framework, the ECU replaced the EUA in all EEC uses, effective January 1, 1981.

Since 1978, the specified amounts of the currencies that make up the ECU have only been changed once in September 1984 when, following the reexamination required every five years, the Council changed the composition of the ECU and incorporated the Greek drachma as required by the treaty of accession of Greece to the EEC and the other European communities. In addition to the inclusion of the Greek drachma, the principal revisions were to decrease the amounts of German marks and Dutch guilders included in the ECU and to increase the amounts of Italian lire and French francs. These changes were made mainly to bring the weights of the component currencies in line with underlying economic criteria and had the effect of compensating for the appreciation of the German mark and the Dutch guilder and the depreciation of the French franc and the Italian lira over the previous five-year period. As a result, since September 17, 1984, the ECU is defined by Council Regulation as the sum of the following amounts of the currencies of the Member States:

0.719	German marks	3.71	Belgian francs
0.0878	United Kingdom pounds	0.14	Luxembourg francs
1.31	French francs	0.219	Danish kroner
140.00	Italian lire	0.00871	Irish pounds
0.256	Dutch guilders	1.15	Greek drachmas

It is important to differentiate between the composition of the ECU as legally defined, which is fixed and subject to change only under strict conditions, and the exchange rate of the ECU, which can vary on a day-to-day basis. As discussed below, and as is the case with most other currencies, the exchange rate of the ECU fluctuates against each component currency as well as non-component currencies.

CIRCUMSTANCES IN WHICH THE COMPOSITION OF THE ECU MAY CHANGE

The 1978 Council Resolution requires that the relative weights (at then prevailing exchange rates, see table, p. 286) of the component currencies of the ECU be examined every five years and, if necessary, the specified amounts of the component currencies be revised. This resulted in the September 1984 revision. In addition, any Member State may request a reexamination if the weight of a currency in the ECU has changed by at least 25% since the previous revision.

In either event, a revision can occur only by unanimous decision of the Council. Any revision is to be made in line with underlying economic criteria. While the 1978 Council Resolution does not specify the economic criteria to be

	March 13, 1979	December 31,					October 31, 1984
		1979	1980	1981	1982	1983	
German mark	32.9%	33.2%	32.3%	33.9%	36.0%	36.7%	32.3%
French franc	19.9	19.9	19.4	18.5	17.6	16.7	19.2
United Kingdom pound	13.4	13.7	16.1	15.6	14.7	15.5	14.5
Italian lira	9.5	9.4	8.9	8.4	8.2	7.9	10.1
Dutch guilder	10.5	10.4	10.2	10.7	11.3	11.3	10.2
Belgian franc	9.2	9.1	8.9	8.8	8.1	7.9	8.2
Luxembourg franc	0.4	0.4	0.3	0.3	0.3	0.3	0.3
Danish krone	3.1	2.8	2.8	2.7	2.7	2.7	2.7
Irish pound	1.1	1.1	1.1	1.1	1.1	1.0	1.2
Greek drachma	—	—	—	—	—	—	1.3
	100.0%	100.0%	100.0%	100.0%	100.0%	100.0%	100.0%

considered, the principal criteria used in the September 1984 revision were the relative gross domestic products of and trade among the Member States. In making the revision, the Council also took into account the need to ensure the continued smooth functioning of the ECU markets.

The 1978 Council Resolution requires that any revision not, in and of itself, modify the exchange rate of the ECU. That is accomplished by choosing a set of specified amounts of the component currencies which ensures that, on the day of calculation, the exchange rate of the ECU under its revised composition is identical to its exchange rate under the superseded composition. For example, the exchange rate of the ECU against the U.S. dollar as of the day of calculation for the September 1984 revision remained at 1 ECU = \$0.742589 under both the revised and the superseded compositions. Because of the revised composition, however, the exchange rate will differ over time from what it would have been under the superseded composition.

While changes in exchange rates of the currencies of the Member States, including revaluations and devaluations, do not affect the fixed composition of the ECU, the exchange rate of the ECU in subsequent trading may change because of the increased or reduced exchange rates of its components.

The opposite table sets forth the relative weights of the component currencies in the ECU, based on the prevailing exchange rates on March 13, 1979 (when the EMS became operative), at each subsequent year-end and at October 31, 1984 (reflecting the revision of the ECU implemented on September 17, 1984). The weight of a currency in the ECU is the ratio in percentage terms between the specified amount of that currency in the ECU and the value of the ECU in terms of that currency. The weights fluctuate as the relevant currency strengthens or weakens on the foreign exchange markets.

It is expected that in the event of the entry of Spain and Portugal into the European Communities, the currencies of those two countries will at some date be included in the ECU.

FUNCTIONS OF THE ECU WITHIN THE EMS

The ECU plays a central role in the functioning of the EMS, which aims to foster close monetary cooperation among the Member States with the intention of making the EEC a zone of monetary stability. The EMS provides for an exchange rate mechanism based on taking appropriate actions to limit exchange rate fluctuations among currencies of the participating Member States within a narrow range around their parity rates. In this context, the ECU is used as a reference point for the calculation of these parities, as a denominator for the claims and liabilities among the participating central banks and as a reserve and settlement instrument created against gold and dollar deposits by those banks. All Member States except the United Kingdom and Greece participate in the EMS stabilization mechanism. The mechanism established under the EMS is limited to stabilization of exchange rates of the currencies of the participating Member States and does not provide for stabilization of those currencies against any other currencies.

EXCHANGE RATE OF THE ECU

Since the ECU is composed of specified amounts of Member State currencies, a value for the ECU can be determined at any time by using the current market rate of each component. For example, the value of the ECU in terms of the Dutch guilder may be calculated by adding to the specified amount of the Dutch guilder in the ECU the amounts of all the other components after having converted them into the Dutch guilder at market rates. A similar procedure is followed to determine the ECU's value in terms of noncomponent currencies.

The Commission calculates daily ECU exchange rates for official use in terms of most of the world's major currencies, including the U.S. dollar, based on the rates in effect at 2:30 p.m., Brussels time, on the exchange markets of the component currencies. These rates are published daily in the Official Journal of the European Communities. They are used for internal purposes of the European Communities and are not necessarily rates at which commercial transactions in ECU can be effected.

The following table sets forth, for the periods and dates indicated, certain information concerning the exchange rate of the ECU in terms of the U.S. dollar, determined by the Commission as described above, for the period from March 13 to December 31, 1979, for the calendar years 1980, 1981, 1982 and 1983 and for the period from January 1 to October 31, 1984.

	At end of period	Average rate[1]	High	Low
1979	$1.43839	$1.37442	$1.44443	$1.31113
1980	1.30963	1.39233	1.45302	1.26638
1981	1.08517	1.11645	1.33166	0.97759
1982	0.96767	0.97972	1.09601	0.90589
1983	0.82737	0.89022	0.98310	0.81333
1984 (through October 31)	0.73574	0.79933	0.87944	0.70976

[1] The average of the exchange rates on each trading day during the period.

III

Hedging and Positioning in International Markets for Financial Assets

H. Lee Remmers

Case 32

Newport Systems Inc.
(*A*)

When George Brown entered his office on Friday October 18, 1985, his secretary handed him a cable indicating acceptance of his firm's offer to supply Helmut Zinn, a West German distributor, with approximately US$535,000 of radios and related equipment for the remote opening of gates and garages in industrial plants and parking lots. The cable also indicated that Zinn would wire the requested deposit of DM150,000 directly to Newport Systems' California bank that same day.

Brown, president and majority owner of Newport Systems, hoped the German export order would mark the beginning of a return to a more satisfactory level of profits. The firm's generally poor results were caused by a

© H. L. Remmers, October 1985. The author wishes to acknowledge the contributions of Mark Eaker and David Eiteman.

recession in the building industry and a lack of marketing effort to find new customers.

Newport Systems was formed in the mid-1960s to manufacture radio-activated controls for opening residential garage doors. California's boom in residential construction and the increase in suburban single family residences with two-car garages created the potential, and the level of affluence of new home buyers in the 1960s and 1970s created a willingness to spend about $500 to be able to open a garage door without having to get out of the car. Sales rose rapidly and profits were more than adequate. By 1980, however, new housing construction tapered off. Newport's high quality meant that the replacement market was virtually zero, and sales began to slip.

Brown realized as early as 1978 that the suburban residential market would not regain its former strength, and he turned to development of an industrial version of his basic mechanism. The industrial model was for use by delivery trucks and other vehicles entering or leaving warehouse loading docks or storage compounds where security was important. An approaching or departing truck would notify plant security by radio of a desire to pass through the gate, but final control of the gate remained with plant security. Security could either activate the gates to open automatically on radio request, a common procedure during busy daylight hours; or they could control the actual gate themselves, opening it after verification by inspection that the vehicle and driver were indeed authorized to enter or leave. The industrial model proved particularly useful in inner-city areas where crime was a problem.

Sales of the industrial model were good at first, but the failure of the construction industry to come out of its relative slump caused sales volumes to remain flat while costs continued to rise. In 1985, Newport suffered a net loss. Financial statements for the years ending 30 September 1984 and 1985 appear in Exhibits 1 and 2.

To use idle capacity, Brown decided in 1984 to try to develop an export market. Although a few foreign sales had been made, they had not been the result of any deliberate sales effort. After discussion with the Department of Commerce International Marketing Center representatives in Los Angeles, Brown contacted Helmut Zinn, an industrial electronics distributor in Hamburg. In May 1985, Brown flew to Germany to meet Zinn and explore further the export potential of the industrial model. Zinn indicated an interest in becoming the German distributor if costs were reasonable and suggested Brown prepare a firm offer.

On 17 July 1985, Brown offered to sell Zinn a shipment of the industrial model gate-openers for DM1,550,000. The offer requested the following payment schedule:

DM 150,000   as cash down payment at the time the offer was accepted by Zinn;

DM 625,000   to be paid three months after the offer was accepted, by which time the first half of the order would have been shipped.

DM 775,000   to be paid six months after the offer was accepted, by which time the remainder of the order should have been shipped.

The offer specified payment in Deutsche marks, which from his earlier meetings with Zinn Brown believed was an important selling point. Shipment would be by airfreight. In the event that Newport was unable to ship within the three- and six-month periods specified in the contract, payment would be made on the first working day following shipment.

Exhibit 1 *Newport Systems Inc. (A) Income statements, years ending 30 September*

	(unaudited) 1985	1984
Sales revenues	3,626,500	3,546,660
Cost of goods sold[1]	2,116,250	2,079,190
Gross profit	1,510,250	1,467,470
Selling & administrative expenses	1,506,130	1,455,200
Earnings before interest & taxes	4,120	12,270
Interest income	980	1,020
Interest expense	19,950	16,185
Other income[2]	12,675	14,640
Earnings before taxes	(2,175)	11,745
Corporate income taxes	—	3,525
Earnings after taxes	(2,175)	8,220

[1]Opening inventory	712,650	658,100
Purchases	1,215,650	1,119,400
Closing inventory	876,800	712,650
Cost of materials	1,051,500	1,064,890
Direct labor	495,150	479,210
Factory overhead	569,600	535,090
Cost of goods sold	2,116,250	2,079,190

[2]Mainly sales of redundant assets

Brown had been impressed by Zinn; this was later confirmed by Newport's bank, which reported that Zinn's credit rating was considered excellent. For this reason, Brown decided not to request any credit guaranty arrangements beyond the downpayment.

The price of DM1,550,000 was arrived at by first pricing the order in dollars and then multiplying this by the spot exchange rate on 15 July — DM2.90 per dollar.

The offer price was computed as follows:

Raw materials and components	229,500
Direct labor	90,400
Factory overhead	100,000
Shipping	18,000
Administrative overheads	48,000
Total cost	485,900
Target profit margin	48,600
Dollar price of bid	534,500
Deutsche mark/dollar rate	× 2.90
Deutsche mark price (rounded off)	1,550,000

Costs were estimated on the assumption that those incurred in manufacturing for export would run approximately the same as for existing business.

As soon as Brown read Zinn's cable accepting the offer, he began to think about foreign exchange risk. Since July when the offer had been made, the dollar had tended to weaken against most major currencies, although the movement had been erratic (see Exhibit 3). Following the meeting in New York on 22 September, where the major central banks agreed to a concerted effort to intervene in the markets, the dollar had dropped abruptly — over 7 percent against the Deutsche mark and 12 percent against the yen. Picking up Friday's edition of the *Wall Street Journal,* Brown noted that Deutsche marks were quoted at 2.6450 the previous day in New York. A quick calculation showed him that the order was worth $586,000, some $50,000 more than when the bid was made. Needless to say, he was elated, and it set him wondering if he was in the right business since this gain amounted to more than the cumulative earnings of the company over the past three years!

Nevertheless, Brown decided to consult his banker to ask her advice about whether or not the future receipts of Deutsche marks should be covered. She suggested three courses of action:

1. Do nothing. After all, she pointed out, the rates could fall back to DM2.90 to the dollar before he would begin to lose.
2. Cover in the forward exchange market.
3. Cover in the money markets.

The three alternatives involved the following:

1. *Do nothing.* This would mean waiting until the sales proceeds were received in January and April and selling the Deutsche marks for dollars at the exchange rate prevailing then. The amount in dollars re-

Exhibit 2 *Newport Systems Inc. (A) Balance sheets*

	(unaudited) 30 September 1985	30 September 1984
Assets	$	$
Current assets		
Cash	9,150	12,500
Accounts receivable	352,520	315,170
Inventory	876,800	712,650
Prepaid expenses	11,650	7,920
·Fixed assets (at cost)	318,000	290,500
Less: accumulated depreciation	126,150	98,750
Fixed assets (net)	191,850	191,750
Total assets	1,441,970	1,239,990
Liabilities and Stockholders' Equity		
Current liabilities:		
Accounts payable	365,994	241,490
Accrued expenses	150,751	88,750
Bank loans	165,500	147,850
Subtotal	682,245	478,090
Stockholders' equity:		
Capital stock	200,000	200,000
Retained earnings	559,725	561,900
Subtotal	759,725	761,900
Total liabilities & stockholders' equity	$1,441,970	$1,239,990

Exhibit 3   *Newport Systems (A) Selected spot rate quotations[1]*

	Deutschmark	Yen
4 January 1985	3.1558	252.28
28 January	3.1585	253.70
15 February	3.2660	256.90
4 March	3.3500	261.20
15 March	3.4000	260.95
29 March	3.0830	251.00
12 April	3.0660	251.50
26 April	3.1430	252.70
10 May	3.1200	252.15
24 May	3.0840	250.90
7 June	3.0585	248.65
21 June	3.0850	248.65
5 July	3.0160	247.30
19 July	2.8600	237.80
2 August	2.8220	237.35
16 August	2.7570	236.55
30 August	2.7820	236.85
13 September	2.8900	241.90
20 September	2.8600	241.10
27 September	2.6750	219.00
4 October	2.6100	213.00
11 October	2.6520	214.70
17 October[2]	2.6450	215.00

[1]Harris Bank—*Foreign Exchange Weekly Review.*
[2]*Wall Street Journal,* 18 October 1985.

ceived was likely to be more or less than at Friday's rate, depending upon events affecting the markets in the meantime. The banker showed Brown the market commentary (see Exhibit 4) which indicated that the direction of the dollar was highly uncertain, a view that Brown had noted being expressed almost daily in the *Wall Street Journal* and other papers he read.

2. *Cover in the Forward Exchange Market.* In the forward market one agrees today to sell (or buy) foreign currency at a fixed price with delivery to be made at a specified future date such as in one, three, or six months. A forward contract would assure Brown of a fixed number of dollars when the sales proceeds were received — the price would be "locked in." The banker quoted Brown a three-month forward rate of DM2.6325 and a six-month forward rate of DM2.6150, which meant that more dollars would be received in the future than at present. Selected exchange rates appear on Exhibit 5.

Includes fee →

Imply that the DM will appreciate

3. *Cover in the Money Markets.* The banker explained that her bank would be able to arrange for Newport Systems to borrow Deutsche marks from either its Frankfurt or London branches. The loan from the Frankfurt branch would be in the form of an overdraft (the rate could change over the life of the loan) priced at 100 basis points above "prime"; the Deutsche mark loan from the London branch would be at a fixed rate for both the three-month and six-month maturities, and priced at 150 basis points above LIBOR.

Brown told his banker that he could probably use about $300,000 from the proceeds of the Deutsche marks loans to finance working capital needs over the next six months or so. He asked his banker if the balance could be used to repay part of the currently outstanding short-term bank loans. She promised to consider this, but assured him that if the bank's Loan Committee did not agree, she would arrange for the balance to be invested in a Eurodollar time deposit in London. Interest rate data appear on Exhibit 6.

OTHER FACTORS

The cash down payment of DM150,000 was sold spot at once, netting $56,475 at the spot price of DM2.6560 per U.S. dollar. These funds would be used to finance the firm's working capital needs.

The existing bank loans represented a partial drawdown of Newport's credit line of $550,000. The loan was priced at prime plus 150 basis points. The loan agreement called for this rate to be adjusted quarterly — on the 15th of March, June, September, and December. At the date of the most recent adjustment, the 15th of September, prime rate was 9.50 percent, to which was added the 150 basis points spread.

[handwritten] Short-term borrowing rate = 11.00 %
(use this to calc. his deposit interest too?)

Exhibit 4 Newport Systems (A) Harris Bank, Foreign Exchange Weekly Review

October 4, 1985

The dollar opened unchanged at DM 2.6750 in quiet trading and stabilized briefly at that level before dropping 1.5% on Tuesday. Upside resistance at DM 2.68 prompted modest dollar selling pressures which quickly escalated after the dollar breeched IMM chart points against the DM and SFr. Favorable increases in August and July leading indicators were largely ignored by market participants since they remain pre-occupied by the threat of central bank dollar sales. Short covering briefly stabilized the dollar at mid-week near DM 2.64 but IMM dollar sales pushed the dollar to the DM 2.6150 on Thursday reflecting market apprehension over possible week-end G-5 measures to further depress the dollar. The dollar closed soft in late trading with dealers unwilling to hold long dollar positions ahead of the Saturday G-5 meeting.

The bearish dollar sentiment that permeates the market reflects widespread agreement that the goal of G-5 officials is to achieve a substantial depreciation of the U.S. dollar prior to IMF annual meeting in Seoul October 8–11. The Bank of Japan has been the most aggressive seller of dollars and its objective seems to be to push yen into a 210–200 range by the Seoul meeting. Such yen strength would imply a strong deutschemark in the 2.55–2.50 range. Obviously the G-5 accord has proven extremely effective since the mere threat of central bank intervention has been sufficient to achieve a dramatic weakening of the dollar with only limited expenditures of reserves by monetary authorities. The dollar has fallen about 8.4% against the mark and 12.6% against the yen with official dollar sales probably totalling less than $4 billion.

The current period of concerted central bank intervention will likely be of limited duration since official dollar sales have historically proven to exert only a short run impact upon the exchange markets. Exchange rate intervention is merely a temporary palliative which exerts no influence on the underlying economic fundamentals which dictate long term currency trends. The G-5 accord included some economic policy initiatives — U.S. budget deficit reductions, U.K. and German tax cuts, Japanese reflationary measures — but similar policy pledges have been made at annual global summit meetings and they rarely are enacted. In the wake of the IMF meeting it is possible that the emphasis of the G-5 officials might shift from exchange intervention to interest rate manipulations. If the dollar trends upward by month-end as Treasury auctions push yields up, the Fed might lower the discount rate to 7% in conjunction with Bank of Japan efforts to push money market rates upward. Bank of Japan Governor Sumita has publicly stated that he would not hesitate to raise interest rates if the yen exhibited signs of weakening.

A dollar trading range of DM 2.50–2.75 seems reasonable for the remainder of 1985 with the dollar probably registering yearly lows during the next several weeks and trending toward the upper end of the range by year-end as the threat of official dollar sales recedes and the pace of U.S. economic activity accelerates.

Earl I. Johnson
Assistant Vice President

October 11, 1985

EXCERPTS FROM OCTOBER 2, 1985 NEW YORK PRESS CONFERENCE

JAMIE K. THORSEN, VICE PRESIDENT & MANAGER, FOREIGN EXCHANGE DIVISION

On Sunday, September 22, monetary officials of the G-5 nations (U.S., U.K., Germany, Japan and France) reached agreement on a package of economic and financial measures designed to reduce the value of the dollar relative to other major currencies. The major instrument for achieving the desired depreciation of the dollar is presumably coordinated central bank intervention. Foreign exchange traders can be expected to test the resolve of the central bankers, and the G-5 accord will prove meaningless if the major central banks are unwilling to engage in large-scale dollar selling operations. A key participant in this joint intervention will be the U.S. Federal Reserve. The exchange markets remain skeptical about the resolve of the Reagan Administration to actively intervene against the dollar, and this skepticism was reinforced by Commerce Secretary Baldridge's comment last week that he does not believe the U.S. is about to embark upon "massive" currency intervention. Last February, the U.S. engaged in modest joint intervention activities totalling perhaps $300 million, and these token dollar sales by the Fed were largely ignored by the market. The scope of U.S. intervention will have to be significantly larger this time to convince foreign exchange dealers that the Reagan Administration is serious in its resolve to lower the value of the dollar. Much of the credibility of the G-5 statement depends upon the willingness of the U.S. authorities to back the rhetoric with action.

Aggressive central bank intervention might push the dollar down to DM 2.50 in the near term, but the impact will be relatively short-lived since prolonged, massive intervention would be prohibitively expensive. The dollar's longer term prospects for 1986 will largely be determined by the underlying strength of the U.S. economy. Many economists believe business activity will rebound during the closing months of 1985, but the financial markets were disappointed by the 3Q flash estimate of 2.8% real GNP growth. Mixed signals may persist from economic statistics this fall, but the U.S. economy should gradually gather momentum in 1986, in response to rapid money growth, lower interest rates and softer oil prices. We expect a slightly improved 3% growth performance in 1986 (after 2.3% in 1985) along with a higher 4.3% inflation rate (3.7% in 1985).

A modest upturn in interest rates should accompany escalating business activity, with Fed officials eventually acting to restrain inflationary pressures.

During 1986, the dollar should trend upward towards an autumn peak of DM 3.00–3.10 with the dollar easing to DM 2.85 by year-end as the pace of economic activity slackens. Favorable interest rates on dollar-denominated financial instruments should continue to attract foreign capital inflows to bolster the dollar, with Japanese institutional bond purchases approaching $30 billion. Investment inflows may slacken by year-end 1986, however, as interest rate levels soften and escalating inflation erodes the real rate of return on dollar assets. The recent slump in the value of the dollar may begin to exert a positive impact on the U.S. trade accounts by year-end 1986, but the 1986 annual trade deficit still may exceed $160 billion.

I have presented a relatively optimistic outlook for the dollar next year, but there are always unanticipated shocks — like the G-5 meeting — which could drastically alter our forecast scenario. Potential shocks for 1986 include 1) a financial crisis within the agricultural economy or 2) Paul Volcker's early departure from the Fed. Rumors periodically surface in the financial markets regarding the resignation of Mr. Volcker as Fed Chairman. The rumor resurfaced last week after the Washington Post reported that the Reagan Administration might ask Mr. Volcker to assume the presidency of the World Bank. When Mr. Volcker accepted his second term appointment in 1983, he indicated that he might not serve out his full term through August 1987. Speculation about his future will likely intensify at year-end, since President Reagan must fill two Federal Reserve Board vacancies due to the departure of Fed Governors Gramley and Partee. Mr. Volcker has won widespread credibility and respect in the world's financial markets, and there does not appear to be any qualified individual who could adequately fill his shoes. The announcement of Mr. Volcker's retirement as Fed Chairman would probably precipitate a 10–20 pfennig drop in the value of the dollar which could easily push it down to the DM 2.50 level. This may well be the level at which the Reagan Administration would like to see the dollar stabilize in order to exert a beneficial impact upon U.S. trade accounts.

The stability of the U.S. Farm Credit System has been jeopardized by the depressed condition of the U.S. agriculture sector and by deteriorating prospects for the farm economy given bumper crops. Several weeks ago, Governor Donald Wilkinson of the U.S. Farm Credit Administration warned that the Farm Credit System would probably require a multi-billion dollar financial assistance package within 18-24 months. Such a massive federal bailout program would force the Fed to pursue an accommodative posture, and the injection of substantial liquidity into the U.S. financial system could easily push U.S. interest rate levels and the dollar downward.

Forecasts - 10/02/85			
	December 1985	June 1986	December 1986
Canada	1.3650	1.3800	1.3600
Germany	2.70	3.00	2.80
Japan	224	250	234
Switzerland	2.24	2.50	2.35
United Kingdom	1.39	1.26	1.34

Note: The above forecasts are not meant to be precise levels, but rather to indicate general currency trends for 1986.

Exhibit 5 *Newport systems (A)*

Foreign Exchange

Thursday, October 17, 1985. The New York foreign exchange selling rates below apply to trading among banks in amounts of $1 million and more, as quoted at 3 p.m. Eastern time by Bankers Trust Co. Retail transactions provide fewer units of foreign currency per dollar.

Country	U.S. $ equiv.		Currency per U.S. $	
	Thurs.	Wed.	Thurs.	Wed.
Argentina (Austral)	1.2484	1.2484	.801	.801
Australia (Dollar)	.7035	.6998	1.4215	1.4290
Austria (Schilling)	.05397	.05305	18.53	18.85
Belgium (Franc)				
Commercial rate	.01871	.01839	53.46	54.37
Financial rate	.01859	.01835	53.80	54.50
Brazil (Cruzeiro)	.0001281	.0001281	7805.00	7805.00
Britain (Pound)	1.4155	1.4095	.7065	.7095
30-Day Forward	1.4114	1.4054	.7085	.7115
90-Day Forward	1.4045	1.3982	.7120	.7152
180-Day Forward	1.3966	1.3907	.7160	.7190
Canada (Dollar)	.7323	.7297	1.3655	1.3705
30-Day Forward	.7322	.7294	1.3658	1.3710
90-Day Forward	.7317	.7289	1.3666	1.3720
180-Day Forward	.7307	.7275	1.3685	1.3745
Chile (Official rate)	.005705	.005705	175.27	175.27
China (Yuan)	.3278	.3278	3.0506	3.0506
Colombia (Peso)	.006293	.006293	158.90	158.90
Denmark (Krone)	.1043	.1029	9.5900	9.7200

Exhibit 5 (continued)

	U.S. $ equiv.		Currency per U.S. $	
Ecuador (Sucre)				
Official rate	.01504	.01504	66.48	66.48
Floating rate	.008877	.008877	112.65	112.65
Finland (Markka)	.1759	.1738	5.6850	5.7540
France (Franc)	.1239	.1220	8.0700	8.1935
30-Day Forward	.1238	.1219	8.0770	8.2015
90-Day Forward	.1234	.1216	8.1025	8.2250
180-Day Forward	.1226	.1208	8.1575	8.2795
Greece (Drachma)	.006452	.006390	155.00	156.50
Hong Kong (Dollar)	.1283	.1282	7.7960	7.8025
India (Rupee)	.08292	.08278	12.06	12.08
Indonesia (Rupiah)	.0008913	.0008913	1122.00	1122.00
Ireland (Punt)	1.1690	1.1550	.8554	.8658
Israel (Shekel)	.0006729	.0006729	1486.00	1486.00
Italy (Lira)	.0005605	.0005534	1784.00	1807.00
Japan (Yen)	.004651	.004600	215.00	217.40
30-Day Forward	.004658	.004607	214.67	217.08
90-Day Forward	.004672	.004620	214.06	216.43
180-Day Forward	.004694	.004643	213.06	215.40
Jordan (Dinar)	2.7427	2.7427	.3646	.3646
Kuwait (Dinar)	3.3738	3.3738	.2964	.2964
Lebanon (Pound)	.05391	.05391	18.55	18.55
Malaysia (Ringgit)	.4069	.4064	2.4575	2.4605
Malta (Lira)	2.2857	2.2857	.4375	.4375
Mexico (Peso)				
Floating rate	.002618	.002632	382.00	380.00
Netherlands (Guilder)	.3350	.3309	2.9850	3.0220
New Zealand (Dollar)	.5820	.5800	1.7182	1.7241
Norway (Krone)	.1261	.1250	7.9300	8.0000
Pakistan (Rupee)	.06309	.06301	15.85	15.87
Peru (Sol)	.00007173	.00007173	13942.00	13942.00
Philippines (Peso)	.05356	.05356	18.67	18.67
Portugal (Escudo)	.006154	.006116	162.50	163.50
Saudi Arabia (Riyal)	.2739	.2739	3.6510	3.6510
Singapore (Dollar)	.4678	.4666	2.1375	2.1430
South Africa (Rand)	.3830	.3650	2.6110	2.7397
South Korea (Won)	.001122	.001122	891.60	891.60
Spain (Peseta)	.006203	.006144	161.20	162.75
Sweden (Krona)	.1261	.1246	7.9300	8.0225
Switzerland (Franc)	.4606	.4529	2.1710	2.2080
30-Day Forward	.4623	.4545	2.1633	2.2003
90-Day Forward	.4649	.4572	2.1508	2.1870
180-Day Forward	.4694	.4613	2.1305	2.1680
Taiwan (Dollar)	.02489	.02489	40.17	40.17
Thailand (Baht)	.03759	.03759	26.60	26.60
United Arab (Dirham)	.2723	.2723	3.673	3.673
Uruguay (New Peso)				
Financial	.008763	.008763	114.12	114.12

"Buy"
offer

	U.S. $ equiv.		Currency per U.S. $	
Venezuela (Bolivar)				
Official rate	.1333	.1333	7.50	7.50
Floating rate	.06840	.06840	14.62	14.62
W. Germany (Mark)	.3781	.3720	2.6450	2.6880
30-Day Forward	.3792	.3731	2.6370	2.6799
90-Day Forward	.3811	.3754	2.6237	2.6637
180-Day Forward	.3846	.3786	2.6002	2.6412
SDR	1.06136	1.05966	0.942186	0.943702
ECU	0.833660	0.825104		

Special Drawing Rights are based on exchange rates for the U.S., West German, British, French and Japanese currencies. Source: International Monetary Fund.

ECU is based on a basket of community currencies. Source: European Community Commission.

z-Not quoted.

Exhibit 6 *Newport systems (A) Selected interest rates*

	1 month	3 months	6 months
U.S. dollars			
Bank time deposits			
(Los Angeles)	7.45%	7.55%	7.70%
LIBOR (London)	7.875%	8.125%	8.25%
Prime Rate	←———	9.50%	———→
Deutsche marks			
LIBOR (London)	4.625%	4.8125%	4.875%
Prime Rate	←———	6.00%	———→
Yen			
LIBOR (New York)	6.4375%	6.50%	6.4375%
Prime Rate	←———	5.00%	———→

Case 32

Newport Systems Inc.
(B)

After leaving his banker's office on Friday morning, George Brown, president of Newport Systems, met a friend of his for lunch. During the course of their conversation, his friend told him of the recent success he had enjoyed in trading currency options and futures. Intrigued, Brown wondered if these might not provide a better alternative for covering the Deutsche mark exposure resulting from the export sale to the West German client (see "Newport Systems Inc. (A)").

Brown phoned his banker to ask her about covering the Deutsche mark sales receipts using futures or options. She told him that whereas an option might be appropriate, the future offered few advantages over a forward contract. Since an understanding of these instruments would require some explanation, Brown decided to return to his banker's office.

She began by showing him the previous day's quotations (Thursday, October 17) from her *Wall Street Journal.* These appear in Exhibit 1. The

Exhibit 1 Currency options, Philadelphia exchange

Option & Underlying	Strike Price	Calls—Last			Puts—Last		
		Nov	Feb	May	Nov	Feb	May
12,500 British Pounds—cents per unit							
BPound	135	r	s	s	0.60	s	s
141.63	.140	3.20	s	s	1.80	s	s
141.63	.145	0.95	s	s	r	s	s
141.63	.150	0.25	s	s	r	s	s
62,500 West German Marks—cents per unit.							
DMark	36	r	s	s	0.09	s	s
37.82	.37	1.20	s	s	0.32	s	s
37.82	.39	0.26	s	s	r	s	s
6,250,000 Japanese Yen—100ths of a cent per unit.							
JYen	.45	r	s	s	0.18	s	s
46.53	.46	r	s	s	0.43	s	s
46.53	.47	0.50	s	s	r	s	s
46.53	.48	0.24	s	s	r	s	s
62,500 Swiss Francs—cents per unit.							
SFranc	.43	r	s	s	0.06	s	s
46.11	.44	r	s	s	0.17	s	s
46.11	.45	r	s	s	0.39	s	s
		Dec	Mar	Jun	Dec	Mar	Jun
12,500 British Pounds—cents per unit.							
BPound	110	31.40	r	s	r	r	s
141.63	.115	26.40	r	s	0.05	0.30	s
141.63	.120	21.40	r	r	r	r	r
141.63	.125	16.40	r	r	r	r	r
141.63	.130	11.50	12.40	r	0.40	r	r
141.63	.135	7.15	r	r	1.20	4.00	r
141.63	.140	3.90	6.20	7.40	3.00	6.05	7.70
141.63	.145	1.80	4.05	5.35	r	8.65	r
141.63	.150	0.80	2.60	r	r	r	r
50,000 Canadian Dollars—cents per unit.							
CDollr	.72	r	r	r	0.17	r	r
73.23	.74	0.27	r	r	r	r	r
62,500 West German Marks—cents per unit.							
DMark	.31	6.75	r	r	r	r	r
37.82	.32	r	r	r	0.02	r	r
37.82	.33	4.92	r	r	0.03	r	r
37.82	.34	3.96	r	r	0.05	r	r
37.82	.35	3.08	r	r	0.10	0.38	r
37.82	.36	2.22	2.85	3.38	0.21	0.60	r
37.82	.37	1.54	2.02	r	0.51	r	r
37.82	.38	0.88	1.65	2.22	0.92	1.34	r
37.82	.39	0.52	1.21	r	1.53	r	r

Exhibit 1 *(continued)*

Option & Underlying	Strike Price	Calls—Last			Puts—Last		
		Dec	Mar	Jun	Dec	Mar	Jun
125,000 French Francs—10ths of a cent per unit.							
FFranc	.125	r	4.15	r	r	r	r
6,250,000 Japanese Yen—100ths of a cent per unit.							
JYen	.40	6.50	r	r	r	r	r
46.53	.41	5.52	5.75	r	r	r	r
46.53	.42	4.60	r	r	0.04	r	r
46.53	.43	3.65	4.00	r	0.08	r	r
46.53	.44	2.77	3.19	r	0.17	r	r
46.53	.45	r	2.60	3.05	r	r	r
46.53	.46	1.34	2.00	2.45	0.77	r	r
46.53	.48	0.50	1.08	r	1.86	r	r
62,500 Swiss Francs—cents per unit.							
SFranc	.43	3.40	r	r	0.17	r	r
46.11	.44	2.71	r	r	0.34	r	r
46.11	.45	1.95	2.82	r	0.67	r	r
46.11	.46	1.30	2.28	r	1.00	1.60	r
46.11	.48	0.54	r	r	r	r	r
Total call vol.		10,358		Call open int.			182,545
Total put vol.		5,141		Put open int.			132,751

r—Not traded. s—No option offered.
Last is premium (purchase price).

Currency Futures

	Open	High	Low	Settle	Change	Lifetime High	Lifetime Low	Open Interest
British Pound (1MM)—25,000 pounds; $ per pound								
Dec	1.4040	1.4105	1.4040	1.4095	+ .0070	1.4395	1.0185	24,312
Mar86	1.3970	1.4025	1.3970	1.4005	+ .0065	1.4310	1.0650	2,241
June	1.3960	1.3970	1.3925	1.3940	+ .0065	1.4250	1.1530	93

Est vol 5,295; vol Wed 6,489; open int 26,646, −352

	Open	High	Low	Settle	Change	Lifetime High	Lifetime Low	Open Interest
Canadian Dollar (1MM)—100,000 dlrs.; $ per Can $								
Dec	.7318	.7326	.7312	.7320	+ .0028	.7568	.7006	4,304
Mar86	.7300	.7315	.7300	.7308	+ .0029	.7504	.6981	528
June	.7290	.7295	.7290	.7296	+ .0030	.7360	.7070	247

Est vol 703; vol Wed 689; open int 5,113, −176.

Exhibit 1 (continued)

	Open	High	Low	Settle	Change	Lifetime High	Lifetime Low	Open Interest
Japanese Yen (1MM) 12.5 million yen; $ per yen (.00)								
Dec	.4633	.4670	.4630	.4667	+ .0040	.4738	.3905	38,446
Mar86	.4658	.4690	.4655	.4689	+ .0041	.4758	.4035	1,299
Est vol 12,777; vol Wed 14,108; open int 39,808, −2,523								
Swiss Franc (1MM)—125,000 francs-$ per franc								
Dec	.4590	.4645	.4580	.4642	+ .0078	.4728	.3525	25,735
Mar86	.4629	.4687	.4625	.4683	+ .0079	.4769	.3790	1,431
Est vol 23,409; vol Wed 18,817; open int 27,248, −1,753								
W. German Mark (1MM)—125,000 marks; $ per mark								
Dec	.3773	.3810	.3765	.3808	+ .0058	.3867	.2971	41,408
Mar86	.3809	.3844	.3804	.3841	+ .0058	.3898	.3040	2,152
June	.3872	.3872	.3872	.3876	+ .0058	.3922	.3335	201
Est vol 28,123; vol Wed 24,537; open int 43,763, −1,151.								

Currency Futures Options Chicago Mercantile Exchange

Eurodollar (CME) $ million; pts. of 100%

Strike Price	Calls—Settle Dec-C	Mar-C	Jun-C	Puts—Settle Dec-P	Mar-P	Jun-P
9050	1.28	1.07	0.88	0.01	0.13	0.36
9100	0.79	0.68	0.61	0.03	0.24	0.54
9150	0.39	0.39	0.38	0.12	0.45	0.78
9200	0.13	0.19	0.21	0.34	0.73	1.01
9250	0.02	0.09	—	0.74	1.10	—
9300	0.01	—	—	1.23	—	—

Est. vol. 3,004, Wed.; vol. 972 calls, 1,124 puts
Open interest Wed.; 16,738 calls, 27,963 puts

British Pound (CME) 25,000 pounds; cents per lb.

Strike Price	Calls—Settle Dec-C	Mar-C	Jun-C	Puts—Settle Dec-P	Mar-P	Jun-P
1350	7.05	8.45	9.35	1.10	3.55	5.15
1375	5.30	7.00	8.10	1.85	4.55	6.25
1400	3.85	5.85	—	2.80	5.80	7.50
1425	2.65	4.70	—	4.15	7.05	—
1450	1.70	3.80	5.00	5.70	8.60	—
1475	1.10	3.00	4.20	—	—	—

Est. vol. 3,501; Wed.; vol. 400 calls; 388 puts
Open interest Wed.; 12,953 calls; 9,032 puts

Exhibit 1 (*continued*)

W. German Mark (CME) 125,000 marks; cents per mark

Strike Price	Calls—Settle		Puts—Settle	
	Dec-C	Mar-C	Dec-P	Mar-P
36	2.24	2.90	0.18	0.56
37	1.48	2.23	0.41	0.86
38	0.87	1.67	0.80	1.27
39	0.47	1.23	1.36	1.80
40	0.22	0.88	—	—
41	0.11	0.61	—	—

Est. vol. 4,942, Wed.; vol. 3,286 calls, 3,094 puts
Open interest Wed.; 32,379 calls, 24,201 puts

Swiss Franc (CME) 125,000 francs; cents per franc

Strike Price	Calls—Settle			Puts—Settle		
	Dec-C	Mar-C	Jun-C	Dec-P	Mar-P	Jun-P
44	2.66	3.52	4.16	0.27	0.76	1.04
45	1.91	2.84	3.51	0.50	1.05	1.35
46	1.26	2.25	2.92	0.85	1.44	1.73
47	0.80	1.76	2.42	1.37	1.91	2.18
48	0.48	1.35	1.99	—	—	2.70
49	0.28	1.02	1.63	—	—	3.29

Est. vol. 845, Wed; vol. 954 calls, 1,124 puts
Open interest Wed.; 11,119 calls, 11,147 puts

Sterling (LIFFE)—b-£25,000; cents per pound

Strike Price	Calls—Settle			Puts—Settle		
	Dec-C	Mar-C	Jun-C	Dec-P	Mar-P	Jun-P
130	11.70	12.46	13.41	0.42	2.41	3.96
135	7.25	9.13	10.36	1.30	4.08	5.91
140	4.06	6.43	7.81	3.11	6.38	8.36
145	1.96	4.34	5.75	6.01	9.29	11.30
150	0.80	2.81	4.13	9.85	12.76	14.68
155	0.28	1.75	2.90	14.33	16.70	18.45

Actual Vol. Thurs, 699 Calls, 175 Puts.
Open interest Wednesday; 9,333, Calls, 15,699 Puts.
   b-Option on physical sterling.

Source: *Wall Street Journal*, October 18, 1985.

futures contracts were traded on the International Monetary Market (IMM) in Chicago. Currency options were traded on the Philadelphia Exchange, the Chicago Mercantile Exchange (CME), and London (LIFFE).

A characteristic of both the futures and options contracts was that they were standardized. Maturity dates were generally the third Wednesday of March, June, September, and December, though the Philadelphia Exchange has recently begun trading other maturity dates. The contracts were of standard size — DM125,000 on the Chicago, London, and Singapore exchanges, DM62,500 on the Philadelphia Exchange. The contracts were all priced in "U.S. Terms," that is, in U.S. dollars per foreign currency unit.

In addition, the exchange traded options had their exercise (or striking) prices stated in one-cent ($0.01) intervals, with usually two or three prices on either side of the current spot exchange rate (see Exhibit 1).

The options traded on the Chicago Mercantile Exchange (CME) were on a *currency futures contract.* Exercise of a call would give the option holder a "long" futures contract — i.e., the equivalent of having bought the future at the exercise price. The exercise of a put would result in a "short" position — equivalent to having sold a future at the exercise price. The amounts and maturities of both the futures and options on futures contracts are identical. One would exercise an option on a future only when it was profitable to do so and receive a cash payment amounting to the difference between the futures price at the time and the option's exercise price.

The exercise of the Philadelphia option contracts, in contrast, would result in the delivery of the *currency* at the exercise price.

One of the problems with the exchange traded contracts is that it can be difficult to exactly match the exposure that is to be covered.

For example, the DM775,000 payment expected in April 1986 would slightly exceed the aggregate value of six DM125,000 contracts. The maturity dates presented another problem; although neither the futures nor the options contracts need to be held to maturity, their sale (or exercise) prior to maturity could result in an imperfect cover for the specific exposure faced by Newport (mid-January and mid-April).

The banker further explained that in the case of a futures contract, Newport would have to open an account with a broker and tie up some funds in a margin account. The margin account would be debited or credited daily as the value of the futures contracts sold or (bought) were "marked to market" each day. Keeping up with this might end up being somewhat of a nuisance to Brown, she suggested.

After pointing out the problems with exchange traded futures and options, the banker thought her bank would be able to arrange an option contract tailored to meet Newport's exact requirements, and asked the foreign exchange department to prepare a quote based on Friday's market conditions. These appear below:

Trade date : 18 October 1985

Put options on Deutsche marks

1. *Amount: DM625,000*
Expiration date : 17 January 1986
Strike price: Premium:
$ 0.37 $ 0.0095 per DM
$ 0.38 $ 0.0135 per DM

2. *Amount: DM775,000*
Expiration date : 17 April 1986
Strike price: Premium:
$ 0.37 $ 0.0150 per DM
$ 0.38 $ 0.0195 per DM

As Brown was leaving her office, the banker gave him a brief memo that she thought he could find of interest (Exhibit 2).

Brown decided to reflect on the various things he had learned during the day and resolved to come to a decision by the first thing on Monday morning.

Exhibit 2

SECURITY NATIONAL BANK
Foreign Exchange Department
125700 Wilshire Boulevard
Los Angeles, CA. 90048

A NEW PRODUCT-CURRENCY OPTION

WHAT IS A CURRENCY OPTION?

A currency option is the right to buy and sell a currency against delivery of dollars at an agreed exchange rate (the "strike" or "exercise" price). The buyer of the option has the right to exercise this option at any date up to and including the agreed expiration date, but no obligation to do so. The buyer of the option pays a premium to the bank for this right.

A currency option is essentially a form of insurance against movements in exchange rates; in this respect it may be considered as an alternative to a forward contract to protect the dollar value of exports and imports.

ADVANTAGES OF CURRENCY OPTIONS?

1) When a currency exposure is hedged by a forward contract, the company is protected against adverse currency movements — the downside risk is eliminated. But at the same time, any upside potential that otherwise might be gained by the company, if rates moved in its favor, is eliminated. The option, in contrast, provides downside risk protection, but allows the upside potential to be retained since the option need not be exercised.
2) The option buyer knows at the outset what his "worst case" will be — the premium he will have already paid. When the main objective is to limit downside risk, this is a powerful advantage. For example, the option premium can often be built into the pricing process thus fixing the minimum margin.
3) Since there is no obligation to exercise an option, it is an ideal instrument to hedge a contingent cash flow such as those arising from a tender.

CURRENCIES AVAILABLE

Security National customers can purchase options to buy (a call) or sell (a put) Deutsche marks, sterling, yen, Swiss francs, Canadian and Australian dollars against U.S. dollars. The maturities can be up to six months, at any strike price (providing it is not too far away from the existing spot rate) and in any amounts above the equivalent of $100,000.

OPTION PREMIUMS

Premiums are payable in advance and are quoted in U.S. dollars per foreign currency unit.

EXERCISE OR CANCELLATION OF OPTIONS

The options can be exercised for value spot at any time up to and including the expiration date. If the option is no longer required prior to or including the expiration date, the bank will be willing to repurchase it at a price to be set by the bank at the time.

Failing exercise or repurchase as set out above, the option will lapse on the expiration date.

Ian H. Giddy

Case 33

Good Eggs

It is two weeks before Easter, 5:05 p.m. on a workday. You are half-way through the elevator door when someone yells that the cash manager of Nestle U.S. is on the line, holding for you. You pick up the phone and listen with half an ear.

"... and we expect to sell a lot of chocolate eggs, imported from Zug, so we'll have about $60 million cash coming in three weeks' time. The Swiss want francs, of course. I need to hedge the exchange rate, so I'm asking you to compare three choices that Werner tells me I have.

"First, a forward contract to lock in the rate. But since Swiss interest rates are so low, I'll end up paying a price one-half a percent higher than today's.

"Second, I could buy Swiss futures with a margin requirement of one percent.

"Third, a call option at a premium of one and one-half percent, with a strike price at today's exchange rate.

"How do they sound to you? What should I do?"

We'll treat as a bank option instead of exchange-traded option.

Ian H. Giddy

Case 34

How to Advance Your Career

You are the cleaning lady at the Empire State Building. One afternoon you are mopping the floor in the trading room of the Empire Financial Group. A phone rings, but everybody's too busy to notice it, so you pick it up.

It is a customer who is interested in selling DM125,000 next December at a guaranteed exchange rate of DM2.78. He's interested in options and futures. This is your big chance. Can you figure out roughly what prices to quote the customer, given the data from *The New York Times*?

© Ian H. Giddy, New York University, 1985.

Exhibit 1 **Wednesday, July 24, 1985 Commodity research
bureau index**

Futures

Financial						
Today 221.2		Previous day 222.5			Year Ago 252.7	

Season						Open
High	Low	High	Low	Close	Chg.	Interest

British pound (1MM)
25,000 pounds; $ per pound

High	Low		High	Low	Close	Chg.	Interest
1.4450	1.0200	Sep	1.4010	1.3875	1.3995	+10	35,088
1.4040	1.0200	Dec	1.3900	1.3770	1.3895	+5	6,434
1.3915	1.0680	Mar	1.3800	1.3740	1.3835	—	962
1.3795	1.1905	Jun	—	—	1.3765	—	37

Last spot 1.4045, off 45.
Est. sales 11,747. Prev. sales 12,785.
Prev day's open int 42,521, up 568.

Canadian dollar (1MM)
100,000 dollars; $ per Canadian dollar

High	Low		High	Low	Close	Chg.	Interest
.7585	.7025	Sep	.7389	.7372	.7383	−20	7,145
.7566	.7006	Dec	.7374	.7359	.7364	−22	734
.7504	.6981	Mar	.7365	.7344	.7345	−21	263
.7360	.7070	Jun	—	—	.7331	−21	93

Last spot .7392, off 25.
Est. sales 1,488. Prev. sales 829.
Prev day's open int 8,235, off 62.

go short

West German mark (1MM)
125,000 marks; $ per mark

2.8329

High	Low		High	Low	Close	Chg.	Interest
.3555	.2930	Sep	.3506	.3476	.3501	—	46,730
.3610	.2971	Dec	.3534	.3506	.3530	—	4,602
.3599	.3040	Mar	—	—	.3560	—	931
.3633	.3335	Jun	—	—	.3601	—	2

Last spot .3478, off 17.
Est. sales 26,892. Prev. sales 37,138.
Prev day's open int 52,265, off 1,699.

2.777

depr. $ appr.

Japanese yen (1MM)
12.5 million yen; $ per yen

High	Low		High	Low	Close	Chg.	Interest
.004268	.003870	Sep	.004198	.004178	.004194	−8	29,813
.004350	.003905	Dec	.004219	.004202	.004217	−8	1,664
.004307	.004035	Mar	.004230	.004228	.004240	−11	39

Last spot .004181, up 01.
Est. sales 10,212. Prev. sales 10,525.
Prev day's open int 31,316, off 760.

Exhibit 1 (continued)

Season						Open
High	Low		High	Low	Close	Chg.	Interest

Swiss franc (1MM)
125,000 francs; $ per franc

High	Low		High	Low	Close	Chg.	Interest
.4830	.3480	Sep	.4283	.4236	.4281	+20	28,420
.4360	.3531	Dec	.4316	.4271	.4316	+22	2,336
.4383	.3835	Mar	.4332	.4315	.4356	+24	59

Last spot .4252, off 07.
Est. sales 25,335. Prev. sales 28,450.
Prev day's open int 30,815, up 651.

Exhibit 2 Treasury bills

Date —1985—		Bid	Ask	Chg.	Yield
Aug	1	6.87	6.81	−0.13	6.91
Aug	8	7.22	7.18	—	7.30
Aug	15	6.90	6.86	−0.10	6.98
Aug	22	6.89	6.85	−0.06	6.98
Aug	29	6.90	6.86	−0.02	7.00
Sep	5	7.06	7.02	−0.08	7.17
Sep	12	7.06	7.02	−0.07	7.18
Sep	19	7.05	7.01	−0.09	7.18
Sep	26	7.03	6.99	−0.04	7.17
Oct	3	7.24	7.20	−0.05	7.40
Oct	10	7.24	7.20	−0.04	7.41
Oct	17	7.24	7.20	−0.03	7.42
Oct	24	7.24	7.20	−0.02	7.43
Oct	31	7.23	7.19	−0.04	7.43
Nov	7	7.25	7.21	−0.02	7.47
Nov	14	7.25	7.21	−0.01	7.48
Nov	21	7.27	7.23	−0.01	7.51
Nov	29	7.27	7.23	−0.03	7.52
Dec	5	7.28	7.22	−0.03	7.52
Dec	12	7.28	7.24	−0.03	7.55
Dec	19	7.28	7.22	−0.01	7.54
Dec	26	7.23	7.19	−0.02	7.52
—1986—					
Jan	2	7.30	7.26	−0.02	7.61
Jan	9	7.32	7.28	−0.03	7.64
Jan	16	7.36	7.32	−0.01	7.69
Jan	23	7.37	7.35	+0.01	7.74

dollar depreciating?

Date —1986—		Bid	Ask	Chg.	Yield
Feb	20	7.38	7.32	—	7.71
Mar	20	7.38	7.34	−0.02	7.75
Apr	17	7.43	7.39	−0.02	7.83
May	15	7.46	7.44	−0.03	7.91
Jun	12	7.47	7.43	−0.01	7.93
Jul	10	7.48	7.46	—	8.00

Source—Federal Reserve Bank.

Copyright © 1985 by The New York Times Company.

Exhibit 3 Financial options

U.S. Treasury bonds (CBOE)

Option & Underlying	Strike Price	Calls—Last			Puts—Last		
		Sep	Dec	Mar	Sep	Dec	Mar
Treasury Notes $100,000 9⅞s 1990-points and 32nds.							
TNote100a	100	0.15	r	r	r	r	r
	101	0.10	r	r	r	r	r
Treasury Bonds $100,000 11¼s 2015-points and 32nds.							
TBnd 100l	106	1.08	r	r	r	r	r
	108	r	1.05	r	r	r	r
	110	0.08	r	r	r	r	r
Treasury Bonds $100,000 11¾s 2014-points and 32nds.							
TBnd100u	110	0.20	1.11	s	r	r	s
Total call vol.			704	Call open int.			15,746
Total put vol.				Put open int.			11,340

Foreign currencies (PHIL)

		Sep	Dec	Mar	Sep	Dec	Mar
12,500 British Pounds—cents per unit.							
BPound	105	r	35.00	r	r	r	r
140.88	110	30.10	r	r	r	0.25	r
140.88	115	25.20	r	r	r	r	r
140.88	120	20.20	r	r	0.10	r	r
140.88	125	15.50	15.50	r	0.30	1.70	r
140.88	130	10.70	r	r	r	3.00	5.00
140.88	135	6.15	r	r	1.90	r	7.20
140.88	140	3.60	5.90	7.85	3.90	r	r
140.88	145	1.80	4.25	r	r	r	r
140.88	150	0.75	2.90	r	r	r	r

Exhibit 3 *(continued)*

Option & Underlying	Strike Price	Calls—Last			Puts—Last		
		Sep	Dec	Mar	Sep	Dec	Mar
50,000 Canadian Dollars—cents per unit.							
CDollr	71	r	r	r	r	0.21	r
73.96	73	1.16	r	r	0.22	r	r
73.96	74	0.51	r	r	r	r	r
73.96	75	0.15	r	r	r	r	2.35
62,500 West German Marks—cents per unit.							
DMark	30	4.80	r	r	r	r	r
34.89	31	3.81	r	r	r	0.17	r
34.89	32	2.95	3.44	r	0.07	0.32	r
34.89	33	1.97	2.66	3.20	0.19	0.58	r
34.89	34	1.41	2.04	2.46	0.46	r	r
34.89	35	0.72	1.50	2.03	0.78	1.32	r
34.89	36	0.40	1.00	1.53	r	r	r
34.89	37	0.17	0.73	r	r	s	r
125,000 French Francs—10ths of a cent per unit.							
FFranc	115	2.00	r	r	r	r	r
6,250,000 Japanese Yen—100ths of a cent per unit.							
JYen	38	r	4.05	r	0.01	r	r
41.85	39	r	3.17	r	r	r	r
41.85	40	1.90	2.31	r	r	r	r
41.85	41	1.12	1.54	r	r	r	r
41.85	42	0.59	1.03	r	0.63	r	r
41.85	43	0.21	0.72	r	r	r	r
41.85	44	0.10	r	r	r	r	r
62,500 Swiss Francs—cents per unit.							
SFranc	33	r	r	r	r	0.01	r
42.62	34	r	r	r	0.01	r	r
42.62	35	7.46	r	r	0.01	r	r
42.62	36	r	r	r	0.01	0.08	r
42.62	37	r	5.80	r	r	r	r
42.62	38	r	r	r	0.04	0.25	r
42.62	39	3.48	4.03	r	r	r	r
42.62	40	2.65	3.30	r	0.16	r	r
42.62	41	1.83	2.62	r	0.34	0.81	r
42.62	42	1.38	r	r	0.80	1.30	r
42.62	43	0.85	1.60	r	1.10	r	r
42.62	44	r	1.23	r	r	r	r
Total call vol.			6,712	Call open int.			178,827
Total put vol.			5,969	Put open int.			124,695

Copyright © 1985 by The New York Times Company.

r = not traded

s = No option offered

Ian H. Giddy

Case 35

Leroy Merz's Options

Wearing shorts is not normally encouraged at the world headquarters of International Computers and Telegraphics, but at 9:30 on a Sunday morning in August, who cares? So thinks Leroy Merz, Assistant Treasurer (International) of I.C. & Tel., as he strides bare-legged across Rockefeller Plaza heading for the thirty-fourth floor of the building that dominates the Plaza's west perimeter.

As Merz had expected, the air conditioning had been off since Friday evening and his office almost drips with New York's summer humidity. "I must get this options memo done," thinks Merz, "and get out of here. Foreign exchange options? A year ago nobody had heard of them, now everyone at the Foreign Exchange Managers Club claims that their firm is plunging in . . . so I had better get the story straight before someone in the

© Ian H. Giddy, New York University, 1985.

319

Finance Committee starts asking questions. Let's see, there are two ways in which I can envisage us using options now. One is to hedge a dividend due on December 15th from I.C. & Tel. Germany. The problem is Germany's new capital controls — who knows if we'll get permission from the Bundesbank to repatriate the full amount? The other is to hedge our upcoming payment to Matsumerda for their spring RAM chip shipment. With the yen at 242 and falling I'm glad we haven't covered that payable so far, but now I'm getting nervous and I would like to protect my posterior. An option to buy yen on September 10 might be just the thing. Gee it's hot in here."

Before we delve any further into Leroy Merz's musings, let us learn a bit about I.C. & Tel., and about foreign exchange options. International Computers and Telegraphics is a $7 billion sales company engaged in, among other things, the development, manufacture, and marketing of microprocessor-based equipment. Although 30 percent of the firm's sales are currently abroad, the firm has full-fledged manufacturing facilities in only three foreign countries, Germany, Canada, and Brazil. An assembly plant in Singapore exists primarily to solder Japanese semiconductor chips onto circuit boards and to screw these into Brazilian-made boxes for shipment to the United States, Canada, and Germany. The German subsidiary has developed half of its sales to France, The Netherlands, and the United Kingdom, billing in local currency, but since the German authorities insist that all export revenues must be converted into Deutsche marks, I.C. & Tel. Hamburg has accumulated a cash reserve of DM899,028, worth US$312,000 at today's exchange rate. (The Deutsche mark is presently at a premium of 6.25 percent against the dollar in the forward market.) While the Hamburg office has automatic permission to repatriate DM3 million, they have been urged to seek authorization to convert another DM1 million by December 15th. The firm has an agreement to buy three hundred thousand RAM chips at Y4000 each semi-annually, and it is this payment that will fall due on September 10th.

The conventional means of hedging exchange risk are forward or future contracts. These, however, are fixed and inviolable agreements. In many practical instances the hedger is uncertain whether foreign currency cash inflow or outflow will materialize. In such cases what is needed is the right, but not the obligation, to buy or sell a designated quantity of a foreign currency at a specified price (exchange rate). This is precisely what a foreign exchange option provides.

A foreign exchange option gives the holder *the right to buy or sell a designated quantity of a foreign currency* at a specified exchange rate up to or at a stipulated date.

The terminal date of the contract is called the expiration date (or maturity date). If the option may be exercised before the expiration date, it is called an American option; if only on the expiration date, a European option.

The party retaining the option is the option buyer; the party giving the option is the option seller (or writer). The exchange rate at which the option can be exercised is called the exercise price or strike price. The buyer of the option must pay the seller some amount, called the option price or the premium, for the rights involved.

The important feature of a foreign exchange option is that the holder of the option has the right, but not the obligation, to exercise it. He will only exercise it if the currency moves in a favorable direction. Thus, once you have paid for an option you cannot lose, unlike a forward contract, where you are obliged to exchange the currencies and therefore will lose if the movement is unfavorable.

The disadvantage of an option contract, compared to a forward contract, is that you have to pay a price for the option, and this price or premium tends to be quite high for certain options. In general, the option's price will be higher the greater the risk to the seller (and the greater the value to the buyer because this is a zero-sum game). The risk of a call option will be greater, and the premium higher, the higher the exercise price relative to the forward rate; after all, one can always lock in a profit by buying at the exercise price and selling at the forward rate. The chance that the option will be exercised profitably is also higher, the more volatile is the currency, and the longer the option has to run before it expires.

Returning to Leroy Merz in his Rockefeller Center office, we find that he has been writing down some numbers while we have been away. During the past week he had telephoned the foreign exchange departments of several major banks and was able to obtain quotes from two of them. They were close to these rates (reported in the latest issue of *The Wall Street Journal*):

	German D-mark		Japanese Yen	
Spot	2.8815	.3470	241.15	.4147
Forward Contracts				
30 day	2.8650		240.03	
90 day	2.8365	.3525	237.75	
Call Option				
Sept.: Strike = 34¢/DM	1.17 (3.37%) Strike = 0.40¢/Yen			
Dec.:	1.93 (5.56%)			
Sept.: Strike = 35¢/DM	0.51 (1.47%) Strike = 0.41¢/Yen		0.85 (2.05%)	.4185
Dec.:	1.23 (3.54%)		1.61 (3.88%)	

	German D-mark		Japanese Yen	
Sept.: Strike = 36¢/DM	0.20 (0.60%)	Strike = 0.42¢/Yen	0.36 (0.87%)	.4236
Dec.:	0.78 (2.25%)		0.95 (2.29%)	

Put Option

	German D-mark		Japanese Yen
Sept.: Strike = 34¢/DM	0.16 (0.50%)	Strike = 0.40¢/Yen	
Dec.:			0.24 (0.58%)
Sept.: Strike = 35¢/DM	0.55 (1.59%)	Strike = 0.41¢/Yen	0.23 (0.55%)
Dec.:	0.91 (2.62%)		0.44 (1.06%)
Sept.: Strike = 36¢/DM	1.28 (3.69%)	Strike = 0.42¢/Yen	
Dec.:	1.54 (4.44%)		

The option prices are quoted in U.S. cents per Deutsche mark. Yen are quoted in hundredths of a cent. Looking at these prices, Leroy realizes that he can work out how much the Deutsche mark or yen would have to change to make the option worthwhile. He has attempted to obtain quotes for buying Japanese yen for the next anticipated payment in March, but has been unable to find a bank willing to sell him a call option on yen that far ahead. That makes him wonder about the depth of this market. "Will I be able to reverse these contracts once I buy them?" he wonders. He scratches his knee. "Perhaps it would be preferable to buy some options on an organized exchange, which will enable me to sell the option if I decide not to use it, and even exercise it before maturity. But everyone tells me these options, now available on the Philadelphia and Montreal exchanges, are quite illiquid and in any case only available in small, standardized quantities. Could I put together enough contracts to make it worthwhile?"

Scraping around on his messy desk, Merz finds *The Wall Street Journal* from which he obtained the above rates. "I'll attach these numbers to my memo," mutters Merz, but the truth is he has yet to come to grips with the real question, which is when, if ever, are currency options a better means of hedging exchange risk for an international firm than traditional forward exchange contracts?

As he is about to put pen to paper, another thought occurs to Leroy. His banker has been arguing persuasively that I.C. & Tel. could take advantage of the German marks they had coming in on December 15, by *writing* a call option on the funds. According to the banker, the firm could receive a premium of about 3 percent for such an option. Then, if the mark falls, I.C. & Tel. would simply keep the premium they receive for the option because the call option would not be exercised. If the mark rises, and the option is exercised, I.C. & Tel. would simply deliver the currency at the prearranged exchange rate — the strike price — which could be set equal to the forward rate if desired. This "covered option writing" idea seems so attractive that Leroy wonders why none of his colleagues at the club have tried it.

Ian H. Giddy

Case 36

Fuji Erupts

You have been hired by Fuji Bank to make sure that, in the future, the bank retains control over its foreign exchange exposure (see Exhibit 1). Your task is to devise guidelines or rules that give Tokyo sufficient information and control to limit risks and losses from foreign exchange activities in its overseas branches. On the other hand, you must not prevent Japan's second-biggest bank from taking the risks necessary to provide its customers with a full and flexible range of foreign exchange services. You also cannot recommend centralizing everything because that would make their Treasury operations too unwieldy.

Can you list some recommendations that will achieve these objectives? If so, you should be prepared to defend them in front of a critical committee of experienced Fuji traders who resent some young MBA telling them how to run their business and who are determined to show that whatever you come up with can be circumvented.

Exhibit 1 Too Far Forward

In little more than two years, Japan's two biggest banks have both blushingly had to admit that one of their foreign-exchange dealers has lost them billions of yen from unauthorized dealing at one of their foreign branches. On November 7, Fuji Bank revealed that Mr. Jahimu Nakazawa, the chief foreign exchange dealer in its New York branch, lost Y11.5 billion ($47.9 million) this summer when he bet that the dollar would crash against the yen. After keeping his losses secret for three months, he was fired. All Fuji's board of directors have taken a 20 percent pay cut for the next six months to demonstrate their shame.

In September 1982, Dai-Ichi Kangyo Bank, the country's biggest, announced that Mr. Haruo Kanda, one of the dealers in its Singapore branch, had lost the bank Y9.7 billion between 1978 and 1982 through unauthorized speculation against the dollar. Mr. Kanda was dismissed and the bank's deputy president publicly apologized for the bank's shortcomings. Japanese banks — so tightly constrained at home — seem much less in control of their foreign controls.

Mr. Nakazawa became convinced in April this year that America's huge trade deficit made a currency realignment inevitable. So, with the dollar at Y226, he bought huge amounts of yen in the forward market — about $500 million worth, to judge by his losses. The dollar promptly strengthened, eventually reaching Y249. Mr. Nakazawa was breaking Fuji's internal rules on trading limits; to conceal his gambling, he made his deals after-hours with banks outside New York. He was helped, Fuji says, by the fact that his branch's computer system was being replaced at the time, and the bank's normal accounting system had become temporarily confused.

Fuji has been forecasting a post-tax profit for the six months from April to September of Y32 billion. Mr. Nakazawa's flutter will hurt: but it will not affect the profit figures when the bank announces its results on November 20. Fuji says it has plugged the hole in its profits by selling securities.

Source: The Economist, November 10, 1984.

Ian H. Giddy

Case 37

Good Hedges Make Good Neighbors

"Chicago closes two hours earlier than it should," thought Bruce Lange, Treasury Manager for Transamerica Corporation, as he gazed at the winter sun setting on the San Francisco Bay from the vantage point of his office near the pinnacle of the company's headquarters building.

It was too late to put in an order to the company's broker at the International Monetary Market. Bruce would have to wait until tomorrow, but that was okay, because he had yet to figure out what order to put in. His boss, Bob Einzig, had suggested the company "get its feet wet" by using the IMM to hedge Transamerica's anticipated $100 million, nine-month borrowing. The funds would be taken down on December 12 for use as working capital at the company's shipping insurance subsidiary in London. Based on recent experience Transamerica could borrow at ⅛ percent over three-month LIBOR either in dollars or in sterling.

Bruce noticed that the IMM quoted both Eurodollar futures and

Eurodollar options. Which would be more appropriate to limit Transamerica's borrowing risk? He thought he had better lay out, step by step, exactly how Eurodollar futures and Eurodollar options each could be used to hedge the nine-month borrowing. Then he could run the two alternatives by Einzig the next morning. Pulling out the Futures and Options columns from the newspaper, Bruce decided he would calculate, based on yesterday's closing prices, what Eurodollar interest rates could be locked in and what cost of hedging, if any, the firm would incur. "But we'd better act quickly," he muttered, noticing that Eurodollar futures yields seemed to be rising. "Perhaps if I meet with Bob early enough, we can do the hedge on the LIFFE exchange in London before those traders in Chicago have a chance to push the market even further up. Let's see, what time would that have to be?"

Exhibit 1 *Futures options*

Monday, November 25, 1985
—Financial—

British Pound (CME) 25,000 pounds; cents per pound

Strike Price	Calls—Settle			Puts—Settle		
	Dec-C	Mar-C	Jun-C	Dec-P	Mar-P	Jun-P
1400	6.25	6.85	7.65	0.05	1.85	3.60
1425	3.85	5.35	6.25	0.20	2.70	4.65
1450	1.80	3.90	5.10	0.55	3.85	5.90
1475	0.55	2.90	4.00	1.80	5.30	7.35
1500	0.15	2.05	—	—	—	—
1525	—	—	—	—	—	—

Est. vol. 2,205, Fri; vol. 1,023 calls, 1,197 puts
Open interest Fri.; 12,692 calls, 14,927 puts

W. German Mark (CME) 125,000 marks; cents per mark

Strike Price	Calls—Settle			Puts—Settle		
	Dec-C	Mar-C	Jun-C	Dec-P	Mar-P	Jun-P
37	2.10	2.64	3.15	0.01	0.26	0.54
38	1.13	1.92	2.51	0.04	0.51	0.81
39	0.33	1.30	1.94	0.24	0.90	1.21
40	0.07	0.87	1.43	0.98	1.43	1.68
41	0.01	0.56	1.06	1.92	2.10	2.22
42	—	—	—	—	—	—

Est. vol. 8,390, Fri; vol. 5,063 calls, 1,306 puts
Open interest Fri.; 41,688 calls, 35,618 puts

Swiss Franc (CME) 125,000 francs; cents per franc

Strike Price	Calls—Settle			Puts—Settle		
	Dec-C	Mar-C	Jun-C	Dec-P	Mar-P	Jun-P
46	1.76	2.72	3.44	0.01	0.52	0.84
47	0.86	2.04	2.80	0.12	0.82	1.16
48	0.28	1.48	2.23	0.53	1.25	1.56
49	0.06	1.03	1.76	1.31	1.79	2.04
50	—	0.70	1.37	—	2.45	2.62
51	—	—	—	—	—	—

Est. vol. 1,405, Fri.; vol. 1,780 calls, 603 puts
Open interest Fri.; 13,969 calls, 14,967 puts

Sterling (LIFFE)—b-£25,000; cents per pound

Strike Price	Calls—Settle			Puts—Settle		
	Dec-C	Mar-C	Jun-C	Dec-P	Mar-P	Jun-P
130	16.24	16.24	16.24	0.00	0.35	1.25
135	11.24	11.24	11.26	0.00	0.99	2.41
140	6.24	7.08	8.02	0.08	2.28	4.17
145	2.02	4.23	5.44	1.07	4.43	6.59
150	0.28	2.28	3.52	4.33	7.48	9.67
155	0.01	1.11	2.16	9.06	11.31	13.31

Actual Vol. Monday, 748 Calls, 695 Puts.
Open interest Friday; 10,867 Calls, 17,474 Puts.
  b—Option on physical sterling.

Eurodollar (LIFFE) $1 million; pts. of 100%

Strike Price	Calls—Settle			Puts—Settle		
	Dec-C	Mar-C	Jun-C	Dec-P	Mar-P	Jun-P
9100	1.00	1.01	0.91	0.00	0.03	0.15
9150	0.51	0.58	0.56	0.01	0.10	0.30
9200	0.12	0.25	0.29	0.12	0.27	0.53
9250	0.00	0.08	0.13	0.50	0.60	0.87
9300	0.00	0.01	—	1.00	1.03	—

Actual Vol. Monday, 2 Calls, 0 Puts.
Open interest Friday; 3,148, Calls, 3,333 Puts.

Eurodollar (CME) $ million; pts. of 100%

Strike Price	Calls—Settle			Puts—Settle		
	Dec-C	Mar-C	Jun-C	Dec-P	Mar-P	Jun-P
9100	1.00	1.01	0.85	.0004	0.04	0.16
9150	0.50	0.55	0.51	0.01	0.11	0.29
9200	0.10	0.24	0.26	0.10	0.27	0.52
9250	0.01	0.08	0.12	0.50	0.58	—
9300	.0004	0.03	—	—	—	—
9350	—	—	—	—	—	—

Est. vol. 1,383, Fri.; vol. 2,389 calls, 1,015 puts
Open interest Fri.; 26,510 calls, 38,912 puts

T-Bonds (CBT) $ 100,000; points and 64ths of 100%

Strike Price	Calls—Last			Puts—Last		
	Mar-C	Jun-C	Sep-C	Mar-P	Jun-P	Sep-P
76	3-56	3-34	—	0-39	1-17	2-03
78	2-34	2-26	2-29	1-10	2-03	3-01
80	1-27	1-36	1-48	2-03	3-06	4-07
82	0-47	0-62	1-11	3-21	4-28	5-28
84	0-24	0-37	0-48	4-58	6-00	7-00
86	0-11	0-21	—	6-44	—	—

Est. vol. 40,000, Fri; vol. 22,657 calls, 31,229 puts
Open interest Friday; 161,153 calls, 159,626 puts

T-Notes (CBT) $ 100,000; points and 64ths of 100%

Strike Price	Calls—Last			Puts—Last		
	Mar-C	Jun-C	Sep-C	Mar-P	Jun-P	Sep-P
84	4-44	4-08	—	0-10	0-31	—
86	2-63	2-46	—	0-27	1-00	—
88	1-39	1-40	—	1-00	1-55	—
90	0-44	0-57	—	2-05	3-02	—
92	0-17	—	—	—	—	—
94	0-05	—	—	—	—	—

Futures Prices

Monday, November 25, 1985
Open Interest Reflects Previous Trading Day.

	Open	High	Low	Settle	Change	Lifetime High	Lifetime Low	Open Interest
Cotton (CTN)—50,000 lbs.; cents per lb.								
Dec	61.85	61.90	61.15	61.15	− .73	73.00	57.51	2,294
Mar86	62.16	62.32	61.59	61.59	− .77	71.50	58.77	9,153
May	62.40	62.60	62.10	62.12	− .53	70.00	59.25	3,341
July	61.00	61.00	60.21	60.21	− .91	70.05	58.20	2,598
Oct	54.40	54.50	54.40	54.10	− .35	65.50	52.40	637
Dec	52.05	52.20	51.65	51.65	− .35	59.25	50.85	5,436

Est vol 2,500; vol Fri 3,057; open int 23,526, −198

	Open	High	Low	Settle	Change	Lifetime High	Lifetime Low	Open Interest
Orange Juice (CTN)—15,000 lbs.; cents per lb.								
Jan	113.40	113.70	112.80	113.25	− .10	180.00	111.70	2,092
Mar	114.35	114.50	113.50	113.85	− .05	177.50	112.75	2,914
May	114.55	114.75	114.05	114.45	−	162.50	113.00	867
July	115.00	115.00	114.75	114.95	+ .15	157.50	111.40	269

Est vol 350; vol Fri 385; open int 6,647, −66

Sugar—World (CSCE)—112,000 lbs.; cents per lb.

Jan	5.50	5.50	5.49	5.44	−	.03	7.75	3.00	519
Mar	6.25	6.29	6.12	6.17	−	.01	8.27	3.34	48,893
May	6.44	6.47	6.30	6.37		—	7.15	3.58	17,427
July	6.60	6.61	6.47	6.50	−	.01	6.69	3.79	7,398
Oct	6.84	6.86	6.71	6.76	+	.02	6.96	4.02	15,140
Mar87	7.40	7.40	7.30	7.35	−	.01	7.53	6.64	4,894

Est vol 6,486; vol Fri 13,048; open int 44,381, +618

Suger—Domestic (CSCE)—112,000 lbs.; cents per lb.

Jan	18.83	18.83	18.83	18.83	−	.17	22.00	18.25	617
Mar	19.10	19.13	19.10	19.13	−	.02	22.00	18.65	2,511
May	—	—	—	19.60		—	21.90	19.15	1,534
July	—	—	—	19.86	−	.09	21.60	19.35	1,416
Sept	—	—	—	19.83	−	.09	21.40	19.35	659

Est vol 450; vol Fri 91; open int 6,761, −43.

—Metals & Petroleum—

Copper (CMX)—25,000 lbs.; cents per lb.

Nov	—	—	—	61.05	−	.05	60.70	60.30	94
Dec	61.45	61.60	61.00	61.15	−	.05	84.25	58.50	21,215
Mar86	62.45	62.60	61.90	62.05	−	.05	80.00	59.50	36,268
May	62.75	62.85	62.30	62.40	+	.05	74.00	60.00	8,496
July	63.00	63.00	62.60	62.65	+	.05	72.55	60.35	5,508
Sept	63.30	63.30	63.30	62.95	+	.05	70.90	60.90	2,468
Dec	63.85	63.85	63.40	63.45	+	.10	70.30	61.60	3,122
Mar	64.30	64.30	64.30	63.95	+	.10	67.90	62.55	625
May	63.70	64.70	64.70	64.30	+	.15	67.30	62.90	265

Est vol 15,000; vol Fri 15,978; open int 78,232, +474.

Aluminum (CMX)—40,000 lbs.; cents per lb.

Nov	—	—	—	44.35	−	.50	—	—	0
Dec	44.90	45.00	44.60	44.45	−	.50	70.60	41.80	794
Mar86	45.85	46.15	45.60	45.60	−	.55	68.85	42.90	1,009
May	46.90	46.90	46.90	46.40	−	.50	62.35	44.20	25
July	47.65	47.65	47.50	47.20	−	.45	63.45	44.50	115

Est vol 300; vol Fri 588; open int 1,967, +50.

Gold (CMX)—100 troy oz.; $ per troy oz.

Nov	329.50	332.00	329.50	332.30	+	5.40	332.00	320.00	4
Dec	330.20	333.40	329.80	332.70	+	5.30	489.50	301.50	27,165
Fb86	334.50	337.80	334.00	337.00	+	5.50	485.50	306.00	28,852
Apr	338.00	341.50	338.00	340.80	+	5.60	496.80	314.70	14,211
June	342.50	345.20	342.00	345.00	+	5.70	433.50	320.50	12,686
Aug	346.30	347.50	346.30	349.20	+	5.80	427.50	331.00	10,988
Oct	351.00	352.00	351.00	353.60	+	5.90	395.70	335.00	8,430
Dec	354.50	358.50	354.50	358.20	+	6.00	388.20	339.00	10,233
Fb87	361.50	362.80	361.50	362.90	+	6.10	393.00	337.30	6,105
Apr	365.70	365.70	365.70	357.80	+	6.20	388.40	355.00	2,586
June	—	—	—	373.00	+	6.30	394.50	365.00	1,178
Aug	374.50	376.20	374.50	378.60	+	6.40	380.50	371.50	1,154

Est vol 50,000; vol Fri 36,882; open int 123,592, −1,121

Platinum (NYM)—50 troy oz.; $ per troy oz.

Dec	—	—	—	356.60	+	5.40	334.00	330.00	1
Jan86	354.70	359.80	354.50	356.60	+	5.40	373.00	293.50	10,835
Apr	358.50	362.50	358.50	359.60	+	4.50	362.50	264.50	5,109
July	360.00	366.50	360.00	363.10	+	4.50	366.50	273.00	1,186
Oct	369.00	369.00	366.00	366.60	+	4.50	369.00	303.50	598

Est vol 6,755; vol Fri 12,136; open int 17,733, +3,040.

Palladium (NYM) 100 troy oz.; $ per troy oz.

Dec	102.75	105.50	102.70	105.25	+	3.95	141.50	91.00	1,802
Mr86	104.50	107.95	104.50	107.35	+	4.55	127.50	91.70	3,779
June	106.00	109.00	106.00	108.60	+	4.55	114.00	91.50	933
Sept	106.50	110.50	106.50	109.85	+	4.55	115.00	91.70	241

Est vol 2,371; vol Fri 959; open int 6,813, −426.

Silver (CMX)—5,000 troy oz.; cents per troy oz.

Nov	628.0	628.0	628.0	627.8	+	6.2	628.0	602.5	4
Dec	627.0	631.8	625.5	628.5	+	6.0	1230.0	599.0	23,419
Jan86	631.0	635.0	631.0	633.0	+	6.0	1215.0	595.0	931
Mar	640.0	645.0	638.0	641.6	+	6.0	1193.0	607.0	22,415
May	647.0	653.0	647.0	649.7	+	6.2	1048.0	619.0	7,603
July	657.5	662.0	657.0	658.3	+	6.2	945.0	629.0	7,878
Sept	667.5	670.5	666.5	667.4	+	6.3	940.0	640.0	8,578
Dec	681.0	684.0	678.0	681.2	+	6.4	799.0	652.0	7,656
Mar87	698.0	698.0	695.0	695.7	+	6.7	770.0	670.0	3,653
May	707.0	707.0	707.0	705.7	+	6.8	752.0	682.0	3,766
July	720.0	720.0	719.0	716.2	+	6.9	746.0	695.0	1,329
Sept	729.2	729.2	729.2	727.2	+	7.0	729.2	711.0	1,009

Est vol 33,000; vol Fri 28,874; open int 88,284, +800.

Silver (CBT)—1,000 troy oz.; cents per troy oz.

Dec	627.0	633.0	625.0	629.0	+	6.0	940.5	590.0	9,839
Feb86	638.0	643.0	635.0	638.5	+	6.5	876.0	602.5	3,798
Apr	647.0	652.0	645.0	648.0	+	7.0	813.5	615.0	2,032
June	655.0	661.0	653.0	657.5	+	7.5	765.0	625.0	4,636
Aug	670.0	670.0	665.0	667.0	+	8.0	765.0	640.0	639
Oct	678.0	680.0	675.0	676.5	+	7.5	720.0	650.0	113
Dec	682.0	690.0	682.0	686.0	+	9.0	727.5	658.0	1,032

Est vol 5,000; vol Fri 6,768; open int 22,120, +1159.

Crude Oil (NYM)—42,000 gal.; $ per bbl.

Apr	.7845	.7920	.7845	.7880	+	.0075	.7920	.7050	631
May	.7850	.7905	.7840	.7880	+	.0065	.7905	.6975	946
June	.7850	.7860	.7840	.7875	+	.0075	.7860	.7370	158
Aug	.7675	.7675	.7675	.7865	+	.0075	.7790	.7300	117

Est vol 2,267; vol Fri 1,559; open int 11,992, −225.

Gasoline, Unleaded (NYM) 42,000 gal.; $ per gal.

Dec	.8070	.8095	.8060	.8061	+	.0001	.8100	.6835	575
Jan86	.7960	.8000	.7960	.7970	+	.0020	.8000	.6822	972
Feb	.7890	.7910	.7865	.7890	+	.0040	.7910	.6750	1,147
Mar	.7861	.7861	.7850	.7860	+	.0082	.7861	.6825	546
Apr	.7792	.7880	.7792	.7870	+	.0080	.7880	.6600	123
July	.7850	.7850	.7850	.7845	+	.0055	.7850	.7325	113
Aug	.7675	.7675	.7675	.7840	+	.0075	.7810	.7260	208

Est vol 375; vol Fri 220; open int 3,810, −37.

—Wood—

Lumber (CME)—138,000 bd. ft.; $ per 1,000 bd. ft.

Jan	145.00	145.60	143.80	145.30	+	.40	187.30	133.60	3,794
Mar	150.40	151.40	149.20	151.20	+	.80	195.00	139.70	1,494
May	155.00	155.50	154.10	155.50	+	.10	176.40	145.20	699
July	158.90	160.00	158.40	159.50	+	.50	183.40	149.50	212
Sept	—	—	—	162.60	−	.20	180.00	152.90	169

Est vol 934; vol Fri 881; open int 6,454, −160.

—Financial—

British Pound (1MM)—25,000 pounds; $ per pound

Dec	1.4595	1.4635	1.4540	1.4625	+	.0015	1.4635	1.0185	26,172
Mar86	1.4480	1.4525	1.4435	1.4510	+	.0010	1.4525	1.0650	7,844
June	1.4390	1.4440	1.4340	1.4410	+	.0010	1.4440	1.1530	254

Est vol 7,094; vol Fri 13,159; open int 34,270, +1,181

Canadian Dollar (1MM)—100,000 dlrs.; $ per Can $

Dec	.7255	.7260	.7249	.7251	−	.0015	.7568	.7006	5,421
Mar86	.7236	.7243	.7230	.7235	−	.0017	.7504	.6981	1,100
June	.7227	.7229	.7218	.7219	−	.0018	.7360	.7070	532
Sept	.7220	.7220	.7206	.7203	−	.0022	.7303	.7176	104

Est vol 613; vol Fri 1,102; open int 7,157, −232.

Japanese Yen (1MM) 12.5 million yen; $ per yen (.00)

Dec	.4978	.4986	.4962	.4981	+	.0006	.4986	.3905	30,450
Mar86	.4984	.4993	.4968	.4988	+	.0007	.4993	.4035	9,275
June	.4998	.5003	.4986	.4999	+	.0007	.5003	.4220	217

Est vol 13,211; vol Fri 16,303; open int 40,040, +763.

Swiss Franc (1MM)—125,000 francs; $ per franc

Dec	.4773	.4784	.4764	.4775	+	.0003	.4784	.3525	29,669
Mar86	.4820	.4831	.4811	.4823	+	.0003	.4831	.3790	4,970
June	.4870	.4875	.4866	.4870	−	.0002	.4875	.4190	379

Est vol 15,174; vol Fri 21,710; open int 35,021, +2,258.

W. German Mark (1MM)—125,000 marks; $ per mark

Dec	.3903	.3912	.3896	.3909	+	.0006	.3912	.2971	45,859
Mar86	.3940	.3945	.3930	.3942	+	.0006	.3945	.3040	7,523
June	.3967	.3979	.3966	.3976	+	.0006	.3979	.3335	434

Est vol 22,619; vol Fri 24,354; open int 53,822, +824.

Eurodollar (LIFFE)—$1 million; pts of 100%

	Open	High	Low	Settle		Chg	High	Low	Open Int
Dec	92.00	92.00	91.97	92.00	−	.01	92.16	88.12	5,904
Mar86	91.98	92.01	91.95	91.98	−	.02	92.15	87.87	8,407
June	91.76	91.78	91.73	91.76		—	91.95	87.64	4,502
Sept	91.45	91.46	91.43	91.45	+	.01	91.66	89.06	1,228
Dec	—	—		91.14	+	.02	91.30	90.20	720
Mar87		—	—	90.84	+	.02	—	—	110

Est vol 2,798; vol Fri 4,054; open int 20,886, +231

Sterling (LIFFE)—£500,000; pts of 100%

	Open	High	Low	Settle		Chg	High	Low	Open Int
Dec	88.62	88.63	88.57	88.58	+	.02	89.85	87.50	2,932
Mar86	89.16	89.17	89.11	89.13	+	.05	89.99	88.20	2,014
June	89.51	89.52	89.47	89.48	+	.04	89.92	88.80	1,040
Sept	89.66	89.68	89.62	89.63	+	.03	89.88	89.19	632
Dec	89.62	89.62	89.62	89.59	+	.07	89.84	89.20	356

Est vol 1,862; vol Fri 883; open int 6,994, +111.

Long Gilt (LIFFE)—£50,000; 32nds of 100%

	Open	High	Low	Settle		Chg	High	Low	Open Int
Dec	112-20	113-01	112-20	112-25	+	0-13	114-08	110-18	6,012
Mar86	112-27	113-04	112-27	112-30	+	0-15	112-19	110-29	1,818

Est vol 499; vol Fri 618; open int 1,669, +23.

Eurodollar (1MM)—$1 million; pts of 100%

	Open	High	Low	Set-tle		Chg	Yield Settle		Chg	Open Interest
Dec	91.99	92.01	91.98	92.00	−	.02	8.00	+	.02	59,884
Mr86	91.99	91.99	91.95	91.97	−	.03	8.03	+	.03	54,634
June	91.73	91.74	91.72	91.73	−	.02	8.27	+	.02	21,774
Sept	91.41	91.43	91.40	91.42	−	.01	8.58	+	.01	7,279
Dec	91.09	91.12	91.08	91.11	−	.01	8.89	+	.01	7,009
Mr87	90.76	90.81	90.76	90.80	−	.01	9.20	+	.01	3,224
June	90.51	90.52	90.50	90.51	−	.01	9.49	+	.01	3,073
Sept	90.24	90.26	90.24	90.24	−	.01	9.76	+	.01	3,209

Est vol 17,061; vol Fri 23,968; open int 160,686, +1,396.

GNMA 8% (CBT)—$100,000 prncpl; pts 32nds. of 100%

	Open	High	Low	Settle		Chg	Yield Settle		Chg	Open Interest
Dec	82-07	82-14	82-07	82-14	−	5	10.674	+	.027	2,378
Mr86	81-07	81-15	81-07	81-15	−	4	10.847	+	.022	1,427
June	80-16	80-19	80-14	80-19	−	3	11.006	+	.017	533
Sept	79-22	79-26	79-22	79-26	−	2	11.150	+	.012	156

Est vol 180; vol Fri 286; open int 4,494, +10.

Treasury Bonds (CBT)—$100,000; pts. 32nds of 100%

Dec	80-21	80-28	80-16	80-22	—	5	10.297	+	.022	145,273
Mr86	79-12	79-20	79-08	79-14	—	5	10.475	+	.022	107,557
June	78-14	78-19	78-09	78-14	—	5	10.621	+	.023	36,957
Sept	77-17	77-22	77-12	77-17	—	5	10.756	+	.024	17,108
Dec	76-22	76-28	76-18	76-23	—	5	10.879	+	.024	8,928
Mr87	75-27	76-04	75-27	75-31	—	5	10.994	+	.024	4,783
June	75-11	75-11	75-10	75-10	—	5	11.097	+	.025	2,053
Sept	74-20	74-29	74-20	74-24	—	5	11.186	+	.025	1,499
Dec	74-09	74-13	74-08	74-08	—	5	11.266	+	.025	276

Est vol 140,000; vol Fri 224,698; open int 324,522, −6432.

Treasury Notes (CBT)—$100,000; pts. 32nds of 100%

Dec	89-13	89-20	89-09	89-18	—	9.650	—	36,952
Mr86	88-18	88-22	88-11	88-21	—	9.806	—	26,585
June	87-20	87-25	87-17	87-25	—	9.957	—	2,533
Sept	—	—	—	86-31	—	10.100	—	2,042
Dec	—	—	—	86-08	—	10.228	—	369

Est vol 18,000; vol Fri 24,742; open int 68,481, +1108.

Ian H. Giddy

Case 38

An Order of French FRA's

Paris is an exciting place, especially since on your second day on the job in your bank's French affiliate, you have been asked to respond to a customer's request for a fifteen-month fixed rate French franc loan. Of course the bank is perfectly willing to make this loan. The only thing is that the French unit has had trouble accessing the interbank market for funds that far out: the best they can get at a reasonable cost — 14 percent to be precise — is a nine-month interbank placement. It seems that everyone is worried about another franc–D mark realignment beyond that period. So the Treasurer decided to go ahead and make the loan at a fixed fifteen-month rate, and fund only the first nine-month leg.

Where's the other leg? It's been dumped in your lap, of course, along with an article about Future Rate Agreements. All you know is that an

© Ian H. Giddy, New York University, 1985.

FRA is a sort of interbank interest rate futures contract, one where two parties agree to fix a future interest rate at a specified level for a specified future period. If, at the start of the specified period, the market rate (in this case French franc LIBOR) turns out to be different from the fixed-in-advance rate, the losing party compensates the winning party in cash.

Your boss knows this; but he wants to appear smarter than he actually is when he meets with the Treasurer, so he's asked you to find out:

(1) How exactly could a French FRA be used to fix the bank's cost of funding for the second leg of the loan?

(2) What would be reasonable quotes for a suitable FRA? Why?

(3) If the bank hedged its cost with an FRA at *x* percent, what would be the minimum rate it could charge on the loan and still make a ¾ percent spread?

(4) Should the customer be charged a fee up front for the cost of hedging? Why or why not?

(5) What would happen if rates fell by, say, 2 percent in the next nine months?

(6) What credit risk, if any, would the bank face if it hedged with one of these agreements?

Being a trader, your first reaction is to stare at the Reuters screen quotations of Euro French franc rates. You figure these rates would be available to your bank at least for up to nine months. But from there on in, you're on your own.

Exhibit 1 *Noonan Astley Eurocurrency Rates*

	US DLR	UK STLG	FR FRANCS	D MARKS
Call	10 – 10-1/8	10 – 10-1/8	—	—
2 Days	12-5/8 – 12-3/4	12-5/8 – 12-3/4	—	6-1/4 – 6-3/8
1 Week	11-3/4 – 11-7/8	11-3/4 – 11-7/8	12-1/8 – 12-1/4	7 – 7-1/8
1 Mo	11-3/8 – 11-1/2	11-7/8 – 12	12-1/8 – 12-1/4	7-1/4 – 7-3/8
3 Mo	11 – 11-1/8	12-1/4 – 12-3/8	13 – 13-1/8	7 – 7-1/8
6 Mo	10-1/2 – 10-5/8	12-1/2 – 12-5/8	14-1/4 – 14-3/8	6-1/2 – 6-5/8
9 Mo	10-1/4 – 10-3/8	12-1/2 – 12-5/8	13-7/8 – 14	6-1/2 – 6-5/8
12 Mo	10-1/4 – 10-3/8	12-1/2 – 12-5/8	13-5/8 – 13-3/4	6-1/2 – 6-5/8
15 Mo	10 – 10-1/8	—	13-1/4 – 13-3/8	6-1/4 – 6-3/8
18 Mo	9-3/4 – 9-7/8	—	13 – 13-1/4	6-1/4 – 6-3/8
			REUTERS	

Ian H. Giddy

Case 39

Wooden Stake

Metrobank's Bucharest office recently arranged a swap deal in which the bank intermediated between the Wooden Stake Corporation, a northwestern U.S. lumber firm that wanted six-year fixed rate sterling funds, and the Bank of Transylvania, which wanted floating-rate dollar funds. Wooden Stake obtained a floating-rate loan linked to LIBOR while Bank of Transylvania issued a fixed rate Bulldog bond; each effectively paid the other's interest with Metrobank coming in between.

1. Show, by means of diagrams, the initial, annual and final cash flows arising from this swap.
2. Show what flows (if any) might have occurred if Wooden Stake had wanted dollar funds instead.

3. What conditions are necessary for such a swap to occur?
4. Assume that dollar and sterling six-year interest rates were 10% and 11% and that the sterling/dollar exchange rate was $1.50 at the initiation of the swap. Eurodollar LIBOR was 8½% at that time. Five years later, sterling has fallen by 2% and sterling rates by 1%. What position would Metrobank be in if Transylvania went under?

Wooden Stake

Initial

W.S.

B of T

Annual

Final

Ian H. Giddy

Case 40

Das Kappenfloten

One day in the Eurobond market a new technique was invented: the stripped capped floater. Briefly, a borrower would issue a regular Eurobond floating-rate note, paying slightly more than LIBOR on a three- or six-month basis, but with an absolute ceiling on the rate payable on the note. The investor's return on the note would be limited by the cap, but if the cap were far enough above current LIBOR levels, he would not object too much and indeed certain investors would be attracted by the twenty-five to fifty basis points above comparable FRN's that the "cap floaters" offered. Then, through an investment bank, the issuer could sell his interest rate protection for an annual or up-front fee to another borrower who would pay an up-front fee for ceiling rate protection. This was called "stripping the cap from the floater."

Late in 1985, the cap floater was regarded as an idea whose time had come — and might be going. But Andy Monk, formerly from Citibank and now working at Deutsche Bank's New York Office, knew better. His customer was Canbank, a major Canadian bank, who wanted to obtain long-term Deutsche mark money to fund its Euro German mark loan portfolio, and Andy and his colleagues had been making enquiries among the German institutional investor community about the possibility of underwriting a EuroDM floating-rate note with a cap.

Deutsche Bank's London people had concluded that Canbank could successfully issue DM100 million FRNs with a cap of 8 percent at an interest rate of ³⁄₁₆ above three-month DM LIBOR, which was presently 4¹³⁄₁₆. This was where the bank's vast distribution power in the German domestic market came in useful. The Canadian bank was willing to issue such a note and to sell the cap — essentially an agreement to pay out the difference between DM LIBOR and 8 percent, should the rate exceed that level — to Deutsche Bank or a suitable counterparty. The Canadian bank could normally issue FRNs at LIBOR flat.

"This is getting exciting," thought Andy. "The only thing now is to find out who would want to buy the DM interest rate hedge and what price would make the deal work." Glancing at the Telerate Screen, he saw that Citibank was selling ten-year dollar interest rate ceilings at 11⅛ percent for a 5.2 percent fee. Dollar LIBOR was now 8 percent.

How should the deal be priced? Andy thought he had better diagram exactly how it worked, and who bears what risk when, before deciding on a minimum price for the cap to be sold.

IV

International Banking and Financial Intermediation

Ingo Walter

Case 41

Schubert National Bank

On a bright Saturday morning in mid-August, Tom Williams sat at his desk on the fifty-fifth floor of the Schubert National Bank building in lower Manhattan. Beyond the rooftops he could see the brisk chop of the water in New York harbor, and his thoughts turned briefly to his family relaxing at the Jersey shore and his plan to spend the day sailing. His thoughts were abruptly brought back to reality by the stack of reports and the sheaf of memoranda before him. As Senior Vice-President in charge of Credit Administration at Schubert National Bank, it was Tom Williams' job to recommend to top management the appropriate level of the Bank's exposure in individual countries.

© This case was written by Ingo Walter, Professor of Economics and Finance, Graduate School of Business Administration, New York University and John H. Loudon Professor of International Management, INSEAD, Fontainebleau, France, as a basis for class discussion. Revised February 1981. Reprinted by permission.

The past week had been a hectic one, with a number of major lending proposals coming to a decision point all at once. It was also clear from scanning the various memoranda on his desk that there were some substantial differences of opinion between the bank's economists, on the one hand, and the individual country lending officers and their supervisors with regional responsibility, on the other hand, about the desirability of some of the proposals from the point of view of the bank's strategic objectives. Tom Williams had called a series of meetings for Monday afternoon, at which the decision on each proposal would be made. Usually these decisions were reached by consensus; but he knew that his views would carry a great deal of weight and, in the absence of a real consensus, he would have to push through a resolution on his own.

Beyond the immediate problem, however, lay two more general issues that had preoccupied Tom Williams for several weeks. For one thing, he had been asked in a meeting with Juan G. Lopez, the bank's president, and Donald S. Schwarz, head of the International Banking Division and his immediate superior, to take a look at all of the bank's lending limits for less-developed countries in the light of Schubert's growth strategy for the 1980s, and to recommend possible revisions. This, he knew, reflected discussions at the last Board of Directors meeting. It was a periodic occurrence, but this was the first time he had faced the issue since getting promoted into his present job.

The other issue was his nagging dissatisfaction with the way the bank was currently doing country risk analysis. He had been to numerous meetings and conferences over the past year, and he knew that there wasn't a major bank in the country that was not currently trying to get a better handle on country risk. The methodology ranged all the way from multiple equation models designed for computer analysis to fundamentally intuitive "horseback" or "gut instinct" approaches. He respected the current approach taken by Schubert's economists, as reflected in the pile of country reports before him. But he wondered whether some innovative approaches might not be devised that would help in reaching sound decisions in cases such as those he now faced.

As he thought about these problems, Tom Williams tried to keep in mind the nature of Schubert National Bank — its history, its strategy in an increasingly competitive environment, and the way decisions on country loans are made.

HISTORY OF THE BANK

Hubertus Schubert was born in the tiny village of Leutershausen in the German state of Baden in 1790, the son of a local forester. The upper Rhine valley at the time was a fertile and prosperous area of farms and villages, with a few larger towns serving as hubs of transportation, commerce, and finance. Bordered on the east by the Odenwald forest and on the west by the wooded hills of the Palatinate, Baden at the time was governed by the Margrave Charles Frederick, who resided at Karlsruhe and who had greatly expanded the size and prestige of his state since coming to power in 1746.

The Schubert family was rather poor, and only four of the nine children survived beyond the age of ten. The household was maintained by a small hunting concession the elder Schubert had obtained from the Margrave and by a salary of fifteen Thaler per month he was paid as a forester. And so Fran Schubert had to maintain a tight rein on the household, with the two daughters and two sons required to do their assigned chores at an early age. Hubertus was the youngest. In later years he would remember phrases like "a Pfennig saved is a Pfennig earned" and "he who doesn't honor a Pfennig isn't worth a Thaler," both of which his father used repeatedly and which he claimed he had coined. Despite the poverty (or perhaps because of it), the Schubert family was known for its almost painful insistence on integrity.

In 1802, at the age of twelve and with four years of schooling under his belt (his academic performance was well below average), Hubertus was apprenticed to Oscar Meier in the local butcher shop. He earned no salary, received a free noontime meal each day, and his father was obliged to pay a monthly apprenticeship fee. Hubertus hated the work, ···hich in those days involved the slaughter of animals on the premises, but it was the only thing available in the area. Despite nine hours of meatcutting six days a week, Hubertus was able to do odd jobs before and after hours. The proceeds were squirreled away (except what he had to surrender to his mother), as were his earnings as a butcher in the first five years after completing his apprenticeship in Herr Meier's shop. The latter was fond of the grape, and died suddenly of acute gastrointestinal distress in 1810. At the age of twenty Hubertus purchased the shop with 25 percent equity and a medium-term self-liquidating loan from the widow Meier for the balance.

For the next ten years business boomed. Competition in the meat business was fragmented by local loyalties and long travel times, and cost-price margins were wide. Alone among butchers, Hubertus' reputation for honesty and quality drew customers from miles around. By partially overcoming his aversion to the meat business, knowing a good thing when he saw one, not getting married, and living with his mother (his father had since died), Hubertus by 1820 owned the shop outright and had amassed a tidy little fortune besides. Indeed, he had become one of the most respected of the region's burghers, and an outstanding prospect for every eligible Fraulein. His choice was the comely Louise Braunschweiger, the only child of a worthy goldsmith and moneylender in the nearby somewhat larger town of Weinheim — the only man in the region who surpassed Hubertus' own reputation for integrity.

During these years political events had produced considerable change. In 1806 Charles Frederick had acquired the title of Elector and Grand Duke, so the region became the Grand Duchy of Baden as part of the Confederation of the Rhine. In 1811 he was succeeded by his grandson Charles, who seceded from the Confederation. Despite the political turmoil, which was to continue, the regional economy continued to do well. In the months following his marriage to the goldsmith's daughter, Hubertus sold the butcher shop at (for him) an unconscionable profit and purchased a half-interest (at a concessionary price) in his father-in-law's business — eventually named Bankhaus Braunschweiger & Schubert. Together, they determined to deemphasize goldsmithing and concentrate on serving customers as a repository of gold and Thalers and a lender of same at interest, all the while maintaining comfortable reserves against the possibility of deposit withdrawals. They also became involved in clearing customers' payments, particularly with correspondent firms in the Hanseatic League cities of Hamburg, Bremen, and Lübeck in the North, and in making loans from time to time to the Grand Duke to finance his military ventures and public works. Some of the best assets in their portfolio were medium-term loans secured by a pledge of revenues from toll gates the Duke had strategically located along his stretch of the Rhine. And they invested part of their own capital — as well as some client money entrusted to them for this purpose and even some regular deposit-based funds — in minority equity participations in local farms and other enterprises. In short, the old man and his son-in-law became a bank.

Time went by, and the business grew. Braunschweiger died of pneumonia in 1835 and Hubertus and his staff of fifty carried on, moving the bank to the larger town of Mannheim on the banks of the Rhine. His wife had given birth to a son and four daughters in quick succession, and by 1850 Bankhaus Braunschweiger & Schubert (BB&S for short) was one of the premier financial institutions in the Grand Duchy, with an impeccable reputation. Hubertus's oldest child and only son, Alois, joined the bank as a clerk at the age of fifteen and began working his way up the ladder as heir apparent. The family was prosperous, well liked, and respected, with the girls married off unfailingly one by one to even more prosperous burghers in the area.

Despite economic growth, political uncertainties often preoccupied the Schuberts and their senior managers. In 1846 a Constitutionalist government was instituted in Baden, and as a spillover from the French revolution of 1848 serious popular insurrection occurred. The military sided with the revolutionaries and the Grand Duke was forced to flee. However, he was able to appeal successfully to the Prussian monarchy, and after several battles he was reinstated. But in 1866 he made the mistake of siding with the losers in the Austro-Prussian War, and Baden was forced to pay heavy reparations and reorganize its army on the Prussian model. In 1867 Baden joined the North German Confederation. These episodes created both problems and opportunities for BB&S, which was generally able to ride out the various crises while taking advantage of the new business possibilities they inevitably gave rise to.

A different kind of crisis also shook the bank during this period. In 1860 Hubertus and Louise Schubert were killed in a train wreck while returning from a relaxing sojourn in Baden-Baden. Hubertus had just turned seventy. Their deaths shocked the community, and gave rise to much speculation about the future course of events at BB&S, by that time having net assets of 6 million Thaler and over one hundred employees. The burden of leadership fell to Alois Schubert, who by the age of thirty-eight had already been exposed to all phases of the bank's operations, had done a stint in the military as a cavalry officer with combat experience, and had spent six years abroad with financial institutions in New York, London, and Paris. He spoke French and English fluently and had few of the "rough edges," in terms of social graces, that his father had never quite managed to shed in his lifetime. Despite minimal formal schooling — which never agreed with him and which the elder Schubert had never valued highly — his reputation in the banking community was beyond reproach. So the choice of leadership for Bankhaus Braunschweiger & Schubert was natural, a choice made entirely by the Schubert family as sole owners.

While BB&S prospered despite local political problems, these years were a time of turmoil around the world as well. Colonialism was in its heyday in Africa and Asia. Civil war erupted in the United States, with different European interests backing one side or the other. The Franco-Prussian War enveloped the Continent in military conflict, and the future of the German Empire forged by Bismarck in 1870 was highly uncertain. Particularly in the banking business, nobody knew what conditions would be like in the *Reich* presided over by Kaiser Wilhelm I. Aversion to uncertainty had been a Schubert family trait for generations — they had nothing against economic and political "risk," which could be assessed and accounted for in business and which indeed they had done quite well in "managing" over the years. But "uncertainty," which he was unable to build into his business planning, was anathema to Alois Schubert. In early 1871, just as Baden joined the new German Empire, he shocked the local business and financial community by selling out to his principal competitor. With Schubert family assets liquidated, equal shares were distributed to the five shareholders. On May 15, 1871, Alois Schubert and his new young wife Mathilde left Hamburg for New York. In the hold of the ship was his entire fortune in gold bullion (fully insured, of course). In later years he would often think about the correctness of his decision to leave Europe. Names like Lazard, Brinkmann, Schroder, Rothschild, and Warburg kept coming to mind. But the decision had been made and there was no turning back.

In New York, Alois Schubert set up shop as a private banker in the Wall Street area in November 1871 as Braunschweiger, Schubert & Co. Served well by friendships he had made in his traineeship years in New York and good contacts that had existed between BB&S and a number of top financial houses, he was soon accepted as a creative and hard-working banker. Despite the problems faced by immigrants everywhere, renewed prosperity was not long in coming — nor were three sons, William (1872), Robert (1874), and Joseph (1876). So at the age of forty-nine Alois Schubert began a new life in a new country.

American financial markets at the time were themselves in turmoil, a legacy of the Civil War and recurring bitter battles between easy-money advocates ("greenbackism") and conservatives, who demanded a return to the gold standard. The latter seemed to have won with passage of the Resumption Act of 1875 that provided for a return to specie payments in 1879, later compromised to freeze the supply of greenbacks at $247 million. Silver dollars were eliminated from coinage in 1873, effectively reestablishing the gold standard, but major silver discoveries later caused a drop in the silver price and a demand for a return to bimetallism. Silver prices remained a hot political issue until 1900, with periodic purchases by the U.S. Treasury inflating the money supply. Meantime, the use of checkbook money grew steadily at the expense of banknotes.

The National Banking System, adopted during the Civil War, provided that any group of persons with enough capital could obtain a charter from the Controller of the Currency by depositing a specified amount in government bonds. City banks were required to maintain 25 percent reserves against deposits under this system, and were not permitted to own real estate or make real estate and security loans. The Schubert National Bank succeeded Alois Schubert's private bank under a National Banking charter in 1885. Despite recurring financial crises, the Schubert National Bank prospered in both commercial and investment banking during the late nineteenth and early twentieth centuries. Alois Schubert took his place a bit behind J. Pierpoint Morgan as a financier of business in the burgeoning American economy. His ties to European banking allowed Schubert to readily tap foreign sources of capital to finance U.S. enterprises, although like others he later began to cut his links in favor of greater reliance on domestic savings and financial intermediation.

At the turn of the century, Alois Schubert retired at the age of seventy-five and in the pink of health — trying to stay that way, he said, to guarantee a more impressive portrait to adorn the bank in years to come. The burden of leadership fell to the three sons, still in their twenties. None had attended universities. All were privately schooled under the old man's close supervision and with extensive periods of training in the bank. William and Robert followed in the footsteps of their father and grandfather as intelligent, courageous, and scrupulous bankers. William's forte was investment banking, while Robert was more adept at commercial banking, and that is how they split the leadership role. Joseph was the black sheep of the family. He marched to a different drummer and entered New York University for what turned out to be ten years of academic work, finishing in 1910 with a Ph.D. degree in economics and a college teaching job in Missouri.

From then on things moved quickly. Alois Schubert died in 1911 at the age of eighty-six. The Federal Reserve Act was passed in 1913, with the Schubert National Bank one of the first members — a move welcomed by the Schuberts because it promised to end pyramiding of bank reserves and increase the stability of the U.S. banking system. There was growing confidence that recurring bank crises and depressions were a thing of the past. The stock market boomed, and Schubert went public with the sale of a 60 percent equity interest on the open market. Besides enlarging the bank's capital base, this served to diversify the family's holdings and to establish the Schubert Family Charitable Trust. William did very well indeed during the speculative 1920s, while Robert cautiously continued to build the bank's deposit base, loan portfolio, international transactions, and client relationships. Joseph remained in the Midwest and rose to the (untenured) rank of Associate Professor at the University of Missouri.

At the annual family gathering on Christmas 1928 Joseph told his brothers about his concern over the state of the economy. Midwest farmers had overbought machinery and equipment, and he doubted that 1929 would be a good year for the farm implements industry. Such a slump couldn't help but percolate through the rest of the economy, and he was afraid that when the feverish and highly leveraged speculators on Wall Street got wind of this the stock market might be in for a significant "correction." William and Robert knew that Joseph was certainly no banker, but they also knew that he was a respectable economist with (even more important) plenty of plain common sense. Beginning early in January 1929, senior management at Schubert National Bank slowly and carefully began to liquidate some of its equity positions and to advise their clients to do likewise, and at the same time took a much more conservative position on securities loans and credits to potentially vulnerable businesses. Earnings dropped rather abruptly, but when the great crash came Schubert felt no need to make abrupt moves like the legendary Ben Smith, who allegedly got out just in time by bursting through his brokers' door shouting "Sell 'em, they're worthless!" And so, as the world economy spiraled into the Great Depression, Schubert National Bank was in better shape than most to ride out the storm. Meantime, Joseph suffered in losing his teaching job at Missouri for not having sufficient scholarly publications, and rejoined the family enterprise as Chief Economist.

The 1930s saw bank regulation considerably tightened, with passage of the National Banking Acts of 1933 and 1935, and the Glass-Steagall Act, which separated investment and commercial banking. As a result, William left the bank to establish the investment banking house of Braunschweiger & Co., which still exists today as a partnership. Robert took the helm at Schubert National Bank, and was succeeded on retirement in 1939 by his second-in-command, John K. Thompson. In the early postwar years the only Schubert left at the bank was Robert's nephew, Missouri-born Albert, the son of the bank's first economist and (not surprisingly) a rapidly rising young vice-president.

With the growth of banking after World War II, the Schubert National Bank has been in an excellent position to play a leading role. Albert Schubert acceded to the presidency in 1955 and to board chairmanship on Thompson's retirement in 1958. He took the reins easily and naturally, in the best tradition of the Schubert lineage, defining his role as a strategic planner and banking statesman. Although shy and introspective by nature, he feels comfortable in personal contacts with heads of state, corporate managers, and high government officials, and his easygoing nature and obvious control inspire confidence and maintain morale of bank employees at all levels. In recent years "Al" Schubert has even become a kind of spokesman for banking and private enterprise as a whole, arguing forcefully and persuasively in the great debates of the day on the appropriate roles of business and government in society. Within the bank Al Schubert is almost ideally complemented by President Juan Lopez, a hard-driving but fair-minded individual with a global reputation as a consummate professional executive and a masterful tactician in the evolving game of international banking.

THE BANK AND ITS COMPETITIVE ENVIRONMENT

At the present time, the Schubert National Bank is among the ten leading commercial banks in the United States, with assets of almost $40 billion and total deposits of almost $30 billion at the end of 1980. Stockholders' equity was $1.9 billion at year end 1980 compared with $1.1 billion in 1976. Income per share has remained about the same for the past four years, and was $5.92 in 1980. Dividend payment has been allowed to rise gradually over time, from $1.79 in 1976 to $2.28 in 1980.

Schubert is actively involved in both wholesale and retail banking in the United States, with thirty-four offices in the New York metropolitan area and contiguous counties. Its market has traditionally been biased toward the wholesale end, however, with retail banking limited to the extent possible to large accounts and mortgage financing. An aggressive corporate lending program is maintained throughout the United States, with loan production offices in major centers such as Houston, Chicago, and Los Angeles. Schubert is known as a hard-driving bank, yet one that maintains a deserved reputation for conservatism in lending decisions. Management's strategy evidently is to compete vigorously in every major market and then to select only the best from among the lending possibilities that present themselves.

An active and high-quality trust department is maintained, and Schubert's operations and systems groups are known to be among the best in the industry. In recent years, Schubert has taken on a number of ancillary activities including travelers checks, foreign exchange and money management advisory services, and the like in order to develop and maintain "full service" relationships with clients. The bank's foreign exchange department is large, sophisticated, and profitable, with the newest technical aids supporting traders' activities in spot and forward markets. As a result, the bank's relationships with individual clients tend to involve a variety of services, and assessment of the profitability of these relationships tends to be quite complex.

Schubert maintains extensive correspondent banking relationships both domestically and internationally, although in recent years the bank's aggressive expansion has led to a growing incidence of direct competition with some of its most valued correspondents. Management feels, however, that such incidents are an inevitable consequence of its growth strategy.

In matters of personnel, the bank is known for the quality of its senior management, most of whom have had twenty years or more of service and were recruited during the early 1950s as the bank was establishing its place among the leading money-center institutions. Middle management, however, is viewed as somewhat less strong, partly the result of some personnel errors in the 1960s involving insufficiently broad-based searches for entry-level talent, and morale problems among junior officers that have led to high levels of attrition, particularly among the most marketable individuals. Many of them moved to competing New York banks and, more recently, to foreign banks aggressively entering the U.S. market.

These problems had been largely corrected by the mid-1970s, however, with greatly intensified recruiting linked to completely revamped training and incentive programs. Schubert leads the industry in opening opportunities to women and minorities. In part because of its retail banking operations, Schubert's annual intake of trainees is rather sizeable. Employment is no guarantee of retention, and considerable involuntary terminations occur after three or four years of service. Management feels that this system of aggressive and open recruiting, excellence in training, rewards for initiative and performance, and selective pruning will provide a solid base from which to draw the future leadership of the bank. Among potential employees, Schubert is known as an institution where individual performance counts heavily. Clients are increasingly coming to view these developments as overcoming the recent spate of problems at the middle-management level.

In the early 1960s, Schubert management made a decision to move actively into international banking. The formation of the European Common Market in 1958, together with rapid economic growth in Europe and the Pacific Basin, made these areas prime targets for expansion. Close ties with American-based multinationals provided a natural market that grew with their rapid overseas expansion in the decade of the 1960s and early 1970s. Schubert also found that it was quite innovative in relation to local European and Asian banks, and was able to make inroads into some of their traditional markets. Management decided to concentrate on these two relatively "open" markets for bank services — it felt that much of Africa was more or less sewn up by French and British banks and in any case had questionable medium-term prospects, while limits on resources and other priorities precluded a major presence in Latin America. In the early 1970s, however, the bank moved aggressively in Latin America, especially Brazil, and was beginning to reexamine its long-term plan for Africa as well. In both of these areas, however, it was faced with well-entrenched competition. Besides the major developed market-economy countries, the bank has had long-standing mutually beneficial relations especially with the governments of South Korea, the Philippines, Malaysia, and Mexico.

During recent years loan demand growth abroad has greatly exceeded demand at home, and at present 53 percent of the bank's operating income is generated by international activities. The development of the Eurocurrency market also played a major role in the bank's evolution toward heavy international involvement. The contribution of international operations to Schubert's income is slightly over 50 percent. The Schubert National Bank's network of branches, representative offices, and other foreign affiliations is extensive. In recent years the international banking environment has become increasingly competitive, including major moves by foreign banks into the U.S. market.

Schubert National Bank is organized along more or less traditional lines, as depicted in Exhibit 1. The operating unit for international operations is the International Banking Division, headed by Donald S. Schwartz.

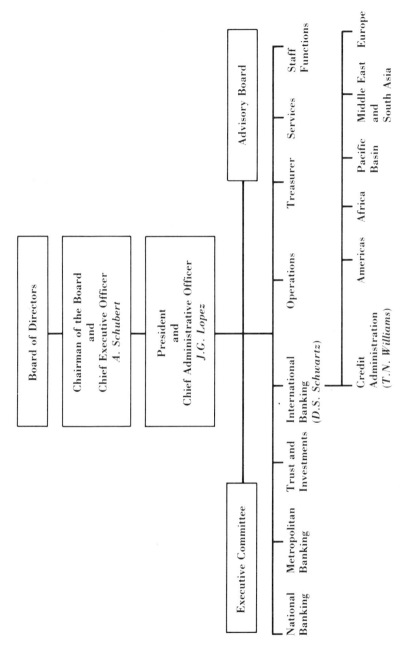

Exhibit 1 Organizational Chart, Schubert National Bank

It is divided into five major reporting areas: Americas, Africa, Pacific Basin, Middle East and South Asia, and Europe. A Credit Administration unit headed by Thomas N. Williams oversees the bank's exposure in all of its international operations. With respect to its overall asset profile at the end of 1980, 31.4 percent was in the United States, 18.2 percent in Canada and Latin America, 1.3 percent in Africa, 16.8 percent in the Pacific Basin countries, 4.4 percent in the Middle East and South Asia, and 27.9 percent in Europe.

ASSESSMENT OF COUNTRY RISK AND EXPOSURE LIMITS

In a recent discussion emerging from a Schubert National Bank's board of directors meeting, senior management appeared concerned about the bank's method of establishing country lending limits as well as individual country lending decisions. International loan charge-offs were significantly smaller than domestic losses. Nevertheless, in the light of several recent negative experiences with short-term credits involving Turkey and Peru and the growth of the International Banking Division, senior credit officers were determined to monitor the bank's country exposure more closely. Moreover, although losses on international loans were less than those on domestic credits, management felt that increasing international loan demand required a more serious approach to the measurement of risks involved in international lending.

COUNTRY EXPOSURE

Senior credit officers at Schubert were quite aware of the growing trend among major banks toward quantifying risk factors in individual country lending decisions. Schubert's international economics group was itself in the process of devising a new set of criteria that might serve to more accurately reflect risk in country lending decisions. Such criteria would have to reflect an awareness of the differences between domestic and international credits, and differences in the available machinery for dealing with problem loans. Although final responsibility for servicing domestic loans is often clouded, the degree of complexity in the case of foreign loans is generally much greater.

Is a loan to a French company under the guarantee of a U.S. company considered a U.S. risk or a French risk? Is a time deposit from the bank's London office to the Paris office of Deutsche Bank viewed as French or

German risk? How are locally funded assets of a foreign branch to be treated? Where do you place the country risk for shipping loans that might be made to shell companies in Liberia or Panama? How is a "comfort letter" or "keepwell" used to determine country risk? After examining each of these questions carefully, Schubert management agreed that for cross-border loans every facility or other risk asset should be assigned to the country that best reflects the location of the entity having the ultimate legal responsibility for repayment of the obligation. All credit facilities extended by one of Schubert's foreign offices, including those funded locally, are incorporated in the credit risk report in order to give a complete picture for the entire bank. The classification scheme used by Schubert National Bank is presented in Appendix One.

The senior officer in charge of each country in which Schubert does business is responsible for assembling exposure information from all bank branches, representative offices, and majority-owned or -managed affiliates on each country in which it has incurred exposure. This information is consolidated and sent to Head Office, with information simultaneously sent to the senior officer in charge of each country where exposure exists. The latter prepares a separate report including the location of Schubert units creating the exposure and likewise sends it to Head Office. Head Office thus receives two reports, one from the Schubert unit creating the exposure and one from the officer in charge of the country where the exposure is located — the latter includes domestic credit facilities extended by units of the bank.

Information used in preparing country exposure reports includes (a) name and industry of the customer; (b) country of domicile of the borrower; (c) type, amount, and tenor (time remaining to maturity: under one year, one to five years, six to eight years and over eight years) of the facility; (d) amount of outstandings under the facility; (e) whether the facility is guaranteed or otherwise supported by another entity, e.g., via "comfort letter" or "keepwell," and the domicile of that entity; (f) involvement of a government or government entity as borrower or guarantor; (g) currency in which outstandings are denominated; and (h) facilities guaranteed by the customer in another country. Double-counting is avoided by separating the reporting into "cross-border" facilities by Schubert affiliates in one country to borrowers in another and "intracountry" facilities to borrowers in the same country. All information is updated by the booking units quarterly, and is consolidated at Schubert head office — it is reported in local currency and translated into U.S. dollars at the time of consolidation.

No liability offsets, in the form of cash deposits taken in by Schubert or its affiliates abroad, are considered in reporting country exposure. Data on such liabilities are, however, maintained in comparable form, so that they can be considered in country-risk analyses. The system captures both direct exposure (loans, investments, etc.) and contingent exposure (letters of credit, guarantees, etc.) as well as unused portions of credit facilities granted to customers. Comfort letters, keepwells, and other implicit guarantees do not serve to transfer exposure to the country of the "guarantor" unless, in the opinion of the lending officer, the commitment is so strong that it is the equivalent of an explicit guarantee. Loans to branches of banks are allocated to the country of the bank's head office, while shipping loans are allocated to the country where legal proceedings could best be instituted against the obligor.

At Schubert's head office, the assembly, consolidation, and dissemination of quarterly country exposure information is the responsibility of the Treasurer's Division. Analysis and monitoring of country exposure is the responsibility of the International Banking Division, specifically the senior officer in charge and the officer responsible for credit administration.

The reporting system utilized by Schubert is capable of providing an instantaneous measurement of country exposure according to two classifications: "maximum country exposure" and "exposure over one year." In addition, the system provides a breakdown of the maturity profile and loan structure (i.e., letters of credit, Euro-currency loans, etc.). It thus permits senior management to closely monitor the bank's country exposure, and is an important factor in its attempt to minimize losses associated with possible defaults, reschedulings, or other "problems" — as had been in the case with regard to Turkey and Peru.

Special emphasis is placed at Schubert on the mix of the present and planned exposure in a country. Short-term trade financing is generally considered to be less risky than term loans. Euro-currency loans to projects with identifiable hard-currency cash flows are preferable to those that generate only local currency. A line of credit, which is subject to review periodically, gives more flexibility than a longer-term commitment. In developing countries, exposure to governments and banks is usually regarded as far better in quality than exposure to private corporations. Aside from the normal credit decisions associated with any loan, decisions on international credits must therefore concern themselves with the creditworthiness of a particular country as well. The concept of country exposure is relatively simple. It is to show the distribution of the present and potential risk assets of a bank on a country-by-country basis. After much wrangling at recent staff meetings, senior management had tentatively defined some basic principles by which one could measure risk associated with country exposure. At Schubert National Bank, it is examined from two different points of view: Credit Risk and Country Risk.

CREDIT RISK

The concept of credit risk is the conventional identification of risk elements associated with any borrower and assumed by the creditor in domestic or international loans. It is "entity-specific" and related to the ability of the borrower to service the debt from normal sources of funds. International credit risk analysis, therefore, involves the ability and willingness of the foreign borrower — business firm, state or local government agency, public authority, etc. — to meet interest and principal payments on schedule. Questions relating to political and legal jurisdiction, as well as conditions affecting the country of domicile of the borrower, are normally beyond the scope of credit risk analysis.

SOVEREIGN RISK

Exposure to sovereign risk arises from the presence of a politically sovereign national government as an actor in the international lending process. It may enter that process either directly via government loans, or indirectly via business or agency loans. There are both economic and political dimensions to a country's "ability" and "willingness" to service externally held debt. The economic dimensions often relate to the availability of foreign exchange for debt-service, and factors affecting that availability. The political dimensions may range from outright repudiation of externally held debt to problems in the political delivery of economic policies that would make possible normal debt-service flows.

Thus, an unguaranteed credit to a private firm or public agency in a particular country embodies elements of both credit and country risk — the firm may be able and willing to pay, but the government may not be willing or able to make available the needed foreign exchange. Government guaranteed debt, on the other hand, embodies only country risk, since debt-service depends entirely on the policies and actions of a politically sovereign foreign state.

At the limit, exposure to sovereign risk at Schubert National Bank is intended to show the possible loss to the bank if a foreign government should expropriate its own or a borrower's assets or uses exchange controls to prohibit cross-border transfers of funds. The basic concept at Schubert is to present a "worst-case" scenario for each country, and then show factors that might reduce the amount of the loss. Considerations such as slow payments, missed payments, loan rescheduling, or refinancing serve to mitigate the maximum loss criterion. But the risk of outright loss is of greatest interest to management, and dictates a "worst-case" approach in assessing sovereign risk.

Maximum country risk in a given case encompasses all outstanding assets that might not be repaid in the event of an expropriation or application of exchange controls in that country. One factor that might conceivably reduce the amount of maximum loss is deposits taken in from residents of the country. Assuming that these deposits might not have to be repaid in the event of a default, the deposits from residents are shown as a possible offset to maximum country risk.

DETERMINING COUNTRY CREDITWORTHINESS

The International Economist's office at Schubert is charged with following developments in all countries in which the bank has an actual or potential interest. A staff economist may be assigned between one and five countries, in addition to his or her other assignments. A country report is published for staff use only, detailing internal and external economic and political conditions in each country. These reports are readily available to all international lending officers. They are usually updated annually, with an interim revision semiannually or when major events appear to make this necessary. For some countries, however, the reports may not be updated for extended periods if there is no particular interest in them or if other work takes precedence. The economist charged with following a country is also available for in-person or telephone consultation. In turn, the economist receives periodic reports on conditions from Schubert branches or other affiliates in his assigned countries, as well as occasional trip reports and periodic on-site visits lasting an average of one week. The country reports generally go into considerable detail on each dimension of national economic performance, and summary conclusions are reached concerning prospects one, three, and five years into the future. On request, these projections can be extended to seven or ten years, although for many countries the economists are hesitant to go this far out.

In addition to in-house research, economists and credit officers at Schubert also make use of external intelligence services, occasional consultants, contacts at other banks and international financial institutions, government officials, and the like. They also remain generally alert to news events. Significant items from any of these sources are usually reported in memorandum form, a copy of which goes into the economist's country file for use in subsequent analysis of country conditions.

Creditworthiness in the view of Schubert management cannot be summed up in one or two simple ratios dealing with a country's external liabilities and assets. Any judgment must be based on a broad array of factors dealing with the country's past and future, its economics and politics, and the kinds of short-term cyclical as well as longer-term structural factors that affect its economy.

There are four basic sets of factors that senior credit officers at Schubert National Bank now utilize in determining countries' economic and political risk profiles. The weight that the international economists at Schubert assign to each of these factors is undetermined, and has been subject to some controversy. The majority of Schubert economists feel strongly that these weights should remain unspecified, since they could be different from country to country and from one time period to the next. The four factors are: (1) domestic demand management, i.e., the policy context in which economic activity in the country take place; (2) fundamental economic factors (raw materials, human, and financial resources) and the growth and development strategy of its main policymakers; (3) the external finance (both stocks and flows) of the country, including the balance of payments and level and structure of its external debt; and finally (4) the outlook for internal and regional political stability and the quality of its political institutions. These factors are presented in somewhat greater detail in the Appendix One.

The economist at Schubert examined many of the traditional indicators such as the debt-service ratio or the ratio of debt outstanding to gross domestic product, but felt that these indicators really do not adequately measure the effects that monetary, fiscal, and exchange rate policies might have on the balance of payments in the short term, or the effects that a country's growth and development may have on export or import trends and foreign exchange availability over the long run.

In re-examining the bank's recent sobering experiences with Turkey, Peru, and a few other "problem" cases, the office of the International Economist at Schubert has developed some "early warning" signals. Should trends in the country's economy be regarded as heading toward these signals, the senior credit officers at Schubert are alerted that the country's exposure limit should be carefully monitored and possibly even changed. These "early warning" indicators are as follows: (1) large fiscal deficits as a percent of GDP; (2) rapid expansion of domestic credit; (3) high inflation rates relative to earlier patterns; (4) reluctance on the part of the authorities to permit the exchange rate to depreciate and to offset adverse inflation rate differentials; and (5) a marked decline in the ratio of domestic savings to GDP.

ESTABLISHING NEW COUNTRY LENDING LIMITS

The size of Schubert National Bank in terms of officer-level personnel is an integral factor in the determination of new country limits. Although the bank is among the top ten in the United States by most measures, divisional lending officers know each other and have established close working relationships. Rather than a highly competitive atmosphere that exists at some other banks, the officers at Schubert traditionally cooperate with each other to the fullest extent possible.

Given the complexity of the country risk assessment problem, establishing new exposure limits can easily become a long and arduous process. But at Schubert it is a rather informal one, involving the office of the International Economist, a senior credit officer, the area manager, and the territory lending officers. The economist assigned to the country under discussion is always involved, although sometimes the International Economist himself participates. Each participant contributes to an informal but intensive "information exchange" during the course of the year and is able to ascertain a multifaceted picture of the country's economic and political direction. When it is time to actually review and possibly revise existing country exposure, the area manager, the senior credit officer, and an international economist will examine a number of items:

First, they will look at the exposure as it now exists using the country risk exposure reporting system described above. Schubert's current exposure profile is presented in Exhibit 2.

Second, they will examine the bank's overall portfolio mix of international and domestic assets. Is this the right mix under prevailing economic conditions? If not, how should it be changed? Does it satisfy the bank's strategic and tactical objectives, as set by senior management, in the international market for bank services given the evolving competitive conditions?

Third, they will analyze current conditions in the country in question, focusing on the inherent economic developments and associated risks, the level of term debt, the political situation, current economic policy and the quality of the officials responsible for its implementation, the opportunities for financing, and finally, an intuitive feeling of the territory lending officer towards the political and economic future. At Schubert, all other things being equal, the subjective judgment of an area officer will be rather heavily weighed in the ultimate decision.

Fourth, in evaluating new limits, the group will pose a question involving future planning. Where would we like to be (in terms of a maximum exposure limit) in five years? This will clearly be based on the country's future potential for growth, as well as the outlook for internal and regional political stability.

Exhibit 2 **International banking division credit exposure by country of risk** *(in thousands of U.S. dollars)*

Territory	Maximum		Outstanding			Unused Commitments	Term Sublimit	Term Exposure	Redeposits
	Country Limit	Country Exposure	Direct	Contingent	Total				
Americas	6,152,000	5,359,300	4,030,500	479,700	4,510,200	849,100	3,731,500	3,341,500	1,118,200
Africa	526,450	446,470	266,800	92,730	359,530	86,940	331,170	302,700	21,300
Middle East and South Asia	1,090,500	933,000	711,600	178,800	890,400	44,600	532,500	417,350	158,300
Pacific Basin	4,923,000	4,258,800	3,260,900	564,600	3,825,500	433,300	2,901,500	2,299,300	668,000
Europe	7,031,050	6,520,990	4,373,900	1,066,800	5,440,700	1,080,290	4,076,900	3,232,900	2,629,000
Total	19,723,000	17,518,560	12,643,700	2,382,630	15,026,330	2,494,230	11,573,570	9,593,750	4,594,800

As of December 31, 1980.

361

Finally, some attention will be paid to the "utilization rate" — that is, the percentage of past and current exposure to the overall maximum exposure ceiling that had been established in previous periods. Based on future credit demand and potential, Schubert officers prefer to maintain the historical ratio. This, in the past, has allowed for some flexibility in any given year without having to re-establish a new limit in midstream.

In summary, new country exposure should satisfy the following criteria: (1) Does it meet the bank's goals as set forth by senior management? (2) Are we comfortable with it or does it seem too low or too high? and (3) Is there ample room for flexibility should credit demand require it?

Independently, each lending officer covering the territory in question analyzes his or her accounts and how the utilization rate has matched up with the current plan. Through continuous contact with account relationships, each credit officer will have a fairly clear picture of both the short-term and long-term needs of the bank's clients. Therefore, arriving at an exposure planning limit is not accomplished in a vacuum, but rather in response to the evolving realities of the market. Generally, country limits are established when Schubert exposure in a particular country exceeds $100,000, and are reviewed annually or when conditions require it. Sublimits are established for facilities extending beyond one year. The office of the International Economist will, quite often, independently recommend to the senior credit officer the direction in which specific country limits should move. Frequently, in countries where growth may be declining or perhaps the economy may be headed for a recession, the economist will suggest a very conservative approach on new limits. Likewise, there may be instances where an economist may feel the bank should "go in heavy." A frequent source of disagreement, however, occurs when a lending officer's views, both about the short-term and long-term picture of the economy, differ from that of the economist, especially with respect to loan demand. The banker will frequently have different reasons for wanting to increase or decrease country exposure, and so the views of the economist and the lending officer occasionally clash.

HOW A PARTICULAR COUNTRY CREDIT IS DECIDED

There are two types of country classifications that confront international lending officers at Schubert: (1) countries where the bank is doing or would like to do business and (2) countries where for reasons of assessed risk, general apprehension, or uninteresting economic prospects, the bank is not actively soliciting business.

Assuming a Schubert lending officer is responsible for a country in which the bank actively wants to do business, he would look for a good credit risk, adequate pricing, and most of all, the character of the borrower.

If, however, the country is not one in which the bank is actively soliciting business, lending criteria tend to be much more conservative. The officer must have a good reason as to why the loan should be made. The credit rating of the borrower must be excellent. The loan must also be priced at or above market. There should be potential for collateral business, or if the borrower is a private firm, the company involved should be one that is important to the bank now or in the future — in the words of one Schubert official, "it has earned a call by us."

SPECIAL PROBLEMS OF DEVELOPING-COUNTRY LIMITS

The management at Schubert'National Bank has traditionally taken a relatively conservative approach towards exposure limits with respect to less-developed countries. The credit officer must show *objective* prudence in loan situations. The International Economist's office will be involved with the country lending officer on a day-to-day basis, and the bank does not hesitate to freeze the current exposure or maximum approval limit if inadequate data exist or "warning signals" appear to be unfavorable. This conservatism has paid off in the past, and management feels it should be reinforced in the light of the prospective debt-service situation in a significant number of developing countries.

MAJOR LENDING OPPORTUNITIES AND LOAN SYNDICATIONS

Schubert National Bank has been in the syndicated loan business for a long time, and indeed was one of the pioneers in syndication techniques. Syndication typically means that a "lead manager" bank (or banks) arranges a rather large loan, some of which is taken up in its own portfolio and the remainder (often the majority) is put out to other financial institutions that constitute a "syndicate" assembled by the lead bank(s). Managing a syndicate is considered lucrative, since the lead bank earns a handsome fee and enhances its competitive position among rival banks. Syndication also allows Schubert to make its exposure limits more flexible in international lending. Schubert led eleven syndications worth $2.5 billion in 1977 and thirty syndications worth $1.2 billion in 1978.

In recent years Euro-currency syndications have become increasingly common — for example, dollar-denominated syndicated loans drawing on dollar deposits in non-U.S. banks (including foreign branches of American banks). Since banks often fund themselves in the Euro-currency market as well, the base rate of interest is the so-called London Inter-Bank Offered Rate (LIBOR), effectively the cost of funds to the bank. Since LIBOR changes constantly, Euro-currency term credits tend to be "floating-rate" loans priced at "X percent over LIBOR." So, for example, a $200 million syndicated Euro-dollar loan has recently been managed by Schubert for the Venezuelan Ministry of Public Works to finance improvements in port facilities at 1 percent over LIBOR. Another, for $20 million at 1.5 percent over LIBOR, arranged for the government of Zaire to help overcome a temporary balance of payments problem brought on by a precipitous drop in world copper prices. Economists at Schubert feel that the interest rate on such loans should properly compensate the banks involved for the assessed level of country risk. The fact is, however, that for competitive reasons this often does not appear to be the case.

Schubert senior management has traditionally taken a rather conservative attitude toward loan syndications. If Schubert is a lead bank in a syndication, its account relationship will tend not to look at the loan any differently than if Schubert were the sole lending agent. Thus, if loan demand in a given country exceeds the maximum exposure limit and the area officers are hesitant to request new limits, they can aggressively take a lead position in a syndication as added flexibility. However, syndications are not always easy to organize, since other banks that are syndicate members will have to make their own assessments of country risk. Syndication memoranda are extremely carefully worded to relieve Schubert of any legal liability should the loan turn bad. Similarly, syndicates are painstakingly put together to match the character of participating banks with the character of the loan. Special care is taken in attempting to include in a syndicate lenders who have already had experience with the borrowing country in question. Still, since the lead bank usually benefits from a syndication in ways other than simply adding another loan to its portfolio, it may find that other banks that are not in line for such benefits perceive the risks and returns quite differently.

Occasionally, a lead bank or group of banks finds that it cannot put together a large syndicated Euro-currency loan successfully under any reasonable terms — an embarrassing event that should be avoided if at all possible. Indeed, a lead bank will sometimes "price itself out of the market" when faced with such a situation, raising the interest rate or worsening the terms in order to discourage the borrower if it is unwilling to take the exposure or unable to form a syndicate. Schubert's traditionally cautious approach has succeeded in keeping the bank out of such circumstances for the most part, and senior management puts a high premium on maintaining that record. But with the growth of developing-country Euro-currency borrowing, this appears to be a growing danger.

Questions

1. What improvements can you suggest in the way Schubert now develops its country reviews? Consider the following factors: (a) sources of information; (b) staff versus line responsibility; (d) sources of bias; (e) usability of the output in banking decisions.
2. How might Schubert improve on the way its country reviews are currently used in decision making in order to achieve a more nearly optimal "portfolio" of exposures to country risk?
3. Design an information-flow and decision-making network for Schubert that combines full recognition of risk, return, and diversification elements with the requirement of short response times often encountered in international lending.
4. How would you decide how many human and financial resources to commit to country analysis and its use in decision making?
5. How would your answers to Questions 1–4 differ for: (a) a smaller, regionally oriented bank; (b) a major Swiss or Japanese bank; (c) the World Bank?
6. Several proposals have suggested much greater control by central banks over international lending exposure by private banking institutions. Comment.

Appendix One

Schubert National Bank's Approach to the Assessment of Country Risk

Country risk assessment at Schubert National Bank is the product of an implicitly weighted rating of four major categories: policy factors, basic economic forces, external finances, and political factors. The weights are not formally specified, and may vary from one country to the next.

POLICY FACTORS
- Quality of economic team; influence and effectiveness of the central bank; impact of economic policy team on political leadership.
- Budget/monetary policies; wage/price policies.
- Current-account adjustment policies; import restraint policies; exchange-rate policies.
- Relations with IMF; willingness to cooperate with international

banking community in providing necessary data, projections, and other information.

A great deal of emphasis should be placed on the quality of a country's economic and financial management, and whether the economic team is able to make its counsel felt among the country's political leadership. If there are not good lines of communication between "technocrats" and politicians, or if for political reasons a country's leadership feels unable to implement the recommendations of the economic policy team, then no matter how good the advice of the technocrats, appropriate policies may not be followed. Moreover, even if there is political impact but central bank and ministry of finance officials are not competent, then a government is not likely to follow policies that are appropriate to changing domestic and international circumstances, or even to the country's basic resource endowment. In the short and medium term, the important policy measures to watch are those dealing in particular with monetary, fiscal, and inflation questions. Since 1973, the promptness of current-account adjustment in response to higher oil prices and world recession has been a major issue. Competent and appropriate policies also assure good relationships with the International Monetary Fund, the International Bank for Reconstruction and Development, and the foreign private commercial banking sector, the most important source of finance.

BASIC ECONOMIC FACTORS

- Balance of growth strategy; policy toward agriculture; appropriateness and efficiency of industrial investment in relation to country's overall resource base.
- Natural resource base.
- Human resource base: population growth, education level, entrepreneurial ability.
- Financial resource base; policy toward stimulating domestic savings; financial market development; relative importance of foreign capital in total domestic investment.
- Export diversification by commodity and region.

Five factors should be stressed in assessing a country's underlying economic strengths and weaknesses. Before enumerating them, it is worth emphasizing that a particular country's situation with respect to all of these is in large part the result of a process of development over many years, and as such cannot be expected to change quickly. What is important for the analysis is to note whether policies and strategies are in tune with basic factors or, if not in tune, whether policy or strategy changes are likely. First, growth strategy followed in years past and at present should have been in accord with the country's natural and human resource base; if not, then production inefficiencies may have occurred that in the future will make it difficult for the country to maintain its international competitiveness — thus requiring increased borrowing or slower economic growth. Second, while natural resources alone do not make for a rich country, they can help, and their potential or actual use should be developed. Third, and more important, is the state of the country's human resources, and in particular, the success with which the labor force can be educated and trained for increasingly complex tasks required as well as the entrepreneurial ability of lending elements in the society. Fourth, it is important that a developing country be able to finance a significant portion of its investment requirements. If it cannot, the foreign borrowing required to support its investment program may result in an overly rapid buildup in external debt. Several factors can contribute to a country's ability to finance its own development: Ideally, the government should keep its *current* expenditures below its *current* revenues, applying the surplus to public sector investment, while realistic interest rate policies and other means should be employed to make it attractive for individuals to place their excess savings in financial institutions. Also, export diversification by country and commodity is important in order to maintain export earnings in case of price or production drops with respect to one commodity, or recession in key export markets.

EXTERNAL FINANCE

- Level and maturity structure of external debt; amortization and interest payments on external debt as percentage of foreign exchange earnings from exports of goods and services.
- Official reserves; three months' coverage of import requirements is considered the minimum desirable level.
- Potential access to medium-term official finance, for example, from the IMF.
- Balance-of-payments prospects and outlook for external debt service burden.

The conjunction of the policy context and the basic economic factors discussed above, as well as the international economic situation, will jointly affect the country's external financial position. This position may be described as having four key elements. First, the balance-of-payments outlook should be assessed in a fairly systematic way. If quantitative projections are to be used, some attempt should be made to test the sensitivity of the implied external borrowing requirements to changes in key assumptions. Second, how rapidly has the country's external debt been growing, what have been its terms — grace periods, interest rates, maturity structures? What do these terms imply for debt servicing requirements? And given the export outlook, what will be the burden of debt service on the balance of payments? Third, is the present level of external official international reserves adequate to permit normal trade financing without undue delays, and to provide some cushion in the event of export shortfall? Generally speaking, a figure of three months' import requirements is considered the minimum desirable level, although in single-commodity economies, more of a cushion may be desirable. Fourth, although not included in a country's officially reported international reserves, it is important to take note of its borrowing rights in the IMF. These are sometimes referred to as "conditional" or "secondary" reserves, in that in order to borrow, a country must make certain commitments to the IMF relating to its economic policies.

POLITICS

Internal and regional political stability. In assessing political stability, foreign lenders look for reasonable assuredness that when political change comes, it will be orderly, and there will be reasonable continuity in fundamental economic policies. These desiderata do not, however, imply either institutional rigidity or the continuance in office of particular individuals. Indeed, such situations could well be inconsistent with the primary goal of orderly change. In addition, the international political context ideally should be such as not to seem to endanger a country's economic viability.

Appendix Two

Subsidiaries and Affiliates

EDGE ACT SUBSIDIARIES

Schubert Bank International, New York
Schubert Bank International, Miami
Schubert Bank International, Chicago
Schubert Bank International, San Francisco

INTERNATIONAL SUBSIDIARIES

Schubank Financial Ltd.	Luxembourg
Schubert Credit Development N.V.	Rotterdam
Schubert Finance Company	London
Schubert Location S.A.	Paris
Deutsche Schubert K.G.	Frankfurt
Schubert Advisory Ltd.	Abu Dhabi
Schulease GmbH	Düsseldorf
Schulease S.p.A.	Milan

Schubert Leasing Ltd.		Hong Kong
Atlantic Finance S.A.		Brussels
Schiffahrtskredit A.G.		Hamburg
Schubert Acceptance Corp. Ltd.		Sydney
Schubertinvest Corporation		Jakarta
Schubert Merchant Bank Ltd.		Kuala Lumpur
Advance Financial Corporation		San Juan
Banco Schubert C.A.		Caracas
Banco Schubert Brasileiro		Sao Paulo

INTERNATIONAL AFFILIATES

Kaufkraftsbank A.G.	(25%)	Frankfurt
Commercial Finance Ltd.	(40%)	Sydney
New Century Financing	(15%)	Hong Kong
Pan-Iranian Bank	(25%)	Tehran
Dynamic Financial Corporation	(45%)	Manila
Bancaria Atlantico	(10%)	Madrid
Corporacion Financiera del Sud	(15%)	Buenos Aires
Banco da Credito	(12%)	Caracas
Resource Capital Corporation	(49%)	Toronto
Pacific Financing Ltd.	(31%)	Singapore
Banque Commerciale de France	(28%)	Paris
Taiwan Development Bank	(15%)	Taipei
Nakamura Financial Advisory Ltd.	(40%)	Tokyo
Peoples' Bank	(15%)	San Juan
Banco do Bahia	(18%)	Salvador
Merchant Bank of Nigeria	(29%)	Lagos

Appendix Three

Consolidated Balance Sheet

	1980	1979
Assets:		
Cash due from banks	$ 5,422,375	$ 4,420,594
Interest-bearing deposits at banks	6,974,316	6,718,953
U.S. Treasury securities	1,180,481	2,184,363
Obligations of U.S. government agencies	201,242	239,451
Obligations of states and political subdivisions	1,687,209	1,348,638
Other investment securities	714,299	612,318
Trading account securities	58,590	402,535
Federal funds sold and securities purchased under agreements to resell	470,275	303,613
Loans and lease financing	19,613,234	16,974,257
Less: allowance for possible credit losses	184,181	182,595
Net loans and lease financing	$19,429,053	$16,791,662
Customers' acceptance liability	1,183,057	974,788

372

	1980	1979
Assets:		
Premises and equipment, net of accumulated depreciation of $106,319,000 in 1978 and $93,912,000 in 1976	151,522	149,692
Other real estate	42,829	93,368
Other assets	967,952	738,885
Total assets	$38,503,200	$34,978,860
Liabilities:		
Demand deposits	$ 9,230,845	$ 8,215,792
Time deposits	4,929,298	3,665,259
Deposits in foreign offices	14,818,385	14,634,549
Total deposits	$28,978,528	$26,515,600
Federal funds purchased and securities sold under agreements to repurchase	3,200,737	3,144,649
Commercial paper	359,245	236,386
Other liabilities for borrowed money	946,592	820,494
Accrued taxes and expenses	575,408	493,450
Liability on acceptances	1,189,520	980,933
Dividend payable	25,868	23,527
Long-term debt	756,977	661,505
Other liabilities	534,940	332,370
Total liabilities	$36,567,815	$33,208,914
Stockholder's Equity:		
Preferred stock, no par value (1,275,000 shares authorized; none issued)		
Common stock, $2.00 par value (authorized 70,000,000 shares; issued 59,006,000 in 1978 and 59,004,000 in 1977	$ 118,012	$ 118,008
Capital surplus	589,893	589,829
Retained earnings	1,236,199	1,069,567
Less: Treasury stock (170,961 shares in 1978 and 149,160 shares in 1977) at cost	$ 1,944,104	$ 1,777,404
	8,719	7,458
Total stockholders' equity	$ 1,935,385	$ 1,769,946
Total liabilities and stockholders' equity	38,503,200	34,978,860

Appendix Four

Consolidated Statement of Income
(in thousands, except per share)

	1980	1979
Interest Income From:		
Loans	$1,209,966	$1,161,006
Federal funds sold & securities purchased under agreements to resell	21,247	11,746
U.S. Treasury securities	132,235	136,677
Obligations of states and political subdivisions	95,723	71,103
Other investment securities	68,246	58,777
Trading account securities		
- obligations of states and political subdivisions	4,776	3,670
- other securities	21,419	37,318

Other sources, mainly interest bearing deposits at banks	396,919	349,180
Total interest income	$1,950,531	$1,829,477
Interest Expense Due To:		
Deposits	$1,046,466	$ 957,189
Federal funds purchased and securities sold under agreements to repurchase	201,785	177,769
Other borrowed money	50,879	54,373
Notes and debentures	40,314	34,257
Total interest expense	$1,339,444	$1,223,588
Interest income net of interest expense	611,087	605,917
Provision for possible credit losses	55,803	80,008
Interest income net of interest expense and provision for possible credit losses	$ 555,284	$ 525,909
Noninterest Operating Income:		
Trading account profits (losses) and commissions	$ 4,050	$ 34,530
Corporate trust, other trust, and agency income	126,468	119,036
Foreign exchange trading income	47,298	39,699
Other operating income, mainly fees and commissions	104,435	102,851
Total noninterest operating income	$ 282,251	$ 296,116
Total operating income net of interest expense and provision for possible credit losses	837,535	822,025
Other Noninterest Operating Expenses:		
Salaries	$ 171,952	$ 166,616
Deferred profit sharing	17,758	16,639
Additional compensation	7,133	6,064
Other employee benefits	56,686	50,071
Net occupancy expense	48,601	44,094
Equipment rentals, depreciation and maintenance	21,560	18,851
Other operating expenses	83,453	78,726
Total other noninterest operating expenses	$ 407,143	$ 381,061
Income before income taxes and securities gains (losses)	430,392	440,964
Applicable income taxes	197,980	203,127
Income Before Securities Gains (Losses):	$ 232,412	$ 237,837
Per share	5.62	5.81
Net securities profits	7,264	3,466
Income tax benefit	4,958	3,378
Net Income:	$ 244,634	$ 244,681
Per share	5.92	5.98
Dividends declared per common share	2.28	2.19

Appendix Five

Contribution to International Operations (1980) (dollar amounts in millions)

Contribution to:	At U.S. offices		At foreign offices		Total
Total operating income					
1978	$ 196.4	8.8%	$ 996.3	44.8%	$ 2,224.7
1977	173.2	8.1	989.5	46.6	2,125.6
Income before income taxes and securities gains (losses)					
1978	60.8	14.4	174.4	41.3	422.3
1977	45.4	10.3	185.9	42.2	440.9
Income before securities gains (losses)					
1978	31.8	12.4	101.9	39.8	256.1
1977	20.5	8.6	95.4	40.1	237.9
Assets at year end					
1978	4,582	11.9	18,065	44.6	38,503
1977	3,323	9.5	15,716	41.0	34,979

	December 31, 1980		December 31, 1979	
United States	$ 7,254	31.4%	$ 5,897	30.2%
Americas	4,205	18.2	3,339	17.1
Africa	300	1.3	273	1.4
Pacific Basin	3,881	16.8	2,948	15.1
Middle East and South Asia	1,016	4.4	898	4.6
Europe	6,446	27.9	6,170	31.5
Total	$23,102	100 %	$19,525	100 %

Appendix Six

Contribution of International Operations
(in millions)

	December 31, 1980			December 31, 1979		
	At U.S. offices	Foreign	Total	At U.S. offices	Foreign	Total
Interest-bearing deposits at banks	$ —*	$ 6,974	$ 6,974	$ 2	$ 6,686	$ 6,688
Investment securities	109	528	637	94	460	554
Loans to or guaranteed by banks	832	1,504	2,336	676	1,352	2,028
Loans to or guaranteed by governments, government agencies, or central banks	399	2,296	2,695	564	1,704	2,268
Other loans, substantially all to business	1,302	6,181	7,483	986	4,956	5,942
Customers' acceptance liability	1,135	36	1,171	906	51	957
Other assets	1,260	546	1,806	580	507	1,087
Total assets	$5,037	$18,065	$23,102	$3,808	$15,716	$19,524
Deposits from banks, central banks, and official institutions	$4,558	$ 9,988	$14,546	$3,501	$10,075	$13,575
Other deposits	812	4,830	5,642	886	4,560	5,446
Total deposits	$5,370	$14,818	$20,188	$4,387	$14,635	$19,021

* Less than $ million.

Appendix Seven

Schubert National Bank Balance Sheet

	1980	1979	1978	1976	1977
Balance January 1	$182.6	$164.0	$147.3	$125.6	$118.2
Provision charged to operating expense	57.9	82.9	117.5	50.1	9.8
Recoveries	5.7	0.9	1.8	5.1	1.3
Loans charged off	48.5	64.6	102.5	33.6	3.8
Net charge-off	42.8	63.7	100.7	28.5	2.5
Sale of subsidiary	—	0.6	—	—	—
Applied to other real estate	13.5				
Balance December 31	184.2	182.6	164.0	147.3	125.6
Recoveries, by type of loan: Domestic:					
Commercial and industrial	5.1	0.4	.5	1.7	0.9
Reit's	—	—	—	—	—
Secured by real estate	0.2	—	—	—	—
Other	0.1	—	0.1	0.1	—

International:					
At U.S. offices	0.1	0.1	0.1	0.2	0.4
At foreign offices					
secured by real estate	—	—	—	—	—
other	0.2	0.4	1.1	3.1	—
Total recoveries	5.7	0.9	1.8	5.1	1.3
Loans charged off by type of loan:					
Domestic:					
Commercial and industrial	6.1	1.5	4.5	21.5	—
Reit's	9.5	12.9	16.1	8.6	—
Secured by real estate	25.4	37.8	11.7	—	0.5
Other	0.1	1.3	62.1	0.4	0.1
International:					
At U.S. offices	0.5	3.0	0.5	—	1.0
At foreign offices					
secured by real estate	1.7	2.8	4.4	3.1	—
other	5.2	5.3	3.2	—	2.2
Total loans charged off	48.5	64.6	102.5	33.6	3.8
Net charge-off	42.8	63.7	100.7	28.5	2.5

Ian H. Giddy

Case 42

Passing the Buck at Banco

"Do I deserve this?" mused Bertram, leaning against the frame of his office window overlooking the Praca de Republica. He heard his secretary leave for the day but made no move, continuing to stare blankly at the overflow of desk paper on his window ledge.

Bertram L. T. Worthington was the general manager of the Sao Paulo branch of Banco Internacional de North America (BINA) Corporation, a subsidiary of a major U.S. bank holding company. Two days earlier a director of one of his bank's biggest clients, Uniao Fabril S.A., had threatened to withdraw his family's deposits, and perhaps his company's business, unless he received written clarification from BINA on the status of his U.S. dollar deposits. It appeared that the fellow got concerned about what

© Ian H. Giddy, Columbia University, 1981. Revised, with permission, by Gunter Dufey, 1982.

would happen to his money if the Brazilian authorities walked in one day and froze all dollar deposits.

Bertram had been told of this by his deputy, recently transferred from the Lisbon branch, Luis Filipe David da Gloria Nunes e Oliveira. The client, it seemed, had argued that since his money was in U.S. dollars, he assumed that he would be able to collect it from the New York office of BINA. This was obvious, he said, since dollar funds were always paid out of New York correspondent balances anyway.

Bertram Worthington was not so sure.

"Ollie, old man," he had said, "what if we had already loaned the dollars to a Brazilian company? Then they wouldn't be in New York." Or would they? he wondered silently to himself. "Also, how can a branch in one country be responsible for all branches that accept dollar deposits in other countries?"

"You forget I have a law degree," replied Dr. Luis Filipe etc. Oliveira. "We are a branch, not a subsidiary. In accordance with corporate law and with general principles of corporate responsibility, a bank may be held liable at its home office for deposits placed in its foreign branches, U.S. v. First National City Bank, 321 F.2d 14, 19–20, Cir. 1963."

"Listen, Ollie, I agree, but according to the separate entity doctrine, a branch is treated for some purposes like a distinct business entity. Deposits placed at a branch are normally payable only at the branch, which means that the law of the jurisdiction where it is located controls the bank's liability on deposits in the branch."

"Oh? Are you going to tell our depositors, in writing, that neither BINA nor the parent bank will repay deposits seized in an offshore branch? What do you think that will do to our image as a global bank?"

Bertram had later obtained some legal advice. He had been informed that a British or American court might well consider sympathetically a claim by a depositor in a foreign branch, even where acts of the host state had resulted in a loss of the depositor's rights or the loss of assets by the foreign branch. Two precedents were highlighted. First, Section 138 of New York State's Banking Law implies that head offices of New York banks have liability for deposits seized in a foreign branch except in proportion to the book value of assets also seized.

Second, in a recent decision, the U.S. Court of Appeals upheld the claims of a group of Vietnamese who had had funds deposited in Chase Manhattan's Saigon branch when that city was overrun by the North Vietnamese in 1975. The claims were upheld despite the fact that the deposits were in local currency, piasters, and that the new government had seized all remaining assets of the branch.

It was no help to Bertram Worthington that virtually all his branch's assets, in both dollars and cruzeiros, were invested in Brazil. If there were an official seizure of Brazilians' deposits, there was little the Sao Paulo branch could do legally. If the head office in London paid out such funds, the bank could find itself subjected to double liability. He thought of advising his client to transfer the funds to BINA's Cayman Islands branch, but his counsel had heard of a case where a New York court had placed an attachment on funds deposited in the Cayman branch of a Brazilian bank, on the grounds that the branch was just a "nameplate" entity, with its funds held and managed by the bank's New York branch.

"I don't want to lose those deposits," thought Bertram. "Next thing, the client will be telling his swimming-pool set, I wonder what Citibank would do? In his shoes I'd put my money in the U.S. of A., where the sheriff is in charge. Let's see what the rates are." He glanced at his rate sheet. "Gees, look what we're paying him! He deserves to take some extra risk. The only question is, how can I put it to him?"

Three-month deposits, One million minimum

New York (Parent) US$	14.125%
London (BINA) US$	14.5%
Cayman Is. (BINA) US$	14.5%
Singapore (Parent's branch) US$	14.625%
Sao Paulo (BINA) US$	14.875%
Sao Paulo (BINA) Cr$	37%

Bertram's stomach rumbled. He turned on his heels and strode over to his desk. B. L. T. Worthington had reached a decision. "This is a job for New York, quoth he, here comes one grande Telexo; Boy will New York be surprised to get one from old Bertie that does not concern the latest round of musical ministers; and if I make this look good, maybe I get promoted to the San Francisco Edge; here goes . . ."

Can you help Bertie get his promotion? Consider what the bank's written statement on its worldwide obligations to depositors should be:

(1) What is the status of deposits in U.S. dollars, compared to those in local currencies?
(2) If in local currencies, should deposits be repayable, at the customer's option, in dollars (or sterling)? At what exchange rate?
(3) Under what circumstances should the bank refuse to repay at the head office or a different branch? If the branch fails? If Brazil freezes all deposits? If there is an illegal insurrection that forces the branch to cease business?

(4) Does it matter whether the deposit is undocumented, or is evidenced by a certificate of deposit?
(5) Does the interest premium over domestic deposits make a difference?
(6) What if the U.S. authorities try to freeze Eurodollar deposits, as happened in the Iranian case?
(7) Should the parent bank provide explicit guarantees on offshore deposits?

Ian H. Giddy

Case 43

How to Relax in Rio

"Well, they're a good credit, and if we want to keep doing business with Condocorp we've got to keep servicing them. Right now, they need that $35 million, and I think we should make the loan."

"A loan! They expect us to make them a loan! They should realize that we're a bank, and banks like us aren't supposed to be making loans, except to bankrupt countries! Can't we find some other way of maintaining the relationship?"

"I don't know. You let me know what you decide." (Click)

Christine Hekman, SVP at Banco Internacional de Norte America (BINA) in Miami, hung up the phone. Lately she had been facing more and more of these situations — where the basic lending business of the bank was proving more and more difficult. Competition from foreign

384

banks, eroding spreads, and cost-plus pricing all made the returns to lending narrower. The only solution was to achieve tighter leverage, but the Fed had been discouraging that approach by putting pressure on the bank to replenish its capital before allowing the loan portfolio to swell much further. In the case of some customers, such as Condocorp, Banco Internacional was approaching the 10-percent-of-capital lending limit. The problem was worse in Latin America, where Banco Internacional was caught up in the Brazilian rescheduling. Hekman's neck muscles tightened as she thought of her last visit to Rio. On the one hand, the federal bank examiners were becoming increasingly critical of BINA's cross-border exposure in Latin America; on the other hand, the IMF and the Fed were insisting on new loans, not to mention extensions of old ones, to Brazil and its buddies.

"What," Christine wondered, "should the bank's strategy be toward new lending?" She reflected that the senior management were increasingly tempted to follow the crowd into non–asset-based financial services, such as discount brokerage and insurance. She was against it. "What the (delete) do we know about all these other businesses?" she had argued at a recent meeting. "We have a team of credit officers and a storehouse of Latin American customer relationships virtually unequalled in the region. Are we going to throw all that away, just when all the competition is making like Houdini escaping from Latin America?"

Hekman had tried to persuade her colleagues that certain countries' export potential would strengthen their debt servicing capacity within a few years, and that spreads would surely widen to attractive levels. But of course she could not be sure, and right now her job was to find a way of capitalizing on all that loan-generating experience and expertise without swelling the bank's assets. She decided to consider three approaches.

First, what were the ways in which the bank could generate fee-based income, not by entering new ventures but by offering services to existing customers, preferably utilizing the credit personnel and their contacts and expertise in the hemisphere?

Second, in cases where we are constrained in the amount of funds we can lend, how can we generate alternative sources of financing for our customers, including those in Latin America, that will benefit both us and them?

Third, having heard of similar instances recently, Christine wondered whether it would be possible to sell off some of the loans the bank had made to certain governments as well as to companies. Was this a realistic option for a bank such as BINA? If so, what were the procedures and problems involved?

Ian H. Giddy

Case 44

Austerity in Venezuela

José Carreras sighed. As assistant to the Finance Minister of Venezuela, José was obliged to spend the evening going over his notes from the various meetings held earlier that day with American commercial and investment bankers. While the Finance Minister and his entourage were being wined and dined by some officials from Chase, José was left behind at the Plaza Hotel in midtown Manhattan. At least the Minister had allowed him to use his large study in the Ambassador Suite. José's job for the night was to analyze various proposals on how to borrow $120 million for ten years. In the past his country had relied on medium-term syndicated loans from large U.S. and other banks. Now, however, those loans were proving very expensive — perhaps it had been a mistake to take them. Venezuela now found itself forced to adopt severe austerity measures in order to manage the higher debt service costs on existing loans. A substantial proportion of the loans had had to be rescheduled. José poured himself a drink to drown out thoughts of the depressed state of the Venezuelan economy, which seemed unable to produce sufficient export growth that would generate enough dollars to repay the American banks, while allowing the economy to recover. "Nobody wants to take the blame for high interest rates and weak world trade," he thought, "but we poor oil exporters have to pay the price."

To get out of this Catch-22 situation, the Venezuelan government was now asking for a new $120 million 10-year loan to finance a specific project: a new, highly efficient oil refinery on the Caribbean coast. This would supply the strong markets on the east coast of the United States and in Western Europe, where economic growth seemed at last to be taking hold.

José gazed through the window at Central Park and the evening rush hour traffic. "*Caramba*," he muttered, "look at them all using up our oil. If only oil prices would rise and interest rates would fall like they're supposed to! But with things going the other way, oil has been our bane as well as our boon. One thing is clear: Syndicated loans, with rates fixed at a spread above LIBOR and fixed amortization schedules, are meeting neither our needs nor those of the bankers. We have to look at something different." José reluctantly returned to the desk to review some alternatives proposed by a group of investment bankers.

Following his mother's advice to stay clear of the local water, he poured himself another whisky-and-soda. He realized that his notes were rather sketchy. No details had been discussed. But in preparation for the following day's discussions, he felt he should point out to his boss the major disadvantages, advantages, and risks of each alternative, preferably in some consistent framework. Also he would have to eliminate those that would prove unacceptable to the providers of funds. Perhaps the first task would be to reorganize the list into some more logical order.

ALTERNATIVE 1: FLEXIBLE MATURITY LOAN

This technique appears to be like a syndicated loan, with a variable interest rate set at a spread above LIBOR, except that the annual payments are preset at a fixed dollar amount. As interest rates fluctuate, the maturity of the loan can be lengthened or shortened. Here, the borrower will always be certain about the *size* of periodic payments, while the *number* of payments will be adjusted according to market conditions.

Loans to developing countries usually provide for the repayment of principal at maturity. In many cases, however, the repayment is scheduled over three or four years before maturity date. Either way, the time set for repayment of the principal moves closer or further into the future in a loan with fixed annual interest payments.

ALTERNATIVE 2: CONSTANT REAL DEBT SERVICE

Here, a *real* interest rate is fixed, while the nominal interest rate fluctuates according to some price index. Instead of the American Consumer Price Index, the Venezuelans would probably prefer an index based on the U.S. dollar value of the country's export basket.

ALTERNATIVE 3: FIXED INTEREST EUROBONDS

Under this type of financing, already used by many LDCs, the interest rate is fixed and cannot be raised by the bankers. On the other hand, since the bonds are sold to the public worldwide, the borrower essentially faces two choices: repay or default. The debt cannot be renegotiated or extended the way a loan can. The default risk of course, is totally borne by the bondholders, which include individual and institutional investors in the country or countries in which the bonds are sold. One aspect of this choice is to decide where, and in what currency, the bond should be issued.

ALTERNATIVE 4: FLEXIBLE REPAYMENT DEBT

Some limited flexibility on repayment is allowed at the discretion of the borrower. The earlier repayments can be much lower than the later ones, to reflect somehow the cash flows generated by, for instance, oil refineries. For example, financing can be achieved through a bond or Eurocredit with a normal repayment schedule calling for equal payments of principal each year, but with a provision that the borrower can opt to repay some lesser amount in one or more years, subject to provisions for catching up in the future years. Such a bond provides a degree of automatic refinancing at the borrower's discretion.

ALTERNATIVE 5: REPAYMENT LINKED TO TRADE FLOWS

This is a bond or loan, but with both the interest and the principal indexed. Specifically, the borrower's debt service is linked to the country's net export position. One problem is that the lender might perceive this arrangement as an incentive for a country not to export. A way to get around this is to index the debt to the volume of world trade.

ALTERNATIVE 6: COMMODITY PRICE-LINKED BONDS OR LOANS

This suggestion, based on Mexico's erstwhile "Petrobonds," was to issue bonds with interest rates indexed to the price of a commodity, in this case oil. This would allow the financing's effective repayment to be linked more closely to Venezuela's oil payments. The question raised, however, is would investors be willing to purchase such bonds — or banks provide such loans — in a period of declining oil prices?

ALTERNATIVE 7: PROJECT SPECIFIC LOAN

In this case the country borrows funds for a specific project, such as a refinery construction. To guarantee repayment, export proceeds generated by the project are put in escrow; furthermore, the lender has first claim on those escrowed proceeds.

ALTERNATIVE 8: EQUITY PORTFOLIO INVESTMENT

Finally, funds can be raised by selling equity stakes in a specific venture. The return on investment is then directly tied to the outcome of the project. The borrower can sell shares to portfolio investors, who get a high return if the project does well and a low return if the project returns do not live up to expectations. Therefore, the investor shares in the profits along with, in this case, the Venezuelan government. In essence, the project risk is shared by both borrower and lender.

Gunter Dufey

Case 45

Issues in International Markets

It was Monday afternoon on Memorial Day weekend. William R. Stein-berg was sitting in his study, preparing for the following day's Asset Liability Policy Committee (ALPC) meeting. As a Senior Vice-President of a major money market center bank, his job was to represent the funding side when major commitments were being considered. Today was exceptional: He had long since learned not to take work home on weekends, but this time he had some thinking to do that required a period of peace and quiet.

He took a set of proposals out of his briefcase and stared at them. Most of them were quite routine, but it was the last one that had prompted his concern. As far as it went, it wasn't that new, either. Over the past three

This case was prepared by Professor Gunter Dufey from publicly available informa-tion as a basis for discussion rather than to illustrate effective or ineffective handling of administrative situations. July 1982. Revised May 1984.

years he had seen a dozen of these deals. They originated with the merchant banking group that the bank had set up years ago in an effort to break into a business that the bank and its domestic competitors were not allowed to pursue at home: the investment banking business, particularly the underwriting of securities. Many large U.S. banks considered such activities to be a natural extension of their financial service franchise; they had always envied their competitors — the Swiss and Germans particularly — who seemed to be quite successful at offering a "compleat set" of services to captive customers, earning good fee income in the process without straining capitalization ratios, which were constantly under attack as being inadequate.

In the early years, the activities of the merchant banking affiliates of U.S. deposit-taking institutions were largely limited to arranging syndicated credits. Here, only the distribution technique could be considered investment banking; in other respects, syndicated credits were simply term loans where the borrower accepted the interest rate risk (the loan was repriced every three or six months at a spread over LIBOR or a similar base rate). And anyone who had nurtured expectations that the merchant banks affiliated with commercial banks would quickly replace the independent securities houses in the rapidly growing market for Eurobonds and Euronotes was quickly disappointed. While relative market shares fluctuated considerably from one year to the next, relative shares of the underwriting market stayed fairly stable over time, as shown in Table 1.

Furthermore, the commercial banks who did the lion's share of the underwriting were headquartered in continental Europe and had traditionally dominated the business of underwriting and distributing securities in their home markets. As late as 1979/80, the merchant banks affiliated with U.S. and Japanese commercial banks played a very modest role in the underwriting of securities in international markets, as evidenced by data in Table 2.

However, there were signs of an impending change. With the advent of the 1980s, some of the more aggressive bank-affiliated merchant banks

TABLE 1 Market share attained by first 20 lead managers in the new issue market for Eurodollar notes and bonds (in percentages)

	1983	1982	1981	1980	1979	1978	1977	1976
Banks[1]	52	58	46	28	51	61	51	48
Investment banks[2]	48	42	54	72	49	39	49	52

[1] Includes bank-affiliated merchant banks
[2] Includes independent merchant banks
Source: *Euromoney,* "International Bond League Tables," various issues.

TABLE 2 Activities of international investment banking houses, all notes and bonds—including FRNS, but excluding New York issues (Sole lead managers receive *full* amount of the issue, joint lead managers receive *equal* amounts)

Period: January–December 1980				Period: January–December 1983			
Position	No. of Issues	Amount ($m)	% Share	Position	No. of Issues	Amount ($m)	% Share
1 Credit Suisse First Boston	38	1859.7	13.2	1 Credit Suisse First Boston	37	3778.7	14.7
2 Deutsche Bank	29	1713.0	12.1	2 Deutsche Bank	37	2533.3	9.9
3 Morgan Stanley	18	1312.4	9.3	3 Morgan Stanley	21	1044.2	4.1
4 SG Warburg	20	843.9	5.9	4 Banque Nationale de Paris	15	1008.0	3.9
5 Goldman Sachs	9	685.0	4.8	5 Dresdner Bank	15	865.9	3.4
6 Paribas	9	678.6	4.8	6 SG Warburg	25	849.4	3.3
7 Dresdner Bank	14	663.3	4.7	7 Morgan Guaranty	20	810.8	3.2
8 Societe Generale	10	621.3	4.4	8 Merrill Lynch	11	803.6	3.1
9 WestLB	10	435.9	3.0	9 Salomon Brothers	19	735.0	2.9
10 Orion Bank	9	417.5	2.9	10 Societe Generale	11	713.0	2.8
11 Daiwa	14	366.8	2.6	11 Citicorp	6	601.2	2.3
12 Citicorp	8	364.4	2.5	12 Nomura	10	597.6	2.3
13 Banque Nationale de Paris	10	351.4	2.5	13 Westdeutsche Landesbank	14	571.9	2.2
14 Hambros Bank	9	330.9	2.3	14 Commerzbank	13	567.5	2.2
15 Credit Commercial de France	7	329.5	2.3	15 Goldman Sachs	15	550.0	2.1
16 Salomon Brothers	8	328.1	2.3	16 Lloyds	3	541.1	2.1
17 Union Bank of Switzerland	6	321.5	2.2	17 Orion Royal	13	506.1	2.0
18 Commerzbank	8	315.8	2.2	18 Amsterdam-Rotterdam Bank	15	480.2	1.9
19 Wood Gundy	7	310.5	2.2	19 Union Bank of Switzerland	10	478.8	1.9
20 Swiss Bank Corporation	7	298.3	2.1	20 Swiss Bank Corporation	13	469.2	1.8

Rank	Name	No.	Value	%
21	Nomura	12	251.4	1.8
22	Lloyds Bank International	4	239.1	1.7
23	Barclays Bank International	2	211.3	1.5
24	Credit Lyonnais	8	202.1	1.4
25	Merrill Lynch	9	187.0	1.3
26	Yamaichi International (Europe)	6	185.8	1.3
27	Kuwait International Investment Company	10	178.2	1.2
28	Smith Barney Harris Upham	4	177.5	1.2
29	Amsterdam-Rotterdam Bank	6	161.0	1.1
30	Kleinwood Benson	7	160.2	1.1
31	Sumitomo Finance International	6	157.5	1.1
32	Caisse des Depots et Consignations	5	151.9	1.0
33	Algemene Bank Nederland	4	140.0	.9
34	Morgan Grenfell	7	139.3	.9
35	Bank Mees & Hope	5	138.5	.9
36	Chemical Bank	5	137.5	.9
37	Dillon Read Overseas Corp.	4	130.0	.9
38	Kuwait Investment Company	4	128.5	.9
39	European Banking Company	4	127.0	.9
40	Morgan Guaranty	6	127.0	.9

Rank	Name	No.	Value	%
21	Algemene Bank Nederland	12	456.8	1.8
22	Daiwa	13	452.4	1.8
23	Banque Paribas	8	338.3	1.3
24	Manufacturers Hanover	7	321.7	1.3
25	Nikko Securities	10	301.0	1.2
26	Lehman Brothers, Kuhn Loeb	3	295.8	1.2
27	Credit Lyonnais	7	251.4	1.0
28	Bank of America	4	243.8	1.0
29	Credit Commercial de France	7	243.1	.9
30	Societe Generale de Banque	11	240.9	.9
31	Hambros Bank	6	224.9	.9
32	Wood Gundy	6	222.4	.9
33	Morgan Grenfell	8	215.0	.8
34	Bank of Tokyo	4	168.8	.7
35	Kidder Peabody	2	158.3	.6
36	Hill Samuel	2	154.7	.6
37	Industrial Bank of Japan	5	151.1	.6
38	Kredietbank	7	144.4	.6
39	Yamaichi	5	134.2	.5
40	Banque Bruxelles Lambert	10	131.5	.5

operating out of Hong Kong had refined a concept known as the "Euro-note purchase facility." Such facilities were originally designed to offer borrowers of exceptional credit standing an attractive alternative to syndi-cated credits. The competition from new entrants into the Euromarket had squeezed spreads for this type of borrower so much that the major U.S. banks, who had dominated this kind of lending, saw only their footings grow, with the result that returns on total assets declined. Furthermore, there was always the danger that AAA-rated governments, their agencies, and corporations of equivalent standing would be driven into the short-term securities markets; and the consequence would be further disinterme-diation and the concomitant loss of a relationship when participation in a syndicated credit was declined. As a solution to this problem, some of the merchant banking affiliates put together deals that permitted the borrower to draw funds against bearer notes, with maturities of up to 180 days. The banks involved would "purchase" the securities for immediate placement with those investors who viewed them as alternatives to prime bank CDs. Further, the managing bank agreed to make a market on a best-efforts basis if an investor wished to liquidate notes prior to maturity.

Borrowers found such facilities quite attractive. They provided flexi-ble, medium-term, floating-rate financing. With commitment fees on un-drawn portions typically ¼ percent per annum, a management fee of ⅜ to ¼ percent flat, modest out-of-pocket expenses for legal work and the paying bank, and notes that were priced at LIBOR plus ¼ percent, the note pur-chase facility was typically less expensive than a similar syndicated loan. At the same time, the borrower had no problems with early repayment and a good chance to gain access to new investors, and there were few if any regu-latory delays and expenses (except when a currency option feature was in-volved) because the note was issued offshore.

For investors, the advantages were yields better than those for prime bank CDs — the notes were typically sold to yield between LIBOR and LIBID — and some assurance of liquidity if the managing bank succeeded in making a secondary market. Under one variant, the bank even offered to repurchase the notes at face value every six months. With this "put op-tion," of course, the investor transferred the borrower's credit risk totally onto the bank (although the borrower might lose some flexibility with re-spect to repayment).

In any case, the nature of the purchase commitment was critical. Without a commitment, or with one that was weakened by "material cus-tomer and market adverse change" language, the borrowers would merely receive distribution services. And this was something in which the tradi-tional investment banks and securities houses excelled. On the other hand, with a "hell or high water" commitment by the banks to purchase the notes, the full risk of financial intermediation would have to be borne precisely at those times when nobody else wanted to make funds available. And this would have to be done at a level of compensation appropriate to the securities business, where all risks are passed on to borrowers and investors once the distribution process has been completed.

At this point, Bill Steinberg's thoughts turned to the last few meetings of the ALPC when similar deals had come up. Then, much of the discussion had centered on a vexing competitive problem. Some of the new customers for such facilities were second-tier names whose paper might be unsold and would therefore stay on the books of the bank for significant periods of time. The appropriate language for such facilities was that governing the usual floating-rate term loan. The problem was that some overeager competitors had begun to offer note placement facilities to second-tier credits on terms appropriate for first-tier borrowers, with protection clauses for term loans.

Bill had not participated in these discussions very actively because he considered the issue to be primarily one involving credit-quality-pricing relationships. However, as he saw the volume of facilities of both kinds building up rapidly, he thought that the funding implications deserved much more attention. He planned to call his colleagues' attention to these issues, but since the matter was quite complex he decided to do a little homework in order to get his own thoughts together. It would not be easy to get the lenders on the committee to focus on funding risks. After all, the offshore dollar market had grown virtually without interruption for more than a decade (see data in Table 3); and even during the Herstatt crisis in

TABLE 3 Relative Sizes of Eurocurrency and U.S. Dollar Markets (Billions of U.S. Dollars)

Eurocurrency market (net size)		U.S. domestic market		
End of period	All currencies	Euro dollar market	Commercial bank time & savings deposits	Commercial bank CD's	Commercial paper & BA's
1965	17	12	141	16	12
1970	65	23	226	26	40
1975	250	195	463	56	66
1979	615	432	653	93	158
1980	705	526	755	116	180
1982	932	740	998	132	246
1983	1011^E	809^E	1142	91	264

* E = Estimated
Sources: Morgan Guaranty, *World Financial Markets,* various issues.
U.S. Federal Reserve System, *Federal Reserve Bulletin.*

1974, the bank had had no problem attracting funds in the interbank market. Most people believed that the pool of offshore dollars would continue to grow, fed by persistent U.S. balance-of-payments deficits and the surpluses of some OPEC countries. But these things might change; with oil consumption falling and prices weak, and expenditures of OPEC countries on a steady rise, it was not inconceivable that this source would dry up.

As a matter of fact, Bill had just seen an analysis by the economics department of the bank indicating that the U.S. balance of payments had not been in deficit even during some years when the offshore market manifested faster growth than domestic markets (Table 5). But how long can this continue, he thought? And the question was becoming even more urgent, as borrowers were beginning to demand these facilities with currency option clauses as a matter of course.

In the first large deal of this kind, the problem was avoided — in a fashion. When the central banks in question (specifically involved were the German, Swiss, and Japanese authorities) indicated their disapproval of having their respective currencies included among the currency options (they did not like at all the idea of short-term, highly liquid pieces of paper being floated outside their national markets), the managing banks had elegantly skirted the problem by putting together syndicated swap facilities through which the notes could be denominated in the desired currencies — in effect, if not explicitly. But how reliable were these forward markets without viable offshore deposit markets? Bill had come to the conclusion that, with the ever-growing use of currency options in loan contracts, a lot of people other than just those concerned with liability management and foreign exchange trading should be asking questions about the existence, growth, and applicable government controls of offshore markets and markets for forward exchange.

Like most senior people in the bank, Bill had received his early experience in domestic lending. He was quite familiar with practices in the U.S. domestic market, where for a long time banks had been granting committed backup lines for commercial paper that their larger corporate customers sold — often with the help of specialized securities dealers — to U.S. institutional investors. And he had learned that the funding risk was quite tolerable, as long as the authorities did not impose quantitative credit restrictions. When times got tough and all but AAA-rated Commercial Paper (CP) issuers were pushed out of the market, funds flooded to the banks in search of safety, and those institutions had relatively few problems in accommodating the increased demand for credit; it was simply a process of reintermediation.

But did it work the same way in the offshore market? The past did not provide a clue. Euro-CP had never been very successful; in its heyday in the

TABLE 4 The OPEC Problem Financial and Real Dimensions (All Figures in Billions US$)

	1973	1974	1975	1976	1978	1979	1980	1981	1982	1983[E*]
Revenues	30	115	110	125	150	220	300	290	230	170
Imports (+Aid)	28	50	70	100	140	160	210	250	265	230
Amount to Invest	2	65	40	25	10	60	90	40	−35	−60
Accumulated Funds	16	80	120	160	200	260	350	390	350	290

* E = Estimated

TABLE 5 Annual Series U.S. International Transactions [1] (Millions of Dollars)

	Trade Flows					Capital Flows								
Year	Merchandise Exports	Merchandise Imports	Service Exports	Service Imports	Current Account Balance	Direct Investment Abroad	Direct Investment in U.S.	Security Purchases Abroad	Security Purchases in U.S.	Bank Claims on Foreigners	Bank Liabilities to Foreigners	U.S. Government Assets Abroad	Foreign Official Assets in U.S.	Monetary Base Effect [2]
1960	19,650	14,758	9,211	8,971	2,824	2,940	315	663	-82	1,148	678	-1,045	1,473	-2,128
1961	20,108	14,537	9,829	9,054	3,822	2,653	311	762	475	1,261	928	303	765	-1,061
1962	20,781	16,260	11,022	9,518	3,387	2,851	346	969	68	450	336	-450	1,270	-1,012
1963	22,272	17,048	11,942	9,999	4,414	3,483	231	1,105	138	1,556	898	1,284	1,986	-539
1964	25,501	18,700	13,325	10,522	6,823	3,760	322	677	-231	2,505	1,818	1,509	1,660	-114
1965	26,461	21,510	14,626	11,291	5,432	5,011	415	759	-489	-93	503	380	134	-1,378
1966	29,310	25,493	15,252	13,106	3,031	5,418	425	720	550	-233	2,882	973	-672	-879
1967	30,666	26,866	16,648	14,740	2,583	4,805	698	1,308	881	495	1,765	2,370	3,451	1,748
1968	33,626	32,991	18,737	15,809	611	5,295	807	1,569	4,550	-233	3,871	3,144	-774	-1,540
1969	36,414	35,807	21,108	18,322	339	5,690	1,263	1,459	3,062	570	8,886	3,379	-1,301	-72
1970	42,469	39,866	23,205	20,184	2,331	7,590	1,464	1,076	2,270	967	-6,298	-892	6,908	-355

1971	43,319	45,579	25,519	20,990	−1,433	7,618	367	1,113	2,265	2,980	−6,911	−465	26,879	−922
1972	49,381	55,797	28,114	23,638	−5,795	7,747	949	618	4,468	3,506	4,754	1,572	10,475	−39
1973	71,410	70,499	38,831	28,720	7,140	11,353	2,800	671	3,825	5,980	4,702	2,486	6,026	−328
1974	98,306	103,649	48,360	33,708	2,124	9,052	4,760	1,854	1,075	19,516	16,017	1,101	10,546	−34
1975	107,088	98,041	48,641	34,795	18,280	14,244	2,603	6,247	5,093	13,532	628	4,323	7,027	469
1976	114,745	124,051	56,885	38,197	4,384	11,949	4,347	8,885	4,067	21,368	10,990	6,772	17,693	759
1977	120,816	151,689	63,521	42,099	−14,068	11,890	3,728	5,460	2,971	11,427	6,719	4,068	36,816	−414
1978	142,054	175,813	78,083	54,067	−14,773	16,056	7,897	3,626	4,432	33,667	16,141	3,928	33,678	693
1979	184,473	211,819	102,299	69,858	−466	25,222	11,877	4,726	6,311	26,213	32,607	4,876	−13,697	2,039
1980	224,237	249,575	117,865	84,225	1,520	19,238	13,666	3,524	8,096	46,838	10,743	13,281	15,442	2,947
1981	236,254	264,143	136,683	97,670	4,471	8,691	21,301	5,429	10,041	84,531	41,262	10,312	4,785	1,907
1982	211,013p	247,344p	139,075p	102,969p	−8,093p	−2,198p	9,424p	7,772p	12,918p	106,711p	62,869p	10,731p	3,043p	1,246

p—Preliminary

[1] For a description of the data see page 3. The signs in this table do *not* indicate whether a particular transaction is an inflow or an outflow. In this table a negative sign indicates a reduction in the stock of a particular class of assets during a particular time period.
[2] Beginning in 1979, official U.S. holdings of assets denominated in foreign currencies are revalued monthly at market exchange rates. As of July 1980 the monetary base effect includes the addition of official U.S. holdings of Swiss franc denominated assets. Consequently, this series after July 1980 is not directly comparable to that reported for previous periods.

Source: U.S. Dept. of Commerce, *Survey of Current Business*, 1982.

early 1970s, its existence seemed to depend on a quirk in the U.S balance-of-payment regulations then in force. And since that time, the Euro-CP market had languished.

Coming to think about it, Bill mused, it is interesting to note that the U.S. (domestic) CP market had provided real competition to the note purchase facility. AAA foreign borrowers had been able to obtain funds as much as ½ to ⅝ percent below LIBOR. And even less well-known foreign borrowers could establish a viable program by having their paper "domesticated" under a letter of credit issued by a major bank.[1] At this stage, Bill Steinberg began to think that senior management should be aware of the factors that might cause the supply of funds in the U.S. commercial paper market to behave differently from those in the offshore market. "After all, it's all U.S. dollars," someone might think.

The thought of the dollar as a currency brought Bill's thoughts back to a more immediate issue. He believed that, in addition to availability clauses, there were some issues underlying pricing formulas using a base rate that should be considered again. Most people in the business had come to rely on a long-established relationship in the dollar market, where offshore deposit rates were higher than domestic rates by a margin that essentially reflected the cost of reserve requirements under Federal Reserve Regulation D. And (effective) lending rates were lower than the U.S. prime rate, when adjusted for compensated balance requirements. Quite often, however, there was considerable unexplained "noise" in rate differentials, and Bill believed it might be worthwhile to discuss such questions, especially since customers had more alternatives once traditional prime-rate loans began to be written with LIBOR options.

As competitive pressures forced the creation of currency denomination options, matters became more complicated. In some markets — e.g., those for Swiss franc and Deutsche mark-denominated facilities — offshore deposit rates were traditionally below equivalent domestic interbank rates, at widely fluctuating differentials. But this had not been the case at all times; during parts of 1981, for example, Euro-Deutsche mark rates exceeded domestic rates. The latter constellation held consistently for Euro-French francs and Euro-Lire, but here again rate differentials had shown considerable variability. And Euro-Yen were an enigma altogether, with many (Japanese) observers even denying that they had ever seen anything like a Euro-Yen.

---

1. It appeared, however, that a quirk in the new U.S. bankruptcy code, which forces investors to return proceeds obtained within 90 days of an issuer's bankruptcy (unless an investor can *prove* that he had no knowledge of the impending event), reduced enthusiasm for such transactions.

At this point, Bill's thoughts were interrupted when his wife stopped in to offer him a cup of coffee. Bill gladly accepted and decided that before dinner he would put together an agenda that would compel everybody on the ALPC to make explicit previously held notions about the workings of the international credit markets before they would be forced to learn through accidents. And considering the rate at which the new deals were flooding in, funds availability risks were building up rapidly.

Study Questions
  (1) Disregarding the credit risk issues, which questions are raised by Steinberg regarding international credit markets?
  (2) How would you order these issues into a coherent agenda that permits an open exchange of views about market risks?
  (3) How would you answer the questions raised?

V

Multimarket Financial Packaging

Ian H. Giddy

Case 46

Yin and Yang

This is a case that calls upon your skills as a negotiator. Because there are three parties involved in the negotiation, each of whom has access to different information, your teacher will distribute the specifics of the case in three parts and to three separate groups of students. Good luck!

Ian H. Giddy

Case 47

Nokia Comes Out of the Forest

Bent over against the first chill of autumn, Paula Perttunen hurried up Helsinki's esplanade toward her office in the Nokia Oy headquarters building. She tried to keep her mind clear so that she could properly evaluate the various financing proposals that had been discussed over a long lunch with the Metrobank investment banking people from London. As Assistant Treasurer (International) for Nokia, the largest private industrial firm in Finland, Paula was responsible for the initial assessment and presentation of financing proposals for Nokia's international investments.

In August 1984, the Nokia Group's products encompassed forest industries, cables, metal products, and electronics, among others, with a recent emphasis on international production and sales of industrial and consumer electronics. A major objective was to reduce dependency on forest products. Forty-eight percent of its estimated $1.7 billion sales in 1984 were outside Finland (Exhibit 1), although 85 percent of the Group's $1.37 billion assets remained within the country (Exhibit 2). Nokia was presently considering an investment of approximately US$210 million in the United States, and Paula Perttunen was digging up ways to finance it. Her immediate task upon reaching her desk was to come up with a financing package for presentation to the Finance Committee the next morning. The bankers had proposed a private placement with a U.S. insurance company or a Eurobond issue or, alternatively, issuing commercial paper that would be coupled with an interest rate swap to give Nokia fixed-rate money. In addition to these, Paula had some others up her sleeve. But first, she

Exhibit 1 *Nokia's International Sales (in millions of Finnmarks)*

Sales in	1983	1982
Finland	3089	2687
Exports from Finland	2214	2080
Foreign subsidiaries	1644	1630
Total	6947	6397

Profile of Foreign Sales by Market Area

Nokia Group exports and turnover of foreign subsidiaries by market area (in millions of Finnmarks)

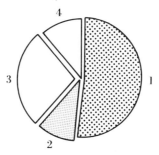

1   Western Europe
2   Other OECD countries
3   CMEA
4   OPEC and other countries

thought, I had better make sure of how much and what kind of financing we need.

WHAT FINANCING WAS REALLY NEEDED?

Nokia was no newcomer to the international capital market. It had borrowed over $200 million in various currencies from international banks, and had issued a $40 million, seven-year Swiss franc bond in 1978. Its shares were even traded on the Stockholm stock exchange. Already well known in the area of modems for data transfer, Nokia had earlier in the year successfully launched a new product, a mobile hand-held radio-telephone, through a subsidiary called Mobira. Initial sales looked good, and Nokia's top management was keen to get a jump on the U.S. consumer electronics market by producing a hand-held, remote computer terminal. This device would combine the modem and radio-telephone technology with a flat-screen display device developed by another Finnish firm, Lohja Oy. Nokia had already set up a new subsidiary, Mobiterm, which had developed a prototype model that was reportedly reliable and cost efficient. Kurt Wikstedt, Nokia's electronics chief honcho and director of finance, was keeping an eye open for a U.S. assembler and distributor when he heard that Mattel, the U.S. consumer electronics firm, was seeking a buyer

Exhibit 2 *Nokia group balance sheet (in millions of Finnmarks) as at June 30, 1984*

Assets		
Cash and receivables	2,512	
Inventories	1,897	
Fixed assets	3,580	
Goodwill	8	
Valuation items[1]	213	8,210
Liabilities		
Current liabilities	2,520	
Long-term liabilities	2,217	
Minority interests in group companies	320	
Provisions for losses[2]	1,076	
Shareholders capital[3]	2,077	8,210

[1] Chiefly unrealized exchange losses.
[2] Including provisions for bad debts, stocks, investments and exchange losses.
[3] Including net profit for the past year of FIM 121 million.

for its troubled Intellivision division. The Board agreed with his view that such an acquisition could give Nokia a central place in the U.S. consumer electronics industry and serve as a base from which to launch the Mobiterm product.

The Bank of Finland and the Ministry of Finance had been informed of Nokia's interest — the authorities maintained discretionary control over all capital movements, especially outward investments (Exhibit 3) — and

Exhibit 3 *Summary of Finnish Government's Role in Finnish Companies' International Borrowing*

Three authorities of the Finnish Government can be involved in a Finnish firm's international financing plans. The first and most important of these is the central bank, the Bank of Finland. The Bank administers Finland's rather strict capital controls, both on capital inflows and on capital outflows. Since Finland has a small capital market, the Bank wants to be sure that it is not depleted by borrowing for foreign investments. Capital outflows would also deplete Finland's rather limited foreign exchange reserves. Thus, only a very limited amount of domestic Finnmark funds could be used to finance foreign investments. The Bank of Finland also influences all major funding abroad by Finnish, private or government-owned. The goals are to ensure that Finnish firms abroad displace neither one another nor the Government itself in tapping the international capital market, and to prevent excessive capital flows that could lead to monetary expansion. Any firm planning to issue equity, long-term debt, or commercial paper abroad must therefore seek the Bank's approval.

A Bank of Finland official described the procedure for gaining such approval as follows. First, the Bank limits the number of potential issuers to major Finnish companies. Each year the Bank conducts a survey of such companies' prospective demand for foreign credits. The firms are assigned "quotas" of foreign funds that they may be permitted to raise. These quotas are based on the Bank's judgment of Finland's total access to the international capital market, and its internal analysis of the credit standing of each company — its profitability, indebtedness, and so forth. Such an evaluation, which can be done on an ad hoc basis for companies planning major borrowing, can take up to two weeks to complete. The Board of Management of the Bank of Finland must approve all amounts above FIM50 million.

When the firm passes muster, it gets approval "in principle." Although the company may now in principle plan to do its financing any way it likes, in practice it must get a second approval each time it does a specific issue. This approval, which only takes a day or two, is designed to prevent bunching of Finnish issues abroad and to make sure that the proposed terms and conditions are fair and competitive.

The second Finnish government agency with an interest in capital flows is the Ministry of Finance. Its role is an informal one. Because the MOF borrows in the name of the Republic of Finland in the Eurobond and commercial paper markets, it will give the thumbs down to any issue that it feels might damage Finland's AAA rating.

Finally, the Ministry of Trade and Industry can also get involved in international capital movements involving equity financing, as for example in a bond issue carrying warrants or a convertible bond. The reason is that the Ministry administers the corporation law, including the severe restraints on property ownership imposed on any Finnish company whose voting stock is more than 20 percent owned by foreigners.

Nokia was seeking an export credit guarantee for the $25 million of equipment that they expected to supply to any new U.S. subsidiary. Preliminary discussions with Mattel were underway, although the purchase price was by no means set in stone. Mattell refused to accept Nokia shares, but had agreed that part of the purchase price could be in the form of a $75 million five-year note at 12¾ percent; the rest would have to be cash. Nokia was being advised in the acquisition negotiations by the American investment banking firm, Goldman Sachs. Wikstedt's intention was to assemble the hand-held terminals at Mattell's plant in Dallas and sell them in the United States initially. After two years, if they were a success in the United States, the terminals would be sold in Europe as well; the aim was to achieve an 80 percent North America, 10 percent Europe sales mix.

Wikstedt had told Paula that Nokia or its new subsidiary, Mobiterm, would have to borrow all but $30 million of the purchase price. The $30 million was funds that had been generated from the European sales of Nokia's Swedish electronics subsidiary, Luxor. On the other hand, it was rumored that Nokia's soft-tissue unit, Nordic Tissues, might soon be sold. This would reap at least FIM700 million, or US$117 million at today's exchange rate of six Finnmarks to the dollar. Wikstedt felt that funding should be such that repayment was deferred for at least seven years. Since Nokia had been burned during the last rise in short-term rates, it was generally understood that Wikstedt's goal was to increase the proportion of fixed rate debt to about 60 percent. At present, all but 28 percent of the company's total debt of FIM5.1 billion was short term or variable rate debt. The currency mix of the company's debt at the end of 1983 was: FIM

49 percent, US$ 28 percent, DM 12 percent, SK 4 percent, GBP 3 percent, SWF 3 percent and other 1 percent.

SOURCES OF FUNDS

Paula began by writing down the likely mix of funds sources for the acquisition:

Purchase price	$210 million
Five-year note to Mattell	($ 75 million)
Cash on hand	($ 30 million)
New debt required:	$105 million

The obvious source of financing, she mused, is a syndicated revolving credit facility — a bank loan. Banque Francaise had been pestering Nokia's treasury people about this, saying that the bank could put together a $75–100 million syndicated credit at a cost of ⅝ percent above LIBOR, the London Interbank Offered Rate, plus the usual front-end fees. Such credits ranged up to twelve years' maturity and could be drawn down when needed. The only problem was that Finland's two biggest banks together owned 21.4 percent of Nokia's stock and had board representation who resisted Francaise's lead management of any loan because they had been excluded from the management group of recent Scandinavian issues led by Francaise.

An alternative source of short-term funds would be for Nokia to issue commercial paper in the United States. To do this, the company would have to get a rating and pay about ½ percent for a back-up line of credit from a bank. Metrobank alone was willing to provide a line for up to $50 million and to assist in the commercial paper, and had argued that this would be a good way for Nokia to become better known in the United States. Despite their recent rapid expansion into the United States (Exhibit 4), Finnish companies still had a very low profile in North America. To assist Nokia in ensuring its paper's acceptability to U.S. institutional investors, Metrobank had offered letter of credit support for a fee of ¼ percent. This would give it an A1/P1 rating. The A1/P1 commercial paper rate was currently about ninety basis points below LIBOR.

Alternatively, a U.S. bank could place short-term Nokia notes directly with U.S. institutional investors, at a cost of a few extra basis points.

Two other possibilities that Paula had discussed with the Metrobank people at lunch involved taking advantage of the short-term assets that the

Exhibit 4 **Subsidiaries of Finnish companies abroad in 1972, 1981, and 1983**

	1972		1981		1983	
	MFG	Total	MFG	Total	MFG	Total
SWEDEN	9	133	28	133	41	287
UNITED KINGDOM	5	45	14	139	15	154
UNITED STATES	1	16	10	113	20	143
WEST GERMANY	5	44	9	124	11	139
NORWAY	1	12	7	69	7	75
DENMARK	3	16	5	41	8	46
FRANCE	2	11	5	38	7	38
THE NETHERLANDS	3	11	2	36	4	60
CANADA	6	10	7	29	9	33
BRAZIL	3	6	5	20	6	21
SAUDI ARABIA	—	—	3	10	4	10
OTHER	0	0	0	0	30	229
	38	304	95	874	162	1235

Intellivision unit had on its balance sheet. Mattell, who had provided an unaudited statement of accounts to Nokia (see Exhibit 5), estimated that about two-thirds of Intellivision's inventory consisted of silver for use in microchip circuitry. Metrobank would purchase the silver from Mobiterm for, say, six months at a time, meanwhile allowing Mobiterm to use the metal in its finished products. At the end of six months Metrobank would

Exhibit 5 **Mattell Inc.—Intellivision Division unaudited balance sheet (millions of dollars)**

Assets		
Cash and marketable securities	11	
Accounts receivable	45	
Inventories	57	
Fixed Assets	98	
Goodwill	13	224
Liabilities		
Short-term bank debt	0	
Accounts payable	33	
Long-term debt	0	
Net worth	191	224

sell the silver back to Mobiterm at the going market price. Metrobank was willing to do this for only 5½ percent per annum, it seemed. Alternatively, a bank would be able to discount Mobiterm's receivables — Nokia had experience with this technique inside and outside Finland — although many of Intellivision's receivables were in Deutsche marks and sterling. Metrobank had expressed an interest in discounting longer-term big-ticket trade receivables. Both approaches were excellent means of taking assets off the books of a company that had credit rating problems.

Paula Perttunen made a list of all these financing methods. However, she wondered, would Widstedt live with the varying interest rates that these would entail? Perhaps just for the part that's financing our receivables or inventory? On the other hand, we should consider taking up Metrobank's suggestion that we create fixed-rate funds out of variable-rate financing by doing an interest rate swap. Let's see, how would that work? And what would it cost? She recalled the conversation at lunch.

Perttunen:	Timo, if we drew down a Eurodollar loan at a spread over six-month LIBOR, how would you fix our cost of funds?
Timo Tyynela (the local Metrobanker):	Well, in a floating-fixed interest rate swap, we would pay LIBOR to Nokia every six months, which you could then use to service your floating interest payments. In return, Nokia would pay us a fixed rate set at, I would guess, fifty basis points above the seven-year U.S. Treasury bond rate. Yesterday, seven-year Treasuries were yielding 11¾ percent.
Perttunen:	Any fees?
Tyynela:	A ½ percent up-front fee is usual, although to meet the competition we've gone down to ¼ percent on occasion. But that's not much if you spread it over seven years. We could do a seven-year deal as big as $125 million for Nokia. The only thing I would say is that you would have to do a minimum of $20 million to make it worthwhile.
Pettunen:	No problem. Could you do these swaps in other currencies?
Tyynela:	Yes, interest rate swaps are being done in most of the major European currencies, and yen, and a few others.
Perttunen:	Finnmarks?
Tyynela:	Anything's possible ... at a price. We could also give you a rate swap based not on LIBOR but on the A1/P1 commercial paper rate; in fact, that would knock about forty basis points off the fixed rate you'd have to pay. In addition we could fix you up with a currency swap, in case you need dollars but feel you have an advantage in the D-mark or Swiss franc market. These would be priced as an interest differential for fixed-rate funds in the two currencies. Take

Exhibit 6 The Finnmark

In 1984 the Finnish currency was assiduously controlled by the Bank of Finland by means of intervention in the spot market and in the forward market, and by stringent capital controls. The spot rate of the Finnmark was tied to a "basket" of currencies based on Finland's trade, excluding trade with the Soviet bloc, which was conducted largely on a bilateral basis. The weights in the basket were as follows as of June 1, 1984:

Deutsche mark   60%
U.S. Dollar   30%
Pound sterling   10%

The exchange rates, in Finnmarks per foreign currency unit, on June 1, 1984 were: DM 2.1345, US$ 5.7790, and 8.0540.

The following chart shows the movement of the Finnmark against basket, including the devaluation that took place in late 1982 in response to Sweden's devaluation:

Bank of Finland Currency Index

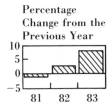

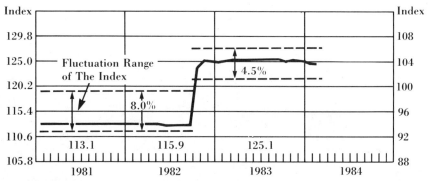

Source: Bank of Finland Monthly Bulletin

a dollar–mark swap. The indicative rate for a seven-year fixed-fixed swap is 4¾ percent. For Swissies it would be 6 percent. For example, if Nokia has D-mark debt on which you're paying 7 percent fixed, we would give you the 7 percent annually in marks and you would give us 11¾ percent annually in dollars. At maturity we would pay you the D-mark amount of your principal and you could pay us the same amount in dollars, calculated at today's exchange rate. Thus, as far as you're concerned it's dollar debt. There's a mere ½ percent fee for these currency swaps.

Pettunen: That's a long answer to a question I never asked, but thanks anyway. Let's order the pancakes.

Paula reflected that she had indeed been told by Dresdner Bank that Nokia could issue a D-mark Eurobond for as much as DM150 million, or about $50 million at today's exchange rate. The amount would be higher if the mark strengthened, as many economists expected would happen soon. Nokia would have to pay perhaps 6½ percent for seven-year D-mark funds under present conditions.

As the Metrobank people from London had pointed out, however, the obvious choice to finance a U.S. venture for Mobiterm was a Eurodollar bond — a Eurobond denominated in U.S. dollars. This market could give the company fixed-rate funds, for maturities up to twelve years. The bankers felt that Nokia's name was sufficiently well known in Europe that it could float an issue as large as $75 million at 13 percent unless the dollar weakened a great deal, in which case a $50 million issue would be the most Nokia could expect. Should the dollar weaken, another source worth considering was the Swiss franc foreign bond market — an issue in Switzerland by a nonresident borrower — where Nokia could probably get $40 million at 5½ percent right away. All of these international bond issues, of course, would entail managing, underwriting, and selling fees, which totalled about 2 percent of the amount issued. And with a Eurobond, or for that matter any bond, there was always the possibility that if the issue were mispriced or badly timed, the price would have to be dropped or the issue withdrawn. Investment bankers, who had done their homework in advance of an issue, should usually be able to avoid this, but that was not always feasible if market conditions changed or if the issuer was a newcomer to the maket. Some issuers tried to "sweeten" their offering by adding warrants, or denominating the issue in a basket of currencies designed to appeal to the individual investor. Paula had also talked to her boss about the merits of doing a convertible Eurobond issue, which could cost 2 to 3 percent below a straight issue and which might strengthen Nokia's capital structure. The problem with the latter was that Finnish laws limited the amount of a local firm's equity that could be held by foreigners to 20 percent, and Nokia was already approaching that limit.

All things considered, the conclusion of the luncheon meeting was that Nokia would be well advised to undertake, with Metrobank's assistance, a private placement of debt with an institutional investor in the United States. Although they had internal limits on foreign holdings, two or three life insurance companies had shown an interest in fixed-rate, medium-term paper of prominent Scandinavian issuers. Metrobank felt their New York specialists could place as much as $150 million of Nokia's paper in this manner. The cost right now would be about 13¼ percent, a little bit higher than a public issue in the United States (a "Yankee bond"), but the fees were a shade lower — about 1 percent of the principal amount. This approach would ensure availability of all the funds needed, and more, with the only drawback being that it would not help Nokia gain the visibility that top management felt it needed in the international capital market. "We must get out of the Finnish forest and into the light," Wikstedt had once growled to Paula.

Paula began to organize her notes and thoughts in preparation for the following day's meeting. First, she felt she should divide the choices into those involving variable interest rates and those involving fixed. Should all the funds be at fixed rates? If so, could this be done by means of swaps? If swaps were used, would this entail any additional risks? If a fixed rate issue were done, should it be a public issue or a private placement? A straight bond or a convertible? Also, through which corporate entity should the debt be issued? And Paula wondered about the wisdom of denominating the issue in U.S. dollars. The dollar had risen substantially against the Finnmark in recent years, and if that were to continue, the value of the debt to be repaid would increase just as the Swiss franc issue had done. Since the Finnmark was more or less tied to the German mark and since D-mark issues bear a much lower interest rate, Paula was sure that the question of borrowing in D-marks would be raised at the meeting. Finally, she wanted to be able to recommend a *package* of financing that would meet the company's needs, that would comply with Finnish government requirements, that would minimize cost and risk while not closing the door to future Nokia financing requirements.

VI

Organization, Control, and Financial Reporting

Raymond Vernon

| Case 48 |

Sola Chemical Company

ORGANIZING THE INTERNATIONAL FINANCE FUNCTION

The year was 1970. The subject before Sola Chemical's board of directors was a set of proposals by Multinational Consultants, Inc., recommending a drastic overhaul in the organization of Sola's overseas business. The board had already agreed, albeit a bit uncertainly, that the International Division would have to be abolished and that its responsibilities for overseas production and overseas marketing would have to be distributed among some new regional divisions. Now the question was: What to do about the finance and control functions for which the International Division had been responsible?

ORIGINS

Ever since World War II, Sóla had been doing what came naturally in the expansion of its foreign business. In the years just after the war, Sola thought of itself as one of five or six companies that made up the leadership in the industrial and agricultural chemicals industry in the United States. At that time, a company with annual sales of $150 million could claim a leadership position. Besides, sales of the company at that time were reasonably well concentrated in only four main product groups. From the perspective of 1970, after nearly twenty-five years of growth and of diversification into new products and new markets, operations in the immediate postwar period seemed extraordinarily neat and tidy.

In the first years after the war, the foreign business of Sola was a limited affair. Mainly it consisted of the sales that a small export department could drum up in Western Europe and Latin America, relying largely on commission merchants, wholesalers, and industrial buyers in those areas. From time to time, Sola would discover that one of its newer products had taken hold in some country, generally at a time five or six years after it had found a market in the United States. After a few years of expansion in any foreign market, however, the attractiveness of the particular line in the area would generally fall away as quietly as it had appeared.

Apart from the seemingly episodic and sporadic lines of business of this sort, Sola's main "foreign" commitment in the years up to World War II was a manufacturing subsidiary in Canada, a subsidiary that Sola had set up in the late 1920s in response to a sharp increase in Canada's industrial tariffs. Except for a few shares nominally held by Canadian directors, this subsidiary was wholly owned by Sola. When the Imperial Preference tariff system was established in 1932, the Sola management had congratulated itself on its foresight in establishing a subsidiary inside the Commonwealth so that it could meet British competitors such as Imperial Chemical Industries on equal terms. From Sola management's viewpoint, however, the Canadian subsidiary could hardly be called "foreign." Situated not far from Windsor, Ontario, it was close enough to Sola's midwest headquarters to be run like any other branch plant. The product policies and marketing policies of Sola seemed to apply about as well to the Canadian plant as any other. True, there were some occasional crises of an unfamiliar sort, as when the Canadians tinkered with the value of their currency in relation to the U.S. dollar, or when they set up unfamiliar provisions in relation to the taxation of profits. But an occasional consultation with the company's bankers and tax attorneys was generally sufficient to deal with crises of this sort.

Quite different from Sola's relationship to its Canadian subsidiary in the years immediately after World War II were its ties to a French subsidiary that had been set up at about the same time. Unlike the Canadian subsidiary, only 53 percent of the equity of this company was owned by Sola, the rest being in the hands of Cie. Chimie Tricolor, a leading French manufacturer whose product lines fell largely within two of Sola's four product groups. Nobody at Sola could quite recall how this particular liaison had first developed. But there was an impression that Sola had been confronted with an ultimatum by the French chemical industry at one point in the 1920s: either she must invite a French business interest to join her in the creation of a French manufacturing subsidiary or she must risk losing a lucrative market that was being supplied by exports from the United States. There was some recollection among Sola's oldtimers that the ultimatum had been backed up by hints from the French ministry of industry that the threats might not prove hollow. In any event, whatever the origins of the French partnership might be, the subsidiary had grown away from Sola over the years. By the late 1940s it was thought of as almost an independent entity, operating under the stewardship of the French partner and negotiating with Sola for product information and technology very much on an arm's-length basis.

So much for the situation at the beginning of the postwar era.

Between that time and 1970, the foreign business of Sola had expanded at an astonishing rate, considerably faster than the United States. And as the foreign business grew, not only the policies and strategies but even the very structure of Sola was greatly affected. Step by step, additional locations had been selected for the establishment of new manufacturing subsidiaries: the United Kingdom in 1952; Germany in 1955; Mexico in 1956; Brazil in 1960; Italy in 1962; Australia in 1965; and so on, until Sola's manufacturing facilities covered fifteen different countries. At the same time, operations in Canada had been considerably expanded, covering more of Sola's product lines. In each of these cases, Sola had preferred to go it alone, without local partners. And after a nasty confrontation or two with the French partners over the management of the French facility, a friendly divorce had been arranged, leaving Sola with a wholly owned manufacturing facility in France in lieu of the old partnership.

Although Sola had not set up more than a portion of the U.S. product line in any one country, the total number of products manufactured overseas was widening every year. In fact, there were even three or four cases in which the U.S. plants had suspended operations on an old staple item, assigning what was left of the business to one of the foreign facilities where the product still seemed to command a market. When that happened, the foreign facility took over Sola's third country markets as well.

While the manufacturing subsidiaries were spreading over the globe, Sola was setting up other units to facilitate the handling of its foreign business. Sola had discovered very early the tax advantages of a western hemisphere trade corporation and had set up a company in Delaware to qualify under the U.S. tax code. A corporation could qualify if it derived practically all its income from trade or business (as distinguished from investment), and confined its business to the western hemisphere outside the United States. The profits of such a corporation were taxed at a rate 14 percentage points less than the standard U.S. rate. To exploit this advantage, U.S. Sola billed its exports to western hemisphere countries from the United States through its western hemisphere trade corporation. As a rule, such exports were billed out by U.S. Sola to the trade corporation at the lowest possible appropriate figure, which Sola calculated in accordance with a formula that included an 8 percent mark-up over cost. This formula had the effect of placing most of the profit on such sales in the trade corporation.

Other arrangements to minimize taxes had been made as well. Back in 1958, before the Revenue Act of 1962 had restricted the use of foreign-based holding companies as "tax havens" — that is, as vehicles for postponing the payment of U.S. taxes on foreign income — Sola's treasurer and tax attorney had pushed through the establishment of a Swiss holding company. U.S. Sola owned Sola-Switzerland, which in turn held nominal ownership over Sola's subsidiaries outside the United States. In those days, Sola-Switzerland could perform all kinds of useful services for U.S. Sola. For one thing, like the western hemisphere trade corporation, it could act as an intermediary in export sales from the United States. When Sola-Switzerland was used as an intermediary, the tax benefits to U.S. Sola were rather different than those associated with the use of the western hemisphere company. Sola-Switzerland's profits were subject to normal tax rates once they got into the U.S. tax jurisdiction. But that did not occur until the profits were declared to U.S. Sola in the form of dividends. Meanwhile, Sola-Switzerland could shuttle the cash generated by export profits to any point in the Sola system that required it.

Sola-Switzerland's cash flow could be built up not only by exports but also by the dividends, royalties, interest and fees generated in the Sola subsidiaries that Sola-Switzerland nominally owned. As long as Swiss law did not tax the income of the Swiss holding company and as long as a U.S. law did not classify the funds as taxable in the United States, Sola-Switzerland was a highly useful mechanism.

That particular arrangement had deferred quite a lot of tax payments for a few years. Subsidiaries could declare dividends and could pay interest, agency fees, administrative charges, and royalties to the holding company without subjecting the income to U.S. taxation; the U.S. tax bite would come only when the income moved upstream as dividends to the U.S. parent. Though the U.S. system of tax credits on foreign-earned income ensured that the income would not be taxed twice when it finally appeared on the U.S. parent's books, still there was something to be gained at times from deferring the U.S. tax. The tax advantage was especially important when the subsidiary's payments to its parent had not been taxed locally because they represented expenses to the subsidiary, or when the subsidiary's income had been taxed at rates well below those in the United States. In those situations, when the payments finally were received as dividends in the United States, some U.S. taxes would be due.

When the Internal Revenue Code was amended in 1962 to restrict the use of tax haven companies, many of the tax advantages involved in the maintenance of such a company disappeared. The provisions that expose the income of such tax haven companies to U.S. taxation are exceedingly complex. But Sola's Swiss holding company clearly fell within its terms. It was controlled by U.S. Sola, and it derived more than 70 percent of its income from the dividends, interest, royalties and other fees received from Sola's operating subsidiaries located in third countries. Accordingly, the income of Sola-Switzerland was fully taxable under U.S. law just as if it had been paid directly to U.S. Sola itself.

One tax advantage associated with foreign holding companies still remained, however. Loath to discourage exports from the U.S. in any way, Congress had exempted from the new provisions such income as the tax haven companies were garnering from their role in the handling of U.S. exports. As long as a spread could exist between the price at which U.S. Sola invoiced its goods for export and the price at which the goods were invoiced for import in the foreign country of destination, there were still tax advantages in assigning the spread to an intermediate company located in a tax-free area.

Despite the fact that Sola-Switzerland had lost much of its original purpose, there was some hesitation about liquidating the Swiss company. It would entail the transfer of the equity of many underlying operating subsidiaries, the transfer of the Swiss company's claims to the long-term and short-term debt of some of the operating subsidiaries, and the shift of the Swiss company's title in patents and trade names abroad that were being licensed to the subsidiaries.

Numerous contractual ties between the Swiss company and the subsidiaries also would have to be dissolved, such as the right of the Swiss company to receive payment for administrative and technical services and for sales agency services. All these rearrangements were bound to generate administrative and legal problems in a number of different countries, where the increasing curiosity and sophistication of the regulatory authorities could be counted on to stir up difficulties.

Accordingly, Sola decided to leave the Swiss holding company in existence and to create several other intermediate companies besides. One would be a Luxembourg company, set up to capture some of the profits on U.S. exports, which still were entitled to tax deferral treatment. Another enterprise would be set up to segregate the income generated by subsidiaries in advanced countries. Under the 1962 law, income originating in subsidiaries in the less-developed areas, unlike income from the advanced countries, could still be kept beyond the reach of U.S. tax collectors to the extent that it was reinvested in less-developed areas. Accordingly, a holding company was set up in Curaçao to own Sola's subsidiaries in less-developed areas and to receive the income of such subsidiaries for routing to destinations where the income was needed. Curaçao's virtue as a holding company headquarters consisted *inter alia* of its willingness to leave such income virtually untaxed as it passed through the holding company on its way to a new destination.

As if this complex cluster of intermediate companies was not enough, Sola decided in 1966 that another intermediate structure would be useful, namely, a holding company created under the laws of Delaware to act as Sola's alter ego in floating bond issues in the European market.

Well before 1966, it was clear to U.S. Sola that its European subsidiaries' voracious appetite would have to be fed by more borrowing from abroad. Sola itself was under a handicap when raising money in Europe, because U.S. internal revenue requirements obliged it to withhold 30 percent of interest or dividend payments to non-resident recipients. That provision placed a heavy handicap on the securities of U.S. issuers in Europe. Sola's Swiss holding company had been used two or three times before as the nominal borrower of dollar-denominated funds from European sources. Operating under the umbrella of a guarantee from U.S. Sola, the Swiss holding company had been able to borrow medium-term money at reasonable rates from private European sources. Though the interest costs had run a little higher than they would have in the United States, these flotations had saved the bother of registration with the Securities and Exchange Commission, the problem of qualification under the "blue sky" laws of the state regulatory agencies, and so on; the difference in costs, therefore, was not as great as the interest rates indicated. At the same time, Sola had developed some excellent European banking ties that might be in a position to help out in the event that the U.S. government really clamped down on the export of capital from the United States. As early as 1958 or 1959, that contingency had become something to worry about, as U.S. officials began to express their misgivings over the condition of the U.S. balance of payments.

By 1965, contingency had turned to reality. "Voluntary" controls had been imposed over the outflow of funds from the United States to subsidiaries in Europe. Although the controls were very loose and left many different ways in which Sola could arrange for the generation of cash flows in its overseas subsidiaries, Sola tried to respond to the spirit of the regulations by raising a larger proportion of its needed funds outside the United States.

One possible step to that end was to continue using the Swiss holding company, as it had been used in the past, to borrow from European sources. But Sola was not eager to expand the use of the Swiss holding company, now that it had lost most of its usefulness as a tax haven. True, such a holding company still had some advantages that U.S. Sola did not share, such as the fact that its payments of dividend and interest to non-U.S. recipients were not subject to the reporting and withholding requirements of U.S. tax law. But the use of such a company also had some disadvantages, when compared with a Delaware company, such as the fact that losses if any could not be consolidated in U.S. Sola's income tax return in the United States.

The upshot was that Sola decided in 1966 to create a second Delaware holding company, with functions carefully designed to retain the advantages of a Swiss holding company as a financing intermediary while avoiding some of its disabilities. The main purpose of the second Delaware holding company was to borrow funds outside the United States with the guarantee of U.S. Sola and to lend those funds to Sola's foreign subsidiaries. As long as the new holding company confined itself to this sort of operation, its only significant income — namely, interest payments from the subsidiaries — was regarded as of foreign origin. Since 80 percent or more of its income was of foreign origin, the Delaware company, like the Swiss company, was not required to withhold any sums in connection with interest payments to non-U.S. recipients. Such profits as the Delaware company might have were within the reach of the U.S. and Delaware tax jurisdiction. But profits were likely to be trivial, given the purpose of the company. Besides, Delaware tax provisions were traditionally benign in such matters, and U.S. tax provisions, ever since the adoption of the 1962 amendments, made only small distinctions between the profits of domestic holding companies and those of foreign holding companies of U.S. taxpayers.

The creation of the Delaware finance company proved to be a very wise step indeed. On January 1, 1968, the so-called voluntary program of capital export controls became mandatory. At the same time, the program was tightened up so that the various alternative means of transferring funds abroad became more restricted. Under the new program, Sola's right to transfer funds abroad was tied to its historical record of investment in the years just prior to 1968. Investment for that base period was defined as capital transfers in cash or in kind made to foreign subsidiaries plus profits retained in the subsidiaries during the period. Once that base figure was calculated, its application was differently defined for different groups of countries. Subsidiaries in the less-developed countries, the "Schedule A" countries, were allowed to continue receiving investment from U.S. Sola at their old levels, even a little higher. Then there was a "Schedule B" group, which the U.S. regulators thought of as being especially dependent on U.S. capital flows — the oil countries, the United Kingdom, Japan, and a few other areas. Added investments from the United States in these areas were cut down but not eliminated; capital flows to these areas were restricted to 65 percent of the base period. Canada, originally in this group, was exempted from the regulations altogether.

The real problem for Sola, therefore, was the European subsidiaries, that is, the subsidiaries located in "Schedule C" countries. These were cut back drastically. At first, added investment from U.S. Sola could only take place through retained earnings. And even the retained earnings could not be used under the rules if this meant a retention rate higher than base period rates or if it meant an investment rate higher than 35 percent of the base period.

If it had not been for the fact that borrowings outside the United States were exempted from the restrictions, Sola would have been in real trouble at first. That exemption carried the company through 1968. And in 1969 and 1970, the restrictions came to be somewhat eased. But the experience impressed on the minds of Sola's management more than ever the need to have an intimate knowledge of the world's sources of capital and to have the flexibility in organization to use the sources as needed. This heightened recognition centered attention on just how decisions were taken on such matters inside the organization.

THE FINANCIAL ORGANIZATION

As Sola expanded its overseas operations, the legal instrumentalities and national environments that concerned it increased rapidly in number. From World War II until 1970, therefore, there was a constant need to restructure the internal organization and procedures that were responsible for formulating and executing financial policies and for controlling financial operations. That restructuring was tied in intimately, of course, with other changes in Sola's organization, including changes in the marketing and production systems associated with a growing overseas operation.

In the early 1960s, the foreign business had grown to such proportions that it was thought advisable to create an international division. The first executive in charge of that division, an aggressive and ambitious manager, decided that one of his major needs was to pull together the haphazard structure that up to that time had been formulating financial policy for the foreign areas. With the approval of Sola's top management, therefore, a new structure was created. Some of the essential elements of the organization tying together the financial function at that stage are suggested by the diagram in Exhibit 1.

A word or two of elaboration is needed in order to relate Sola's structure in the early 1960s, portrayed in Exhibit 1, to financial decisions as taken at that time.

Major investment decisions, such as decisions to create a new foreign subsidiary or substantially to increase its capitalization, were generally recommended in the first instance by the international manager to Sola's president; he, in turn, usually sought the advice of his board of directors, as well as the advice of many other sources.

Major policies aimed at reducing taxes on overseas operations were usually initiated by the international treasurer, discussed wtih U.S. Sola's treasurer and tax attorney, then cleared with the finance committee.

Policies with regard to borrowing by foreign subsidiaries were no problem. Apart from accounts payable and accrued liabilities and except for a rare local loan initiated by the international treasurer, such transactions did not arise. Subsidiaries were not authorized to borrow; indeed they were not thought of as managing their own cash flow. Funds were channelled to the subsidiaries by the international treasurer as needed. Before 1965 these funds had come mainly from the parent or the Swiss holding company, in the form of short-term dollar debt. Later on, after the Delaware company was formed and had begun to raise dollars through the sale of Eurobonds, it became the principal creditor for Sola's foreign subsidiaries.

Apart from decisions on whether and how to provide the subsidiaries with their working capital needs, the other major area of financial operating policy was how to withdraw funds from a subsidiary that held surplus cash. In this case, the main problem was viewed as minimizing the tax burden associated with withdrawal, and the main policy variable was the choice between dividends, royalties, interest, and management fees. That choice was made by the tax attorney, on the basis of data provided by the international treasurer.

The international controller, as Exhibit 1 suggests, bore a somewhat

Exhibit 1 *Sola Chemical Company. Financial offices in the structure of Sola Company, 1962*

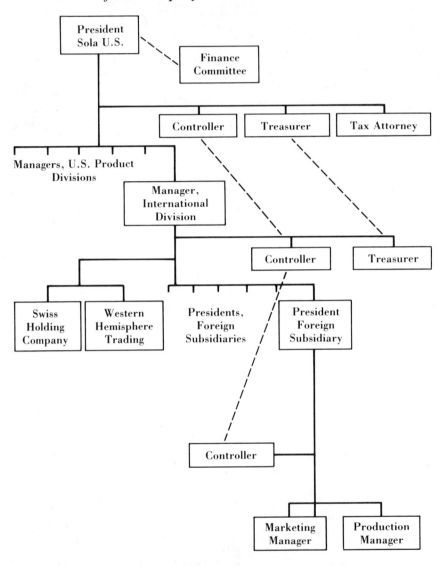

different relation to the organization than the treasurer. Unlike the treasurer, the controller had representatives in each of the subsidiaries. This difference reflected the fact that the treasurer saw his function as that of managing the money flows of the system, whereas the controller saw his function as that of monitoring the performance of its various parts. The first function, so it seemed, could be performed well enough from the bridge of the enterprise, whereas the second function required getting down into the various holds below.

PROPOSALS FOR REORGANIZATION

As a rule, the international treasurer's problems were not the sort of subject that got discussed very much among Sola's directors. When a major investment abroad was involved, that of course was fairly well explored. But the discussion mostly involved questions of strategy, rather than financing and cash flow problems. These were left pretty much for the finance committee and the treasurer's office to worry about. As far as the finance committee was concerned, that group was free to admit that its ability to second-guess the treasurer's office on overseas' financing was quite limited. The subject was just too specialized, it appeared. So the international treasurer proved to be performing a vital function.

Fortunately for Sola Chemical, it had filled that post very well indeed. Milray Thaler had been international treasurer ever since 1958 when the post was first created. He had come out of the old export department, seasoned by years of selling in a world of inconvertible currencies. He had learned all about the ways in which blocked currencies could be turned into usable cash, and ways in which avoidable taxes could be avoided. As international treasurer, he ran a tight organization. He kept close touch with the problems of every subsidiary, especially their problems of cash flow. As far as he could see, the foreign subsidiaries had been well provided for, without having to worry about money and credit questions for which they were hardly equipped. And as far as taxes were concerned, the foreign side of Sola had done marvelously well in avoiding the avoidable.

Despite that fact, by 1970, the financial organization was showing certain signs of strain. By that time, Thaler's unflagging efforts to hold down taxes and to generate money where it was most needed had made a shambles of the periodic profit and loss statements of the subsidiaries. The U.S. system of controls over the export of funds to subsidiaries had increased the complexities of financing. The objective of holding down the total tax bill was now constrained by restrictions on the outflow of capital from the United States. The importance of distinguishing between the treatment of subsidiaries in different countries also was increasing. The differences between less-developed countries and advanced countries, and between countries in Schedules A, B, and C, were important. Added wrinkles, such as Canada's special status under the U.S. capital export control program, had to be kept in mind. The difficulties were heightened further by the fact that some countries, especially the United States and Germany, were beginning to take seriously their various fiscal provisions relating to the international pricing of goods and services. Provisions such as Section 482 of the U.S. Internal Revenue Code, authorizing the tax authorities to use arm's-length prices in interaffiliate transactions, were beginning to be applied seriously. Thaler's consultations with the tax people and his demands on Sola's treasurer were constantly rising in number and urgency.

In addition, Thaler's difficulties with the controller's area seemed on the increase. The more strenuous the efforts of the treasurer, the more difficult the problem of the controller. If the reported profit and loss statements of the manufacturing subsidiaries could be taken at face value, most of them were operating at practically no profit; the only exception was the subsidiary in Canada. What actually was happening depends on what the word "actually" meant. Profits were appearing in the western hemisphere trading company, in the Swiss holding company, in the Swiss holding company in Luxembourg, and in Curaçao. Whether these profits were "actual" or not depended on what one thought of the validity of the prices charged for products traded among the affiliates, as well as the royalty charges and administrative fees. Sometimes there was a basis for testing these prices and fees against analogous arm's-length transactions. But more often, the goods or services involved were sufficiently distinctive so that no independent arm's-length standard could readily be found, assuming an effort were made to find one.

On top of this problem was the fact that Sola's subsidiaries in Europe, facing the elimination of trade barriers in the EEC and EFTA, found themselves competing in one another's territory with similar product lines. Here and there, the problem had been reduced by the timely intervention of the international manager. Once or twice, where specialty items were involved, the subsidiaries had agreed to allocate production tasks between them without bothering to involve the international office. In situations of that sort, the transfer price was fixed according to the bargaining strength of the subsidiaries and the transaction was recorded as if it were undertaken with an outside vendor. But as the number of subsidiaries and the number of product lines kept rising, this *ad hoc* approach was beginning to prove inadequate.

For the controllers in the local subsidiaries, all these problems presented growing headaches. The performance reports were beginning to make less and less sense, unless adjusted in various ways. Adjustments, however, required the refereeing role of the international controller when it involved a decision affecting the relative performance of two foreign subsidiaries, and it required the involvement of U.S. Sola's controller when the decision affected the U.S. company's reported performance. As a result of the accumulation of decision rules arising out of these adjudications, controllers' reports were beginning to bear less and less relation to the financial statements.

With these considerations and others in mind, Multinational Consultants, Inc., a prominent international consulting firm, was called in to advise on the reorganization of Sola's foreign business. After studying the operations of the company for a number of months, Multinational Consultants produced a voluminous report covering the problems of the foreign side of Sola's business. Among other things, it had a number of observations regarding the operation of the financial function, observations that boiled down to three propositions:

1. The treasurer's function had become much too complex and diffuse to be managed effectively from the center. Opportunities were being missed and errors committed. Among the errors cited, for instance, was the failure of the international treasurer to develop a systematic policy toward the threat of currency fluctuations. The opportunities missed as a result of the absence of such a policy were not the sort that were necessarily visible in Sola's financial statements. But once in a while, missed opportunities could be detected. One of these was the failure to hedge against a sterling devaluation in 1967, when the likelihood of the devaluation seemed extraordinarily high; this alleged oversight was said to have cost the company $350,000 in translation losses. Other opportunities overlooked, according to MCI, were those inherent in the possibilities for borrowing in local markets.

   The tight cash flow controls from headquarters, MCI guessed, reduced the likelihood that such opportunities were being recognized and exploited.

2. The treasurer was much too preoccupied with tax savings and too little concerned with reducing the cost of funds.

3. The financial data essential for the use of the treasurer's office was markedly different from the data needed for the performance of the controller's function, more so than in the case of complex operations within the United States proper. This difference was due to the fact that the units of Sola were in so many different jurisdictions with different rules covering taxation, access to capital, and so on. Essentially, the controller would be obliged to develop a separate score card, gauging the performance of profit centers on the basis of data that were compiled primarily for controls purposes.

As a first step toward achieving the needed shifts in direction, Multinational Consultants, Inc., proposed a number of major organizational changes. It was proposed that the international division should be broken up into several foreign area divisions, each of which would have status on a par with a U.S. product division. The international treasurer and the international controller would be moved upstairs into the offices of Sola's treasurer and controller respectively. A new layer of treasurers, controllers, and tax attorneys would be created at the area division level.

Under the new system, the lowest control center on the foreign side would be a given product line in a given area. Where more than one subsidiary in an area was involved in the product, the control center would combine the activities in the product of all such subsidiaries. Presumably, the treasurer could not ignore the performance of the subsidiary, since that performance would affect its tax liability. But for the controller's needs, an area-product approach to performance would be taken. Exhibit 2 indicates how the financial offices would sit in the revised Sola structure after reorganization.

Practically everyone on the foreign side of the Sola organization reacted to the proposals with some degree of hostility or reserve. The international manager saw himself as risking a major demotion: Either he would be moved upstairs into the staff of the Sola's president, or would be placed at the head of the "Europe and Africa" area. In either case, his status would be a notch lower. Of all the officers reacting to the change, however, it was Milray Thaler, the international treasurer, who felt most threatened.

Thaler was furious at the report of Multinational Consultants. A few days after it had been circulated in Sola, Thaler produced a 26-page reply, refuting the report point by point. Some of the extracts from his rebuttal were especially provocative.

> 2. *Of course, the international side of the treasurer's function is growing more complicated. Governments get smarter every day. Regulations get more complicated. With Section 482 on one side and OFDI on the other, it is not easy to do business abroad. But what kind of an answer is MCI offering us? To set up a treasurer in every area, so one area doesn't know what the other is doing? Who will tell German-Sola to stop trying to make a record for itself by gouging Argentine-Sola with its high invoice prices for petrochemicals? And who will stop the subsidiaries from always trying to build up their equity, instead of building up accounts payable? Much better to give me a few more high-level assistants who have had a little experience with such complicated matters so that we can stay on top of such problems.*

> 3. *Maybe production and marketing need some decentralizing at the regional level. After all, the users of industrial chemicals in Nairobi are not exactly the same types you find in Hamburg or Rio. But the management of money is another matter; that should be centralized. Money is money once you get it out of the clutches of a country and make it convertible. A dollar out of Peru is a dollar out of Turkey, and it ought to be managed that way.*

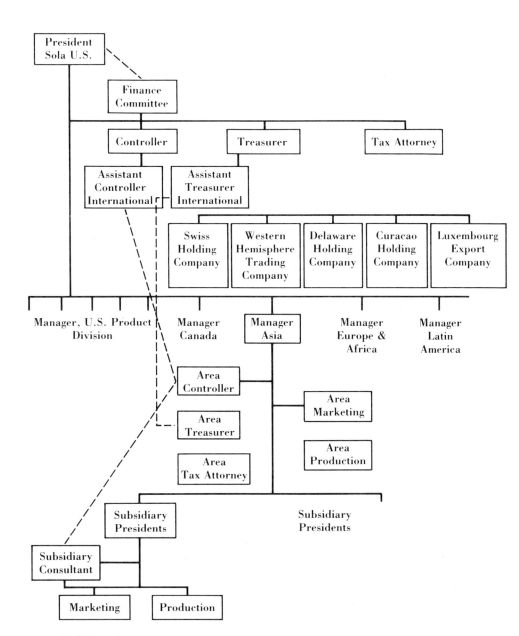

Exhibit 2 *Financial Offices in Proposed Reorganization of Sola Company, 1970*

5. How would a regional treasurer know how to use the Curaçao or Luxembourg companies, or why? Today, if Sola-Switzerland needs to pay a dividend to U.S. Sola, I can easily drum up the money by way of Curaçao and I know how to compare it with Berne's cash flow prospects.

14. That famous $350,000 translation loss from the devaluation of sterling is getting a little ridiculous. Translation losses are not money, they are bookkeeping. They mean nothing to Sola's cash flow. Tax payments are a different matter. There is where real money can be saved. If I were to worry about every currency that might devalue tomorrow, I would eat up the time of the company and the office chasing paper butterflies.

15. Once the controller starts making up his own score card and the treasurer makes up a separate one, it will be impossible to know where we stand. The controller has everything he needs, without the headaches of a special set of books, if he gets copies of the treasurer's instructions to the subsidiaries. If he wants to adjust his records because of these instructions, so that the effect of tax transactions and cash flow transactions are cancelled out, it is easy enough for him to do it.

16. Above all, once you start putting the profit centers in the regional offices, you are a dead duck. Europe is not yet a country. Neither is Latin America. The authorities in the central banks and in the national tax administrations are not about to give up their powers and go away. These are the offices you have to keep your eye on if you are going to survive in the international business.

M. Edgar Barrett

Case 49

Multiquimica Do Brasil

"I'm really concerned about our position in Brazil. Our pharmaceutical products are being hurt by both local and foreign producers and our foreign exchange policies may well be to blame." So said Don Howard, controller of the foreign operations of the pharmaceutical group of Multichemical Industries, Inc. "Look at Levadol, for example, our sales are falling while those of Hoffman et Cie are up."[1]

This conversation took place in February 1983 as Don was reviewing the 1982 results of the foreign operations of the pharmaceutical group with the group's general manager, Paul McConnell. The men were in the company's corporate offices in Houston, Texas.

1. Hoffman et Cie was a large, multinational firm based in Bern, Switzerland.
© 1983 by M. Edgar Barrett. This case was prepared by Mary Pat Cormack and Professor M. Edgar Barrett as a basis for class discussion. It is not intended to illustrate either effective or ineffective handling of an administrative situation.

435

Exhibit 1   *Multiquimica Do Brasil Financial Data:*
Consolidated Corporate Results (in millions of dollars)

	1982	1981
Income statement		
Sales		
Agricultural chemicals	$ 658	$ 600
Industrial chemicals	583	513
Petrochemicals	652	585
Pharmaceutical products	1,210	1,086
Subtotal	$3,103	$2,784
Cost of goods sold	1,300	1,169
Selling and administrative expense	884	793
Depreciation	296	262
Research expense	292	250
Subtotal	$2,772	$2,474
Operating income	$ 331	$ 310
Interest expense	45	42
Other income—net	41	30
Subtotal	$ 4	$ 12
Income before taxes	327	298
Income taxes	126	110
Net income	$ 201	$ 188
Balance sheet	1982	1981
Current assets	$1,016	$1,001
Net property, plant, and		
equipment	1,536	1,338
Other assets	241	139
Total assets	$2,793	$2,478
Current liabilities	363	297
Long-term debt	394	309
Deferred income taxes	140	124
Stockholders' equity	1,896	1,748
Total liabilities and stockholders' equity	$2,793	$2,478

Source: Multichemical Industries Inc. 1982 Annual Report.

BACKGROUND

Multichemical Industries Inc. sold seventy-five different products in over fifty countries during 1982. Sales for the year were $3.1 billion (see Exhibit 1 for financial data). The company's principal product groups were: pharmaceuticals; industrial chemicals; agricultural chemicals; and petrochemicals. Multichemical's overseas subsidiaries accounted for 35 percent of sales in 1982, with the majority of the activity taking place in Europe.

Multiquimica do Brasil (MB) was responsible for all sales and manufacturing that took place in Brazil. Thus, its managers had responsibility for products in several of the firm's product groups. Sales during the year were $65 million, 6 percent of foreign sales. This wholly owned subsidiary was formed in 1977 with the initial purpose of establishing manufacturing facilities for agricultural chemical, industrial chemical, and pharmaceutical products in Brazil. Prior to that time, Multichemical had been active in Brazil through export sales. In other words, products that were manufactured in the United States had been sold in Brazil through local, independent importers. Multichemical did not operate either manufacturing facilities or a division office in the country until 1977.

The new subsidiary began manufacturing and selling herbicides in 1977. MB did not show a profit until 1980. The losses that were incurred were primarily attributable to two factors: the large startup costs associated with a new business and a weak economic period in Brazil. As a result of the losses sustained during the 1977 to 1980 period, MB was entitled to a substantial amount of tax loss carryforwards on its Brazilian tax return.[2]

In late 1979, the company installed a manufacturing plant to process Levadol, an aspirin-free pain reliever. Such facilities were included in the original operating plans for MB. They were scheduled, however, for the early 1980s. They went onstream sooner than originally planned due to an increase in the amount of duty on imports.

The manufacture of this product involved shipping the raw materials in bulk form from the United States. The raw materials were formulated, converted into tablet form, and packaged in the Brazilian plant and then sold to distributors. MB sales of Levadol in 1982 were $6.8 million.

PRODUCT AND PRICING FLOW FOR LEVADOL

The raw materials for Levadol were shipped from a domestic subsidiary of Multichemical to MB. The invoiced price for transferred goods during

2. The term "tax loss carryforward" refers to the fact that net operating losses, to the extent that they exceed taxable income of the preceding three years, can be carried forward, thus reducing future taxable income.

1982 averaged $60/case equivalent. The invoice was denominated in U.S. dollars.

The cost of goods sold on MB's books for Levadol averaged $131/case. This figure included the $60/case raw material costs, plus $31/case for import duty and $40/case to formulate, convert, and package it.

The product was sold to wholesalers serving both drug stores and chain stores, usually on ninety-day payment terms, for a price of approximately $218/case. The $87/case difference between the sales price and the cost of goods sold consisted of marketing costs (roughly 20 percent of sales), administration, distribution, and interest expenses and approximately a 5 percent profit margin before taxes. The distributors, in turn, usually added a 10 to 20 percent margin. This was designed to both cover their costs and provide a profit margin.

DOLLAR LINKAGE BILLING

On their tax and fiscal books, MB benefited from a system known as dollar linkage billing. A statement on the invoice that was sent from the domestic subsidiary to MB said, "payable at the exchange rate in effect on the date of the receipt of goods." (Management books, on the other hand, were kept on the assumption that the invoice was to be paid in dollars — thus, effectively, using the exchange rate in effect at the time of payment.)

Brazilian law, at the time, required 180-day payment terms on imports. Since the Brazilian cruzeiro lost value in relation to the dollar on a more or less continuous basis, a foreign exchange loss would normally show up on a Brazilian firm's cruzeiro-denominated books. Given the above-mentioned system, however, the foreign exchange loss showed up on the U.S. tax books.

DOMESTIC SALES WITHIN BRAZIL

Even within the context of the Brazilian domestic market, MB's reported profit in dollar terms was affected by the more or less continuous devaluation of the cruzeiro. The major problem here was tied to the fact that competition had forced MB to offer ninety-day payment terms to their customers. Given the fact that the cruzeiro was formally devalued approximately once every ten days, any domestic subsidiary with terms of ninety days was faced with a translation loss whenever its books were translated back into dollar terms.[3]

---

3. This "translation loss" would be caused by the fact that the *dollar value* of the original *cruzeiro denominated* sale would exceed the *dollar value* of the actual *cruzeiro denominated* collection of the account receivable some 90 days later.

In an attempt to deal with the situation, MB put into place a method known as "forward pricing." Under the assumptions of this method, MB's management predicted the amount of cruzeiro devaluation that would occur during the forthcoming ninety days. This estimate then served as the basis for raising the then-current sales price. In other words, they passed along the expected loss due to the devaluation of the cruzeiro to the customer. As a result of this policy, product prices were revised at least monthly.

HEDGING POLICIES

From 1977 to 1979, the annual inflation rate in Brazil was in the general range of 30 to 50 percent. In 1979, however, Brazil — which imported the vast majority of its crude oil — began to feel the effects of the increasing price of crude oil. As a result, the domestic inflation rate took off *and* the cruzeiro was devalued by 30 percent during the year. MB reacted by pushing up its prices, a policy which it continued to adhere to throughout 1982.

Beginning in late 1979, the corporate treasurer's office of Multichemical began to "encourage" MB to borrow locally. Such a policy was designed to match assets and liabilities in cruzeiro terms and thus offset the translation loss on assets with a translation gain on liabilities. By having the subsidiaries borrow locally, the corporate treasurer was hoping to eliminate the risk of having to report large translation losses on the corporate income statement. Local borrowing, in essence, helped to smooth the corporation's reported income stream by substituting a periodic interest expense for less frequent, but presumably larger, losses due to translation. There was a cost, however. The nominal interest rate in Brazil in 1982 was approximately 160 percent. (See Exhibit 2 for foreign exchange and inflation rate data.)

PERFORMANCE MEASUREMENT POLICIES

Multichemical had recently changed its internal reporting system. Previous to the change, operating managers had been held responsible for the performance of their units as measured by the "operating income" figures. This meant that items such as other income, other expense, interest expense, and translation gains and losses were not focused upon in the quarterly business results review meetings. Over time, the senior management at the corporate level had come to feel that this system of performance measurement ignored the impact of some business decisions which could (or should) be taken by some of the operating managers in question.

Exhibit 2 *Multiquimica Do Brasil*
Yearend foreign exchange rates (per U.S. dollar)

	Brazilian Cruzeiro	Swiss Franc
1976	12.34	2.45
1977	16.05	2.00
1978	20.92	1.62
1979	42.53	1.58
1980	65.50	1.76
1981	127.80	1.80
1982	252.67	1.99

Source: International Financial Statistics, International Monetary Fund.

Consumer price index numbers and yearly percentage changes

	Brazil		Switzerland		U.S.	
1976	254.3		147.3		146.6	
1977	357.3	.41	149.2	.01	156.1	.06
1978	494.2	.38	150.8	.01	167.9	.08
1979	742.5	.50	156.2	.04	187.2	.11
1980	1321.2	.78	162.5	.04	212.4	.13
1981	2584.9	.96	173.1	.07	234.1	.10
1982	6394.7*	1.47	182.8	.06	248.2	.06

* Estimated
Source: Monthly Bulletin of Statistics, United Nations, February 1983, p. 200

After a thorough study of both the then-existing internal reporting system and a set of alternative systems, a new system was designed and introduced. "Full Responsibility Accounting," as the new system was called, was made effective with the 1983 data. Under the terms of this new system, both individual product managers and product group managers were to be held responsible for the relationship between their profit after tax figures and the net assets under their control on both a worldwide and a "major" country basis. The term "net assets" for a particular subunit of the overall corporation was defined as net property (gross property less accumulated depreciation) plus net working capital. Thus, both individual product managers and product group managers now bore some of the responsibility for such items as interest expense, translation gains and losses, and the amount and composition of both short- and long-term assets.

The new system was designed with the intention that it would, among other things, force top management to delegate expansion and curtailment decisions to lower levels. The individual product managers and their superiors (the product group managers), sometimes in conjunction with an (geographic) area manager, were to have total responsibility for the assets that they employed in the process of producing, distibuting, and selling their particular product. The firm's capital budgeting and operational budgeting systems were to be altered such that the full year's capital expenditures would be approved at once and there would be agreement reached during the operational budgeting cycle as to the appropriate levels for inventories and receivables for the budget year in question.

While the new system was very focused upon a return on assets figure, two other measures were to receive emphasis under the terms of the new program. Both net income and cash flow were to be measured and monitored. The former would be measured against a budgeted target and the latter would be assessed in respect to an understanding of the underlying strategy for the subunit. Thus a subunit with a growth strategy might be expected to generate little or no cash (or indeed, even use cash) over a short- to medium-term time period.

Of particular concern to product group managers, such as Paul McConnell, was the fact that he was now responsible for both translation gains and losses *and* interest expense, the latter of which could be very high in the case of local borrowing. Fortunately, the translation losses that were to be reported were to be highly specific in nature. That is, they were to be directly traced to specific items on the local subsidiary balance sheets and, thus, would be tied to items directly related to the pharmaceutical group's products. Interest expense and translation gains, on the other hand, were not easily identified with such specific items. This lack of easy identification was caused by the fact that the corporate treasurer would sum all of the Brazilian borrowings and then allocate both translation gains and interest expense to each product group based on a formula tied primarily to sales.

COMPETITION

MB had been able to successfully position Levadol such that a significant amount of the population asked for Levadol when they wanted an aspirin-free pain reliever. This had become an important issue as the product became more widely stocked by the various grocery chains and cooperatives (with their open, free-standing shelves). Every year MB sold a greater amount of Levadol through grocery stores than it had the year before. During 1982, it was estimated that 60 percent of the retail sales of all aspirin-free pain relievers in Brazil took place in grocery stores, while the remaining 40 percent were sold through some type of drug related outlet.

During 1982, MB lost both volume and market share on Levadol. Over

36,000 cases of Levadol were sold in 1980. Fewer than 32,000 were sold in 1982 (see Table 1 for volume and market share data). Although it was considered a premium product, an increasing number of distributors were reacting to the recession by substituting lower cost product.

MB's primary competition during 1982 was the Swiss firm Hoffman et Cie which sold a similar, but not identical, product. Hoffman's product was priced slightly lower than Levadol. The Swiss Franc (in relation to the cruzeiro) had not revalued as fast as the U.S. dollar over the most recent two-year period (see Exhibit 2). Thus, the apparent incentive for Hoffman to raise its price to cover a translation loss was not as great as MB's. Also, Hoffman had been known to be somewhat more concerned with market share than with short-term reported profit.

Other reasons for Hoffman's strength had to do with the company's size in Brazil. In addition to having a large percentage of the pharmaceutical market, it also had a very large share of the market in agricultural chemicals. Its field sales force was about three to four times the size of MB's. Also, Hoffman gave somewhat longer payment terms. Hoffman's management apparently felt that they could squeeze the profit margin in pharmaceuticals a bit because of their strong position and high profits with agricultural chemicals.

In addition to Hoffman and other foreign based firms, two local producers sold a generic substitute. The raw materials for the generic product were sourced in Brazil. The local patent covering this product had already expired. One result of this was that the industry was currently afflicted with an overcapacity of manufacturing facilities for products such as generic brand pain relievers. The price of the generic aspirin-free pain reliever had risen 16 percent in the past two years. On the other hand, the price of Levadol had risen 20 percent, making the price difference $18/case (see Table 2).

TABLE 1 Aspirin-free pain relievers (percentage of market share by major competitors)

	MB	**Hoffman**	**Generic**	**All Other**	**Total Volume**
					(thousands of cases)
1977	3%	7%	31%	59%	125
1978	8	12	25	55	152
1979	9	17	21	53	202
1980	15	25	17	43	240
1981	13	32	13	42	287
1982	10	32	15	43	320

TABLE 2 Average wholesale price of aspirin-free pain relievers
(U.S. dollars per case)

	MB	Hoffman	Generic
1980	$182	$180	$172
1981	201	198	187
1982	218	212	200

CONCLUSION

"My greatest fear at this moment in Brazil is that we're being finessed by firms with a better knowledge of international business. Levadol should not be losing market share to Hoffman," said Paul McConnell. "I could understand some loss of market to the locals, but even there we should be able to sell the customer on our product superiority. Hoffman has a premium product. But it's not as good as ours."

Jarl Kallberg

Case 50

Universal Truck and Tractor

BACKGROUND

The Universal Truck and Tractor Corporation (UTT) is a U.S.-based corporation with headquarters in New York City. The firm ranks in the second half of the Fortune 1000 listing of corporations and is primarily involved with the manufacture, distribution, and sale of agricultural equipment and machinery.

Since its founding in 1904, UTT has developed a respectable market share although it is not the industry leader. Its products are considered to

This case is based on some aspects of Chapter 8 of Kallberg and Parkinson, *Current Asset Management*, John Wiley, New York, 1984. While UTT is a fictitious entity, it represents an amalgam of a number of international firms that we are familiar with. The major goal of this case is to develop an integrated viewpoint to working capital management in the international setting.

be of the highest quality, with technical features among the most advanced in the industry. The customers for UTT's products are regional dealers in the United States and major dealers in the overseas markets that UTT has reached through export as well as local sales efforts. Customers are extremely loyal and provide frequent suggestions for product enhancements and new market developments.

UTT has two manufacturing plants: one in Syracuse, New York and the other in Turlock, California. These two plants have long enjoyed relative autonomy in their operations, although some activities have traditionally been handled by central staff. Plants purchase supplies locally and handle their own payroll. Major purchases of raw materials and manufacturing equipment are made by central purchasing. Sales and marketing efforts are performed by five local offices in the United States and by major offices in Brussels (for all of Europe) and Singapore (for all of Asia). In all foreign countries where UTT sells, there is at least one sales and service office.

The central credit and invoicing department is run by a credit manager and his staff. This department sets credit terms and policies for all customers and prepares and distributes invoices based on information from local sales orders and shipping documentation from both plants. It manages outstanding receivables, taking any necessary dunning or follow-up actions. Foreign sales representatives function in a similar manner to their domestic counterparts, making sales and then relaying all orders to New York for processing. Any letters of credit or related types of sales are handled in New York.

In the United States essentially all customer payments are made by check to a central lock box UTT maintains with its lead bank: Gotham Trust in New York City. The bank delivers check copies, envelopes, and other contents (such as the invoice) to the credit staff daily. Local offices and salesmen occasionally receive checks, which they remit to the lock box. Related documentation is sent to the central credit staff.

Disbursements are processed by central accounting from information supplied by central purchasing and related staff departments. All checks are drawn on a disbursement account at Gotham Trust. Both plants maintain local disbursement accounts with large local banks in their cities: Upstate National (Syracuse) and West Coast National (Turlock). Both accounts are funded by wire transfer weekly according to a schedule supplied to central cash management by plant accountants. Payrolls are handled by each plant at the banks given above. Funds are transferred to each account on the biweekly pay days based on a phone call two or three days prior from the local payroll manager. Payrolls for other employees are handled through a central payroll group, with the majority of checks drawn on another New York bank, Metropolitan State Bank. This account is funded on pay days by wire transfer from Gotham Trust.

Export collections are received by either check or wire transfer. While billing for original equipment is in $US, billing for spare parts is in the local currency. UTT maintains four international collection accounts with banks in New York City (Gotham, Metropolitan, New York National, and American International) since remittances can come in to any of them. These banks are supposed to notify UTT treasury staff or credit staff when payments have been received. They typically notify the credit staff as this group has more frequent interaction with the bank's international department. All checks are processed by central credit staff and are then sent to Gotham for deposit. A few checks are received by the lock box as well. Foreign currency checks are purchased by Gotham at competitive exchange rates.

Daily the cash manager establishes cash positions at each major UTT bank (the four international receiving banks and the two plant banks). Funds are moved to Gotham as a central cash pool. Each bank is called by the cash manager or his assistant each morning to obtain the beginning balance for the current day's activity. Both plants call in any variations from their cash forecasts. By late morning the credit staff provides the cash deposit figure for the current day based on a call from the lock box area of the bank. The credit staff will also send over a "buck slip" via internal mail to inform the cash manager of international receipts (based on phone calls from the banks). The main account at Gotham is used to wire funds to other banks as required, and the cash manager completes these transfers by noon. International transfers are handled the same way, although they are typically done later in the day.

Banking relations are handled by the treasurer, although the credit manager must approve any changes in collections. UTT maintains lines of credit with each of its major New York banks and keeps 5 percent (of the portion of the credit line that is utilized) in compensating balances. The company has seasonal short-term borrowing needs in addition to a substantial amount of long-term debt.

In Belgium the UTT office deals with the Bank of Belgium, a major Belgian bank with expertise in international finance. All transactions are made through this bank, whose major U.S. correspondent is American International. The relationship is a long and valued one, as the bank helped UTT establish its offices in Brussels and is quite helpful in supplying credit and other information on potential customers. In Singapore the UTT office uses a major local bank, the NPB Bank. As in Belgium, all transactions are made through this bank; its major U.S. correspondent is West Coast National.

Spare parts inventories are maintained in both Brussels and Singapore. Each location maintains a stock of approximately 11,000 items, although each year (when new models are distributed) the number of spare parts increases by approximately 1,000. All items are shipped from New York City, with the average time to Brussels being three weeks and to Singapore, five weeks. Written authorization from headquarters is required for all inventory replenishments with value more than $US one million. This usually delays the order by about five days. Guidelines for inventory policies are established at headquarters. Inventory turnover targets are set at four per year on all items; safety stocks are to be maintained at 25 percent of annual demand. Receivables turnover standards are likewise set by headquarters at four per year. In Europe salesmen are paid fixed salaries while in Asia they are paid a salary plus a commission on the $US value of sales. In the U.S. salesmen receive a regular salary plus a small commission on all orders.

Headquarters has established standard credit policies. Overseas accounts past due are not now subject to any penalties, but each month New York sends dunning letters to major offenders. In some exceptional cases they will call the customer or even ask the local office to help. This contrasts with domestic U.S. policy, which refuses to ship to any account more than sixty days past due and charges 4 percent over prime on those accounts. Standard terms on both original equipment and on spare parts are net ninety days in the United States and Europe (although sales offices often assist customers in obtaining financing with local banks). In Asia local trade credit standards are adopted, using the standards for the machine industry.

Sales have shown only a slight increase in recent years. The pattern during any year is typically seasonal, with a peak in summer and a winter low. The company's profits have been fairly stable. There are no major expansion plans. The following exhibits provide basic data on banking, treasury, receivables, and inventory management functions.

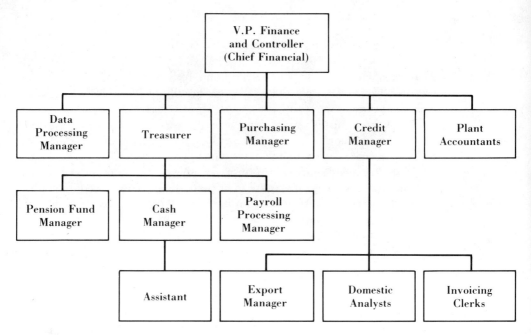

Exhibit 1 Organization

Exhibit 2 *UTT financial statements (millions)*

	1982	1983	1984
Balance Sheet			
Cash and short-term investment	36.7	33.3	28.2
Accounts receivable	167.5	187.6	215.8
Inventory	245.5	252.5	260.5
Other current assets	2.5	2.7	2.3
Total current assets	452.2	476.1	506.8
Fixed assets	402.5	377.7	345.5
Total assets	854.7	853.8	852.3
Accounts payable	172.2	185.4	221.2
Notes payable	126.5	88.9	26.2
Current portion of long-term debt	29.1	31.2	33.2
Other current liabilities	1.7	1.9	1.8
Total current liabilities	329.5	307.4	282.4
Long-term debt	275.1	286.2	298.5
Total liabilities	604.6	593.6	580.9
Equity	250.1	260.2	271.4
Total liabilities and equity	854.7	853.8	852.3
Profit and Loss Statement			
Total revenues	700	730	765
Cost of goods sold	375	386	397
Total expenses	231	247	260
Net income before taxes	94	97	108
Net interest income/(expense)	(25)	(26)	(28)
Depreciation	42	45	51

Exhibit 3 *Quarterly revenues ($US millions)*

Quarter	1982	1983	1984
First	70	75	72
Second	200	220	235
Third	280	290	304
Fourth	150	145	154

Exhibit 4 *Quarter revenues for 1984 ($US millions)*

	Q1	Q2	Q3	Q4
United Kingdom				
Spare parts	1.2	1.1	1.4	0.8
Total sales	14.0	20.5	23.3	8.3
Germany				
Spare parts	3.0	3.4	4.4	4.1
Total sales	6.0	8.5	18.0	9.1
France				
Spare parts	2.9	4.8	9.8	3.4
Total sales	3.1	7.0	14.1	4.1
Malaysia				
Spare parts	0.1	0.1	0.2	0.2
Total sales	3.4	2.0	2.0	4.7
Australia				
Spare parts	2.6	2.2	1.4	1.9
Total sales	9.6	4.1	1.4	12.1
Philippines				
Spare parts	0.3	2.2	0.7	0.1
Total sales	0.3	2.7	0.7	0.1
United States				
Spare parts	20.2	29.4	40.4	25.1
Total sales	35.6	190.2	244.5	115.6
Totals				
Spare parts	30.3	43.2	58.3	35.6
Total sales	72	235.0	304.0	154.0

Exhibit 5 *Receivables and revenue data year-end 1984 ($US millions)*

	Annual Revenue	Current	Receivables Aging 0–30 Days OD	31–60 Days OD
United Kingdom	66.1	13.6	5.1	0.8
Germany	41.5	10.1	0.8	0.4
France	28.3	8.2	4.3	1.1
Malaysia	12.1	4.3	0.3	0
Australia	27.2	5.8	0	0
Philippines	3.8	0.4	0.3	0.1
United States	586.0	130.2	20.4	6.7

Exhibit 6 Inventory data

Location	Shipments	Value of shipments	Year-end inventory
Singapore	16	13.1	5.4
Brussels	20	36.1	10.3

Data shown are for spare parts inventory; figures are in US millions.

Exhibit 7 DSOs for the Machinery Industry (1984)

Australia	53.1
France	130.7
Germany	99.1
Malaysia	92.4
Philippines	60.3
United Kingdom	112.3
United States	104.4

Exhibit 8 Monthly net investment/(borrowing) activity ($US millions)

Month	Average
January	(30)
February	(60)
March	(105)
April	(125)
May	(125)
June	(110)
July	(95)
August	(50)
September	(10)
October	20
November	40
December	30

Borrowings were at an average rate of 11.02%; investment was at an average rate of 9.34%.

Exhibit 9 *Sample international mail times*

| | Receiving points | | | | |
Mailing Points	New York	London	Brussels	Frankfurt	Singapore
London	7		4.5	6	
Paris	6	3.5	4	4	
Brussels	5	4.5	2.5	3	
Frankfurt	7.5	6	3		
Sydney	8				8
Singapore	11.5				
Kuala Lampur	13				5.5
Manila	9.5				7.5

ASSIGNMENT

You are to put yourself in the position of the assistant treasurer of UTT. Essentially you are responsible for all of the domestic and international cash and treasury function. You have been asked to formulate responses to the attached two memoranda. (The responses can be separate or, if desired, both could be incorporated within a general analysis of the cash and treasury areas of UTT.)

Areas of particular importance include:

- The integration of all of the components of working capital.
- The design of the information flows within the corporation.
- The degree of centralization/decentralization that is appropriate.

Memorandum 1

May 8, 1985

To: Assistant Treasurer
From: Treasurer
Re: Analysis of working capital performance and procedures

As you know we are in the process of generating our long-term plans and budgets. One of the areas coming under scrutiny will be the short-term finance function, in particular the current asset performance. This area has not been reviewed in the past three years and in the opinion of some members of UTT's senior management, it is felt that some of our policies are outmoded.

I would like you to prepare a report to senior management addressing the above concerns; in particular, this report should contain:

- An overview and evaluation of UTT's current practice in the working capital area. [It would make sense to divide this and perhaps other sections of your report into the functional areas: cash, inventory and receivables management.]

453

- Suggestions for improved policies. It might make sense to frame your recommendations in terms of what you know should be done, what you think should be done, and areas where you feel further study is required. Be sure to address the problems of implementability in detail.

Memorandum 2

To: Assistant Treasurer
From: Treasurer
Re: Use of the direct debiting option for German spare parts

As you are aware, most of our spare parts sales to Germany are to a few major customers who provide a relatively regular stream of revenues. During the past year however, there appears to have been some deterioration in their payment behavior. (Although I admit there is some disagreement on this point.) I would like you to investigate whether or not German payment behavior (at least as exhibited by the data available) has indeed been worsening. Addendum #1 gives the latest year's aging schedule for those customers that are on net 30 terms. (Note that these data are only for spare parts and are thus not comparable to our usual net 90 terms for original equipment.)

In any case, we are re-evaluating our receivables policies in Germany, and subsequently all foreign countries. The information above is very relevant to our discussion of new techniques. One of the options UTT should consider is direct debiting since this practice is common in Germany. (See Addenda #2 and #3.) I think it is appropriate to conduct a pilot project on direct debiting which could possibly be extended to other countries if successful. (Just in terms of bank and internal processing costs, we feel that we can save at least $3.00 per item by direct debiting.)

There are of course a number of costs and benefits to this type of program. I would like you to evaluate these and to present a recommendation for the German (and possibly other countries') direct debit program. Some of the alternatives are the creation of new credit terms or the establishment of a factoring arrangement. If new credit terms or incentives to move to direct debiting are to be offered, what should they be?

Memorandum 3

To: Assistant Treasurer
From: Treasurer
Re: International Lockbox/Intercept Points

I have become increasingly concerned with the extremely long delays in receiving available funds from checks being remitted from overseas. It has been suggested that we consider establishing one (or more) international lockbox/intercept points to reduce the float on these remittances.

At least two U.S. banks have established products for this purpose. One is a mail-intercept lockbox network with four intercept points: London, Toronto, Hong Kong, and Singapore (in addition to seven U.S. points). Items intercepted at these foreign sites are couriered to a New York processing center for processing within twenty-four hours. These deliveries will obviously eliminate the lags in mail times: checks are purchased at a discount by the bank giving us immediate funds while compensating the bank for the clearing float.

The second type of system combines mail intercept with international lock-box processing. Items again are couriered (to Los Angeles) where they are processed by foreign lockbox banks. The foreign sites include Hong Kong, London, Madrid, Manila, Seoul, Singapore, Taipei, Tokyo, Toronto, and Vancouver.

Given our current and projected flow of remittances from abroad, does it make sense to consider one or both of these options? While we have some of the data required to perform a complete study, I need to know the type of data we would need to gather to attempt this evaluation. Even more important, I would like to know whether or not there are enough potential benefits to justify this type of study.

Memorandum 4

May 11, 1985

To: Assistant Treasurer
From: Treasurer
Re: Collections in the Philippines

After a review of some of the payment performance data available, a number of questions arise with respect to the rather poor performance in the Philippines. This country represents an important overseas market for us, yet the continuing problems with billing in a very weak currency, poor payment behavior, in addition to excessive float times, make it somewhat of a problem. Our New York credit staff has noted the following concerns that are crucial to our ability to provide adequate service while maintaining profitability.

1. Telephone service, both local and international, is poor, thus interfering with our ability to follow up poor accounts.
2. Mail service is extremely slow, even within Manila. Times to rural points often exceed ten days.

459

3. Weakening commodity prices have impacted the ability of our customers to service their obligations.
4. Stringent controls on foreign currency have been imposed.
5. The 1981 Dewey Dee Scandal has disrupted the local short-term borrowing picture.
6. Central Bank approval is required for letters of credit for our exports. These restrictions mandate a minimum payment term of 360 days and three-year deferred terms on equipment valued at $US20,000 or more.
7. While check clearing times within Manila are about two and a half days, it can take ten days to clear items drawn on remote banks.
8. Local banks are inefficient, especially with regard to documentation, credit facilities, forex, and float.
9. Over the total agricultural sector, DSOs have been averaging forty-five days overdue.
10. Large customers have been demanding a "credit overcharge" — an addition of up to ten days on stated terms.
11. Several methods exist within the Philippines for accelerating payments. These include: use of salesmen to pick up payments from customers, offering discounts, forcing shorter credit terms, usng couriers to pick up checks, opening accounts at the banks of major customers, faster billing procedures, and imposition of penalties for late payment. None of these practices are utilized by UTT.
12. Salesmen are paid a commission on total sales; this gives them no incentive to investigate the creditworthiness of their clients.
13. Handling delinquent accounts is awkward. While payments are delayed, nonpayment is not yet a severe problem.

With respect to these points and in light of all of the other revisions that we have been contemplating within the international division, what possible changes can you suggest in the way we handle these collections?

Addendum 1

Monthly Aging Records for German Spare Parts Customers

- All figures have been converted to millions of $US.
- These figures represent all German customers receiving net 30 terms. On average 400 transactions are received per month. These terms represent about one-third of all spare parts sales. [Other customers may receive longer terms in connection with long-term sales agreements; some customers have negotiated early payment terms.]

Month	Sales of Spare Parts	Current	Overdue Categories		
			1–30	31–60	61–90
January	.24	.12	.02	.03	.02
February	.21	.20	.03	.01	.02
March	.30	.19	.04	.02	.00
April	.45	.27	.05	.03	.01
May	.32	.40	.07	.03	.02
June	.30	.26	.05	.04	.02
July	.40	.28	.03	.03	.02
August	.43	.38	.02	.01	.01
September	.36	.41	.02	.01	.00
October	.23	.34	.02	.01	.00
November	.19	.22	.01	.00	.00
December	.11	.18	.01	.00	.00

Addendum 2

Speeding Receivables in a Friendly Environment: Collecting in Germany

When it comes to managing receivables, Germany is a cinch. The country has good sources of credit information and efficient mail and funds-transfer systems. Even more remarkable, German customers are almost alone in the world in not making a sport of delaying payments for as long as possible. In the words of one local treasurer, "Sometimes we stretch payment a little, but in Germany the most important thing is to preserve your reputation with suppliers."

But even though there is little excuse for credit and collection difficulties here — or perhaps because of it — many firms have failed to tightly manage their German receivables. Several German companies interviewed by *BIMR* offered the following pointers on how to exploit the opportunities of the friendly German environment.

SETTING CREDIT TERMS

Credit terms in Germany are short, usually thirty days from date of invoice. Discounts for early payments are common — typically 2–3 percent on cash received within eight to fourteen days — but although penalty charges for late payments are often stipulated in a contract, the clause is rarely enforced. One firm interviewed by BI has kept its DSOs down to twenty-five days by offering a 2 percent cash discount for payments within fourteen days. "Today," the spokesman claimed, "fifty percent of our customers pay within fourteen days and get the discount."

But the technique must be applied cautiously: "Many of our customers consider the 2 percent discount part of the price. So we have a strict campaign to weed out those who take the discount but pay in twenty-four or twenty-five days. We send out nasty letters, and we've convinced most of them that they must pay within fourteen days if they want the discount."

To avoid payment delays, firms should make sure that customers clearly understand their credit terms. For example, some companies choose to interpret the terms of sale as thirty days from *receipt* of invoice, rather than from *date* of invoice. An electronics firm has standard terms of thirty days net with a 3 percent discount at ten days. But because it takes up to a week for customers to receive the invoice, some customers effectively gain seven days' extra credit by quietly applying their own interpretation to the terms.

ORGANIZING FOR IMPROVED CONTROL

Most companies would do well to emulate the receivables management system of the German subsidiary of a U.S. chemicals company that has reduced DSOs and bad debts while keeping bank float to a bare minimum. The firm has set up a rigorous credit and collection program that incorporates internal checks and balances to minimize customer risk. According to the treasurer, these tight internal controls are the key to his success.

The credit manager is obliged to follow these rules:

Screen customers tightly, using a credit-rating agency, bank references, and other sources. Only the credit manager may approve orders.
Assign risk-evaluation codes to each account for entry into the computerized receivables files.
Set separate credit limits for each customer. Not even an old customer can get a new order once he goes over his limit.
Give salesmen low credit ceilings as an incentive to convince customers to take shorter payment terms. "We find that quick collections help reduce our bad-debt risk," said the treasurer.
Use the sales force to help collect when there is a problem, and penalize salesmen with too many overdue accounts. (However, collecting from the customer is the primary responsibility of the credit division of the treasury department, with only backup support from sales.)

Get on the phone several days before a large invoice is due to make sure payment comes in on time.

Demand a bank guarantee from risky customers.

GETTING MORE FROM YOUR BANKS

Important as setting credit terms and organizing internally are to good receivables management, a company's best efforts can be undermined by a sloppy approach to bank services. One of the most important goals of any cash manager is negotiating value-dating conditions for its banks' clearing services. Germany has four major clearing systems, and when payments are routed from one to another, sizable clearing delays can result. To make matters worse, the banks often use the least efficient transfer methods to maximize float. As a result of this, value dating on checks and transfer orders can range from two to six days.

Nevertheless, many firms interviewed by BI have been able to extract same-day or next-day value from their banks. "We don't deal with banks unless we get same-day value," asserted the CFO of one of Germany's largest companies. The finance director of a smaller firm has also obtained good terms: "Value dating is usually standard, but you can squeeze something out of the banks if you try. We get next-day value on both in-town and out-of-town checks, which is pretty good."

Finally, companies should use specialized collection services provided by banks, such as lockboxes, courier services, and direct debiting. Direct debiting, in particular, is increasingly popular in Germany. Although customers tend to resist cooperation, the controller of an electronics firm suggested how this can be overcome: "We have about five customers who have given us permission for direct debiting because we give them a 5 percent discount, as though they were paying in advance."

Business International Money Report, March 15, 1985, p. 83.

Addendum 3

Why In-House Factoring Is a Simple Way to Centralize

EUROPEAN TREASURY SYSTEMS

Companies establishing reinvoicing centers to centralize and streamline cash and exposure management face a thicket of tax, legal, organizational, and bureaucratic obstacles. For many companies, an in-house factoring company can achieve the same goals without the hassles of reinvoicing.

In-house factoring systems provide a number of advantages to companies with European operations. While the centers may be set up as simple arrangements to discount intracompany receivables, they can also be developed into full-fledged treasury vehicles offering many of the capabilities of reinvoicing. "We looked into reinvoicing and we looked into factoring," said the financial manager of the Geneva-based company. "We determined that we could set up a factoring company that would be as useful for treasury management as a reinvoicing center."

In-house factoring offers companies these advantages:

(1) Factoring centers are usually simpler and less extensive to establish and

operate than reinvoicing centers. Since only one invoice is needed for factoring, rather than the two required for reinvoicing, administrative work and costs are reduced. "Right off the bat a reinvoicing center doubles the paperwork," one treasury manager commented. "Unless you're going to totally automate the system, whch you can bet will cost, it doesn't make any sense. Factoring can achieve the same things with less work." And even automated reinvoicing systems can go awry, as another cash manager pointed out: "There are always bugs in the system — things you didn't think about."

Factoring also has organizational benefits over reinvoicing, since it provides central control without infringing on the freedom of subsidiaries. In many factoring systems, for example, subsidiaries do not have to participate. But because the factoring company offers attractive rates on financing and investing — and is willing to take on exchange risks — subsidiaries find it in their best interest to use the treasury vehicle's services.

(2) Factoring avoids transfer-pricing problems and other tax and legal hurdles. Because factoring merely involves the discounting of trade receivables — and not the transfer of title from subsidiaries — it avoids the tax and legal problems associated with transfer pricing. The assistant treasurer of one pharmaceuticals firm explained: "We looked at reinvoicing. But since transfer pricing is such a touchy issue in our industry, we encountered a great deal of reluctance on the part of our divisional people. We look at factoring as something that can be accomplished much more easily." A financial executive for another firm agreed: "Factoring companies do not have the stigma of transfer pricing — of shifting profits. Therefore, factoring companies undergo less government scrutiny than reinvoicing companies."

However, in-house factoring systems are not without tax problems. Companies debating whether to establish a factoring company should consider the consequences of charging intracompany interest rates and service fees.

(3) In-house factoring removes currency exposure from operating units and centralizes it. By paying the exporting sub in its own currency and receiving payment in the currency of the importing sub, the factoring unit can assume and centrally hedge forex risks. For example, one well-known U.S. company began factoring in 1982 in response to FAS No. 52. The firm's treasurer explained why: "We have a lot of intracompany activity, and when we had an intracompany transaction, we had a nonfunctional currency on somebody's books. The purpose of the factoring company is to factor all the intracompany nonfunctional currency receivables and pay the company in its functional currency."

Some factoring companies hire currency professionals who are better equipped to carry out forex trading and hedging than local financial managers. According to the spokesman for a factoring company that just hired away the former head trader of a leading European bank, "You need to have the foreign exchange manager as a pillar. He's a very important man and maybe the most difficult to find."

(4) Factoring reduces funds-transfer and currency-conversion costs. Because factoring units handle financial transactions centrally, they often have increased leverage with their banks and can thus negotiate low funds-transfer costs and

narrow forex spreads. For instance, one Swiss factoring company can transfer funds promptly to manufacturing units free of charge — thus saving the costs of telex transfers, which can be as high as several hundreds of dollars per transaction in some European countries.

"For example, if Italy had to pay Australia," the Swiss financial manager explained, "the bank charges for the transfer would be high. So we do all transfers by telex. We transfer in Australian dollars in Australia and in Italy we pay our account in Italian lire." The Italian bank does not charge for the services because it gets a sizable portion of the factoring company's forex business. According to the spokesman, it is relatively easy to negotiate for free transfers: "We say, 'We give you foreign exchange business but we don't pay bank charges on any transfers.' We've negotiated that with all our banks."

The Swiss factoring company also nets intracompany transactions, further reducing funds-transfer and currency-conversion costs.

Business International Money Report, April 19, 1985.